OFFICIAL HISTORY OF THE WOMEN'S AMATEUR ATHLETIC ASSOCIATION

OFFICIAL HISTORY OF THE WOMEN'S AMATEUR ATHLETIC ASSOCIATION

Mel Watman

SPORTS
BOOKS

Published in Great Britain by
SportsBooks Limited
1 Evelyn Court
Malvern Road
Cheltenham
GL50 2JR

Most of the photographs have been
supplied by Mark Shearman

Cover designed by Alan Hunns.

A catalogue record for this book is available from
the British Library.

ISBN 9781907524332

Printed and bound in England by TJ International.

CONTENTS

FOREWORD

By Dame Mary Peters

IT IS WITH pleasure that I contribute this foreword to a book which has long been awaited ... a definitive history of British women's athletics. The Women's AAA was primarily the governing body for England (my country of birth, incidentally, although I have lived most of my life in Northern Ireland) but its influence spread much wider – to the whole of the United Kingdom and beyond. Competing in the WAAA Championships was always a special occasion for me. My first Championships were in 1956 and the last in 1973, and I was fortunate enough to win 17 titles indoors or out at the hurdles, shot and pentathlon between 1962 and 1973.

This book, written with such enthusiasm by Mel Watman – who was on hand to report on so many of my best moments in athletics, most notably at the 1972 Olympics in Munich – has revived countless memories of competitions, friends and rivals.

I was an active athlete for many years, from the 1950s to the 1970s, but Mel's account goes back much further, to those plucky pioneers of the 1920s who dared to appear in public wearing shorts! Among them was Vera Searle, who was such a prominent personality in the WAAA during my competitive days. The most influential official of all was Marea Hartman, who was my team manager on so many occasions and who I was privileged to succeed as Olympic team manager in 1980 and 1984.

The WAAA may no longer exist as a separate entity but its legacy lives on and women's athletics in the UK continues to flourish. Everyone connected with that side of our great sport will find much to enthral and inspire them within these pages ... a glorious nostalgic wallow!

INTRODUCTION

AFTER MORE THAN 40 years I am making amends. Back in 1968 I wrote a book, *History of British Athletics*, which was well received but which caused me considerable embarrassment. The problem was that because of publishing deadlines and the amount of time I had spent researching and writing about the men's side of the sport I was able to include only a quickly assembled and cursory outline of British women's athletics history ... 213 pages devoted to the men, a mere 14 to the women. As someone who was instrumental during his years with *Athletics Weekly* in ensuring that women's athletics coverage was accorded equal treatment I was only too aware of the imbalance in the book.

Now, thanks to the Amateur Athletic Association, I am able to rectify a situation that has bugged me for decades. I was commissioned to write the Official Histories of both the AAA (which was published in 2011) and the Women's AAA, and in this volume I have expanded that remit to present what is in effect a history of women's athletics in the United Kingdom from the 1920s right through to the British team's splendid medal spree at the 2012 World Indoor Championships and Jessica Ennis's brilliant victory at the London Olympic Games.

As I researched this work, so my admiration grew for the female pioneers of the sport. The First World War and its aftermath fundamentally changed society at every level and during the 1920s the role and status of women were enhanced in many ways ... but not without a struggle against deeply entrenched male chauvinist attitudes. Remember, it was only in 1928 that – thanks largely to pressure by the suffragettes –

women were accorded the same voting rights as men. It was during this period of campaigning for female emancipation that the Women's AAA came into existence in 1922. It could not have happened without the drive and vision of a few enlightened men, but from the outset the WAAA – having been rebuffed by the AAA – decided it would be better anyway to go it alone.

That policy served them well for many years, the WAAA being at the forefront of women's athletics' development internationally as well as at home, but after the Second World War the WAAA became a curiosity as the only governing body exclusively for women anywhere in the world. That independence was fiercely guarded by such formidable figures as Vera Searle, who had herself been one of those daring young women in the twenties who would appear in public in shorts, but slowly – ever so slowly – the more progressive elements in the WAAA who felt the sport would be better served by amalgamating the men's and women's governing bodies won the day and marriage with the AAA took place in 1991.

In this book, which has been such a privilege and pleasure to write, reviving wonderful memories of the great champions who have graced our sport, I have attempted to trace the evolution of women's athletics in the UK and have concentrated on recording and perpetuating the achievements of so many splendid athletes over the past 90 years. It is so important that they should be remembered and honoured, and hopefully serve as an inspiration for the generations of athletes to come.

I dedicate this book to all who have competed in WAAA Championships, and to the band of officials and coaches who have not only made that participation possible but without whom there would be no athletics.

Mel Watman
August 2012

ACKNOWLEDGEMENTS

IN COLLECTING MATERIAL for this book I have drawn heavily on my own files, accumulated over a period of 60 years, and such magazine sources as Athletics Weekly, Athletics Today, Athletics International, The Modern Athlete, Women's Athletics and World Sports, numerous newspapers and a multitude of publications by the National Union of Track Statisticians (NUTS), in particular Progressive British Records (Women's Records, 1992, by Eric Cowe, John Brant & Peter Matthews) and *Track Stats* (edited by Bob Phillips), as well as various NUTS Annuals and ATFS (Association of Track & Field Statisticians) & IAAF publications.

The website www.gbrathletics.com has been particularly useful with its lists of champions originally compiled by Martin Rix, and I am also grateful for the immensely helpful co-operation of publisher Randall Northam (SportsBooks Ltd), legendary athletics photographer Mark Shearman, Ian Tempest, John Brant, Peter Lovesey, John Temperton, Wilf Morgan, Mark Curthoys (Oxford Dictionary of National Biography), Clive Williams, Lionel Peters, Dr Greg Moon, Hazel Rider, Margaret Ó hÓgartaigh and various AAA officers, in particular Norma Blaine, George Bunner, Chris Carter, Susan Deaves, Walter Nicholls and Ken Oakley.

As a professional, objective athletics journalist I suppose I shouldn't have any "favourites" – but of course certain athletes, by dint of their personality and demeanour as well as their physical ability, have fallen into that category and none more so than Dame Mary Peters. I am delighted and honoured that she has associated herself with this book. Older readers will have their own fond memories of Mary P and I can assure those who may not have been around when she was competing that there was no more determined yet charming athlete. Her smile would light up a whole stadium. I would also like to thank my long suffering wife Pat for her patience and support during the year or more it took to research and write this book. My promised retirement has had to be deferred yet again!

Among other books I have consulted are:

Brant, John & Wasko, Janusz – *World Women's Athletics 100 Best Performers Year Lists 1921-1962* (2012)

Cowe, Eric – *International Women's Athletics 1890-1940* (1985) and *Early Women's Athletics: Statistics & History* (1999)

Daniels, Stephanie & Tedder, Anita – *A Proper Spectacle: Women Olympians 1900-1936* (ZeNaNA Press & Walla Walla Press, 2000)

Holmes, Kelly – *Black, White & Gold* (Virgin Books, 2005)

Huxtable, Andrew – *A Statistical History of UK Track & Field Athletics* (NUTS, 1990)

Hyman, Dorothy – *Sprint to Fame* (Stanley Paul, 1964)

Hymans, Richard – *Progression of World Best Performances & Official IAAF World Records* (IAAF, 2003)

Lewis, Denise – *Personal Best* (Century, 2001)

Lovesey, Peter – *The Official Centenary History of the AAA* (Guinness Superlatives, 1979)

Matthews, Peter & Buchanan, Ian – *All-Time Greats of British & Irish Sport* (Guinness Publishing, 1995)

McWhirter, Norris & Ross – *Get To Your Marks!* (Nicholas Kaye, 1951)

Naughton, Lindie – *Lady Icarus* (Lady Mary Heath) (Ashfield Press, 2004)

Pallett, George – *Women's Athletics* (Normal Press, 1955)

Peters, Mary – *Mary P* (Hutchinson, 1974)

Phillips, Bob – *Honour of Empire, Glory of Sport: History of Athletics at the Commonwealth Games* (The Parrs Wood Press, 2000)

Pickering, Ron & Watman, Mel – *Athletics 74, 75, 76* (Queen Anne Press); *Athletics 77, 78, 79* (Macdonald & Jane's) and *Athletics 1980* (Athletics Weekly)

Acknowledgements

Pozzoli, Peter – *British Women's Athletics* (Arena Publications, 1963)

Rand, Mary – *Mary Mary* (Hodder & Stoughton, 1969)

Rix, Martin & Whittingham, Rob – *British All-Time Lists* (Umbra Software, 1998)

Sheridan, Michael – *British Athletics 1946–1949* (2004), *British Athletics 1950* (2000 & 2004), *British Athletics 1951–1959* (2008) and *Who's Who of British International Athletes 1945–1960* (2010)

Tomlin, Stan – *Olympic Odyssey* (Modern Athlete Publications, 1956)

Watman, Mel – *The Encyclopaedia of Athletics* (Robert Hale, 1964, 1967, 1973, 1977, 1981); *History of British Athletics* (Robert Hale, 1968), *Olympic Track & Field History* (*Athletics International* & Shooting Star Media, 2004), *All-Time Greats of British Athletics* (SportsBooks, 2006) and *The Official History of the AAA* (SportsBooks, 2011)

Webster, F A M – *Athletics of Today for Women* (Warne, 1930)

Whittingham, Rob, Jenes, Paul & Greenberg, Stan – *Athletics at the Commonwealth Games* (Umbra Athletics, 2002)

M. W.

BIRTH OF THE WAAA

THE WOMEN'S AMATEUR Athletic Association, founded in 1922, was among the earliest of governing bodies for the female side of the sport, but women's athletics dates far, far back ... to the days of Ancient Greece. Although prohibited on pain of death from even watching the Olympic Games, women held their own four-yearly Heraea Games, named after Hera, wife of Zeus. The festival included foot races of about 150 metres and, as described by Captain F.A.M.Webster in his groundbreaking book, *Athletics of Today for Women* (1930), "girls ran with hair unbound and wore short tunics to the knee which left the right shoulder bare to the breast."

In England, there is mention of girls' races in Kent as early as 1639 and, following the restoration of the monarchy in 1660 and the demise of Puritanism, races for women – at distances ranging up to half a mile – were staged at rural fairs, wakes and other public gatherings. Prizes of clothing, usually smocks, and money were awarded. According to the noted athletics historian Eric Cowe, "some women took these races very seriously but were constrained by the need to display a degree of modesty in their choice of clothing. Some eyebrows were raised at the sight of women competing in 'shifts and under-petticoats' but generally the women managed to maintain their 'respectability' in the often isolated rural villages." By the time Victoria ascended the throne in 1837 the country's growing industrialisation and urbanisation led to the demise of such country pursuits and women's races were deemed unseemly.

Just as the public schools, recognising the sport's value in bringing out some of the best qualities in a boy, played a significant role in the creation of athletics competition as we know it today (annual sprint, hurdle and steeplechase races were staged at Eton from 1845), so from the 1880s a more genteel form of women's athletics, suitable for young ladies of breeding, originated in the form of "sports days" at such prestigious girls' schools as North London Collegiate, Cheltenham Ladies College and Roedean.

In his meticulously researched book *Early Women's Athletics: Statistics & History* (1999), Eric Cowe wrote that "the first known timed track performances by British women date from athletic events organised by the proprietor of Hengler's Circus during a visit to Dublin in 1891. Organised as publicity for the circus, Hengler's Cirque Sports were held at Ballsbridge, Dublin, on August 12. Two handicap races for women over 100 yards and 440 yards were held."

The first marks of note occurred just before the First World War. Margaret Belasco, the 15-year-old daughter of a rabbi, high jumped 4ft 10 in (1.47m) at the Inter-Kent School Sports at Chatham on 6 June 1914, a height she replicated in the Ramsgate County School for Girls Sports 12 days later, although it is probable that she jumped over a rope rather than a bar. Margaret died aged only 21, after a brief illness, in May 1920. Later that month her 18-year-old sister Joan Belasco was reported to have cleared the remarkable height of 5ft 4in (1.62m) in the Inter-Kent School Sports at Ramsgate over a rope weighted at both ends with sand ballast. That jump, although not acceptable for any category of official record, was not bettered in competition until 1932.

It was just after the Great War that women's athletics started to be organised on a national basis. Previously the most noteworthy result was 12.4 for 100y by Agnes Webb at Cheltenham in 1913, a time that was reduced to 12.0 by Phyllis Scarlett in Birmingham in 1920. Nowhere near as fast, but a more celebrated pioneer, was Elaine Burton from Yorkshire who, at 15, won what was termed the North of England Championship in Manchester in 1919 with a time of 13.0. That was a few months after Constance Markievicz, an Irish nationalist politician, became the first woman to be elected to the House of Commons, although she did not take her seat. At that time Ireland was still part of the UK. Possibly the first woman in England to wear shorts and spikes, Elaine was the daughter of and trained by 1908 Olympic 400m hurdles finalist Sergeant-Major Leslie Burton. She served as Labour MP for Coventry South between 1950 and 1959, and in 1962 she became Baroness Burton of Coventry, a member of the House of Lords (for the newly created SDP from 1981) until her death in 1991, aged 87. Another early post-war result was a 55.2 4x110y relay by a Women's Royal Air Force team at the otherwise all-male 1919 Inter-Services Championships.

The French can claim credit for creating the first national governing body for women's athletics, 33-year-old Alice Milliat founding the Fédération des Sociétés Féminines Sportives de France while the war was still raging in 1917. Within a year or two athletic activity was starting to blossom in several countries, although the concept of women running, jumping and throwing was slow to be accepted by many of the men who controlled the sport and those female pioneers, like the suffragettes of that time, had to fight hard for their rights.

The year of 1921 saw the establishment of international competition for women, the driving force again being Alice Milliat. At Easter the First Monte Carlo Games were staged on a rough and ready grass track marked out on a pigeon shooting ground in front of the celebrated Casino. France, England, Switzerland, Italy and Norway sent teams. Two enlightened men were responsible for organising the English squad: timekeeper and starter Joe Palmer and Major W.B.Marchant, the Regent Street Polytechnic's Director of Physical Education. The most promising young women attending PE classes at the Regent Street and Woolwich Polytechnics were invited to train at Paddington Recreation Ground under the supervision of Palmer, known affectionately as Mr Joe. None of them had a background in track and field athletics.

As Mary Amies, WAAA Hon. Secretary between 1953 and 1960, reminisced: "Mr Joe's enthusiasm and patient understanding brought early results and some of the girls quickly learned the rudiments of starting, baton changing, jumping and hurdling, which I understand was taught over a pole resting on two sticks. Training then became serious and eventually seven girls were selected, and with a basketball team made up the first party of women athletes to leave England as a representative team, although of course an unofficial one."

There were 11 events on the programme which started in Monte Carlo on March 25 and star of the English squad was team captain Mary Lines who won the 60m (8.2 after a world best 8.0 heat), 250m (world best of 36.6) and long jump (British best of 4.70m), contributed to victories in both sprint relays, finished second in the 800m (on a track measuring just 175 metres!) with a British best of 2:32.8 ... and played on the victorious basketball team! Coached by Mr Joe, the 27-year-old Lyon's Corner House waitress had never run a race prior to 1921. Another to excel was Hilda Hatt (17), joint winner of the high jump with 1.40m (a British best over a bar in official competition), runner-up in the long jump with 4.60m and a member of the successful relay squads. As Lord Decies, then President of the Women's AAA, wrote in 1930: "I do not think they [the English team] realised it, and I am sure no one else on the ground did, but they were the pioneers of a great movement. On the way home [on a train travelling through France] these girls (afterwards known as the London Olympiades) formed the first women's athletic club."

That was true in terms of being the first club exclusively for women but earlier in 1921 a ladies' section was formed at London's Kensington Athletic Club, the credit going mainly to Teddy Knowles. Sophie Eliott-Lynn was an early member, as was Vera Palmer, and in 1923 the women went their own way to become Middlesex Ladies – these days amalgamated with the men and known as Ealing Southall & Middlesex AC, Kelly Holmes' club when she became a double Olympic champion in 2004.

The success of the Monte Carlo meeting had other important consequences as Alice Milliat then set about creating the Fédération Sportive Féminine Internationale (FSFI), which with the support of England, Italy, Spain, Czechoslovakia and the USA as well as France came into being in Paris on 31 October 1921, the international governing body for women's athletics until the IAAF took over in 1936. The new organisation unified technical rules, decided on a schedule of events and became the body empowered to ratify world records. The previous day, at Stade Pershing in conjunction with the conference which led to the birth of the FSFI, an English team beat France. Mary Lines shone again with wins in the 100y in 11.8, 300m in 43.8, 4x110y relay in 51.8 and 4x220y relay in 1:53.0, all world best times.

With women's athletics now established internationally it was time for England to put its own affairs in order. The General Committee of the AAA (founded in 1880) decided it would be advisable for women's athletics to be governed by a separate body – in other words, it wanted no part of an activity that many members deemed unfeminine – and so, following a proposal by shot and discus star Florence Birchenough, Major Marchant and Mr Palmer organised a meeting at the Regent Street Polytechnic and the Women's AAA was formed in October 1922. The other founder members were Mary Lines, Teddy Knowles, Harry Wadmore and Charles Churchill. The WAAA's declared aims were:

The co-ordination and control of women's athletics in England.

The assurance that women should compete only in suitable surroundings and desirable conditions.

The registration of duly authenticated national records.

The giving of advice as to the choice of suitable events for competition and also as to training.

The improvement of the physique and physical efficiency of the nation.

As Captain Webster wrote: "Within a short time the WAAA had several hundred clubs in affiliation; men's clubs were running women's sections, and soon the new governing body, under the presidency of Lord Hawke, found itself legislating for upwards of 23,000 girl athletes." Sophie Eliott-Lynn claimed in 1925 there were 25,000 members drawn from over 500 clubs.

Vera Palmer, who was 20 when the WAAA came into existence, set her first world record in 1923 and later as Vera Searle became one of the most influential figures in WAAA history. She reflected on those early days when interviewed by Gwenda Ward (herself an Olympic high jumper in 1964) for the *AAA News* in 1989. "The men didn't want anything to do with us. They were afraid of a lot of fierce looking women interfering!" In October 1922 the women's application to affiliate to the AAA was refused. 'You'll be better off on your own' the women were told. "And they were right," Vera emphasised. "Many times women officials from Europe have told us how lucky we are to be separate from the men. 'You don't know what it's like having to work with them', they say." Vera was to cling to the belief that the WAAA was better off as an independent body for the rest of her long life.

In another interview, reproduced in the book *A Proper Spectacle*, by Stephanie Daniels and Anita Tedder, Vera said: "I would think it would be safe to say that 99% of the medical profession in this country [in those pioneering days] were against women taking an active part in athletics. They said you were leaving your womanhood on the track, and it was quite possible none of us would ever have children. That made me laugh. How could they know anything about it? They'd never seen any women running, either before or after their races."

A report in *The Times* stated that the WAAA was formed "in response to what was thought to be an urgent necessity. At the suggestion of the AAA, women's events had been promoted for some years by men's clubs at their meetings, and universities had held women's sports for several seasons, but it was felt that all these uncorrelated athletic energies should be combined and standardised. This is the chief object of the Association: its aims are to ensure that women and girls compete in suitable surroundings and under desirable conditions, and to prevent the exploitation of women's athletics for advertisement and money making, and to foster the true amateur spirit. The more trying events, such as tug-of-war and distance races of over half-mile, have been banned by the Association, which also provides for the health of the competitors by including a rule to the effect that a coat or wrap shall be worn between events."

Although the women were happy to go their own way, right from the start enlightened men played an important role in officiating and coaching, including the celebrated trainer Sam Mussabini, who put Vera Searle through the same routine of exercises he would demand of Harold Abrahams when preparing him for the 1924 Olympics. Mussabini was also a member, along with two doctors, of a Medical Commission set up by the WAAA in 1923 to assess the suitability or otherwise of adding the pole vault and triple jump to the women's programme of events. They were rejected, but the following year the Commission approved cross country "in moderation and with proper training." The WAAA adopted the AAA rule book in its entirety, merely substituting 'she' for 'he' where appropriate.

The opening major event of the 1922 season was the second Monte Carlo Games in April and English athletes again played a prominent role. Mary Lines took the 250m (39.0) and long jump (4.66m) but was beaten in the 60m (for which there were 23 heats!) by French-born team-mate Norah Callebout (8.2), who was taken to England when six months old, only became a naturalised Briton in January 1922 and lived to 1995 when she was 99. Daisy Wright, aged 35, won the 65m hurdles in 11.4, Hilda Hatt was joint winner of the high jump at 1.37m and Ivy Lowman took the pentathlon comprising 60m, 300m, high jump, javelin and shot, the throws being decided on the aggregate distance of left and right hand. The javelin technique in those early days bore no resemblance to today's event. Athletics historian Ian Tempest deduced from Sophie Eliott-Lynn's description that "in the 1920s it was common for women to throw the javelin with both hands on the spear. A throwing hand would hold the end of the javelin while the other arm is extended upwards along the spear at an angle of 45° with the thumb and first finger pointed and the other fingers curved to form a 'glide' for the javelin. The throwers must have looked like pole vaulters on the run-up, carrying the javelin low and parallel to the ground but, on reaching the throwing point, weight was transferred onto the right foot, the javelin was lifted to a 45° angle, and was thrown."

Although one centralised WAAA Championships meeting was not instituted until the following year, several "Championship of England" events, under the WAAA's auspices, were farmed out to various meetings during the 1922 season. Mary

Lines won the 220y (26.8) at Waddon in Surrey, 440y (64.4) at Paddington and 880y (2:26.6) at Crystal Palace – all three of them world records.

The big event of 1922 though was the inaugural Women's World Games in Paris in August. The French, led by Alice Milliat, had in 1919 requested women's events be included in the following year's Olympic Games in Antwerp. That was refused by a misogynistic International Olympic Committee, as was FSFI's demand for a women's programme to be added to the 1924 Games in Paris. The IOC's blinkered attitude reflected the view of its founder, Baron Pierre de Coubertin, who once declared "women have but one task, crowning the winner with garlands." As a gesture of defiance the FSFI organised what it first referred to as the "Women's Olympic Games" but later renamed as Women's World Games following objections by the IOC and IAAF. Only five nations were represented (England, USA, France, Czechoslovakia and Switzerland) but the occasion proved a huge success. Over 20,000 spectators attended the one-day event and several world records were established with English athletes easily topping the points table ahead of the USA. Norah Callebout won the 100y in 12.0 (11.6 heat), Mary Lines the 300m in 44.8 and long jump with 5.06m, Hilda Hatt tied for first in the high jump (1.45m) and England (Lines, Callebout, Daisy Leach, Gwendoline Porter) took the 4x110y relay in a world record 51.8.

What kit did they wear in those days? A letter to team members from 25-year-old Sophie Eliott-Lynn, who apart from being a future world high jump record holder was one of the founders of the WAAA, advised: "Will you please provide yourself with close fitting black knickers reaching to not more than four inches from the ground when kneeling, a loose white tunic of stout material belted, with elbow sleeves, reaching to 10-12 inches below the waist. The use of stockings is optional, but most of the team will compete without them. It is advisable to bring two pairs of running pumps and a warm coat." What would they have thought of today's Lycra and bikini-like uniforms?

As 1922 drew to a close, the British record book had been totally rewritten. According to Eric Cowe's priceless research, these were among the best marks registered, with the supremely versatile Mary Lines the brightest star. 60m – 7.8 (& estimated 7.7) Mary Lines; 100y – 11.6 Lines & Norah Callebout; 220y – 26.8 Lines; 250m – 35.8 Alice Cast; 440y – 64.4 Lines; 880y – 2:26.6 Lines; 100y hurdles – 14.8 Hilda Hatt; high jump (over crossbar) – 1.47m Ivy Lowman & Sophie Eliott-Lynn; long jump – 5.06m Lines; 8lb (3.628kg) shot – 9.08m Florence Birchenough. The 220y, 440y and 880y performances were also world bests.

Despite continuing opposition and prejudice from certain male officials and organisations, English women's athletics was off to a flying start and undoubtedly benefited by being run principally by women dedicated to the cause. As would be seen when, grudgingly, women were finally admitted to the Olympics in 1928 but confined to just five events (the WAAA boycotting in protest), it was the female administrators who encouraged their athletes to expand the sport by trying a wide range of disciplines.

An early convert to the development of women's athletics was Capt Webster, a brilliant writer on athletics and a pioneering coach, who began training women in previously neglected field events from August 1922. In his *Athletics of Today for Women* he wrote: "Results have shown the fallacy of the argument that vigorous open-air exercise impairs the natural beauty of women. The trim-figured athletic girl of today can afford to smile at her seniors who solemnly prophesied a lamentable shapelessness as the result of playing games."

Although influenced by his social environment and class as an Army officer, Webster's enlightenment shines through as he writes: "It is hard to see how it can be contended that the throwing of a light javelin, weighing 600 grammes, can impose a greater strain upon a woman than the use of the overhead tennis service, since both actions call for the employment of exactly the same set of muscles. Again, how can it be said that a short cross country race of two and three quarter miles is likely to prove any more harmful than a day out with the beagles. Nothing I have yet seen among women has convinced me that an average normal and perfectly healthy woman has relatively less powers of endurance than a man. In fact, the end of a hard day's hunting or a long night dancing will usually find the male rather more 'shop-soiled' than his sister."

In other passages, he writes (this was in 1930): "I suppose there are people still living who can remember when croquet was the only game considered fit for the fair sex", and "It is worthwhile to mention that since the WAAA was formed in 1922 there has not been recorded a single case of injury or strain, except among such girls as have wilfully ignored or broken the fundamental rules of training."

It was a telling response to such doubters as 1924 Olympic 100m champion Harold Abrahams who once wrote: "I do not consider that women are built for really violent exercise of the kind that is the essence of competition. One has only to see them practising to realise how awkward they are on the running track." On another occasion, in the late 1930s, he confessed to "a deep-seated opposition to women's athletics." To his credit, though, Abrahams did eventually eat his words and after watching in admiration as Fanny Blankers-Koen won four gold medals at the London Olympics of 1948 he became an avid supporter of women's athletics, serving for many years as the WAAA's legal adviser.

WHO COULD HAVE PREDICTED THESE RECORDS?

In 1922, when the WAAA was founded, organised women's athletics was in its infancy and performances were understandably under-developed. The most famous athlete in the world at that time was the "Flying Finn" Paavo Nurmi, who had smashed the world 10,000m record in 1921 and set new records at 2000m, 3000m and 5000m in 1922. Nobody in their right mind could have predicted that his record times would ever be surpassed by a woman. In fact, in those events where a direct comparison can be made, practically every men's record that stood in 1922 is inferior or comparable to the present day women's equivalent.
100m: men's record in 1922 – 10.4, women's record – 10.49 (1988); 200m: 21.2 – 21.34 (1988); 400m: 47.4 – 47.60 (1985); 800m: 1:51.9 – 1:53.28 (1983); 1500m: 3:54.7

– 3:50.46 (1993); mile: 4:12.6 – 4:12.56 (1996); 3000m: 8:28.6 – 8:06.11 (1993); 5000m: 14:35.4 – 14:11.15 (2008); 10,000m: 30:40.2 – 29:31.78 (1993); marathon: 2:32:36 – 2:15:25 (2003); high jump: 2.01m – 2.09m (1987); pole vault: 4.12m – 5.06m (2009; although not directly comparable due to advances in pole technology); long jump: 7.69m – 7.52m (1988); triple jump: 15.52m – 15.50m (1995); 4x100m: 42.2 – 40.82 (2012); 4x400m: 3:16.6 – 3:15.17 (1988).

THE TWENTIES

WOMEN'S ATHLETICS IN Britain and throughout the world flourished and developed apace during the rest of the "Roaring Twenties". Just look at how various world records or bests progressed between 1920 and 1929: 100y: from 12.0 to 11.0; 100m: 12.8-12.0; 200m: 29.0-25.4; 800m: 2:30.2-2:16.8; high jump: 1.42-1.60m; long jump: 5.41-5.98m; shot: 8.75-12.85m; 4x100m relay: 53.0-49.0.

A landmark event was the first full-scale WAAA Championships meeting in 1923, held at the Oxo Sports Ground at Bromley in Kent, the outstanding performer being Mary Lines who won five events. Later WAAA Championships in the twenties were staged at Woolwich, Stamford Bridge (the home of English men's athletics) and Reading, the last named venue being the furthest from London until Birmingham in 1985. Also held in 1923 were the first county championships (Essex).

The 1923 season opened early again with the third and final Monte Carlo Games. The entire England team was composed of London Olympiades members and victories were gained by Norah Callebout (7.9 60m, 41.0 250m plus two relays), Ivy Lowman (10.3 65m hurdles, 1.47m high jump) and 16-year-old Sylvia Stone (4.85m long jump).

LOAC also comprised the England team which beat Belgium and France in a match in Antwerp with Mary Lines scoring a huge number of points by winning the 80m (10.4 after a 10.2 heat), 250m (35.6), 83m hurdles (13.8) and long jump (5.04m) as well as a leg on the victorious 4x200m relay team. Mary was absent from a match in Paris when France was defeated again, and this time the big news was provided by 19-year-old Rose Thompson (dubbed "The Rose of England"), who had finished second to Mary Lines in the WAAA 100 yards. She clocked 11.4 to equal the official FSFI ratified world record. Rose, who later married international 400m runner Jack Gillis (one of the starters at the 1948 Olympics) and herself became a prominent and long-serving WAAA official, was a member of the Manor Park Ladies AC which eventually became the celebrated Essex Ladies club. There was a world best also by 22-year-old Vera Palmer with 35.4 for 250m – half a lap of the track.

SOPHIE THE HIGH FLIER

Making her international debut in the match against France in 1923 was the versatile Mrs Sophie Eliott-Lynn, who although primarily a high jumper contested the 100y hurdles, shot and javelin. Her life story was remarkable if ultimately tragic. She was born Sophia Theresa Catherine Mary Peirce Evans in County Limerick, Ireland on November 10 1896 and when only a year old she effectively lost both her parents as her mother was battered to death by her husband, who was declared guilty but insane and confined to Dublin's Central Lunatic Asylum for the rest of his life. Brought up in County Limerick by her aunts, she took up athletics in 1916 as a 19-year-old student at the Royal College of Science in Dublin and later during the First World War her adventurous spirit became evident as she volunteered to be a motor cycle dispatch rider and driver for the Women's Auxiliary Army Corps in France. In 1919, aged 22, she married 41-year-old Captain (later Major) William Eliott-Lynn. After a spell in

British East Africa, where her husband owned a farm, she separated from him and returned to Ireland where in 1921 she graduated with a first class degree in agriculture.

The following year she embarked upon a successful athletics career in Britain, the highlights of which were an officially ratified (by FSFI) world high jump record of 1.485m in 1923 and WAAA titles in the high jump and javelin. In 1925, as a Vice-President of the WAAA, this seemingly indefatigable lady of many talents wrote a book entitled "Athletics for Women and Girls", published a book of poetry, was among the BBC's first radio broadcasters and learned to fly. Barely five months after the death by drowning of Major Eliott-Lynn in 1927 and now aged 30 she married 75-year-old millionaire and former MP Sir James Heath, a man wealthy enough to indulge his new wife's expensive love of flying. The following year, the daredevil Lady Mary Heath as she now called herself, began setting various women's aviation records in a small open 30 horsepower biplane, notably an epic 9000-mile flight, spanning four months, from Cape Town to London. The first woman to gain an officially recognised commercial pilot's licence in Britain and the first woman to make a parachute jump, she became a world-famous personality, known in America as "Queen of the Skies". However, she came close to being killed in August 1929 when she crashed during an air race in the USA. Meanwhile, her marriage had run its course and after being divorced in Reno from Sir James in May 1931 she wed for a third time six months later in Kentucky to 32-year-old American pilot 'Jack' Williams. That marriage also collapsed, and back in England her increasingly frequent drunkenness and mental illness led to her tragic demise. In May 1939, alone and destitute, she fell down the staircase of a London tram and died in hospital the next day, aged just 42. The full story of her tumultuous life is told in the book "Lady Icarus" by Lindie Naughton, published in 2004.

Women's athletics' increasing popularity – tinged perhaps with curiosity – was evident in 1924 when journalist and former British mile record holder Joe Binks, on behalf of the sport's great benefactor, the *News of the World*, promoted the International Women's Games (successor to the now discontinued Monte Carlo Games) on August Bank Holiday at Stamford Bridge, drawing an enormous crowd of 25,000. Mary Lines scored a triple success – 250m in 34.2, 120y hurdles in 18.2 after a world record 17.6 heat, and 5.07m long jump – while Rose Thompson and Gwendoline Porter took 100y races in a swift 11.5 and Edith Trickey the 1000m in 3:08.2. Stamford Bridge was again the venue for an international match in 1925 where home athletes won eight of the ten events on the programme against Canada and Czechoslovakia, including world records by Vera Palmer in the 250m (33.8) and Edith Trickey at 880y (2:24.0). First in the 8lb shot with a British record aggregate distance (right and left hand combined) of 18.38m was 20-year-old WAAA champion Mary Weston – who in 1936 underwent an operation to become Mark Weston. Historian Eric Cowe has revealed that Weston was never a woman, being male from birth, but as a consequence of abnormalities in the genital region and medical ignorance of the condition was brought up as a girl. Mark Weston married soon after his operation and went on to become a father.

The second Women's World Games in Gothenburg in August 1926 were supported by eight nations and as in the previous edition the English team finished a clear first on points. Four victories were achieved: Eileen Edwards won the 250m in a world record 33.4 with Vera Palmer second, Edith Trickey the 1000m in 3:08.8, Daisy Crossley the 1000m walk in 5:10.0 and the 4x110y relay team of Doris Scoular, Eileen Edwards, Florence Haynes and Rose Thompson clocked 49.8 for a world record.

The official report rhapsodised over the Games. "Every event was marked, from the firing of the pistol, by a despatch and precision that could only have been attained by the intelligent and conscientious work of the leaders, backed by the discipline and sporting spirit of the competitors. The Games were spread over three days, in which the sunshine added to the unbroken enjoyment. In races, jumping and throwing contests alike were manifested not only the desire to conquer, but the ability to accept defeat – sure signs of true sportswomanship. When the contests were over and the results summed up, the British flag flew on top, flanked by the French and the Swedish. In the competition between the nations, the British team had won the prizes offered by H.M. The King of Sweden and H.R.H. The Crown Prince."

Other world records to fall to English athletes that year came in the 220y (25.8) by Eileen Edwards and high jump (1.55m or 5ft 1in) by Phyllis Green, who did not bid for selection in Gothenburg because she refused to compete on a Sunday, while one of the great figures of athletics in the twenties and thirties began to emerge in the shape of Muriel Gunn, who at 19 and in her first season of long jumping briefly held the world record with 5.48m and ended the season with an unratified 5.57m. The following year she jumped 5.57m again and this time it was accepted by the FSFI as a world record, surpassing the officially recognised 5.50m by Kinue Hitomi at the 1926 Women's World Games although the latter had earlier been credited with 5.75m in Tokyo.

Fashion note: in his highly informative book *Women's Athletics*, published in 1955, the well known coach and former international long jumper George Pallett remarked that, at those Gothenburg Games, "Hitomi, whose abbreviated shorts, with blouse tucked in, gave a business-like appearance compared with the British girls, who still wore knee-length shorts, with their blouses loose outside them, was watched with eager interest." The 19-year-old Japanese, who became a good friend as well as arch-rival of Muriel Gunn, went on to become the first international superstar of women's athletics. Not only did she raise the world long jump record to 5.98m in 1928, unsurpassed officially for 11 years, but also set world marks at 100m, 200m, 220y, 400m, standing long jump, triple jump and triathlon (100m, high jump, javelin). There was seemingly no limits to her talent; as the long jump wasn't on the programme for the 1928 Olympics she tried a new event for her, the 800m, and finished second! Tragically, she died of pneumonia in 1931, aged just 24.

Looking back half a century later, Vera Searle remarked: "I don't deny the girls look far more attractive in their tight fitting gear these days, but I can assure you we had our admirers too. Obviously I would have been faster had I not had to race with so much spare in the shorts flapping in the breeze – but this was our regulation racing dress then."

Vera always remained cautious about women running long distances, and although an annual cross country championship was instituted in 1927 the longest track championship remained at 800m/880y until the mile was added to the programme in 1936. However, one remarkable and mysterious individual blazed her own trail. Violet Piercy was her name and in October 1926 – believed to be 36 at the time – she reputedly ran the marathon distance (although not validated) from Windsor to Battersea Town Hall as a solo time trial in 3:40:22. More than 80 years later athletics historians are still arguing over the authenticity or otherwise of that performance. She was timed at 73 minutes for 10 miles and 1:39:15 for 12 miles in 1927, and it's known that she competed unofficially in the 1928 Polytechnic Marathon from Windsor to Stamford Bridge but retired after reaching 20 miles in 3:31 - well outside 4:30 marathon pace. In 1933 she was reported to have run from Windsor to North London (finishing on the stage of the Golders Green Hippodrome!) in 4:25, later that year running 22 miles from Colnbrook to Mitcham in 3:45, while in 1936 she apparently finished two hours behind the winner (2:35:20) of that year's Polytechnic Marathon from Windsor to the White City.

The struggle to get women's track and field events into the Olympics was prolonged and bitter. The success of the Women's World Games had emphasised the right of female athletes to be invited to the Amsterdam Olympics of 1928; after all, women had been competing in tennis, golf and yachting in 1900, archery from 1904, swimming from 1912. Nevertheless, the main opposition came from Britain, one of five countries which voted against Olympic participation when the issue was debated at the IAAF Congress in August 1926. However, 12 nations voted in favour, so the women were in. The next problem, though, was the number of events to be allocated. The IAAF offered just five (100m, 800m, high jump, discus and 4x100m relay) as against 22 for the men.

Alice Milliat, the FSFI President, was unhappy at this token gesture but the FSFI Committee, meeting in December 1926, voted 5-1 in favour, the dissenting voice being Britain's.

So the Olympic year of 1928 was one of frustration for Britain's female athletes, although in the wider world there was satisfaction that the voting age for women in Britain had been lowered from 30 to 21. While Douglas Lowe and Lord Burghley were away in Amsterdam winning gold medals our many world class female athletes stayed at home, the WAAA refusing to send a British team. The governing body had the support of the athletes. As Vera Searle recalled some 60 years later: "We showed the bloody men where to get off. We circulated the clubs. An unbiased letter, telling them the situation. They all said the same; a full programme or we don't go. I was proud of them."

Britain may have been absent but 21 nations were represented with the USA and Germany fielding the largest teams. World records were set in four events: by Lina Radke of Germany in the 800m (2:16.8), Ethel Catherwood of Canada in the high jump (1.59m), Halina Konopacka of Poland in the discus (39.62m) and the Canadian 4x100m relay team (48.4). The other title went to 16-year-old American schoolgirl Betty Robinson with 12.2 in the 100m.

Such was the entrenched position of several of the men who were members of the IAAF that at its Congress held at the conclusion of the Games six out of 22, including the British delegate, Harry Barclay, voted in favour of dropping women's athletics from the Olympics entirely. However, it should be pointed out that Mr (later Sir Harry) Barclay, who at the time was Hon. Secretary of both the AAA and WAAA, was representing the WAAA's position. A motion put forward by the FSFI for a programme of ten events was defeated 14-8 and because of an exaggerated reaction to some of the competitors' post-race fatigue the 800m did not reappear until 1960! Harold Abrahams wrote in the BOA's Official Report of the Games: "I myself witnessed no signs of collapse such as have been described." Slowly, ever so slowly, the Olympic women's programme was extended – six events in 1932, nine in 1948, 10 in 1960, 12 in 1964 – but it was not until 2008 that effective parity was reached: 24 men's events and 23 for women, only the 50 kilometres walk being omitted.

Highlights from each of the WAAA Championships meetings
1923–1929

1923 (held at Bromley)

MARY LINES CONTINUED on her merry way as the supreme female star of English athletics by claiming five titles at these inaugural Championships held on August 18 at Bromley, Kent. Following an 11.8 heat she won the 100y in 12.0 narrowly ahead of the up and coming Rose Thompson, who had been timed at 11.5 at Erith earlier in the season and would go on to equal the world record of 11.4 in Paris a month later. Mary also took the 440y in 62.4 and the 120y hurdles in 18.8 – both world bests – together with the long jump at 4.86m and a 220y leg for LOAC's victorious 660y medley relay team. Eileen Edwards' 220y time of 27.0, ahead of Rose Thompson and Vera Palmer, was second only to Mary Lines (26.8) on the nascent world all-time list. The other winners were Edith Trickey, who scored an unusual double in the half mile run (2:40.2) and walk (4:35.0), Hilda Hatt (1.45m high jump), Florence Birchenough (two handed aggregate of 16.16m with the 8lb shot) and Sophie Eliott-Lynn (two handed aggregate of 35.76m with the 800gm javelin). Prizes were presented by WAAA President Lord Hawke, the celebrated former cricketer, and WAAA Vice-President Baroness Orczy, famed author of *The Scarlet Pimpernel*.

1924 (Woolwich)

EILEEN EDWARDS (21) WAS awarded the sensational 100y time of 11.3, which would have constituted a new world record, but it was never submitted for ratification due to a slight downhill slope and probable wind assistance. It was on this track in similar conditions a few weeks earlier that Harold Abrahams was credited with a world record equalling 9.6, a time he never regarded as a legitimate performance. Eileen Edwards also took the 220y in 27.6, and later in the season she would set world records of 26.2 for that event, 33.9

for 250m and 60.8 for 440y. That last mark was greeted with incredulity, according to Capt Webster. "Men who heard of this performance accepted it grudgingly as a freak run and swore that no woman would ever beat the even minute for the quarter-mile distance." Five years later that minute barrier was broken and these days times of inside 50 sec for 400m arouse little comment! Aged 30 and in her final season, Mary Lines added three more titles as she won the 120y hurdles in 18.4, long jumped a possibly wind aided 5.17m and helped LOAC to a 660y relay victory, but wound up third in the 100y. Edith Trickey retained both her 880y titles but in the much quicker times of 2:30.4 running and 4:17.4 walking. Another double winner was Sophie Eliott-Lynn, high jumping 1.45m and producing a two handed javelin aggregate of 52.78m which was not put forward for ratification as a British record because of a "slightly assisting head wind".

1925 (Stamford Bridge)

A 17-YEAR-OLD South London schoolgirl, Phyllis Green, emerged as the most exciting talent on the scene. At the inaugural "Daily Mirror Trophy" meeting at Stamford Bridge in June she high jumped a world record equalling 1.51m and broke Mary Lines' British long jump record with 5.24m, she notched up another 1.51m in Brussels the following month, and at the Championships she scissored over a barrier-breaking 1.52m – five feet even. Her London Olympiades clubmate Edith Trickey became the only athlete to win a third consecutive WAAA title, her 880y time of 2:26.6 equalling Mary Lines' world record although three weeks later on the same track she improved to 2:24.0. Edith, who finished second to Vera Palmer (61.4) over 440y, did not defend her half mile walk title, which went to Florence Faulkner in a record 4:15.0. In the absence of Eileen Edwards, who was away in South Africa representing England at hockey, Vera Palmer also took the 220y in 26.8 while the 100y went to Rose Thompson in 11.8. Vera enjoyed a great season as she topped the British year lists at 60m (8.0), 100y (11.6), 250m (world best of 33.8) and 440y (61.4).

1926 (Stamford Bridge)

THE ONLY BRITISH record to fall at this edition was for the 880y walk with Women's World Games winner Daisy Crossley clocking 4:06.0. A previous champion at the heel and toe discipline, Edith Trickey won the half mile run (2:28.0) for the fourth consecutive year, and for a third time her runner-up was Gladys Lane who had in 1925 briefly held the unofficial world record of 2:24.8. Gladys was killed during the Second World War while driving an ambulance. Vera Palmer, who would live to a great age (she died in 1998 aged 97) and make a huge contribution to the WAAA, scored a 220y (26.8) and 440y (61.8) double in what proved to be her final season of individual competition. Later that year she married Wilfred Searle, Vice-President of Middlesex Ladies, and began her long career as a leading administrator by serving as WAAA Hon. Secretary from 1930 to 1933. Three other double champions were Phyllis Green with a 1.47m high jump and 5.03m long jump, Florence Birchenough in the shot and discus, and Florence Haynes who edged Rose Thompson in a 12.0 100y and was on the winning LOAC 660y relay team. Two of the star turns in Gothenburg, Eileen Edwards and Muriel Gunn, did not compete.

1927 (Reading)

EDITH TRICKEY WAS crowned half mile champion for the fifth and final time, although her mark of 2:32.4 was on the slow side as she was unpressed. Runner-up Anne Williams, who had won the inaugural national cross country title earlier in the year, finished some 20 yards behind. Eileen Edwards was in top sprinting form as she took the 100y in a wind-aided 11.4 and the 220y in 25.8 which equalled her own world best although the previous month in Berlin she had set a superior officially ratified 200m time of 25.4. Off a grass surface at Palmer Park, Phyllis Green high jumped 1.58m (5ft 2 1/4in) which metrically equalled the world record established by Canada's Ethel Catherwood the previous year but the 19-year-old's mark was not accepted as such because the imperial measurement was 3/16ths of an inch less than

Catherwood's. She never competed again. She became a missionary, married a Presbyterian Minister, George Nicol, in 1946 and died in 1999, aged 91. Favourable winds blew Muriel Gunn to a 14.6 100y hurdles and 5.41m long jump. It was a pity that Phyllis chose not to defend her long jump title as the previous week she had registered her best ever leap of 5.52m, while three weeks after the Championships Muriel jumped 5.57m, which was ratified as a world record by the FSFI. Other national (hereafter referred to as UK) records set in 1927 included 11.4 100y (equal) by Gladys Elliott, although Eileen Edwards was estimated to have run a sensational 10.9 or 11.0 when finishing third off scratch in a handicap race, and 13.2 for the new 80m hurdles event by Hilda Hatt.

1928 (Stamford Bridge)

THERE WAS AN international flavour to the meeting as some world class athletes bound for the Amsterdam Olympics added to the occasion. The centre of attraction was Japan's Kinue Hitomi, who took part in six events on the one day and won the 220y in 26.2, after equalling the world record of 25.8 in her semi-final, and the 600gm javelin with a UK all-comers best of 35.97m. However, in her speciality, the long jump, Muriel Gunn defeated her comfortably, 5.68m (UK record) to 5.36m by Hitomi who had set a startling world record of 5.98m in Osaka two months earlier. Muriel also won the 100y in her best time of 11.6. Another distinguished visitor was South Africa's Marjorie Clark, winner of the 100y hurdles in a world best of 13.8 and the high jump at 1.52m. Runner-up in the high jump (she would win in 1929 and 1931) was 20-year-old Marjorie Okell – who later was Secretary of the Northern WAAA until succeeded by Margaret Oakley in 1966 and who, although she had been blind for many years, presented flowers to the medallists at the 2002 Commonwealth Games in Manchester. She lived until 2009, aged 101. Race of the day was the 440y in which Florence Haynes equalled Eileen Edwards' world record figures of 60.8 but had only inches to spare over Annie Stone. Another Florence, WAAA founder member Birchenough (affectionately known as Birch), became the only athlete to win a title at every WAAA Championships meeting since their inception in 1923, notching up her sixth and final discus success.

1929 (Stamford Bridge)

AS AT THE previous year's meeting the 440y brought the spectators to their feet as in a spectacular finish Marion King, who had already set a world record of 60.6 in her heat earlier in the day, crashed through the minute barrier with 59.2, a time (though estimated in her case) shared by runner-up Annie Stone. Capt Webster described the race, which was not run in lanes, as "one long, breathless thrill" and there was a general feeling that this was the greatest of all women's track performances to date. Another very close race was the newly standardised 80m hurdles, replacing previous championships contested at 120y, 75m and 100y. Hilda Hatt prevailed over Muriel Cornell (née Gunn) by inches with a UK record of 12.4, which she trimmed to 12.3 when Germany defeated England in a match in Düsseldorf the following month. Muriel raised her European long jump record to 5.77m – second only to Kinue Hitomi on the world all-time list. Another UK record fell in the mile walk with Lucy Howes timed at 8:18.0, while Ivy Walker (17) equalled the oft-tied 100y record of 11.4. Mary (later Mark) Weston won all three throws: shot (two hand aggregate), discus and javelin.

UK RECORDS AT 1 JANUARY 1930

60m: 7.7 Rose Thompson 1926; 100y: 11.4 Thompson 1923, 1926 & 1929, Eileen Edwards 1926, Gladys Elliott 1927 & 1929, Ivy Walker 1928 & 1929, Elsie Maguire 1928, Daisy Ridgley 1928, Marjorie Wannop 1928, Marjorie Pope 1928, Muriel Cornell 1929, Marion King 1929; 100m: 12.4 Ridgley 1928, Florence Haynes 1928, Thompson 1928; 200m: 25.4 Edwards 1927; 220y: 25.8 Edwards 1926 & 1927, Edna Potter 1928, King 1928; 250m: 33.4 Edwards 1926; 440y: 59.2 King (& Annie Stone, estimated) 1929; 800m: 2:23.8 Ruth Christmas 1929; 880y: 2:24.0 Edith Trickey 1925; 1000m: 3:08.2 Trickey 1924; 80mH: 12.3 Hilda Hatt 1929; HJ: 1.58 Phyllis Green 1927; LJ: 5.77 Cornell 1929; 4kg SP: 10.49 Mary (later Mark) Weston

1929 (otherwise 9.65 Florence Birchenough 1929); 1kg DT: 34.00 Weston 1929 (otherwise 31.51 Birchenough 1926); 600gm JT: 29.70 Weston 1928 (otherwise 28.88 Louisa Fawcett 1928); 4x100m: 48.7 England 1929; Mile Walk: 8:18.0 Lucy Howes 1929.

THE THIRTIES

WITH NO WOMEN'S events being included in the inaugural Empire Games in Hamilton, Canada, the main event in 1930 was the third Women's World Games in Prague. As a future WAAA Hon. Secretary, Mary Amies, put it: "Many other countries were taking the sport seriously, more seriously than we were, and our erstwhile supremacy in the international field began to wane. So much so that we could only finish a poor third behind Germany and Poland." Having won 13 medals (five gold) in 1922 and 14 (four gold) in 1926 the English team had a history of success but fast rising international standards and the increase in participating nations from eight last time to 17 on this occasion resulted in slim pickings for the squad selected by the WAAA. Just four medals were obtained, the one winner being front running Gladys "Sally" Lunn in the 800m (2:21.9). Muriel Cornell finished second (5.76m) to Japan's Kinue Hitomi (5.90m) in a wind-assisted long jump; the 4x100m relay team of Ethel Scott (born in London of a Jamaican father, thus becoming Britain's first black female international), Ivy Walker, Eileen Hiscock and Daisy Ridgley placed second in 50.5 to Germany's 49.9 (the GB team ran 49.7 in the heats); and Nellie Halstead was third in the 200m in 26.0 after running 25.6 in a heat.

These days international athletes fly everywhere but travel in 1930 was a much slower and less comfortable process. Hurdler Kathleen (Kay) Tiffen recalled: "The boat and train journey had been long and tiring, and it was followed by another, equally tedious, as the team travelled on to Berlin. Most of the trains had wooden seats with no upholstery and all we could get to eat was Frankfurter sausages and rolls."

Having lost to Germany, 53.5-45.5, in Düsseldorf the previous year, the English team gained revenge in a return match at Birmingham's Perry Barr Stadium earlier in the 1930 season – but it was close: 51-49. There were two particularly notable individual successes: Gladys Lunn convincingly beat 1928 Olympic champion Lina Radke in a 2:22.8 800m and Muriel Cornell extended her European long jump record to 5.85m.

LONG JUMP STAR MURIEL CORNELL

It was in 1926 that Muriel Gunn burst onto the British athletics scene. At the age of 19 and in her first season of competition as a founder member of the ladies' section of Mitcham AC she opened with a modest long jump of 4.65m in June but such was her rate of improvement that in August she succeeded Phyllis Green as British record holder with 5.48m! Indeed that was ratified by the FSFI as a world record although Japan's Kinue Hitomi had jumped 5.75m in Tokyo a couple of months earlier. Muriel went on to finish a close second with 5.44m to Hitomi's new official world record of 5.50m at the Women's World Games in Gothenburg and was unfortunate not to come away with the gold medal. She jumped beyond 5.50m but, turning to speak to a congratulatory official while she was still in the pit, she made another mark in the sand and her distance was downgraded. The first woman to use the hitch-kick technique effectively, she ended an amazing season by jumping 5.57m in late September but although that was never ratified as a world record it was regarded as a European record.
Muriel registered 5.57m again in 1927, and that was ratified as a world record, but in May 1928 the ill-fated Hitomi (she would die aged just 24) pushed the record out of sight with 5.98m. Nevertheless, Muriel easily beat her at the WAAA Championships, 5.68m (a European record) to 5.36m. Soon afterwards, in August 1928, she married fellow Mitcham athlete and club founder Stan Cornell. She continued to improve. In 1929 she retained her WAAA title with 5.77m and had a marginal foul of over six metres in a match against

Germany, but her best year proved to be 1930. She lengthened her European record to 5.80m before winning against Germany with a leap of 5.85m which would remain unsurpassed by a Briton until Shirley Cawley's 5.92m for the bronze medal at the 1952 Olympics! Her final season in the top flight was 1931, when she ranked second in the world with 5.77m. Capt F.A.M.Webster in his book "Athletics for Women" (1946) described Muriel Cornell as the finest stylist of either sex in the long jump, adding "many have excelled the distance she jumped, but none surpassed her in pace, judgement, and mid-air balance, nor in the accuracy of her timing."

In January 1933 she gave birth to a daughter, Lorna, who herself became WAAA junior (under-15) long jump champion in 1947 although her main sport was tennis, twice winning the Wimbledon junior title. With the Women's World Games (for which she became organising secretary) and the Empire Games being staged at London's White City Stadium in 1934 Muriel resumed training, one of the first mothers to aspire to return to international athletics, but hopes of a successful comeback were dashed by a severed Achilles tendon. Instead she contributed to her sport in other ways. She served as Hon. Secretary of the WAAA for 11 years from 1934, the year in which she became the first woman to be elected to what became the British Amateur Athletic Board, while in 1935 she was the first WAAA representative on the British Olympic Association Council. She was British women's team manager at the 1936 Olympics … and in 1939 was appointed to the same position for the following year's Games, which of course never took place. After the war Muriel played a significant role in setting up a national coaching scheme and officiated at the 1948 Olympics. She died in 1996, aged 89.

Nellie Halstead, a Lancashire mill worker, was the dominant athlete of 1931 with her 440y world record of 58.8 just one of three WAAA titles she won on the same day. She also scored a sprint double (8.0 60m and 25.8 200m plus a leg for two winning relay teams) in what was called "the Olympiad of Grace" in Florence, a meeting which drew athletes from 11

European countries and was really a forerunner of full-blown European Championships. She played her part in England's 53-48 victory over Germany in Hanover, taking the 200m in a UK record of 25.2 and participating in the 4x100m relay team whose time of 48.5 was a national record. Other winners included Gladys Lunn with 2:18.9 in the 800m and Violet Webb who, at 16, tied the UK 80m hurdles record of 12.0. Muriel Cornell brought her brilliant international career to an end with a worthy 5.77m jump but she lost both the contest and the European record to an inspired opponent in Germany's Selma Grieme, who registered 5.91m.

In November 1931 the WAAA decided to send a team to the 1932 Olympics in Los Angeles even though there were to be only six women's events. The 800m was dropped but the 80m hurdles and javelin were added to the existing 100m, high jump, discus and 4x100m relay.

The British Olympic team had already been selected prior to the WAAA Championships, the last to be staged at Stamford Bridge, on July 9. The stars of that meeting were Nellie Halstead with what was at the time considered a phenomenal world 440y record of 56.8 and Ethel Johnson who clocked an unratified world 100y record of 11.0, and they along with Gwendoline Porter, Eileen Hiscock and Violet Webb left Waterloo Station on July 13, sailed from Southampton to Quebec on the Empress of Britain for five days (in the third class tourist section while Prime Minister Stanley Baldwin and his Cabinet were in first class on their way to the Ottawa Conference) and then travelled a further 3000 miles by train, with stopovers in Toronto and Chicago, to arrive in Los Angeles on July 25 – five days before the opening of the Games. What an adventure that must have been. Unfortunately Ethel ruptured a thigh muscle in training and finished a distant last in her Olympic 100m heat, costing her a place in the relay team which finished third behind the USA (46.9) and Canada (47.0) in 47.6, a time which was inside the previous world record. Eileen Hiscock (12.3) and Violet Webb (11.9) finished fifth in the 100m and 80m hurdles respectively. Violet, still only 17, broke the UK record ... and her daughter, Janet Simpson, would emulate her by winning an Olympic 4x100m relay bronze medal in 1964. Such was the state of the economy in 1932 that on her return home Violet was asked to pay 17/6 (87.5p) for her Olympic tracksuit – that's the equivalent of over £43 by today's values.

It was at London's Battersea Park in 1932 that the first decent mile time by a woman was recorded. No one had run inside 5:55 until Ruth Christmas, who had set an unratified world 880y record of 2:22.7 in 1929, was timed at 5:27.5 in the first race at the distance sanctioned by the WAAA. It was a handicap event and Ruth, running from scratch, finished over half a minute behind the winner, her unofficial time being the consensus of watches held by coaches and journalists present. Ruth, who lived to the age of 96, was a fine athlete but in WAAA championship events – mainly because she was a contemporary of Gladys Lunn – she was almost always the bridesmaid never the bride. She won the half mile title in 1933, in Lunn's absence, but was second in 1929, 1930 and 1931, while at cross country she was runner-up in 1930, 1932 and 1933. She had better luck when, after marrying a Frenchman, Ruth Christmas-Paysant won French titles at 800m and cross country and in 1936 she represented France in a match against Italy. Her elder sister Esther Raven, a fellow member of London Olympiades who was third in the national cross country in 1933 and 1935 and ran a 5:34.0 mile in 1935, was the mother of the controversial novelist Simon Raven (1927-2001).

A significant development in 1933 was that the WAAA Championships went metric so that performances could more easily be compared to those of other European athletes. This was a progressive move by the women, as the AAA stuck resolutely to English distances (100 yards etc) until as late as 1969. However, the WAAA made an exception by introducing a mile rather than 1500m championship in 1936, but exercising the female prerogative of changing one's mind switched back entirely to English distances from 1952 until 1967 inclusive!

The 1934 season was the most important yet in the WAAA's brief history for two major events were staged at London's White City, showcasing women's athletics as never before in England. First came the second edition of the Empire Games, the first to feature women's events. The English team performed admirably, although it has to be admitted that only four other countries sent teams: Scotland, Canada, South Africa and Rhodesia. Eileen Hiscock won the 100y in 11.3 (11.1 heat) and the 220y in a world record 25.0 which survived as a UK record until 1949; Gladys Lunn completed a most unusual double (the 880y in 2:19.4 and javelin with 32.19m), Phyllis Bartholomew triumphed in the long jump with 5.47m; and Nellie Halstead (220y), Eileen Hiscock (110y) and Elsie Maguire (110y) finished first in the 440y medley relay in 49.4.

The fourth and final FSFI Women's World Games, which the WAAA was responsible for organising, brought the home athletes down to earth with a bump. Not a single victory was achieved even in the absence of an American team, with Germany – building up for the Berlin Olympics two years hence – winning no fewer than nine of the 12 events. Mary Milne struck silver in the high jump with 1.52m and there were bronze medals for Ethel Johnson (60m in an unofficial 7.7, equalling Rose Thompson's UK record), Eileen Hiscock (100m in an estimated 12.1, which would have been a UK best, and 200m), Gladys Lunn (800m) and Violet Webb (80m hurdles in an unofficial UK record equalling 11.9). The 800m winner in a world record 2:12.4 was Zdenka Koubková of Czechoslovakia and Gladys Lunn was unfortunate not to have received the silver medal, and perhaps even the gold. Some 30 years later, in a private note, Gladys's fellow Birchfield Harrier and leading official Dorette Nelson Neal, wrote of that race: "Lunn was pushed on to the green by Koubková, recovered back on to the track and caught her again, only to be elbowed round the bend and nearly on the green again. Lunn was thoroughly disgusted and 'gave up' and the Swedish girl [Märtha Wretman] passed her. I wanted to have a protest put in but this was received with a scandalised 'we can't do that sort of thing'." There were no official place times but the IAAF's World Record Progression book offers estimated times of 2:15.8 for Wretman (whose nephew Anders Gärderud would become Olympic steeplechase champion 42 years later) and 2:17.0, well inside her UK record, for Lunn, who reportedly walked over the line. The German team totalled 95 points to 33 by Poland and 31 by England. Nineteen countries were represented.

In his book *Running Round The World*, published shortly after his death in 1966, Jack Crump – one of the most influential figures in British athletics after the Second World War – remarked: "I was a judge at these Women's World Championships and I must say that I was a little suspicious about the femininity of some of the competitors from Europe." He was right to be wary in the case of Zdenka Koubková, who was later revealed to be a man, Zdenek Koubek, and in 1943 that world 800m record of 2:12.4 was annulled.

Capt Webster enthused over what he described as "the most wonderful women's athletic meeting that the world has yet witnessed", but was critical too. "It is a great pity that lack of advertising and lack of the dissemination of information to the press prevented more than a few thousand spectators from being present." Reporting on the Games in *The Superman*, a magazine he edited, he did not pull his punches: "I am afraid the English girls must attribute their defeat to the bad management of their administrators. For Mrs Cornell and her vast work for sport, both as Hon. Sec. of the Games and of the WAAA, I have nothing but the most wholehearted admiration; she is not to blame. But the fact remains that the WAAA as a body has been content to bank upon their track athletes pulling them through; nothing has been done to provide our girls with coaching and they have not been given nearly enough scratch competition this year in preparation for the Games. Of the English girls, Mary Milne alone showed fire and skill, the rest were mediocre. We have as good natural material in this country as ever came out of Germany, Poland or Czechoslovakia, but it remains to be seen whether those people who are charged with the administration of English women's athletics have the sense to make proper use of our excellent natural talent."

Although the WAAA had always cherished its independence from the AAA and would hold its annual summer championships quite separately from the men, right through until 1988, the two governing bodies did join forces to stage combined National Indoor Championships at Wembley's

Empire Pool from 1935 to 1939. Equal second in the high jump at 1.47m in 1935 was Dorothy Odam, just turned 15. She would tie for the title with Mary Dumbrill (née Milne) the following year and was outright champion for the next three years. One woman did even better, Ethel Raby taking all five long jump titles on offer.

BRITAIN'S FIRST OLYMPIC MEDALLIST

The distinction of becoming the first British woman to gain an Olympic medal fell to Dorothy Odam whose promise had first been spotted by Muriel Cornell, who arranged for her to join Mitcham AC at the age of 11. As the 16-year-old baby of the team in Berlin in 1936 and on her first trip abroad ("I'd never been further than Bognor"), she placed second in the high jump. In fact she was unlucky to come away with the silver rather than the gold medal for she cleared the winning height of 1.60m at the first attempt, while Hungary's Ibolya Csák managed it at the second try and Elfriede Kaun of Germany at the third. All three failed at 1.62m, so under the present rule Dorothy would have been the winner. But in 1936 a jump-off was decreed and Csák – who this time succeeded at 1.62m whereas Dorothy could go no higher than 1.60m – claimed victory. A few days later the IAAF passed a new rule governing ties and, had that been in effect in Berlin, Dorothy would have been hailed as Britain's first female Olympic champion … fully 28 years before Mary Rand. Team manager Muriel Cornell commented that the youngster had "jumped faultlessly and without apparent nervousness throughout the competition."

Reflecting on the atmosphere at those Games, Dorothy has written: "In Berlin there was an air of tenseness. The burning question was whether to salute Hitler or not and the whole Games inevitably had a political flavour. The accent was too much on nationalistic pride and too little on pure love of sport. Moreover, those Games were highly organised, with typical Teutonic efficiency, and it was sometimes irksome to be ordered about." Of her own high jumping in Berlin, she admitted "really, I knew nothing about the event.

I just jumped as high as I could, using the scissors style. No coach, no teaching, but I was so proud to be in that team. I didn't understand centimetres, so I didn't know what I was jumping. I just kept on clearing the bar, until it was me and a Hungarian. There was hardly a mention when I got home with a silver medal. Different days."

Earlier in 1936, competing in dreadful weather conditions, Dorothy had equalled the listed world record of 1.65m, although it was never ratified, and in 1937 she again topped the world list with 1.63m. In 1938 she won the Empire Games title in Sydney at 1.60m and the following year she cleared 1.66m in the Southern Championships at Brentwood School Playing Fields ("off grass into a pile of sand") for what was eventually accepted as a world record. Not that it was officially ratified until 1947 because the IAAF had recognised a jump of 1.67m in 1938 by Germany's Dora Ratjen, who was later revealed to be a man. As Dorothy recalled: "They [the IAAF] wrote to me telling me I didn't hold the record, so I wrote to them saying, 'She's not a woman, she's a man'. They did some research and found 'her' serving as a waiter called Heinrich Ratjen, so I got my world record back again."

In 1940 Dorothy married Richard Tyler, a former quarter miler and rugby player, and served in the Women's Auxiliary Air Force (WAAFs) as a lorry and bus driver (for the famous Dambusters Squadron) and physical training instructor from 1941 to 1945. She gave birth to sons in 1946 and 1947 and then proceeded to make an astonishing comeback after an absence of eight years. She would return better than ever, as we shall see in the next chapter.

Schoolgirl Dorothy Odam, still only 16, became the first British woman to win an Olympic athletics medal when she placed second in the high jump, with the same height as the winner (1.60m), at the 1936 Games in Berlin. Although none of the three sprinters (Eileen Hiscock, Barbara Burke and Audrey Brown) reached the 100m final that trio plus Violet Olney came away with silver medals from the 4x100m relay in 47.6, having set a UK record of 47.5 in their heat a long way behind Germany's world record breaking 46.4. To the spectating Adolf

Hitler's consternation the home team fluffed the last change when way ahead and victory went to the USA in 46.9. It was some Games for the Brown family as Audrey's brother Godfrey finished a very close second in the 400m and anchored the winning 4x400m relay team. Shortly after the Games, in Wuppertal, Kay Tiffen (a commercial artist who was later to marry Cecil Dale, a future British team manager) broke the UK 80m hurdles record with 11.8 in one heat, only for Violet Webb to clock 11.7 in the next. Neither had survived the semi-finals in Berlin. The winning Olympic time? 11.7.

Kay Tiffen provided an interesting view of those days in an article in *Modern Athletics* magazine in 1958. Mentioning that at the 1936 Olympics she was given a little trowel in a leather case, she recalled that "we used to dig starting holes as conscientiously as the modern athlete fixes the starting block." She added: "The warming up programme was, however, very primitive compared with present-day standards. I used to carefully jog a lap; do a couple of hurdling exercises and a 50 yard sprint; then take a long rest. I was terrified that I might wear myself out before the competition. Yet, strangely enough, despite these methods I only once pulled a muscle during 12 years of top-class competition. Maybe I was not running fast enough!" Violet Webb, who retired from competition before marrying Harry Simpson in 1937, provided another glimpse of a less demanding era: "I wore the same spikes for two Olympic Games and training in between, although sometimes I trained in my slippers."

Despite her great achievement, Dorothy Odam was met with apathy on her return home. As she recollected in the excellent oral history, *A Proper Spectacle*: "When I came back from the Olympics in 1936, no one was interested. A few neighbours asked me how I got on. It didn't mean very much even to me. I was used to winning so I probably was a bit disappointed that I only got silver and I didn't get gold. I didn't realise then how much it would mean in the future not to have won gold. In 1939 I broke the world record in the middle of a school field. Even then I only got two lines in the Stop Press. I think there would have been more about it if I had been a man. Women weren't given much press coverage."

Summing up the state of British athletics in an article for *World Sports* in October 1936, Muriel Cornell wrote: "The standard of women's athletics is still on the upgrade, but if only we could get more public sympathy and interest, athletics taught by competent coaches in the schools, more tracks and equipment, professional coaches and sports organisers, more money in order to develop and help in the formation of new clubs, and, finally, more international meetings, I feel sure that when the next Olympic Games comes along the women athletes would bring a large proportion of medals back to England." Who knew then that the next Olympics would be all of 12 years away ... and would be held in London?

These were far sighted views, but there were others in the sport who remained far too cautious. In her 1934 book, *Improve Your Athletics – A Book For Modern Girls*, Anne Williams, the first WAAA cross country champion in 1927 and former coach to Polytechnic Ladies AC, wrote: "It is not advisable to allow schoolgirls to race a sprint longer than 100 yards ... In schools in which there are girls of 16 and over, a 220 yards race can be inserted as a competitive event. When girls of 16 race against grown women at this distance, harm is likely to be done ... No schoolgirls should be allowed to take part in long-distance or cross country races, but cross country runs can be taken with care and strict supervision as a normal activity ... It is not advisable for girls under 18 years of age to compete in the running long jump."

It was in 1936 that the era of the FSFI drew to a close. It had served its purpose well, establishing women's athletics internationally, but now it was time for the IAAF to take over the responsibility. At the time it was dissolved, the FSFI had 30 member countries: England, France, Czechoslovakia, Italy and USA joined in 1921, Switzerland 1922, Belgium, Canada, Latvia, Lithuania and Yugoslavia in 1924, Sweden in 1925, Austria, Germany, Japan, Luxembourg and Poland in 1926, Argentina, Estonia, Greece, Netherlands, Romania and South Africa in 1928, Australia, Hungary, New Zealand and Palestine in 1930, Ireland, Norway and Rhodesia in 1936.

One of the guarantees given to the FSFI was that the Olympic programme for women would be extended from the six events in Berlin to nine, the new disciplines being the 200m, long jump and shot. It was intended to implement that at the 1940 Games scheduled for Tokyo, but the world had other things on its mind at that time and the augmented programme was introduced in London in 1948.

In 1937 the British Amateur Athletic Board, whose primary function was the promotion of international competition and consisted of five representatives from the AAA (England & Wales), three from the Scottish AAA and two from the Northern Ireland AAA, co-opted two representatives from the WAAA although they had a voice only on matters concerning female athletes. That remained the situation until 1959 when the AAA's representation was increased to six and instead of the two co-opted WAAA members the recently formed British Women's Amateur Athletic Council was awarded two seats on the Board, with full voting powers except on financial matters.

The Women's World Games, which the FSFI had wanted to organise in 1938, were abolished with the demise of that pioneering body, but two other meetings of significance were held that year. The Empire Games, staged on a grass track at Sydney Cricket Grounds in February, comprised eight women's events and for the first time English men's and women's teams travelled together, the journey to Australia taking all of six weeks. The athletes did their best to keep fit on board ship but, as Kay Tiffen wrote, "the sea air did not help and the more exercise we did the more we ate and I for one certainly arrived with a few pounds of extra weight. However, it was a marvellous experience, if not athletically too successful."

Although the only other countries represented were Australia, New Zealand, Canada, South Africa and Scotland, there was just one English victory, the high jump being won by Dorothy Odam – still only 17 – at 1.60m with team-mate Dora Gardner second at 1.58m. The only other individual medals for the England team, which was managed by Rose Gillis (the former sprint star Rose Thompson), came from Ethel Raby, second in the long jump with 5.66m, and Gladys Lunn – who, deprived of any event longer than 220y, snatched bronze in the javelin! Gladys recollected that at those Games the English athletes were given all of 2s 6d (12.5p) a day pocket money (that's about £6 on today's values), but the allowance wasn't much more generous at the 1966 Games when athletes received a daily allowance of 10 shillings (50p, or about £7.50 today). Representing South Africa in Sydney, British Olympian Barbara Burke won the 80m hurdles in 11.7.

The first European Championships for women, held in September in the politically unsettling atmosphere of Vienna (the men competed separately in Paris), was on a much larger scale with athletes from 14 nations. Although Godfrey Brown, Sydney Wooderson, Don Finlay and Harold Whitlock struck gold for the men, the women's team – admittedly lacking Dorothy Odam – returned without any medals at all. Highest placed, at fourth, were Dorothy Saunders in the 100m, Dorothy Cosnett in the high jump and Ethel Raby in the long jump. To make matters even worse, the 4x100m relay team – which had crossed the finish line third – was seemingly unfairly disqualified.

Highlights from each of the WAAA Championships meetings 1930–1939

1930 (Stamford Bridge)

ALTHOUGH MOST OF the country's strongest women's clubs were in the London area – such as London Olympiades, Middlesex Ladies and Mitcham (shortly to be joined by Spartan Ladies, founded by Teddy Knowles in 1930) – the two star performers of these Championships came from the North and Midlands. Bury's Nellie Halstead (19) took the 220y in a world record 25.2, well clear of 100y (11.4) winner Eileen Hiscock, and Gladys "Sally" Lunn (22) of Birmingham's Birchfield Harriers, whose best the previous year was merely 2:39.0, set new world record figures for 880y of 2:18.2. Gladys's clubmate Dorette Nelson (later Mrs Nelson Neal), a future WAAA official and coach of great influence, led at the half distance. Elsie Wright improved from 61.4 to 59.8 to win the 440y, while Muriel Cornell not only won the long jump with 5.63m but also the 80m hurdles in 12.4, having equalled the world record of 12.2 earlier in the summer. The event of the highest standard was the high jump where four women cleared 5 feet (1.52m) or higher. The Dutch world record holder at 1.60m (5ft 3in), Carolina Gisolf, won with 1.57m with Mary Milne – who had the previous year become at 15 the country's youngest international – runner-up at 1.55m.

Writing in *The Sunday Times*, Harold Abrahams – vowing to "set aside all that prejudice I still feel about women holding championships in track and field events" – admitted: "I enjoyed the sports yesterday very much indeed. The women competitors (many of them seem quite children) are dead keen, and you get the impression right through that they are really enjoying what they are doing. The tense atmosphere of men's championships has not yet crept into women's athletics (though I fear it soon will), and consequently there is something rather more attractive about it." Alas, the rest of the report was less positive as the 1924 Olympic 100m champion "noticed especially how unsuited the feminine form is to the throwing events" and recommended that the "heavy" events be dropped.

1931 (Stamford Bridge)

NINE YEARS AFTER Harry Edward achieved a similar triple at the AAA Championships on this track, Nellie Halstead made history by winning the 100y (11.4), 220y (25.5) and 440y in a world record 58.8 on one afternoon! Gladys Lunn, who had during the cross country season won both the national championship and the first international race against France and Belgium, retained her 880y title in 2:22.4. The most dramatic event was the mile walk, which ended with the disqualification of Jeanne Probekk just 15 yards from the tape after she had led all the way. As *The Times* reported: "She repeatedly stalled off determined challenges by the holder, Miss Connie Mason, a clubmate, but when the latter drew almost level with only 30 yards to go, Miss Probekk appeared to become flustered, and developed a half-run with tragic consequences." Connie Mason's winning time was equally startling as she smashed through the eight minute barrier, clocking 7:45.6 as compared to Lucy Howes' previous world mark of 8:12.2 in 1930 and her own best of 8:14.4. Elsie Green set a UK record of 12.0 in the 80m hurdles and Muriel Cornell signed off with a leap of 5.51m for her fifth consecutive long jump title, a sequence that has never been bettered.

1932 (Stamford Bridge)

THE LAST WAAA Championships to be staged at Stamford Bridge (the men had already moved to the White City) proved particularly memorable on account of a staggering world 440y record by Nellie Halstead. She took a cool two seconds off the record, which she had equalled in a heat earlier in the day, with a time of 56.8 – a time which was not bettered until 1954! She also won the 220y in 25.6 but did not defend her 100y laurels, which passed to Ethel Johnson (11.1) who in a heat clocked a world record (but unratified) time of 11.0. Gladys Lunn, who had retained her cross country title with 43 seconds to spare, took the 880y in 2:20.4 to top the world 800m/880y list for the year. Mary Milne, now all of 18, won her first high jump title at 1.55m. Edith Halstead, Nellie's older "sister", became javelin champion but, as with Mary (Mark) Weston, she was actually born male but brought up as a girl. Following a corrective operation in 1944, Eddie Halstead got married and became a father. However, despite some references to the contrary, Nellie Halstead was born, lived and died as a female.

1933 (White City)

MOVING TO THE new home of British athletics and contesting metric distances throughout all the events for the first time, these Championships proved relatively lacklustre. The only performances of top international quality were Nellie Halstead's 58.8 400m, a time only she had ever bettered, and a 12.0 80m hurdles by Elsie Green which equalled the world best for the year by herself and Violet Webb among others. Eileen Hiscock scored a sprint double, taking the 100m in 12.2 and 200m in 25.8. In the 100m she was followed in by Nellie Halstead (12.3) and Lily Chalmers (12.3), the latter going on to win the 200m title in 1937 and 1939 ... while in 1951, in her 40th year, she was third quickest

Briton over 220y! Casting off the disappointment of her late, late disqualification in 1931 and finishing a distant second to Connie Mason in 1932, Jeanne Probekk not only won her first track title, 1600m in 7:51.2, but also the inaugural road walking championship. Mystery of the year was high jumper Dora Greenwood. In June she was credited with a UK record of 1.60m when winning the Southern title at Brentwood, a four-inch improvement on her previous best, followed three days later by an even more sensational world record equalling (but unratified) clearance of 1.65m at a Southend club meeting. At the WAAA Championships the following month, however, she was only second to Mary Milne with 1.47m and never again achieved anything of note.

1934 (Herne Hill)

EILEEN HISCOCK TUNED up for her Empire Games double at the White City five weeks later with a 100m victory in 12.2. Another double gold medallist in waiting, Gladys Lunn, took the 800m in 2:18.3 but was well beaten in the javelin by Edith Halstead. The latter's sister, Nellie Halstead, gave the 400m a miss and captured the 200m title in 25.6, while Phyllis Bartholomew long jumped 5.55m for her third consecutive WAAA title prior to claiming gold at the White City. Elsie Green retained her 80m hurdles title in 12.0, and Jeanne Probekk clocked a world best of 7:38.2 in the 1600m walk. The high jump winner at 1.55m was Gretel Bergmann, a 20-year-old German member of Polytechnic Ladies. She had hoped to represent Britain at the Berlin Olympics two years hence but, as she recalled over half a century later, "I was blackmailed in 1934 to return to Germany under threats to my family and the whole Jewish sports movement. I had absolutely no choice but had to do what I was told to do." Ordered to train for the Games in order for the Nazis to head off boycott threats by pretending there was no religious or racial discrimination, she was shaping up as a potential medallist after equalling the German record of 1.60m but, because she was Jewish, she was barred from the Olympic trials. The German authorities said she was injured, but that wasn't true. And as if that was not bad enough, the Germans selected an athlete called Dora Ratjen to take Gretel's place ... and 'she' was actually a man, later revealed to be Heinrich Ratjen. Gretel is still alive; she emigrated to the USA in 1937, became an American citizen in 1942 and currently resides in New York aged 98.

1935 (White City)

THE EVER ASTONISHING Nellie Halstead, who in 1931 had won the WAAA 100y title and set an unratified world record equalling time of 11.0 from scratch in a handicap race, not only became national cross country champion but on the track won the 800m in the UK record time of 2:15.6 – a mark that was unsurpassed until 1952. But for the confusion over Zdenka Koubková's 2:12.4 on this track the previous year ('she' later transpired to be a 'he') it would have been ratified as a world record. Eileen Hiscock repeated her 1933 sprint double with times of 12.2 and 25.3, her 100m heat time of 11.9 remaining unbeaten by a Briton until 1956, and two other proven winners who triumphed again were Elsie Green with 12.3 in the 80m hurdles for her fifth consecutive title and Mary Milne, high jump champion for a third time with 1.55m ahead of her youthful Mitcham clubmate Dorothy Odam (1.52m).

1936 (White City)

AS A 16-year-old schoolgirl, Dorothy Odam made tremendous progress to equal the listed world high jump record of 1.65m at the Southern Championships at Brentwood in June (the enigmatic Dora Greenwood placing third at 1.52m), but a modest clearance of 1.53m sufficed for her first outdoor national title. The even younger Betty Lock (15) won the 60m in the UK record time of 7.6 for the first of four consecutive wins in this event, but declined Olympic selection. She didn't contest the 100m which went, as did the 200m and 80m hurdles, to Barbara Burke (12.3/25.2/11.9), that last time matching the UK record. Burke's national status has always been contentious. Although born in London, she was taken to South Africa as a child and that was the country she represented at the Empire Games of 1934 and 1938 and for whom at 17 she set world records of 11.0 for 100y and 24.8 for 220y at high altitude Pretoria in 1935. However, as South Africa decided not to send a team to the Berlin Olympics she returned to her native land in order to gain selection in the British team. The 400m was won by Olive Hall in 58.6, a time bettered only by Nellie Halstead, who on this occasion moved up yet another distance to finish second in the inaugural mile championship! Nellie, who had retained her cross country title ahead of Lillian Styles (six times champion and four times runner-up between 1927 and 1937), finished some five yards behind another legendary runner in Gladys Lunn, whose time of 5:23.0 was a world best for an event still in its infancy. One week later in Birmingham, despite a thunderstorm and torrential rain, Olive Hall won an 880y handicap race off scratch in 2:17.4 – a world record although due to some bureaucratic mix-up it never received official IAAF recognition until the 1950s, and that was thanks to the doggedness of Harold Abrahams!

1937 (White City)

DOROTHY ODAM WAS the star attraction at this meeting, which served as selection trials for the forthcoming Empire Games in Sydney in February 1938. She didn't disappoint as her winning leap of 1.63m topped the world year list. An excellent second place performance of 1.60m by Dora Gardner ranked her equal third in the world. She would finish as runner-up to Dorothy also in the last two pre-war championships but return victorious in 1945 and 1946. Another whose career would straddle the war period was Winnie Jeffrey, the 100m winner in 12.2; as Winnie Jordan she would be champion again in 1945, 1947 and 1948. Lily Chalmers became the first Briton to crack 25 sec for 200m with her 24.9 on a loose cinder track, although that lasted as a UK record for only three weeks as Dorothy Saunders, just fifth at the White City, took the World Student Games title in Paris in 24.8, second fastest in the world that year. Gladys Lunn scored an extraordinary triple in what would prove to be her farewell appearance at these championships, defeating Nellie

Halstead over 800m in 2:18.5, lowering her world mile best to 5:17.0 and throwing the javelin 32.97m! She rounded off her distinguished international career as team captain at the Empire Games. A keen golfer, she died aged 79 while enjoying a round at Birmingham's Great Barr Golf Club. Back at the Championships, Barbara Burke won the hurdles in a modest 12.1, having officially equalled the world record of 11.6 in Berlin a few days earlier, and Ethel Raby went very close to Muriel Cornell's UK long jump record with a leap of 5.79m, ranking her third in the world that year.

1938 (White City)

STILL ONLY 17, the quick starting Betty Lock – already with one indoor and two outdoor 60m titles under her belt – completed a sprint double, equalling her championship record of 7.6 at 60m and taking the 100m crown in 12.2. A month later, in Amsterdam, she clocked 7.4 (only 0.1 outside the world record and a British best until Andrea Lynch ran 7.2 in 1974) en route to a personal best of 12.1 in a 100m heat. In the final she produced another 12.1, narrowly defeating a 20-year-old Dutchwoman named Fanny Koen. We would be hearing a lot more of her under her married name! The great Nellie Halstead bowed out with yet another title, the 800m (2:20.4), while Dorothy Odam retained her high jump laurels, pressed all the way by Dora Gardner as both cleared 1.57m. Barbara Burke had returned to South Africa and Kay Tiffen was absent but these were a great championships for Mitcham, for not only were there titles for Betty Lock and Dorothy Odam but Bevis Reid and Kitty Tilley finished first and second in both the shot and discus. That pair dominated British throwing for many years. Bevis (later Mrs Shergold) won the shot six times and the discus five times between 1938 and 1951; Kitty (later Mrs Dyer) collected five shot titles between 1934 and 1946. Before they came on the scene the UK records stood at 9.98m and 34.15m; by the end of the thirties Bevis had thrown 12.35m (improving to 13.25m in 1949) and 36.07m (39.88m in 1951). This was the year in which the WAAA rule on suitable clothing was amended to read: "Every competitor must wear a tunic or blouse, and if sleeves are not worn, must fit to the edge of the shoulder and closely around the arm and neck. Dark shorts must be worn and the inside leg measurement shall be at least 4in, level across the bottom when worn and not more than 4in wider than the largest part of the thigh."

1939 (White City)

THESE WOULD PROVE to be the last WAAA Championships for six bleak years, and all credit to a number of resilient winners who despite losing what would probably have been their best athletic years managed to return to top class competition after the war. Foremost among them was Dorothy Odam, for whom another Olympic silver medal lay nine years ahead. A few weeks earlier she had won the Southern high jump title with a world record 1.66m and she almost matched that with 1.65m. Ethel Raby, who long jumped 5.64m for her fifth consecutive victory, would win once more in 1946, while Bevis Reid and Kitty Tilley again finished one-two in the shot and discus. Betty Lock, who retained her sprint titles in 7.6 and 12.2, would also return (as Mrs Brickwood) after the war, placing second over 60m in 1949; and Lily Chalmers, winner at 200m (25.6) and 400m (59.5), would go on to finish second and third over 400m in 1945 and 1946. One UK record fell when cross country champion Evelyne Forster ran away with the mile in 5:15.3, a time which stood also as a world best until 1952.

UNITED KINGDOM RECORDS AT 1 JANUARY 1940

60m: 7.4 Betty Lock 1938; 100y: 11.0 Ivy Walker 1930, Nellie Halstead 1931, Eileen Hiscock 1931, Ethel Johnson 1932; 100m: 11.9 Hiscock 1935 & 1936; 200m: 24.8 Dorothy Saunders 1937; 220y: 25.0 Hiscock 1934; 400m/440y: 56.8 Halstead 1932; 800m: 2:15.6 Halstead 1935; 880y: 2:17.4 Olive Hall 1936; 1000m: 3:00.6 Gladys Lunn 1934; Mile: 5:15.3 Evelyne Forster 1939; 80mH: 11.7 Violet Webb 1936; HJ: 1.66 Dorothy Odam 1939; LJ: 5.85 Muriel Cornell 1930; 4kg SP: 12.35 Bevis Reid 1939; 1kg DT: 36.07 Reid 1939; 600gm JT: 36.81 Kathleen Connal 1937; 4x100m: 47.5 British Olympic team 1936; Mile Walk: 7:40.8 Jeanne Probekk 1934.

THE FORTIES

WITH MUCH MORE important matters confronting the nation there was only spasmodic athletic activity during the Second World War. John Brant's tireless researches have revealed a few reasonable marks during that period, including a 62.3 400m by Winnie Jeffrey and 2:26.1 880y by Miriam Clarke in 1941, an 11.7 100y by Zoe Hancock in 1943 and a 5:39.0 mile by Phyllis Richards in 1944. Despite having less than £7 in its bank account the WAAA lost little time in starting up again once victory in Europe had been achieved in May 1945. The body moved quickly to organise its first post-war Championships in August 1945, whereas the AAA did not resume the men's Championships until July 1946. Junior (under-15) Championships were inaugurated in just the high jump and long jump to start with in 1945, with the first Intermediate (under-17) titles decided from 1948.

It was a case of catch-up for Britain's women athletes as competitors from several countries had managed to perform at a high level despite the limitations caused by a global war. While many, like Dorothy Tyler (and, on the men's side, Sydney Wooderson), lost what should have been the best athletic years of their lives, one athlete in particular set new standards of excellence. That was Fanny Blankers-Koen, who in Nazi-occupied Holland set world records or bests of 10.8 for 100y (1944), 11.5 for 100m (1943), 11.3 for 80m hurdles (1942), 1.71m high jump (1943) and 6.25m long jump (1943). The Russians were also prominent although as they were not members of the IAAF at the time their performances were not ratified. However, statisticians noted such impressive world beating marks as 2:12.0 for 800m (1943) and 4:38.0

for 1500m (1944) by Yevdokiya Vasilyeva and 49.88m discus throw by Nina Dumbadze in 1944. In Germany, Anneliese Steinheuer set a ratified javelin record of 47.24m in 1942.

An event of considerable significance for women's athletics in the UK occurred in December 1945 when the monthly magazine *Athletics* appeared for the first time. This, the forerunner of *Athletics Weekly*, was founded and edited by Jimmy Green and although run on the proverbial shoestring immediately provided an invaluable service to the sport, particularly at club level. The very first issue demonstrated that the women's side of the sport would not be neglected, as there were action photos of Phyllis Richards and Dora Gardner winning WAAA titles in the 880y and high jump respectively. It was noted that Winnie Hughes was WAAA Hon. Secretary in succession to Muriel Cornell, and that the number of clubs affiliated to the Southern Counties WAAA (Hon. Secretary: Teddy Knowles) had been increased by ten during the past nine months and it was hoped that the pre-war strength of just over 90 clubs would be attained. The Hon. Secretaries of the other area associations were Dorette Nelson Neal (Midland Counties) and Ruth Taylor (Northern Counties).

The major happening in 1946 was the revival of the European Championships and, for the first time, the men and women competed alongside each other in Oslo's Bislett Stadium. Reporting for *Athletics* magazine, Harold Abrahams wrote: "I have never been considered much in favour of women's athletics, but I want to say without reservation that the spirit of our small women's team was something which aroused even my admiration. They were a splendid example of what the team spirit should be." The star was Winnie Jordan (née Jeffrey), who finished second to Yevgeniya Sechenova of the USSR (that country competing for the first time on the international stage) in both the 100m and 200m with times of 12.2 and 25.6.

Ever since its inception *Athletics* had carried the official notices of the AAA, and from its March 1947 issue the WAAA were offered the same service of disseminating information to club members. In a message from the Chairman, Dick Taylor wrote: "I am pleased to note a revived interest in women's athletics after the serious set-back during the war, when so very few sports meetings included competition for them. All parts of the country are functioning again and the WAAA is giving every encouragement in the sport. Naturally many pre-war athletes have retired, but the new generation promises to be equally capable of reaching past standards. The idea that competitive athletics was harmful for women is now proved wrong by the many competitors, now married, who are encouraging their own children in the sport. In fact, many such mothers are of the opinion their period of competition has proved beneficial rather than otherwise. Twenty-five years ago women were merely tolerated, if not scorned, in athletics, but England, like other countries, has now recognised them as an integral part of the sport."

A major step forward in 1947 was that the WAAA was admitted as a member of the BAAB, recognised by the IAAF as the overall governing body for the UK. Women's athletics was moving apace, and as Jimmy Green wrote in an editorial in May 1947: "We shall probably see and hear more of the ladies' side of athletics this year than ever before. The plans of the WAAA and other clubs and associations are going ahead with enterprise and enthusiasm. It will be surprising if considerable talent is not unearthed during the season and there is little doubt that our girls will more than hold their own in the 1948 Olympics. Already I hear from Geoff Dyson of one Olympic hope for the hurdles in Maureen Gardner, the Oxford sprinter. Still a novice, so far as hurdling is concerned, he describes her as already being in the Violet Webb class."

This was the WAAA's silver jubilee year and it was celebrated with a win over France in Paris. Victory was all the sweeter as the British men's team lost by 73 points to 56. The women's encounter, astonishingly the first international match since 1931 (and the first time the women's side had competed together with the men in a match), consisted only of six events – as against 15 for the men – and it could not have been much closer as the result hinged on the final event. With victories by team captain Winnie Jordan (12.7 100m), Maureen Gardner (UK record 11.5 80m hurdles) and the 4x100m team of Sylvia Cheeseman, Margaret Walker, Gardner and Jordan (48.0), Britain prevailed

26-24. Two days later Britain swept aside Luxembourg in a match which saw Jean Desforges, Britain's second best hurdler behind Maureen Gardner, make her international long jump debut. Finishing second to her opponent from Luxembourg with an exceedingly modest 4.94m hardly marked her out as the athlete who would in 1953 become Britain's first six metre jumper and European champion the year after that. In another significant initiative during 1947, Muriel Cornell was appointed WAAA Honorary Coaching Organiser.

As the year ended the BAAB issued a list of Olympic Possibles – "athletes from whom it is believed the team to represent Great Britain in the 1948 Olympic Games will, to a very great extent, be finally selected." Among more than 50 names were such established figures as Winnie Jordan, Maureen Gardner, Sylvia Cheeseman and Dora Gardner, all of whom did indeed make the team with Maureen going so agonisingly close to victory in the hurdles, but surprisingly Dorothy Manley – who would finish second in the 100m – was named only as a high jump possible although she ranked fourth in the UK at 100 yards in 1947 with 11.6. Two other future Olympic silver medallists at Wembley did not make the list at all. Audrey Williamson literally came from nowhere in 1948 to finish as runner-up in the 200m, while Dorothy Tyler (née Odam) had not been considered as she had given birth to sons in 1946 and 1947.

Excitement ran high among WAAA officials as the Olympic season commenced with the Games being staged in London for the first time in 40 years. Nonetheless, certain rules which would be unthinkable today had to be upheld and the Association issued a rebuke to athletes wearing – gasp – white shorts. "White shorts must not be worn. Failure to comply with this rule may mean the ordering off of the competitor concerned." The rule in question insisted that shorts be of a dark or strong colour.

With Winnie Hughes as women's team manager, assisted by Connie Leslie, and Dora Gardner as team captain, the 20-strong British Olympic team performed with enormous credit at Wembley. From a programme of just nine events (the men had 24) four silver medals were obtained, three of them in the wake of the fabulous Fanny Blankers-Koen.

The "Flying Dutchwoman" dominated the Games in a style reminiscent of Jesse Owens in Berlin in 1936. Like him she won four gold medals, in her case in the 100m, 200m, 80m hurdles and 4x100m relay – the first and only woman to win four titles in a single Olympics – and had she competed in the high jump and long jump, at which she was world record holder, it's feasible she could have gone home with six golds! She displayed great form as the Olympics approached, setting world records of 11.5 for 100m and 11.0 for the hurdles in June 1948, but what really motivated her as she prepared for the Games was a printed remark of British team manager Jack Crump that she was too old to win at the Olympics. "It was just the thing to rouse me, to make me go out there and prove to them that even if I was 30 years old and the mother of two children, I could still be a champion."

First came the 100m, where on a slow track and into the wind she won by almost three metres in 11.9 from Britain's Dorothy Manley (12.2), who exceeded all expectations to claim the silver medal thanks to getting the best start of her career. Dorothy, who worked as a shorthand-typist for the Suez Canal company in the City of London, took her summer holiday allowance to compete in the Games. Everything was so much more casual in those days. As she related to Neil Wilson in the *Daily Mail* in 2011: "I never thought about the Olympics. I felt no great expectations. Of course, I was terribly nervous about competing in such a big stadium, but then I was always nervous before competition. I didn't expect to win a medal. I'd never won the women's national title. The trials were a fiasco for me. I was left at the start and finished fifth. I was a bit surprised to be picked." She recalled that the only kit she was given was a blazer and skirt for the Opening Ceremony. "My mother made my vest and shorts. I remember there was a strict rule about our skirts not finishing more than four inches above the knee! My parents bought my spikes." Dorothy later ran under the married name of Hall and in 1979, a widow for the past six years, she married the 1950 Empire Games 880y and European 800m champion John Parlett – whom she had first got to know over 30 years earlier at an Olympic training camp at Butlins. It was one of the great romantic stories in British athletics.

Fanny's next test was the hurdles, a race which she nominated as the most memorable – but most nerve-racking – of her career. "Never shall I forget the day of the heats," she recalled. "I went to the warm-up track behind Wembley Stadium that morning as the Olympic 100m gold medallist but nobody could ever have felt less like a champion. My knees trembled. Never had I been so nervous before a race. I went through my warming-up as usual, but my mind was not on it. All the time I was waiting for a glimpse of my rival, Maureen Gardner, whom I had never seen before. She arrived by car, and made a considerable impression on me when I saw that she had brought her own hurdles. An athlete who carries her own hurdles around must really be in the top class, I thought.

"There were no other hurdles available on the training track and because I felt in need of a little practice over the flights before the first heat, I summoned up my courage and asked if I could use hers. We shook hands and I noticed immediately that I was not the only one who was nervous. Both of us were on tenterhooks. Just how good Maureen was I was soon to see. In her semi-final, she scraped a hurdle and lost her balance, but she still managed to achieve third position and a place in the final. My husband was cautious. 'Fanny,' he said, 'no long jumping for you tomorrow. You must concentrate on the hurdles, because this English girl knows her business'."

She certainly did, and the 19-year-old ballet teacher from Oxford, in only her second season at the event, was ready to run the race of her life. Not that her final preparation was ideal. As she recounted: "I arrived at Wembley by Underground train only just in time for the briefest of warm-ups, after fellow passengers had given up their seats to enable me to stretch out on the journey from Baker Street Station!" The final was a thriller and for a while it looked as though she would become the first British woman to win an Olympic athletics title. Fanny got away to a dreadful start but managed to draw level with Maureen approaching the fifth hurdle. Then disaster loomed up again for the Dutch star: "I was going so fast that I went too close to the hurdle, hit it, and lost my balance. What happened after that is just a blurred memory. It was a grim struggle, in which my hurdling style went to pieces. I staggered like a drunkard."

It was close, but by a matter of inches Fanny had won as both athletes were timed at 11.2, a UK record for the silver medallist. "Maureen and I shook hands. It had been a wonderful race and I was proud to have beaten such a brilliant athlete. We left the ground and went to our waiting coaches. My husband was feeling as delighted as I was. 'Well done, Fanny', he said, 'you aren't too old, after all' – and he left his congratulations at that! But there was Geoff Dyson, giving Maureen a long, long kiss. Ah well ... as somebody standing near said afterwards, 'that's the difference between an engaged couple and a staid old married pair!" Maureen, who married Dyson six weeks later, would finish second again to Fanny in the 1950 European Championships. Tragically, she died of cancer aged only 45.

Next on Fanny's Wembley agenda was the 200m, an Olympic event for the first time. By now she was tired and homesick, and wanted to withdraw. Husband Jan coaxed her into continuing and, on a muddy track which held her time down to 24.4, she won by an enormous six metre margin over Audrey Williamson (25.1), who won an Olympic silver medal in her first and only appearance for Britain. Audrey Patterson (USA) was placed third but in 1975 statistician Bob Sparks gained access to a photo finish print and discovered that it was Australia's Shirley Strickland who was actually third, although the official result has never been amended. Shirley may have been excused for believing a gold medal was coming her way after her team emerged from the final change-over of the relay in the lead with Holland only fourth. But Fanny was not to be denied, and she stormed through for her fourth victory and an indelible place in Olympic history. The British team of Dorothy Manley, Muriel Pletts, Margaret Walker and Maureen Gardner finished fourth in 48.0.

The other British runner-up was high jumper Dorothy Tyler, now 28, who duplicated her placing of 12 years earlier. Only eight months after giving birth to her second son, she raised her UK record to 1.68m (5ft 6in), her own physical height, with a second-time clearance, but the USA's Alice Coachman went over at the first attempt to take the title. Third place went to the multi-talented French concert pianist Micheline Ostermeyer, who had already won the shot and discus titles!

Dorothy was in a plaintive mood when interviewed for *Track Stats* by David Thurlow in 2000. "I missed both the 1940 and 1944 Olympics planned for Tokyo and Helsinki, and there was no reason why I should not have won both. I certainly would have jumped higher. The war took six years out of my life, and everyone else's, too, of course, but it was also six lost years technically. The straddle and western roll would have come in much earlier in the UK and I would have learned the roll earlier and would have gone much higher, but I did not change until 1951 when I came under Arthur Gold's coaching."

The Games, which had been awarded to London in March 1946, proved a huge success despite the organising committee having little more than two years to prepare amid the austerity and restrictions of immediate post-war Britain. The biggest crowds ever to watch athletics in the UK, often in excess of 80,000, flocked to Wembley each day. Sigfrid Edström, the Swedish President of the International Olympic Committee, summed up London's achievement in a message printed in the British Olympic Association's Official Report.

"The staging of the Olympic Games in London this year was recognised as the most crucial occasion in the history of sport. How could such a project in the Grand Manner be accomplished in the threadbare and impoverished world of 1948? It was a challenge to the British genius for improvisation, for Britain had to hold the Games in a city afflicted with an unparalleled housing shortage – yet homes had to be found for tens of thousands of foreign visitors, not to mention some 6000 athletes. The great test was taken; and the organisation rose gloriously to the supreme challenge. The visitors were housed and fed; the athletes were made at home in camps where every care was taken of their waking and sleeping hours. Wembley Stadium itself, where day after day huge crowds assembled, surpassed in magnificence and convenience any previous homes of the Games. The first Olympic Games for 12 years have come and gone – an unqualified success."

Reflecting on the Games, the WAAA stated: "When we look back on our many difficulties (lack of funds, training grounds and coaches, the closed down period during the war, etc) we are rightly pleased with the performance, and proud of our team and officials for the splendid show they put up. We should like to congratulate them all."

Although the Olympic women's programme was extended to include the 200m, long jump and shot, there was still no attempt to cater for endurance runners. Ludicrously, the 200m would remain the longest event at Olympic level until the 800m was reintroduced in 1960. The 400m was added in 1964, 1500m in 1972, 3000m (changed to 5000m in 1996) and marathon in 1984, 10,000m in 1988 and the 3000m steeplechase in 2008. The European authorities were always ahead: at the European Championships the 800m was introduced in 1954, the 400m in 1958, the 1500m in 1969, the 3000m in 1974, the marathon in 1982, the 10,000m in 1986, the steeplechase in 2006. However, it was the WAAA who led the way with national championships at 400m (440y) and 800m (880y) from 1922, cross country from 1927, 1500m (mile) from 1936, 3000m from 1968, 5000m and 10,000m from 1981, marathon from 1978 and steeplechase from 2002.

That women's athletics in 1948 was still light years away from being fully accepted as the equal in status of men's athletics was exemplified by the programme for the British Empire v USA relays and field event team match at the White City shortly after the Games. This the American men won by 11.5 events to 3.5 (there was a tie in the high jump). As for the women, they were allotted just two non-scoring events: 80m hurdles and 4x110y relay.

Attention was drawn to this continuing antipathy in the WAAA notes in the October 1948 issue of *Athletics*. The unidentified writer stated: "I was pleased to see in Jack Crump's article in *World Sports* that he agrees that there are still some of the older officials who are against women's athletics. We know this only too well. If it were not for the help of some of our friends who are also members of the AAA, we should not be in the position we are today, but there are still a few who are living in the past and doing much harm with their prejudice."

The decade ended on a high note when England beat France and the Netherlands at the White City in August 1949, the first post-war women's international on home soil.

Held in conjunction was a 3x880y relay in which a Southern Counties team of Doris Born, Eileen Garritt and Valerie Ball set world record figures of 7:07.8.

Highlights from each of the WAAA Championships meetings 1945–1949

1945 (Tooting Bec)

HELD JUST DAYS after the ending of the war with Japan, it was not surprising that performances were pretty modest. Indeed it was a miracle of organisation and determination that the meeting could be staged at all so soon after the cessation of hostilities with a war-ravaged Britain struggling to pick up the pieces of a normal existence. The meeting was dominated by athletes who had managed to keep some semblance of fitness throughout the war years. Winnie Jordan, who as Miss Jeffrey was 100m champion in 1937, scored a sprint treble in 12.8 (100m), 26.7 (200m) and 61.8 (440y). In the 100m and 440y she was followed home by Lily Chalmers, the 200m winner in 1937 and 200m/400m champion in 1939. Little noticed in fourth place in the 100m was a 16-year-old from Oxford Ladies AC by the name of Maureen Gardner, of whom much more would be heard. The high jump brought together again four-time champion Dorothy Tyler and her three-time runner-up Dora Gardner. This time it was Dora who prevailed with both clearing 1.52m. Another pre-war star, Kitty Dyer, who as Miss Tilley was shot put champion in 1934, 1935 and 1937, not only won that event but also her only discus title. Kathleen Connal, a Squadron Officer in the Women's Auxiliary Air Force, was second in the javelin. The WAAA champion in 1936, 1938 and 1939 and holder of the British record with 36.81m in 1937, she was awarded the OBE in the 1946 New Year Honours List.

1946 (White City)

WINNIE JORDAN ATTEMPTED to retain the 100m and 200m titles but had to settle for second place behind two 17-year-olds, Maureen Gardner (12.6) and Sylvia Cheeseman (25.7) – both of whom would develop into bright stars of the early post-war period and provide a wonderful image for women's athletics. Maureen would later marry AAA Chief Coach Geoff Dyson and Sylvia would wed 1952 Olympic steeplechase medallist and co-founder of the London Marathon, John Disley, who was coached by Dyson. However, Winnie would reach peak form for the season at the European Championships in Oslo, where she collected two silver medals. Phyllis Richards (2:21.0 800m), Dora Gardner (1.55m high jump) and Kitty Dyer (10.20m shot) retained their national titles, while Ethel Raby, champion from 1935 to 1939, reclaimed the long jump laurels with a leap of 5.05m. Margaret Lasbrey, the South African champion in 1939 and 1940, won the javelin with a throw of 34.44m. In 1950 she played hockey for England but later returned to South Africa.

1947 (Chiswick)

THE MEETING SHOULD have been staged at the White City (owned by the Greyhound Racing Association) but because of a coal crisis there was a government ban on midweek sport and two greyhound meetings had to be switched to weekends and the WAAA event was moved to the Polytechnic Harriers' Stadium. Maureen Gardner, still only 18, provided the highlight as she won the 80m hurdles in 11.5, breaking Violet Webb's UK record of 11.7 from 1936, but the time was never ratified because it was considered to be wind assisted. Not that it mattered, for she was to clock a legitimate 11.5 on three further occasions that summer. However, Maureen lost her 100m title despite running 12.1 ... beaten by inches by Winnie Jordan (12.1). Sylvia Cheeseman held on to her 200m title in 25.0 with Winnie a close second. Two 18-year-olds, both future European champions, attained top three placings for the first time: Jean Desforges (later Pickering) was second in the hurdles in 12.2 and Sheila Alexander (later Lerwill) high jumped 1.50m for third. An interesting name among the winners of junior (under-15) titles was long jumper Lorna Cornell, 14-year-old daughter of the great Muriel Cornell. Later in the year she was nominated an an "Olympic possible" but she left the sport early and would find greater fame as a tennis player.

1948 (Chiswick)

WHO WOULD HAVE guessed that Dorothy Manley and Audrey Williamson would, a few weeks later, have Olympic silver medals hung around their necks? Dorothy did top the British rankings at both 100y (11.1 in May) and 100m (12.0 a week before the Championships in June) but was relieved to gain Olympic selection at 100m after being left at the start and finishing only fifth behind Winnie Jordan (12.6), Doris Batter, 17-year-old Muriel Pletts and Maureen Gardner. Audrey, of the Women's Royal Army Corps, didn't impress that much in the 200m. In this her first season of serious competition she was timed at 25.8 behind Sylvia Cheeseman and Margaret Walker (both 25.7) ... and yet at the Games, her only international appearance, she would improve immensely on a heavy rain-soaked track to clock 25.1 (following a windy 24.9 semi) to finish second, admittedly a distant second, to Fanny Blankers-Koen. That essentially was it for Audrey, who never broke 26 sec again and concentrated more on long jumping, albeit at a modest level, until 1953. Three days after clocking a wind assisted 11.2 in a club meeting at Oxford, Maureen Gardner retained her hurdles title in an unremarkable 12.0, while Dorothy Tyler reclaimed the high jump title after a gap of nine years with a leap of 1.62m. Scottish-born Bevis Reid, who had won her first shot and discus titles ten years earlier, made history by achieving victories in all three throws: championship records of 12.34m and 36.74m, plus a javelin throw of 31.10m. A clubmate of Dorothy Tyler's at Mitcham AC, she was working at the time as Secretary of the British Council in Rome. Competing in her first WAAA Championships, 18-year-old Valerie Ball won the 400m in 60.8 – and she would go on to retain that title for the next five years although her main claim to fame would eventually come at double that distance.

1949 (White City)

THE NUMBER OF entries, at 197, was a record, as was Bevis Reid's shot and discus distances of 12.36m and 36.96m, both championship bests. Earlier in the season, competing in Italy, she had set UK records of 13.25m and 39.45m. Another double winner was Sylvia Cheeseman, who took the 100m in 12.1 ahead of Dorothy Manley, having three weeks earlier won her fourth consecutive 200m title (25.4) in an event that was farmed out to the WAAA Intermediate & Junior Championships at Bromsgrove. Later in the season Sylvia would smash the UK records for 200m and 220y with a sparkling 24.5 at Southampton, which was very close to Fanny Blankers-Koen's 24.3 200m which topped that year's world list. In the absence of Maureen Dyson (née Gardner), Jean Desforges recovered from the disappointment of missing Olympic selection by notching up the first of her four hurdles titles in 11.9 and later in the summer clocked 11.4 which ranked her equal third in the world. Dorothy Tyler, who won a superb WAAA high jump contest with 1.60m, a height cleared also by Sheila Alexander and Bertha Crowther, ended up with the world's highest clearance of the year at 1.65m. Bertha went on to claim the inaugural WAAA pentathlon title. Doris Batter won the 60m in 7.7, a time shared by Betty Brickwood, who as Betty Lock was champion from 1936 to 1939 but was still only 28. Valerie Ball chalked up the second of her six consecutive one-lap titles, although her time of 59.4 would surely have been much quicker had she not been obliged to run a heat (60.8) just 35 minutes earlier.

UNITED KINGDOM RECORDS AT 1 JANUARY 1950

60m: 7.4 Betty Lock 1938; 100y: 11.0 Ivy Walker 1930, Nellie Halstead 1931, Eileen Hiscock 1931, Ethel Johnson 1932; 100m: 11.9 Hiscock 1935 & 1936; 200m/220y: 24.5 Sylvia Cheeseman 1949; 400m/440y: 56.8 Halstead 1932; 800m: 2:15.6 Halstead 1935; 880y: 2:17.4 Olive Hall 1936; 1000m: 3:00.6 Gladys Lunn 1934; Mile: 5:15.3 Evelyne Forster 1939; 80mH: 11.2 Maureen Gardner (Dyson) 1948; HJ: 1.68 Dorothy Tyler 1948; LJ: 5.85 Muriel Cornell 1930; SP: 13.25 Bevis Reid 1949; DT: 39.45 Reid 1949; 600gm JT: 39.32 Diane Coates 1949; Pentathlon: (scored on 1954 tables) 3901 Bertha Crowther 1949 (LJ-5.33, 200-27.5, 80H-12.5, SP-8.28, HJ-1.60); 4x100m: 47.5 British Olympic team 1936.

THE FIFTIES

THE NEW DECADE had hardly begun before the first major athletics occasion was staged: the Empire Games in Auckland in early February. Sylvia Cheeseman, a professional journalist as well as being UK 200m record holder, provided an illuminating diary for the magazine which from January 1950 had become *Athletics Weekly*. She reported that on December 16 1949 six English women athletes (team captain Dorothy Tyler, Jean Desforges, Doris Batter, Dorothy Hall née Manley, Margaret Walker and herself) together with team manager Ruth Taylor left Waterloo Station for Southampton and the five-week long sea trip on the S.S.Tamaroa, while Bertha Crowther would be flying out some weeks later. "When the team stepped on the train duly packed with their respective passports, ration books, identity cards, tickets and vaccination certificates, it was after a good few weeks of rushing around, being measured for uniforms, seeing to passports, being vaccinated (which, in some cases, put the girls out of action as regards training for a week), and filling in dozens of forms from various councils, committees and individuals. They were also fortunate enough to be presented each with an 'off duty' dress by a London firm, the material for each dress being chosen individually, and the dress being made up by the firm in the latest styles."

What was the daily schedule on board? 6.30 am – woken up with a cup of tea; 7.30 – up on sun deck in tracksuits for exercises; 8.30 – breakfast, followed by sunbathing or deck-tennis; 11.00 to midday – more drilled exercises; 1.00 – lunch, followed by a siesta (the route was via the Caribbean and Panama); 5.00 to 6.00 – further exercises, followed by salt water baths and then dinner; 9.30 – Horlicks and sandwiches; 10.30 – bedtime. "There is plenty of entertainment to be had on board," wrote Sylvia, "and we never have a dull moment, especially as there are two pianos on the ship and three of the girl athletes can play. The supply of soft drinks seems to be inexhaustible and the food is very good and abundant." Stops were made at Curacao and Panama, where the athletes were able to stretch their legs and train.

The time of year, long journey and heat encountered en route played havoc with the form of most of the athletes and only the high jumpers did themselves justice. Dorothy Tyler retained her title of 12 years earlier with the same mark of 1.60m, a height cleared also by second placed Bertha Crowther. Dorothy Hall, who had been primarily a high jumper before being converted by her coach Sandy Duncan into an Olympic 100m silver medallist, jumped 1.52m for fourth after failing to survive her 100y heat on the grass track. In fact none of the runners reached an individual final. There were just eight women's events (nothing longer than 220y) and the only countries represented, as in 1938, were England, Scotland, Australia, New Zealand, Canada and South Africa. The team arrived back in England on April 8, having been away for nearly four months.

For two of the athletes, Sylvia Cheeseman and Doris Batter, the trip carried unpleasant memories because Mrs Taylor, the team manager, reported to the WAAA that the pair were not amenable to discipline and the WAAA General Committee suspended them without even hearing their side of the story. It was not the governing body's finest moment. A tribunal was set up by the two leading officials of the day, Harold Abrahams and Jack Crump, to consider the athletes' appeal and for the first time the allegations made were fully investigated. The tribunal's report stated: "It is almost inconceivable that the General Committee of the Women's AAA should have entirely ignored one of the most elementary principles of justice. They found that these two athletes were 'not amenable to discipline' on the uncorroborated and unchallenged evidence of the team manager. No opportunity was afforded the two athletes of cross-examining or repudiating the statements of Mrs Taylor, and indeed they had no knowledge (until after they had been condemned and their punishment decided upon) of what the charges were." After investigating the complaints the tribunal decided that they "proved to be of small significance" and did not "warrant the conclusion that they should not be included in athletic teams." The findings concluded: "We assume the General Committee ... will now rescind the decision of June 9 and that the two athletes may then regard the incident as permanently closed." The assumption was correct, but to this day Sylvia (Disley) remains incensed about the original injustice.

Back home, at about the same time as the Empire Games, the AGM of the WAAA agreed to the formation of a separate Association to govern cross country and road walking events. The new body would be financially independent but would be affiliated to the WAAA, and the Women's Cross Country & Road Walking Association duly came into being in September. Mrs Palmer did not offer herself for re-election as Hon. Treasurer, a post she had held since 1931, and her successor was 29-year-old Marea Hartman – a former sprinter with Spartan Ladies who in time would become the most influential figure in British women's athletics.

In April 1950 Len Ward, Athletic Development Officer for the City of Stoke Education Department who was the WAAA's Hon. Chief Coach, announced that "in order to ensure the provision of adequate coaching facilities for women athletes throughout the country, the WAAA has decided to give opportunity for qualification in any of the following groups of events and, where stated, individual events. (A) Sprinting up to and including 440y; (B) relay racing; (C) Hurdling; (D) Distance running – 880y & mile; (E) Jumping events; (F) Throwing events. Qualification will be by examination and 'WAAA Hon. Coach' badges will be available for purchase by those who are successful in reaching the required standard."

The 1950 European Championships in Brussels proved a huge success for the British team. The men came away with six titles and the women added two more thanks to Sheila Alexander, the high jump winner with 1.63m on countback ahead of Dorothy Tyler, and the 4x100m relay squad of Elspeth Hay, Jean Desforges, Dorothy Hall and 16-year-old June Foulds who just held off a spectacular anchor leg by Fanny Blankers-Koen to set a UK record of 47.4. Both June (12.4) and Dorothy (25.0) collected bronze medals in the sprints and Maureen Dyson (11.6) took silver in the hurdles – all three titles going to the "Flying Dutchwoman". The other British medallist was Bertha Crowther, second in the inaugural pentathlon. The proud team manager was Mrs Gillis, who as Rose Thompson was a record breaking sprinter herself in the 1920s.

At the AGM in 1950, Sheffield United Harriers, backed by the Northern Counties, proposed that the WAAA rules should be altered to allow athletes to wear "more becoming" clothing similar to that used by Continental competitors. The motion was referred back for further consideration and at the following year's AGM the appropriate rule was amended to read: "A competitor's clothing must be clean and so designed and worn as not to make an indecent display of the competitor's person. Such clothing must include dark shorts. A track suit or wrap must be worn from dressing room to point of competition and between events."

Decisions taken at the 1952 AGM included changing the age for Juniors and Intermediates to under 15 and under 17 on March 31 in the year of competition and not the date of the meeting, thus falling in line with the English Schools AA; approving of the recently formed Welsh WAAA and taking steps to include it within the WAAA on a proper constitutional basis (Welsh Women's Championships were held for the first time in June 1952); and with immediate effect reverting to yards (100y, 220y etc) at the WAAA Championships. Indoor athletics returned for the first time since 1939 with an experimental meeting at London's Harringay Arena in March 1952. However, another ten years would pass before National Indoor Championships were restored at Wembley's Empire Pool. Later in 1952 the WAAA's prestige received a boost when it was announced that Princess Margaret had consented to become the Association's Patron.

As in 1948, the women's team outshone the men at the 1952 Helsinki Olympics, claiming three medals from the measly total of nine events on the programme. The high jump continued to be Britain's parade event. Despite suffering from a high temperature, cough and a calf bleeding from a spike scratch, Sheila Lerwill (née Alexander) put up a great fight. Third-time clearances at 1.63m and 1.65m kept her in contention for the gold medal but South Africa's Esther Brand, a scissors jumper who had briefly held the world record at 1.66m in 1941, had cleared 1.65m at the second attempt and clinched the title by making 1.67m. Thelma Hopkins, only 16, placed fourth at 1.58m, the same height being cleared for equal seventh by Dorothy Tyler, who was short of training after a groin injury and was hampered by a pulled stomach muscle.

An unexpected bronze medal came Britain's way in the long jump where Shirley Cawley, the WAAA title winner with 5.61m, uncorked the leap of her life at a most timely moment, her 5.92m breaking the UK record of 5.85m which Muriel Cornell had held since 1930. There were bronze medals too for Sylvia Cheeseman, June Foulds, Jean Desforges and Heather Armitage with their UK relay record of 46.2 ... a time faster than the pre-Games world record of 46.4. Luck was with them, though, for they would have finished fourth had the hot favourites, Australia, not suffered a disaster at the final change-over. That compensated in part for Jean Desforges' misfortune in the 80m hurdles. After clocking a sensational if wind-aided 10.9 in her semi-final (the UK record stood at 11.2) she was looming as a medal prospect but in the final she was hampered by an ill Fanny Blankers-Koen in the adjoining lane. The Dutchwoman smashed into the first two barriers and failed to finish, leaving Australia's Shirley Strickland to win the title in a legal, world record breaking 10.9, with a distracted Jean fifth in 11.6.

Those early years of the 1950s were a good time for world records by British women. The crowning achievement was Sheila Lerwill's 1.72m high jump at the 1951 WAAA Championships ... and among the small crowd at the White City that day was the author of this book, aged 13 and thrilled to witness his first world record! Other world marks fell in less developed events, including several somewhat esoteric relays.

There was a rather complicated situation regarding the 880y world record. The 800m record was held by the Soviet Union's Nina Pletnyova (later Otkalenko) with 2:08.5 in June 1952, but the IAAF record for 880y stood at 2:15.6 (worth about 2:14.8

for 800m) by Sweden's Anna Larsson in 1945. There was some excitement not to mention confusion when Enid Harding was timed at 2:14.4 off scratch in an 880y handicap race at the White City in August 1952, while on the same track in cold and wet conditions the following month Valerie Ball ran 2:14.5 to outkick Enid (2:15.3). Officialdom decreed that Valerie's time was a world but not a British record, while Enid's mark was accepted as a British record but refused recognition as a world record because the IAAF would not consider a performance made in a handicap race! Diane Leather ended the dilemma in 1954 when she ran 2:09.0 at the WAAA Championships.

The mile, practically a British preserve in those days, saw the world best (the IAAF only began ratifying official records at that distance from 1967) improved on numerous occasions. Anne Oliver, at 16, won the 1952 WAAA title in 5:11.0 with Enid Harding succeeding her as national champion in 5:09.8, and later in 1953 Anne clocked 5:08.0 and Diane Leather 5:02.6. Romania's Edith Treybal got into the act at the end of that year with 5:00.3 but after that it was all Leather as the tall, front running Birchfield Harrier clocked 5:00.2 and a barrier breaking 4:59.6 in 1954 and 4:50.8 and 4:45.0 in 1955. Again before the IAAF began ratifying records at the distance, Diane registered unofficial world bests of 4:30.0 and 4:22.2 at 1500m en route to her mile records in 1955.

On the administrative front, Winnie Hughes – who had held office since 1946 – stepped down as WAAA Hon. Secretary at the 1953 AGM, to be succeeded by Mary Amies.

"The advance made by women athletes in recent years has fully kept up with that of the men and, if only because of their gallant efforts at the last two Olympic Games, they deserve all the encouragement possible," wrote *The Times* athletics correspondent, O.L. Owen, when previewing the 1953 WAAA Championships. He continued, somewhat patronisingly: "They have, indeed, earned their place in British athletics, even if not everybody is agreed that some of the heftier and more exhausting of the men's events are entirely suitable for women. As runners, hurdlers and jumpers, at any rate, this country has produced some outstanding examples like Maureen Dyson, Jean Desforges, Valerie Winn [née Ball],

Sylvia Cheeseman, Dorothy Tyler and Sheila Lerwill." The newspaper's report led with Enid Harding's world best mile time of 5:09.8 but mentioned "the public support was poor and, recalling the crowd of over 50,000 at Wembley for a recent women's hockey match, and the growing popularity of the women's events at the Olympic Games, one could not help feeling that more could be done to awaken the interest of schoolgirls and young business women in athletics."

Reporting for *The Times* on the WAAA Championships at the White City in 1956, Owen's youthful successor Neil Allen enthused over the standard of performance, but wrote: "The crowd was pitifully small, with not more than 1500 present. It is a sad fact that the public will flock to joint men's and women's athletics as though the latter was an added attraction, but competition for women alone – even the championships – has no draw. This is all the more ironic when it is remembered that Britain's team are second only to Russia, and in the track events (which have the most appeal) there are great athletes in sprints, hurdles and the middle distances." This anomaly never was resolved.

THE WAAA AS VIEWED BY GEORGE PALLETT

A snapshot of the WAAA was presented by Sheila Lerwill's coach, George Pallett, well known also as an official and pre-war international long jumper, in his book Women's Athletics, *published in 1955.*

He wrote: "The present organisation of the WAAA has grown up with the years. The most interesting feature is that almost unbelievably the whole of the administration of women's athletics in Great Britain is done by honorary officials. The Association has not a single paid employee and no offices as headquarters. The Honorary Secretary of the Association for the time being receives correspondence at her private address. The WAAA controls athletics only in England and Wales. The body recognised by the IAAF for international purposes is the BAAB, which deals with international athletic matters on behalf of both men's and women's Associations and athletes in Northern Ireland,

Scotland and England and Wales. Only in the Empire Games and in cross country does England normally compete as a separate entity internationally, although new ground was broken in 1953 by an international match between England and Holland in a floodlight meeting at White City. Scotland has its own WAAA, formed since the 1939-45 war, but Northern Ireland was only in 1953 thinking of forming an Association. In 1953 Wales formed a national WAAA, but it is closely linked to the WAAA of England, and is represented on the English WAAA General Committee. The WAAA has its own representatives on the BAAB, but Northern Ireland and Scotland are represented through delegates from the men's Associations of those countries. Within the WAAA certain powers are delegated by the parent body to Territorial Associations, of which there are three – the Southern WAAA, the Northern WAAA and the Midland WAAA. The WAAA consists of all clubs and Associations affiliated to these Area Associations. Since 1950 control and organisation of road walking and cross country running has been delegated to the Women's Road Walking and Cross Country Association, which was formed in that year. The work of the WAAA is carried out by a General Committee consisting of the officers of the Association (elected at the AGM) and a number of delegates, depending on the number of affiliated clubs, from each of the Territorial Associations. Each affiliated club or Association can send one representative to a General Meeting of the WAAA."

Dealing with the WAAA's Coaching Sub-Committee, Pallett wrote: "Unlike the men's AAA, there are no professional coaches paid by the WAAA. An Honorary Chief Coach, who works in his spare time, has been appointed, and apart from lecturing and organising coaching courses, he sets examinations for persons who wish to become senior honorary coaches, i.e. who can show ability to coach to international standard. These in turn can examine for the qualification of honorary coach, i.e. which requires ability to coach to good club standard. There is a wide gap between the two qualifications. To assist the Chief Coach, a National Coaching Secretary has been appointed, and each Territorial

Association has a coaching secretary; indeed, some County Associations have set up coaching sub-committees."

The two major occasions of 1954 proved bountiful in terms of medals. At the British Empire Games in Vancouver, which now included the shot and discus but still nothing further than 220y, Thelma Hopkins (representing Northern Ireland) won the high jump with 1.67m, with an ailing Dorothy Tyler second at 1.60m. Thelma took silver in the long jump with 5.84m, Jean Desforges registering the same distance in placing third as her second best jump was 5.74m to Thelma's 5.75m. Silver went also to Sue Allday in the discus (40.02m) and the England 4x110y relay team of Shirley Hampton, Shirley Burgess, Heather Armitage and Anne Pashley (46.9), while Hampton at 220y (25.0) and Desforges in the hurdles (11.2w) won bronze medals.

The European Championships in Berne included for the first time an 800m, and the internationally inexperienced Diane Leather ran well to finish second in 2:09.8 to world record holder Nina Otkalenko (2:08.8) after setting a UK record of 2:08.9 in her heat. The British heroines, though, were gold medallists Thelma Hopkins (1.67m) and Jean Desforges (6.04m long jump), both of them coached by the legendary Franz Stampfl, who had been much involved in the preparations for the first four minute mile and would later guide Chris Brasher to the 1956 Olympic steeplechase title. Bronze medals were claimed by Anne Pashley in a UK record equalling 11.9 100m, Shirley Hampton in a UK record 24.4 200m and Pam Seaborne in the hurdles (11.3). Pam, who in 1955 married British pole vault and decathlon record holder Geoff Elliott and subsequently settled in Canada, broke Maureen Gardner's UK record with 11.0 at the end of the season.

For Jean Desforges it was close to the end of a brilliant career; in October 1954 she married Ron Pickering, who was to become a renowned coach and television commentator, and since her husband's death in 1991 she has raised over a million pounds through the Ron Pickering Memorial Fund to dispense to young athletes. She was awarded the MBE in

2010 for her services to athletics. Their son, Shaun Pickering, developed into an Olympic shot putter and a successful coach in his own right.

The 1956 Olympics in Melbourne yielded two silver medals for the ten-strong women's team managed by Mary Amies. Irish hockey international Thelma Hopkins, who in Belfast in May had straddled over the world record height of 1.74m, was expected to vie for the gold medal with Iolanda Balas, the stork-like Romanian who in July added a centimetre to that world record, but both were outclassed by the inspired American, Mildred McDaniel. She was the only contestant to clear 1.70m and then proceeded to break the world record with 1.76m. No fewer than six jumpers made 1.67m, with Thelma (carrying a slight injury) and the USSR's Mariya Pisareva incurring no failures up to and including that height and tying for the silver medal. Balas placed fifth on countback ... amazingly, she would not lose another competition until June 1967! Becoming the third UK athlete to finish runner-up after Dorothy Tyler (1936 and 1948; who at age 36 finished equal 12th with 1.60m in Melbourne) and Sheila Lerwill (1952), Thelma enjoyed a magnificent year. Although born in Hull she was raised in Belfast from the age of nine months and was acknowledged as Northern Ireland's greatest athlete until Mary Peters (also born in England!) struck Olympic gold in 1972. At that Belfast meeting in May she also long jumped 6.12m, which would have been a UK record had not Sheila Hoskin leapt 6.14m in London the same afternoon, and for good measure she clocked a wind-aided 11.2 for the hurdles.

The other Olympic silver medal came in the 4x100m relay. Heather Armitage (sixth in 12.0 after a UK record-equalling 11.6 semi-final), June Paul, née Foulds (fifth in 24.3 after a UK record 23.8 heat), Anne Pashley (eliminated in her 100m heat) and Jean Scrivens (eliminated in her 200m semi) hadn't fared as well as hoped for in the individual sprints, but they put up a magnificent performance to smash the UK record with 44.70, thanks to excellent baton passing, finishing just half a metre behind Australia's world record breaking 44.65. Alas, there were still no races for women beyond 200m. Had there been, Janet Ruff (400m), Diane Leather and Phyllis

Perkins, née Green (800m/1500m) could have been in medal contention against strong Soviet opposition.

At the 1957 WAAA AGM Dorothy Tyler was presented with a gold watch in recognition of her 21 years as an international. Confirming her retirement from major competition, Dorothy said she would continue to assist Mitcham AC as well as serve athletics as a judge and coach. In fact she ranked as fifth highest in Britain in 1961 with 1.63m and threw the javelin for her club at the inaugural Southern Women's League match in 1973 aged 53! Still an active golfer, she was present in 2009, a few months short of her 90th birthday, at a ceremony to induct her into the England Athletics Hall of Fame. She was belatedly awarded the MBE in 2002.

A premature death which rocked the close-knit women's athletics community was that of June Bridgland of Southampton AC. In 1956 she had set a best on record time of 10:52.2 for an event in its infancy, the 2 miles; in 1957 she enjoyed her greatest triumph by winning the national cross country title and that summer she ran 4:36.0 for 1500m to rank fourth on the UK all-time list behind Diane Leather, Maureen Smith and Phyllis Perkins. She met her death in October 1958, falling from a train on which she was travelling from Southampton to London to race in the Southern Counties Road Relay Championship. She was 23. The previous month, Olympic sprint relay medallist Eileen Hiscock had died at 49.

It was a tragic end to what had otherwise been a momentous year, for medals galore had been won at the 1958 British Empire & Commonwealth Games in Cardiff in July and the European Championships in Stockholm in August. The England team, decked out in white shorts for the first time, provided one of the highlights at Cardiff Arms Park when the 4x110y relay squad of Madeleine Weston (18), Dorothy Hyman (17), June Paul (24) and Heather Young, née Armitage (25) beat the Australians by some seven yards in a world record breaking 45.3. There were gold medals also for Sheila Hoskin in the long jump (windy 6.02m) and Sue Allday in the discus (45.91m); silvers for Young (UK 100y record of 10.6), Carole Quinton (windy 10.7 hurdles), 18-year-old Mary

Bignal (5.97m long jump) and Allday (14.44m shot) and bronze medals for Weston (10.7), Young (UK 220y record of 23.9) and Averil Williams (UK javelin record of 46.77m). There was a near miss in the high jump by 19-year-old Dorothy Shirley; she equalled her personal best of 1.65m, same height as the bronze medallist, but lost out on countback. Former world record holder Thelma Hopkins could manage only 1.57m in eighth place, while her Northern Ireland team-mate Mary Peters (19) hardly looked like a world beating athlete in the making as she tied for tenth with 1.47m along with eighth in the shot (11.21m) and a leg on the relay team which finished last in the final.

The European Championships yielded one gold, two silver and two bronze medals – and but for untimely injuries there could well have been two more victories. Ceylon (Sri Lanka) born Heather Young was in superlative form in the 100m, equalling the UK record of 11.6 in her semi-final and winning the final in 11.7 to become the first British woman to carry off a European title in an individual track event. She would have been favourite to complete the sprint double but a strain sustained in the 100m final caused her to withdraw from the 200m heats. Still, British hopes for success in that event looked bright when June Paul was fastest in the semis with 24.0, but at the start of the straight in the final her Achilles tendon snapped and she was carried off on a stretcher. The title was won in 24.1. Had Heather and June been fit to run then surely Britain would have been in strong contention for the relay gold; in their absence Madeleine Weston, Dorothy Hyman, Marianne Dew and Carole Quinton ran bravely to take second (46.0) behind the USSR's 45.3. The other British silver went to Diane Leather who, after passing the bell in last place, overtook everyone except the Soviet winner to clock a UK record of 2:06.6. The bronze medallists were high jumper Dorothy Shirley, who raised her personal best to 1.67m, and Moyra (Molly) Hiscox, who had recently set a world 440y record of 55.6 at the White City. Finishing two seconds behind Maria Itkina (USSR), whose 53.7 was just 0.1 sec outside her far more meaningful world 400m record, Molly lunged for the line inches ahead of Shirley Pirie (née Hampton). Shirley was given the same time of 55.7 and another so-close fourth placer was Carole Quinton in the hurdles with 11.0 after setting a new UK record of 10.9 in her semi. Sue Allday placed a creditable fifth in the shot with a UK record of 14.66m and Mary Bignal smashed Thelma Hopkins' UK pentathlon record with 4466 for seventh position and would have finished many places higher but for a very weak shot put of 9.07m.

Several important decisions were made at the 1959 WAAA AGM. During 1958 the formation of a Joint AAA and WAAA Coaching Committee, as a result of which women holding the WAAA Coaching Award were able to apply to be examined as AAA coaches, had made for closer co-operation between the two coaching organisations, and another step forward was made with the formation of the British Women's Amateur Athletic Council with two members granted full voting powers on the BAAB ... except on financial matters. The clothing rule was amended to read: "In all events competitors must wear clothing which is clean and so designed and worn as not to be objectionable. The clothing must be made of a material which is non-transparent even if wet." Two new championship events were approved: Intermediate 220y and Junior 150y. That distance of 150y for girls under 15 would remain the longest to be sanctioned by a cautious WAAA until an 800m championship was instituted in 1967. Vera Searle, who had been WAAA Hon. Secretary from 1930 to 1933 and since then had been a tireless worker for the Southern Counties WAAA and the Women's Cross Country & Road Walking Association, was elected to the new post of Vice-Chairman.

Highlights from each of the WAAA Championships meetings 1950–1959

1950 (White City)

TO WIN NATIONAL titles at running and walking on the same day is unusual to say the least, but it occurred at this meeting when Joyce Heath not only won her third consecutive 1600m walk championship (8:17.0) but just over an hour later triumphed also in the mile run in 5:25.8. The best performance of the day came from Ceylon (Sri Lanka) born Valerie Ball, a student at the Royal College of Music whose 400m time of 57.5 was the fastest by a Briton since Nellie Halstead's 56.8 for 440y in 1932. Her training? Twice a week during the summer, the sessions lasting between 30 and 60 minutes, and none at all in the winter which was devoted to playing hockey! Two of her Spartan clubmates excelled also. June Foulds, who had equalled the UK 100y record of 11.0 three days before her 16th birthday, became 100m champion in 12.6 (12.4 semi-final) and Sheila Alexander, the first female straddle jumper, cleared a personal best equalling 1.62m. A strong finish by Dorothy Hall carried her to a narrow victory over Sylvia Cheeseman in a 25.2 220y and even closer was the 80m hurdles where Maureen Dyson, recovering just in time after hitting the first barrier, pipped Jean Desforges in 11.6. Diane Coates smashed the javelin championship record with 39.02m and the following month, at the Southern Inter-Counties, broke her UK record three times to finish up with 42.42m. At the same meeting Sheila Alexander replaced Dorothy Tyler as UK record holder with a jump of 1.69m, highest in the world that year.

1951 (White City)

AN INTERNATIONAL NETBALL player who did not take up athletics until she was 18, Sheila Alexander came under the coaching influence of George Pallett in December 1947 with a high jump best of 1.50m. "It was my view," Pallett wrote in his book *Women's Athletics*, "that the scissors style of jumping, outmoded and uneconomical for men, was not the best for women, and after consultation with a medical specialist in women's health troubles, I put it to Sheila that, if she changed to the straddle style, at least a British record was a possibility in time, but that as a change would take months to become really effective she might not qualify for the Olympic Games." She did miss the London Games but in 1950 she became European champion and broke Dorothy Tyler's UK record with 1.69m for second place on the world all-time list. The following year was even more notable for Sheila. In March she became Mrs Michael Lerwill and in July she enjoyed her greatest moment at the WAAA Championships. At her first attempt she succeeded at 1.72m to add a centimetre to the world record which had been held by Fanny Blankers-Koen since 1943. Dorothy Tyler had to settle for second place at 1.60m but still won two WAAA titles: the long jump with 5.58m and, later in the season, the pentathlon with a UK record score (per the 1954 tables) of 3953 points. Three of Sheila Lerwill's clubmates won titles too: June Foulds in the 100m (12.3), Sylvia Cheeseman in the 200m (25.0) and Valerie Ball in the 400m (58.2). It was quite a year for Spartan Ladies as later in July a team of Valerie Robins, Sheila Turner, Foulds and Cheeseman set a world 4x220y relay record of 1:43.9, improving to 1:43.4 in September with a squad comprising Foulds, Robins, Ball and Cheeseman. The last named, who had tied the UK 100y record of 11.0 early in the season, ran the first leg for an England team completed by Barbara Foster, Margaret Brian and Dorothy Hall which lowered the world record to 1:41.4. Maureen Dyson picked up her fourth hurdles championship in 11.7, while Joyce Heath retained her walk title in 7:50.0 but placed only fifth in the mile run which was won by 18-year-old Hazel Needham in 5:23.4. Hazel's sister Sylvia placed fourth in the discus, having finished second the previous year and who at 15 had become one of Britain's youngest ever internationals. She would win the title in 1957. Another 16-year-old who would develop into a senior title winner, Anne Pashley, finished third in the 100m. At the other end of the age scale, Bevis Shergold (32) – who as Miss Reid won her first WAAA discus title in 1938 – broke the UK discus record with 39.88m. The most remarkable veteran of the year, though, was 1934 Empire Games bronze medallist Lily Chalmers, who at 39 ranked third in Britain at 220y (25.4) and equal seventh at 100y (11.3)! Just starting out, though, was Phyllis Green, winner of the national cross country title at age 17. She would go on to win WAAA titles at 880y and mile and set a world best for 1500m with 4:35.4 in 1956.

1952 (White City)

THE MILE CONTINUED to be a British preserve and thus the time of 5:11.0 by Anne Oliver (16) not only broke Evelyne

Forster's 1939 UK record of 5:15.3 but also constituted a world best. Hazel Needham looked all set to retain her title but Anne produced a great finishing burst over the final 40 yards. Hazel (who later became WAAA Hon. Treasurer under her married name of Hazel Rider) was also well under the old figures with 5:12.6. Another UK record fell in the javelin, which Diane Coates propelled to a distance of 45.30m. George Pallett was a judge of that event and wrote in his book *Women's Athletics*: "Diane likes a target and used the author, who thought he was at a safe distance for an English javelin thrower until the spear whistled past his ear for a new British record!" Aged 19, like Coates, Heather Armitage was timed at 10.9 for 100 yards (the WAAA had ditched metric events except for the 80m hurdles), which would have broken the UK record, but it was adjudged wind assisted. Martin Greensill, interviewing Heather for *Track Stats* in 2007, revealed that she won that title without wearing any shorts! "Her school shorts were too long and thick, and also lacking a running vest she just ran in her knickers and an Aertex shirt!" Despite a swollen knee Sylvia Cheeseman (25.0) won the 220y in 25.0 for her sixth title at that distance or 200m, while Valerie Ball extended her run of successes to five with a 59.3 quarter mile. The 80m hurdles crown returned to Jean Desforges but she was hard pressed by her 16-year-old Essex Ladies clubmate Pam Seaborne, 11.4 to 11.5. The high jump fell short of the exceptional heights of the previous year but it was a fine competition with Dorothy Tyler (1.65m), now a western roller thanks to the coaching of Arthur Gold, this time getting the better of Sheila Lerwill (1.62m) with a 16-year-old from Northern Ireland by the name of Thelma Hopkins third at that height. Shirley Cawley, the only woman in Geoff Dyson's personal training group now that his wife Maureen had retired, took her only WAAA long jump title with a leap of 5.61m ... like Sheila Lerwill, she would perform far better at the forthcoming Olympics in Helsinki.

1953 (White City)

DIMINUTIVE, FAST STARTING Anne Pashley (18) – who years later would become a noted opera singer, performing as a soprano at Covent Garden, Glyndebourne and all over

Europe – added her name to the long list of co-holders of the UK 100y record of 11.0 and finished second to Ann Johnson (25.0) over 220y. The elegant Valerie Winn (the former Miss Ball, daughter of a baronet, had married England wing three quarter Chris Winn earlier in the year) gained her sixth and final one-lap title in 57.6. Anne Oliver did not defend her mile title, instead claiming the 880y in 2:15.0, and Enid Harding relieved her of the UK record and world best with 5:09.8. Diane Leather, who had won the national 2½ miles cross country title by the biggest ever margin of 76 seconds, would end the season with a mile record of 5:02.6 but at the Championships she finished a distant third in the half mile. The high jump went to Sheila Lerwill at 1.65m on countback from Thelma Hopkins with Dorothy Tyler third at 1.60m. Jean Desforges enjoyed a successful meeting, taking the hurdles in 11.5 and the long jump with 5.76m. That wasn't all, as two months later she collected the pentathlon title with the UK record score (on 1954 tables) of 3997 which included an excellent long jump of 5.93m but only a modest hurdles time of 12.4. Two weeks earlier, in Germany, she had broken Shirley Cawley's UK record with a barrier-breaking jump of 6.10m, a quarter inch over 20 feet.

1954 (White City)

ADMITTEDLY IT DIDN'T quite measure up to Nina Otkalenko's 800m figures of 2:07.3 but Diane Leather's world 880y record of 2:09.0 (equivalent to around 2:08.2 for 800m) was a brilliant achievement. In her wake Anne Oliver was also inside the old record with 2:11.4, while Valerie Winn (2:11.7), Norah Smalley (2:12.4) and Betty Loakes (2:13.0) all finished under the old UK record. Three weeks earlier the lanky Birchfield Harrier, coached by Dorette Nelson Neal, had made history by becoming the first woman to break five minutes for the mile (23 days after Roger Bannister's first sub-four) when she ran 4:59.6 in the Midland Championships ... less than an hour after winning the 800m in a UK all-comers record of 2:14.1! Her mile lap times were wildly uneven at 68.8, 78.2, 79.3 and 73.3. Diane, who originally joined Birchfield in 1952 merely to get fit for hockey, was the first outstanding British female athlete to be coached by a woman. Her clubmate Beryl Randle also shone at the Championships with a world mile walk best of 7:38.4. Beryl (née Day) was one of the great figures in this event. She was second in 1946 (at 17) and 1948 and third in 1947 and 1949 before winning in 1952, 1953, 1954 and 1955. She went on to finish second in 1956 and third in 1958. Sixth in the 1954 mile walk (she would place fourth a full decade later) was Norma Blaine, destined to become Birchfield Harriers' first female chairman, a coach for over 40 years and be awarded the MBE in 2011 for services to athletics. Other highlights included another double by Jean Desforges (11.4 and 5.83m), and she would also retain the pentathlon title, a 5:09.6 mile by Phyllis Green and a 57.1 quarter by Gloria Goldsborough. That was close to Nellie Halstead's 1932 UK record of 56.8, which fell later in the summer to the ubiquitous Diane Leather at 56.6. Sheila Lerwill won the high jump for the fourth and final time with 1.65m ahead of Dorothy Tyler (1.62m). The discus title, as in 1955, went to one of the most exotic figures in the sport, University of London languages student Maya Giri ... born in Eastbourne of an Indian father and Russian mother.

1955 (White City)

"ATHLETICALLY, THE 28th annual WAAA Championships were quite outstanding, but as is usual at these meetings where only women are taking part, the stadium was almost empty and the necessary atmosphere for a really exciting meting was absent." That was how the *Athletics Weekly* report began, and it remained a fact that women-only meetings never did attract good crowds. However, the WAAA always preferred a policy of segregation for its Championships and not until 1988 did a combined meeting come into being. There were two double winners: Margaret Francis, who had broken the UK 100y record with 10.8 in Manchester ten days earlier, repeated that time but with wind assistance, and also took the hurdles in 11.3; while Thelma Hopkins won both jumps with 1.65m (Dorothy Tyler second at 1.62m) and 5.76m. Diane Leather went after her world record of 2:09.0 in the 880y but a 62.3 first lap was too ambitious and she had to settle for

2:09.7. At the tail end of the season she set UK records of 56.3 for 400m and 2:06.9 for 800m as well as a world best mile time of 4:45.0 (laps of 71.0, 69.6, 72.2 and 72.2). Janet Ruff took the quarter in 56.9 and Phyllis Perkins (the former Miss Green, then married to 1958 English cross country champion Alan Perkins) retained the mile title in 5:05.2. Jean Scrivens, the 220y winner in 24.9, lowered the UK record to 24.4 and 24.3 later in the season. Another UK record to fall in 1955 was Jean Desforges' pentathlon score (on 1954 tables) of 3997. Thelma Hopkins won the Northern Ireland title in Ballymena with 4289 … with a 16-year-old by the name of Mary Peters a remote third. All of seventeen years later Mary would become an "overnight sensation" by winning the Olympic title with a world record score!

1956 (White City)

THE FORMER INFANT prodigy June Foulds, now married to Olympic fencer Raymond Paul (she would later marry singer Ronnie Carroll), hit peak form to complete a superb sprint double. In the semi-finals of the 100y both she and Anne Pashley equalled the UK record of 10.8 and in the final she overtook the ever quick starting Pashley to register a heavily wind-assisted 10.6, with both Anne and Heather Armitage on 10.7. In only her first season of serious furlong racing, June was credited with a wind-aided 23.8, way inside Jean Scrivens' UK record of 24.3, with Jean runner-up in 24.0. However, there were authentic UK records in two other events: Janet Ruff clocked 56.5 for 440y, a "world best" although actually it was over two seconds inferior to the 400m record of 53.9 by the USSR's Maria Itkina, and Sue Allday (née Farmer; now married to British hammer international Peter Allday) threw the discus 47.02m. The UK record holder in the shot with 14.00m, she won that event also with 13.39m. Other top performances included a 5:01.0 mile by Diane Leather, taking it relatively easy after a recent injury, and a wind-assisted 11.1 hurdles by Pam Elliott (née Seaborne), who withdrew from the Melbourne Olympic team as she was expecting a baby. With Thelma Hopkins an absentee as she was taking university exams, the high jump saw one great champion,

Dorothy Tyler, win her eighth and final WAAA title at 1.60m, and a future legend in 16-year-old Mary Bignal of Millfield School take second place at the same height. The junior 100y held in conjunction with the meeting threw up another all-time great in the making as Dorothy Hyman (15) won in 11.3.

1957 (White City)

IN WARM, HUMID conditions the meeting was spread over two days to accommodate also the Intermediate (under-17) and Junior (under-15) Championships. There was much excellent sprinting, even though June Paul was well below peak fitness, both titles passing to Heather Young (née Armitage) in 10.9 and 24.2. The latter was a new UK 220y record although June's 23.8 200m in Melbourne was some 3/10ths quicker in real terms. Later in the season Heather tied the UK 100y record of 10.8. Winning by half a second, Dorothy Hyman annexed the Intermediate title in an outstanding 10.9. For the second year running at this meeting international hockey player Janet Ruff broke the UK 440y record, this time with 56.4. Besides Young there were two other double winners. Thelma Hopkins took the hurdles in 11.4 and the high jump with 1.65m, while Diane Leather won the 880y in 2:09.4 and the mile in 4:55.3 on the same afternoon. Diane enjoyed another highly successful season for she set a UK 800m record of 2:06.8 when winning against formidable opposition in the Britain v USSR match and established a world 1500m best when officially timed at 4:29.7 en route to a 4:50.6 mile, although two years earlier she was unofficially clocked at 4:22.2 on the way to her world mile best of 4:45.0. Perseverance paid off for Sylvia Needham, who had finished second in the discus in 1950 (at 15), 1955 and 1956. Taking advantage of Sue Allday's absence, she claimed the title with 40.22m. Mary Bignal, although only third in the high jump at 1.62m, revealed more of her exciting potential as she set an English record of 4046 in her first ever pentathlon and raised her personal best to 1.65m when winning in a match against Poland. She also won the English Schools high jump title, while at that meeting another future Olympic gold medallist in Ann Packer finished fourth in the Intermediate 150 yards.

1958 (Motspur Park)

THE MOST EYE-catching performance at the more intimate venue of the University of London Sports Ground came in the 100y where an over-the-limit wind blew the petite Madeleine Weston (18) to a 10.6 victory over Heather Young (10.7), June Paul (10.7) and 17-year-old Dorothy Hyman (11.0) – the foursome destined a few weeks later to break the world record for the 4x110y relay. Heather retained her 220y title in 24.5 just ahead of June (24.6), while Shirley Pirie (née Hampton) took the 440y in 56.4, a time she registered also in her heat to equal Janet Ruff's UK record. The wife of distance running legend Gordon Pirie would later set an intrinsically superior UK 400m record of 55.5. In a close finish, Joy Jordan prevailed over Diane Leather in 2:13.3 for the first of five successive half mile titles, while just 0.2 sec covered the first three in the mile won by Maureen Smith in 5:02.6 ahead of national cross country champion Roma Ashby and world mile record holder Derek Ibbotson's wife, Madeline. The most untroubled track winner was Carole Quinton, who enjoyed a six-yard margin when clocking a windy 10.9 for the hurdles. Sue Allday completed the second of five shot/discus doubles with throws of 14.15m and a UK record of 47.70m. Mary Bignal claimed the high jump title with 1.65m, her strongest individual event at that stage of her career, and placed second in the long jump to Sheila Hoskin, 5.96m to 5.88m. A more spectacular high jump achievement was the 1.60m clearance in the Junior championship by Gwenda Matthews, the day after her 14th birthday! Gwenda later competed under her married name of Hurst, and as Gwenda Ward (by then married to the well known athletics personality and writer Tony Ward) she served as a member of the IAAF's Women's Committee from 2003 to 2007.

1959 (Motspur Park)

THE BALMY CONDITIONS were conducive to good performances and several athletes took advantage. Dorothy Hyman gained her first senior titles with times of 10.8 and 24.5 (24.2 semi) and Margaret Pickerell improved by almost a second to take the 440y in 55.9. It wasn't a great day, though, for the UK record holder (55.6) Molly Hiscox; she dropped out of her semi-final 80y from the finish and burst into tears. However, better times lay ahead for her, including late season UK 400m records of 55.1 and 54.0. Joy Jordan took the 880y in 2:09.5 for second on the UK all-time list (she later broke Diane Leather's UK record, ending up with 2:08.1) and international footballer Joan Briggs front ran to a mile victory in a personal best of 5:02.2. Carole Quinton twice clocked 11.1 in the rounds of the hurdles but the final only half an hour after the semis went to Mary Bignal by inches in 11.3. Mary also won the long jump with 6.04m and was second (first Briton) in the high jump at 1.62m. This was the year in which, coached by John Le Masurier, she became UK record holder in the long jump with 6.19m, won the WAAA pentathlon with a UK record score of 4679, ranking second in the world ... and over 30 years before it became an official women's event even played around with the triple jump, reaching 12.22m. Sue Platt notched up the first of her eight javelin titles with a UK record of 49.04m, which she extended later in the season to 49.65m. Meanwhile, other stars of the future were starting to attract attention, for at the English Schools Championships Ann Packer (17) won the Senior 100y in 11.4 and 14-year-old Janet Simpson (daughter of 1932 Olympic relay medallist Violet Webb) the Junior 150y in 17.2. Somewhat older, at 21, was national cross country champion Joyce Byatt, who some 20 years and more later would develop into one of the world's top marathon runners ... Joyce Smith. Hers was to be a remarkably long and diverse career. Winner of the Hertfordshire county schools long jump title, she gave up athletics when she left school in 1952. Fortunately, one day in 1954 she wandered over to the local track and joined Hampstead Harriers. She returned to the sprints and long jump, but soon found she was better at running longer distances. However, it wasn't until her then boyfriend Bryan Smith started coaching her in the spring of 1958 that her career really took off and in 1959, following her cross country success, she displayed her prowess on the track, defeating her idol Diane Leather in a 4:36.6 1500m. Much more will be told of Joyce Smith in later chapters.

UNITED KINGDOM RECORDS AT 1 JANUARY 1960

100y: 10.6 Heather Young 1958; 100m: 11.6 June Paul 1956, Anne Pashley 1956, Heather Young 1956 & 1958; 200m: 23.8 Paul 1956; 220y: 23.9 Young 1958; 400m: 54.0 Molly Hiscox 1959; 440y: 55.6 Hiscox 1958; 800m: 2:06.6 Diane Leather 1958; 880y: 2:08.1 Joy Jordan 1959; 1500m: 4:29.7 Leather 1957 (unofficial 4:22.2, 1955); Mile: 4:45.0 Leather 1955; 80mH: 10.9 Carole Quinton 1958; HJ: 1.74 Thelma Hopkins 1956; LJ: 6.19 Mary Bignal 1959; SP: 14.96 Sue Allday 1959; DT: 47.70 Allday 1958; JT: 49.65 Sue Platt 1959; Pentathlon: (scored on 1954 tables) 4679 Bignal 1959 (LJ-6.06, 200-24.5, 80H-11.3, SP-9.95, HJ-1.65); 4x100m: 44.7 British Olympic team 1956; Mile Walk: 7:38.4 Beryl Randle 1954.

THE SIXTIES

THIS PROVED TO be a momentous decade for British women athletes. Thirty two years after their first Olympic foray there was at last a gold medallist to acclaim; no, two! Between 1932 and 1956 Britain accumulated a total of 12 Olympic medals, but just between 1960 and 1968 the tally was 11 … although admittedly there were now more events on the Olympic programme for women. After a shameful absence of 32 years the 800m was revived for the 1960 Games in Rome, while the 400m and pentathlon were introduced in 1964 in Tokyo. There were numerous successes also for British athletes at the European Championships and Commonwealth Games, and there were world records, too, to celebrate: by Ann Packer at 800m, Anne Smith at 1500m and mile, Betty Moore (an Australian who represented Britain) at 80m hurdles, Chris Perera at the still experimental 100m hurdles, Mary Rand (née Bignal) at long jump, plus relay records at 4x110y, 4x200m, 4x400m, 3x800m and 3x880y.

However, there was a sad start to this memorable decade when in January 1960 Winifred Hughes, who had been the WAAA's Hon. Secretary during those austere and challenging immediate post-war years, died at the age of 65. As her successor, Mary Amies, wrote in *Athletics Weekly*: "Athletes of today have to thank Winifred Hughes for her pioneer work after the war years and it was she who made life easier for those who have followed her." Mrs Amies herself was succeeded as Hon. Secretary in 1960 by Marea Hartman, who during over 40 years of unstinting service to the WAAA and other organisations became the personification of British women's athletics. Her contribution to the sport was such that in her final year of life, 1994, she was created a Dame – the first to be so honoured for services to athletics.

MAREA HARTMAN – ATHLETICS' FIRST DAME

Gladys Marea Hartman was born in London on June 22 1920, two years before the foundation of the WAAA. Her parents worked in the hotel industry; her Swiss father was head of banqueting at the Savoy and her mother held a similar position at the Waldorf. She was a good if not outstanding athlete while reading economics at the University of London just before the war. As she told Neil Allen in an interview for The Times in 1972: "I went down to the Motspur Park track frankly because I wanted an excuse to get into a pair of shorts. I joined Spartan Ladies club and soon I was running in sprint relays for them." She also represented Surrey.

After the war, which claimed the life of her RAF fiancé, she turned her attention to the running of the sport. She started off in 1945 as Hon. Treasurer of Spartan Ladies and early in 1950, aged 29, she was elected Hon. Treasurer of the WAAA. She gradually became one of the most influential of administrators: she attended the 1956 Melbourne Olympics as an aide to team manager Jack Crump, in 1958 she was women's team manager at the European Championships in Stockholm and would remain British team manager for another 20 years, spanning one of the most successful periods with Olympic gold medals for Mary Rand, Ann Packer and Mary Peters and European titles for Heather Young, Dorothy Hyman, Lillian Board and the 4x400m squad.

It was in Stockholm that she became convinced that sex tests were necessary. "Our own girls felt that they were at an unfair disadvantage and they had an understandable sense of distaste about sharing dressing rooms with these sad borderline cases," she told Neil Allen. "Our own team is very popular in Europe because apart from doing well, our girls dress smartly and look thoroughly attractive and feminine." Largely through her efforts sex tests were brought in some years later, and – coincidentally or not – a number of prominent Eastern European athletes retired from the international stage.

How Marea ever found the time to juggle with her numerous responsibilities was a mystery, although she did concede "if I wasn't single I wouldn't be able to do it all." She estimated she spent 35 hours a week on athletics business, and yet her 'day job' for 38 years was the important and demanding one of personnel officer of the gigantic Bowater Corporation in Knightsbridge, overlooking Hyde Park. Well into her fifties she would go out running twice a week – "I find it a vital relief to all the tensions of modern life."

As John Rodda wrote in "The Guardian": "She had a jolly, florid personality and her permanent smile had a way of winning points at the negotiating table. In team management she was a firm but gentle disciplinarian." Although she went on to chair the IAAF's Women's Commission, become Hon. Treasurer and later Chairman of the BAAB, and – after the WAAA finally amalgamated with the men in 1991 – be elected as the first female President of the AAA of England, Marea was at her happiest in the midst of those she called "my girls". As she once remarked in the 1970s, "I don't want to be sentimental but I have a vast, continually changing family of youngsters who keep me feeling young."

Marea Hartman and her colleagues cherished their independence from the men, even though the WAAA relied heavily on coaches and officials of the male persuasion, and when, in 1960, the AAA approved an investigation into the possibilities of forming a United Kingdom AAA, the WAAA along with the Scottish AAA and Northern Irish AAA made it clear that they were perfectly happy with the present arrangements. At the 1963 AAA AGM it was announced that General Committee had decided that exploration of a UKAAA was not practicable at that time.

In March 1967 the AAA and BAAB commissioned a Committee of Inquiry, chaired by Lord (Frank) Byers, the Liberal Party leader in the House of Lords and a former British Universities 440y hurdles record holder. Its terms of reference were "to examine the problems of development of athletics under the jurisdiction of the AAA and BAAB, including matters of organisation, administration, finance, coaching

Her Majesty The Queen, Patron of the Amateur Athletic Association
(c) www.royalimages.co.uk

MARY LINES, the first star of British women's athletics, pictured in 1924

FLORENCE BIRCHENOUGH
Throwing the javelin in the style of
the day at the first England v France
match in 1921

MARY LINES
winning the 300 metres at the 1922
Women's World Games in Paris

ROSE THOMPSON wins the 100 yards in 11.5 at the International Women's Games
at Stamford Bridge before a crowd of 25,000 in 1924

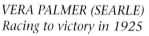

VERA PALMER (SEARLE)
Racing to victory in 1925

MURIEL GUNN (CORNELL)
World long jump record breaker

PHYLLIS GREEN, aged 17, scissors over a record 5 feet (1.52m) at the 1925 WAAA
Championships

NELLIE HALSTEAD
An astonishingly versatile runner who set world bests between 1930 and 1935 at distances from 100 yards to 800m, won an Olympic bronze medal in the 4x100m relay in 1932, and captured 13 WAAA titles between 1930 and 1938 at 100 yards, 200m or 220 yards, 400m or 440 yards, 800m and cross country!

JEANNE PROBEKK
Winning the 1933 WAAA 1600m walk
title. The following year she set a world
best of 7:38.2 for the distance

GLADYS ("SALLY") LUNN
Set world bests at 880 yards, 1000m and
the mile, and Empire Games winner at
880 yards and javelin in 1934. Photo
courtesy Birchfield Harriers

First three in the 1932 Southern Cross Country Championships. From left: winner
LILLIAN STYLES (six times national champion), runner-up RUTH CHRISTMAS and
Ruth's sister ESTHER RAVEN

Pictured in Berlin just weeks before war was declared in 1939: (back row from left) MARJORIE SMITH, BETTY LOCK, team manager, EVELYNE FORSTER, LILLIAN CHALMERS; (front) DORA GARDNER, DOROTHY ODAM (high jump winner with 1.65m) and a German journalist

DOROTHY MANLEY (now PARLETT) Runner-up to Fanny Blankers-Koen in 1948 Olympic 100m

BEVIS SHERGOLD (née REID) British shot and discus record breaker before and after the war

Britain's highly successful 1950 European Championships team. Left to right (top) DOROTHY TYLER (2nd high jump), SHEILA PRATT, JEAN DESFORGES (1st 4x100m), ELSPETH HAY (1st 4x100m), BERTHA CROWTHER (2nd pentathlon); (centre) SHEILA ALEXANDER, later Lerwill (1st high jump), MAUREEN DYSON (2nd 80m hurdles), DIANE COATES, MARGARET BRIAN, VALERIE WEBSTER, team manager ROSE GILLIS (née Thompson); (bottom) JUNE FOULDS (3rd 100m, 1st 4x100m), PATRICIA DEVINE, MARGARET ERSKINE and DOROTHY HALL (née Manley)(3rd 200m, 1st 4x100m)

SHIRLEY CAWLEY
1952 Olympic long jump bronze
medallist

DIANE COATES
First Briton over 40 and 45 metres

BERTHA CROWTHER, inaugural WAAA pentathlon champion in 1949 and silver
medallist at the 1950 European Championships

SYLVIA CHEESEMAN (DISLEY)
*Set UK records at 100 yards, 200m and
220 yards*

VALERIE BALL (WINN)
*Six consecutive WAAA titles at 400m or
440 yards*

*JEAN DESFORGES (left) and MAUREEN DYSON in an 80m hurdles battle at the
White City. Maureen (née Gardner) was the 1948 Olympic silver medallist, while Jean
(who married Ron Pickering) went on to become European long jump champion in 1954*

SHEILA LERWILL
The first female straddle stylist, who set a world record of 1.72m in 1951 and was Olympic silver medallist the following year having won the European title in 1950

THELMA HOPKINS
Her achievements were similar to Sheila Lerwill's; European champion in 1954, she tied for second at the 1956 Olympics after setting a world record that year of 1.74m

DIANE LEATHER
Anchoring a 3x880 yards relay team
which broke the world record in 1953

HEATHER ARMITAGE
Finishing a close second to Betty Cuthbert
(right) in 1956 Olympic 4x100m

The evergreen DOROTHY TYLER, who as 16 year-old Dorothy Odam was
Olympic silver medallist in 1936. She was runner-up also at the 1952 Games,
was Empire Games champion in 1938 and 1950. She still ranked as high
as number five in Britain in 1961, by which time she had switched from
the scissors (above) to the western roll

World relay record breakers who received their awards from BAAB President Prince Philip at Buckingham Palace in 1955. From left: DIANE LEATHER, SHIRLEY HAMPTON, ANN JOHNSON, NORAH SMALLEY, ANNE OLIVER, SYLVIA CHEESEMAN, JEAN NEWBOULT, ANNE PASHLEY and JUNE FOULDS

JOY JORDAN
Set a world half mile record of 2:06.1 in 1960

SUE ALLDAY
UK shot and discus record breaker. Photo: Charles Sharon

DOROTHY HYMAN winning the Commonwealth Games 220 yards title in Perth in 1962

MAUREEN TRANTER (left), DOROTHY HYMAN (centre) and DAPHNE ARDEN do battle over 220 yards at the 1964 WAAA Championships.

BARBARA INKPEN (later Lawton), who between 1969 and 1973 raised the UK high jump record from 1.76m to 1.87m.

*One of the supreme moments in British athletics history: ANN PACKER wins the
1964 Olympic 800m title in the official world record time of 2:01.1*

services and competition, and to make recommendations thereon." Conclusions of the Byers Report, published in May 1968, included: "Firstly, we find the case for one governing body for athletics in the UK to be proved beyond doubt, and secondly, we recommend that a new administrative organisation headed by a 'Director of British Athletics' should be established. ... The 'British Athletic Federation' would represent England and Wales, Scotland and Northern Ireland, the Women's Associations, the Cross Country Unions, the Race Walking Association, the Tug of War Association and the Schools. It would affiliate to the IAAF as the governing body for athletics in the UK."

Marea Hartman was not impressed. She was quoted in the Daily Mail as saying "I don't see how the formation of a British Athletics Federation could help us. We should continue to govern ourselves. Who better understands women athletes than women officials?" She confirmed her viewpoint in an interview with Cliff Temple, editor of Women's Athletics, a monthly stablemate of *Athletics Weekly* which appeared between May 1968 and April 1969. "We get a fair crack of the whip from the BAAB, and we see no reason to change. The BAF, as laid out in the Byers Report, could not be formed without the agreement of the WAAA and we, as a body, do not see the need for such a Federation."

Later in 1968 the Executive Committee stated: "The WAAA cannot accept this Report, as we do not consider it would be of any benefit to us. We did not ask for an enquiry into women's athletics or the WAAA and, as a matter of courtesy only, attended a meeting with members of the Enquiry Committee. We are happy working with the BAAB in connection with all international matters and cannot see any reason for changing this procedure." Despite the Byers Report's recommendations, the WAAA along with the AAA and BAAB would remain separate organisations until the 1990s.

Another thorny subject was whether the AAA and WAAA Championships should be combined into one meeting. A poll of International Athletes' Club members in 1961 voted 57-23 in favour of a mixed meeting and at their AGM proposed combined Championships be staged in 1962. That led nowhere as the WAAA was implacably against the idea (although, curiously, the Indoor Championships had been a mixed affair ever since 1935), and it wasn't until as late as 1988 that the women consented to share the outdoor stage with the men.

Another area of the sport which would puzzle today's younger generation concerned tracks. Cinder and grass tracks at the mercy of our damp climate remained the norm and it wasn't until 1967 that the first En-Tout-Cas all-weather track, made of plastic and rubber crumbs, opened at the Leicester Sports Centre. At the inaugural meeting, despite almost incessant rain, the track held firm and athletes flocked to use it. The first Tartan track in Europe was laid at Crystal Palace in 1968 and the WAAA Championships switched to "The Palace" that summer, three years before the AAA followed suit.

On the coaching front, the sixties got off to a calamitous start when within the space of a few months in 1961 AAA Head Coach Geoff Dyson and National Coaches Jim Alford and Lionel Pugh resigned. Denis Watts and John Le Masurier became the Senior National Coaches and men of the calibre of Bill Marlow, Ron Pickering, Tom McNab, Wilf Paish, John Anderson and others were appointed during the decade to uphold the AAA Coaching Scheme's prestige. All of them coached women as well as men, while Ken Oakley performed valuable service also as the WAAA's National Coaching Secretary from the early sixties, having succeeded Evelyn Baker who due to serious illness resigned after many years of work in that role.

Ken Oakley writes: "Strong links were developed with the leading women's PE colleges, particularly Bedford and Lady Mabel College in South Yorkshire. This led to many students there and in the 'Wing' PE sections of other Colleges of Education qualifying as WAAA coaches, so ensuring that women's athletics was promoted and popular in secondary schools. Links were made with the Schools AA at national and local level. By the 1960s efforts were made to obtain financial support from the Department of Education and during Denis Howell's appointment as the first Sports Minister (1964-1970) Marea Hartman and myself were able to negotiate a grant of £20,000 for coaching development. This continued annually until amalgamation, unfortunately without any increase in value." A UK Coaching Scheme came into effect in 1972, all WAAA coaches becoming instead BAAB coaches.

The 1960 Olympics in Rome brought one particularly crushing disappointment. Having improved the UK long jump record to 6.27m in May, at a time when the world record stood at 6.40m, Mary Bignal was being hailed as a possible gold medallist. Her prospects were enhanced further when in Rome she led the qualifiers with 6.33m, only to wind up a shell-shocked ninth in the final later that day with 6.01m. The gold medal went at 6.37m, the silver at 6.27m. The problem was that she fouled her first two jumps. Her confidence shattered, she measured out her run-up anew but it was of little avail and she failed to qualify for another three jumps. Four years later she would atone for that failure ... and how!

There was heartache also for javelin thrower Sue Platt. Shortly before the Games she extended her UK record to 51.60m but on the big occasion she was inspired in the third round to land her spear at around the 54m mark, good enough for the silver medal. But she was so excited and eager to see how far she had thrown that she unwittingly stepped over the line, and up went the red flag. Ken Oakley believes Sue lost the medal due to a difference between the AAA/WAAA and IAAF rules and their interpretation. He explains: "Under the IAAF rule the athlete must not cross the scratch line. However, in Britain the athletes had been allowed and often encouraged to cross the line and retrieve their javelin once they saw the white flag signalling a valid throw. In Rome, Sue threw, saw the judge signal white and then went forward to collect her javelin. In subsequent years English officials waited until the athlete retired back and went forward around the extended scratch line, one metre on each side of the runway, to collect their implement."

However, three British athletes returned with medals they were not expected to win. One of the supreme stars of the Games, Wilma Rudolph (USA), won both sprints by an enormous margin, but running out of her skin Dorothy Hyman placed second in the 100m in a wind-aided 11.3 (11.43 on electrical timing) after setting a UK record of 11.5 (11.65) in her semi-final and followed with bronze over 200m in 24.7, having posted another national record of 23.7 (23.82) in her heat. Carole Quinton also rose to the challenge with the hurdles race of her life, finishing a close second to Irina Press (USSR) in a UK record equalling 10.9 (10.99), while Mary Bignal also ran above herself in fourth place to compensate a little for her long jumping demise. No one could get anywhere near Romanian world record holder Iolanda Balas in the high jump but Dorothy Shirley maintained the British tradition of silver medals in this event, started by Dorothy Odam in 1936, by tying for second with Poland's Jaroslawa Jozwiakowska with a personal best of 1.71m.

The WAAA moved cautiously over the matter of permitting youngsters to run longer distances but a start was made in 1961 when, among other similar events, the Northern Women's CC&RWA conducted an experimental one and a half mile cross country race for girls of 14 and 15, and that distance was given official blessing two years later, as was one mile cross country for girls of 12 and 13. On the track, in 1967, the half mile was added to the WAAA Junior Girls Championships, although it wasn't until 1969 that the 150 yards was replaced by the 200m and Intermediates were permitted to race at 400m. At the senior level the WAAA was always at the forefront of expanding and refining the programme of events. There had been an 880y championship since the beginnings in 1922, cross country was introduced in 1927, the mile was added in 1936 and 3000m in 1968, although the first club race at 2 miles dated back to 1953. There was pioneering work also relating to the hurdles. In 1961 Pat Nutting (later Pryce) won an experimental race (at 81.75m) over 3ft hurdles, as against the normal 2ft 6in, and it was she who won the inaugural WAAA 200m hurdles title in 1961 and 100m hurdles (2ft 6in) in 1963. In 1967 the height of the 100m barriers was raised to 2ft 9in.

The year of 1962 was one of ups and downs. At the AGM in February the report delivered by Hon. Treasurer Hazel Needham, the 1951 WAAA mile champion, was a gloomy one. "Our position is still most unhappy from a financial point of view," she announced. The Association had incurred a deficit of £219 in 1961, following a shortfall of £345 the previous year, and total assets had shrunk to £2,677. "In common with other sporting bodies," she stated, "we are involved in heavier expenditure, due to rising costs in postage, telephone charges and fares, and a drop in our two main sources of income, affiliations and donations. The apparent decline in public interest in the sport is reflected in the poor attendances at our meetings and the decrease in our income."

Better news at the AGM came from Chairman Dick Taylor, who revealed that the Championships in July would be sponsored by Bovril Ltd, an association which continued throughout the 1960s. During that period of sponsorship an annual week-long high level course for both coaches and talented athletes was held at Lilleshall. These courses, organised by George Stratford of Bromley Ladies and directed by Ken Oakley, proved to be very popular and helped many up and coming coaches to gain valuable experience.

Another positive was the staging at Wembley's Empire Pool of the first National Indoor Championships (AAA and WAAA combined) since 1939, with long jumper Sheila Parkin, a Sheffield schoolgirl, becoming at 15 one of the youngest ever champions. Thanks to sponsorship, and to celebrate 40 years of the WAAA, invitations were extended to some overseas stars to compete at the 1962 outdoor Championships, and for the first time a few MEN'S events were added to the programme. There were many excellent performances but again the attendance at the vast White City Stadium was meagre. Dorothy Hyman was in particularly splendid form as she equalled the UK records in both the 100y (10.6) and 220y (23.8), and was even more impressive at the same venue when Britain edged Poland 54-52 in a thrilling match. She lowered the UK 200m record to 23.5 and on the second day, despite a flooded track and a strong headwind, she returned an extraordinary 11.8 for 100m – which some observers felt would have been 11.4 at worst in decent conditions.

Unsurprisingly, it was Dorothy who was the British star of the 1962 European Championships in Belgrade. Having tuned up with a UK record equalling 11.5, she reached new heights by taking the 100m title in an only just wind assisted (2.3m/sec) 11.3. Even Germany's tall blonde goddess of the track,

Jutta Heine, was left wallowing in her wake. Dorothy had hoped to take the 200m also (she had recently equalled the European record of 23.4) but was foiled by the weather. She led into the finishing straight but Heine was better equipped to deal with the 2.3m/sec headwind and won by 0.2 in 23.5. Dorothy was coached by Denis Watts, who would later guide Ann Packer to the greatest prize of all. Speaking of Ann, she was a revelation in Belgrade. Considered fortunate by some even to make the 200m team considering her personal best was merely 24.9, she ran a wind assisted 24.0 in her heat, a legal 24.2 semi and placed sixth in the final in 24.4.

There were other pleasant surprises: Joy Grieveson travelled out with a best 400m time of 54.7 and returned as UK record holder with 53.9 and silver medallist; 16-year-old Linda Knowles, whose pre-1962 best was just 1.52m, placed third in the high jump with 1.73m; while Mary Rand (née Bignal), who had only resumed training earlier in the summer after giving birth to a daughter, snatched long jump bronze with 6.22m. She, along with Packer, Hyman and Daphne Arden, also gained bronze in the relay (44.9). Joy Jordan was given the same time as the second and third finishers in the 800m – a UK record of 2:05.0 – in fourth place, while yet another team member to excel was Mary Peters. Still a work in progress, she was second in the pentathlon after day one and ended up fifth with her best score yet of 4586.

Dorothy Hyman maintained her brilliant form for the Commonwealth Games in Perth in November 1962, winning the sprint double. Her slow 100y time of 11.2 can be explained by a vicious headwind of 5.8m/sec (in 100°F/37°C heat), after running a windless 10.7 semi, and she went on to take the 220y in a UK record equalling 23.8 into a 3m wind. A silver medal followed in the 4x110y relay (along with Ann Packer, Daphne Arden and Betty Moore), the England team losing by inches in 46.6 to Australia. The versatile Packer had placed sixth in the hurdles, in which Moore had finished second (11.3) to Australia's Pam Kilborn whose 10.9 was an amazing time into a 7m wind. England's other winner was Sue Platt (50.25m) in the javelin, with Rosemary Morgan second (49.62m), and bronze medals went to Joy Jordan with a UK record of 2:05.9 in the 880y and to Sue Allday in the shot (13.56m).

There was no stopping Dorothy Hyman and Mary Rand in 1963, both ranked number one in the world in the 100/200m and long jump respectively. Dorothy clocked 11.3 and 23.2 – European record times that no Briton would better for ten years; while Mary moved to second on the world all-time list with 6.44m. Both featured in the British team which set a world record of 45.2 for the 4x110y relay, their colleagues being Madeleine Cobb (née Weston) and Daphne Arden. Mary also set UK records in the 80m hurdles (10.8, with Pat Nutting given the same time) and pentathlon with scores of 4712 (Ann Packer second with a personal best of 4294) and 4726. The latter was also making her mark at 400m in her first season at the event. She ran 53.4 close behind Joy Grieveson's European record of 53.2 and in a celebrated late season match against the Russian Federation in Volgograd Ann won in 53.3 against Joy (53.4) and former world record holder Maria Itkina (53.7) to establish herself as among the 1964 Olympic medal favourites.

Among the honours heaped on Dorothy Hyman in 1963 was the BBC's prestigious Sports Personality of the Year Award. Such has been the esteem in which so many of the UK's most successful women athletes have been held that six others went on to receive the accolade: Mary Rand in 1964, Mary Peters in 1972, Fatima Whitbread in 1987, Liz McColgan in 1991, Paula Radcliffe in 2002 and Kelly Holmes in 2004. Seven female winners, out of 17 for athletics since Chris Chataway was the first in 1954, is an extraordinary tally. No other sport has produced more than six winners (motor racing), while next with five are football and boxing. Sally Gunnell (1993 and 1994) and Denise Lewis (1998 and 2000) have been voted runners-up, while Jessica Ennis was placed third in 2009 and 2010.

Former Spartan Ladies high jumper Edith Holland succeeded Hazel Rider (née Needham) as WAAA Hon. Treasurer at the 1964 AGM, the previous financial year having yielded a small profit, the first since 1957. Other developments included the decision to lengthen the distance of hurdle races for Juniors and Intermediates to 80y and 80m respectively and that

WAAA age groups would fall into line with those of the English Schools AA; i.e. Juniors under 15 and Intermediates under 17 at midnight on September 1-2 in the year of competition. Later in the year the WCC&RWA altered the second part of its name to refer to Race, rather than Road, Walking.

The year offered a glimpse into the far future when a brave pioneering Scot, Dale Greig (27), completed the tough Isle of Wight marathon in 3:27:25, competing unofficially by starting four minutes before the men. An ambulance followed her around the course and her feat made the front page of the *Sunday Express*. Not everyone was so impressed, though, as the Southern Counties WAAA sent a letter reprimanding Ryde Harriers for allowing her to run. Dale, the Scottish cross country champion, held the world's best time for less than three months but it stood as a British best for 11 years. She went on to break further barriers, becoming in 1972 the first woman to complete the 55-mile London to Brighton race (8:30:04), seven years before females were officially allowed in the event. In 1974 she won the inaugural World Veterans marathon title in Paris, the first marathon in which men and women were permitted, officially, to run together.

Before the year of 1964 was out, Britain would bask in the glory of two much more publicised world records thanks to Mary Rand and Ann Packer, who set them in the cauldron of Olympic competition in Tokyo and thus achieved the ultimate in athletics: an Olympic gold medal with a world record performance. One was largely anticipated; the other far less so.

After leading the long jump qualifiers with an Olympic record of 6.52m, Mary got down to serious business in the final on October 14. She opened with a UK record of 6.59m, improved that to 6.63m in the fourth round and then, on her fifth attempt, produced an extraordinary jump of 6.76m. As her coach John Le Masurier commented: "Technically it was superb – a fast approach, with the body becoming vertical as she crouched into a powerful take-off. A perfect hitchkick with the feet stretched forward for landing and just sufficient forward speed remaining to allow her to stand up in the sand." It was a performance ahead of its time, for there was a headwind of 1.6m/sec blowing at the time and the clay runway was rain soaked. Off a synthetic surface and with that amount of wind in her favour it's possible she would have jumped very close to seven metres – the sort of distance that would not be attained for another dozen years. Dorothy Odam/Tyler and Maureen Gardner had come very close but it was Mary Rand who became the first British woman athlete to win an Olympic gold medal.

You wait all those years and then two come along at almost the same time. Six days later it was Ann Packer's turn. She had already been very busy at the Games but, coached by Denis Watts and having trained ferociously the previous winter with her fiancé, European 400m champion Robbie Brightwell, she was well equipped for the challenge. Despite preparing for a completely new event, the 800m, as well as the 400m, she was faster than ever and buoyed by a personal best 200m of 23.7 she was in confident form in the Olympic one-lap event. She won her heat in a UK record of 53.1, took her semi in a European record 52.7 and in the final on October 17 finished a hugely disappointed second to Australia's Betty Cuthbert (52.0) despite clocking 52.2. Only North Korea's absent and mysterious Sin Kim Dan had ever run the distance faster. Reversing her 400m strategy, she took it as gently as possible in the 800m preliminaries, running 2:12.6 in her heat and 2:06.0 in her semi. That reticence paid off on October 20, for although on paper she was the slowest of the eight finalists with a best of 2:05.3, she ran with impeccable judgement and high energy levels. Sixth at the bell in 59.1, she was third at 600m in 90.7, second around the final turn. She was still five metres behind Maryvonne Dupureur entering the final straight, but as the Frenchwoman began to flag so Ann's stride lengthened and her spirits soared. With a beatific smile on her face, she broke the tape five metres clear in a world record 2:01.1. Apart from a 2:11.0 win for the Commonwealth against the USA and Japan in Osaka five days later that was her final race. Shortly after the Games she became Mrs Brightwell and declared "running a home is more important than running races." The couple have three sons; the eldest, Gary, ran a 47.90 400m as an 18-year-old, while Ian and David became professional footballers with Manchester City.

That Osaka match could have been an anti-climax for Mary Rand but instead she came within an inch of her new world record with 6.74m. Hers had been a phenomenal Olympics. Two days after her historic long jump she started the pentathlon and again performed brilliantly to become only the second woman to exceed 5000 points. She totalled 5035 (10.9 hurdles, 11.05m shot, 1.72m high jump, 6.55m long jump and 24.2 200m) and finished ahead of Irina Press in three of the five events. However, she conceded so many points to Press in the shot – no fewer than 384 – that the muscular Soviet athlete ran out the winner 211 points clear with a world record breaking score of 5246. Mary Peters, whose own golden moments were still eight years away, placed fourth with 4797. There was still the 4x100m relay to come and here Mary Rand – along with Janet Simpson (emulating her mother Violet Webb), Daphne Arden and team captain Dorothy Hyman – took the bronze medals with a UK record of 44.0. Overall the British women's team – with Marea Hartman as manager – placed second on the points table to the USSR.

MARY RAND: THE FIRST GOLD MEDALLIST

There was seemingly no end to Mary Rand's talents. As a member of London Olympiades, she excelled as a sprinter, hurdler, high jumper and pentathlete, triple jumped decades before it became a standard event for women, and even competed in a mile walk race! Her crowning glory, though, was the long jump and in Tokyo in 1964 she set a world record of 6.76m in becoming the first British female athlete to win an Olympic gold medal. It's a salutary fact that the best mark in 2011 by a UK-born jumper was just 6.54m.

As Mary Bignal, born in Wells (Somerset) on February 10 1940, she first attracted attention while a pupil at Millfield School and in 1957, when only 17, she set an English record in her first pentathlon. At the time of the 1960 Olympics she was being regarded as a possible long jump winner and she led the qualifiers with a UK record of 6.33m ... only to flop in the final, placing ninth. After fouling her first two jumps she lost her nerve and registered only 6.01m. It was a shattering disappointment, redeemed only slightly by an unexpectedly high fourth place in the 80m hurdles.

She married Olympic sculler Sidney Rand in 1961 and only four months after the birth of their daughter she took the long jump bronze medal at the 1962 European Championships. In 1963 she was a member of the British team which set a world record in the 4x110 yards relay and she posted UK records in the 80m hurdles, long jump and pentathlon, while her exploits in 1964 prior to the Olympics included equalling the European 100 yards record of 10.6. At the Games she collected a complete set of medals, for after the long jump triumph she placed second in the pentathlon and helped Britain place third in the sprint relay.

British athletics' original "golden girl" never recaptured that form and retired when injury prevented her making the Olympic team in 1968. Resident in the USA for over 40 years but without ever quite losing her Somerset burr, Mary subsequently married Bill Toomey (the 1968 Olympic decathlon champion) in December 1969, divorced again and wed John Reese in 1992. A poll conducted in 1998 by the NUTS (National Union of Track Statisticians) to determine the greatest UK female athletes of the past 40 years resulted in Mary being voted no 1 with 298 points with Sally Gunnell second (277) and Ann Packer and Mary Peters joint third with 186.

ANN PACKER: FOUND BEST EVENT JUST IN TIME

Just in time Ann Packer discovered her best event. Whereas the star of the 1948 Olympics, Fanny Blankers-Koen, began her career at 800m but became a legendary sprinter, hurdler and jumper, Ann started as a sprinter, hurdler and jumper but found fame at 800m. And whereas the Dutchwoman was 30 when she achieved Olympic immortality, Ann retired immediately after her 1964 Olympic success, aged only 22.

Born at Moulsford (Oxfordshire) on March 8 1942, she could look back on a remarkably varied career. She won the 100 yards at the 1959 English Schools Championships, was WAAA long jump champion in 1960 and was a finalist in 1962 at 200m in the European Championships and 80m hurdles at the Commonwealth Games. In 1963 she moved up to 400m, swiftly bursting into world class, and finally in 1964 she took up the 800m with astonishing results.

A PE teacher and member of Reading AC, Ann realised she would never become a world beater as a sprinter but thanks to training considerably harder that winter she emerged a much stronger athlete in 1963 and was only 0.1 sec outside the European and UK 400m record with 53.3. During the winter of 1963-64 she trained even more ferociously with her fiancé, European 400m champion Robbie Brightwell. Her Olympic objective was to win the 400m, but to test her enhanced stamina she opened her season at 800m, winning in a promising 2:11.1. She subsequently ran 2:05.3 and suddenly had become a genuine Olympic prospect at that distance as well as 400m.

In Tokyo, after winning her semi in a European record 52.7, she had to settle for silver in the inaugural Olympic women's 400m final as Australia's Betty Cuthbert held her off, 52.0 to 52.2. Although on paper she was the slowest of the 800m finalists, she had plenty of motivation. Not only did she wish to atone for the 400m reverse but she also wanted desperately to present a gold medal to her fiancé to compensate for his disappointment at finishing fourth in his 400m final. Despite her novice status, she ran a superbly judged race. Maryvonne Dupureur of France was still five metres ahead entering the home straight but Ann overtook her to win in a world record 2:01.1.

Just as Mary Rand was fortunate to have been guided by such a technically brilliant and understanding coach as John Le Masurier, so Ann derived the benefit of being advised by the equally knowledgeable and unassuming Denis Watts, who could claim to be the UK's most successful coach of women athletes. He helped many internationals, male and female, achieve their potential but his three greatest partnerships were with Dorothy Hyman, Ann Packer and Lillian Board.

With no major international championships the big event of 1965 was the inaugural edition of the European Cup, but that turned out to be a massive anti-climax after the highs of

Tokyo as the British women's team failed even to qualify for the final. Still it wasn't all doom and gloom. The MBE was awarded to Mary Rand, Ann Packer and Dorothy Hyman for their services to athletics; the National Indoor Championships switched from the cramped Wembley facility to the luxury of a banked 220y track at RAF Cosford; and it was announced at the WAAA AGM that a profit of £509 had been made during the previous financial year.

There were three important international occasions in 1966 but British women failed to make much of an impression in any of them. Only two athletes were sent to the inaugural European Indoor Games in Dortmund with Mary Rand finishing second in the long jump and third in the 60m and high jump. Representing the Republic of Ireland, Ballymena's seemingly ageless Maeve Kyle (actually 37) – a coach and Hon. Treasurer of the N Ireland WAAA as well as still being a formidable runner – placed third in the 400m. The Commonwealth Games in Kingston, Jamaica produced only one gold medallist as Mary Rand won the long jump with 6.36m. Sheila Parkin was second with 6.30m and other silver medallists were Deirdre Watkinson in the 440y (with a UK record 54.1), Dorothy Shirley in the high jump (1.70m), Mary Peters of N Ireland in the shot (16.30m) and the England 4x110y relay squad of Maureen Tranter, Janet Simpson, Daphne Slater (née Arden) and Jill Hall in 45.6. Jill finished third in the 100y (10.8), as did Anne Smith in the 880y (2:05.0). Coming so soon after those Games, the European Championships in Budapest proved a disaster for a team of weary and jaded athletes. Even Mary Rand was unable to make the medal rostrum, finishing fourth in the pentathlon (4711) and 11th in the long jump (6.16m). The only other Briton to place as high as fourth was former junior international swimmer (and future British team manager) Pam Piercy, with a personal best of 2:04.1 in the 800m. Britain's big hope in that event, Anne Smith, did not compete. Following a dispute with team management she was sent home and the BAAB suspended her from international competition until 1968.

It was at the 1966 Commonwealth Games that athletes encountered the newly introduced sex test. In her 1974 autobiography, *Mary P*, Mary Peters provided a graphic description of the humiliating process. "I went into a bare room which contained two women doctors, one examination couch and one large enamel bowl containing some white, cloudy antiseptic in which the doctors apparently washed their hands after each examination. What occurred next I can only describe as the most crude and degrading experience I have ever known in my life. I was ordered to lie on the couch and pull my knees up. The doctors then proceeded to undertake an examination which, in modern parlance, amounted to a grope. Presumably they were searching for hidden testes. They found none and I left. Like everyone else who had fled that detestable room I said nothing to anyone still waiting in the corridor and made my way, shaken, back to my room." By the time of the 1968 Olympics that procedure had been supplanted by a saliva test and prior to the 1972 Olympics a hair follicle from the head was examined instead. Tests have since been abolished, except where there are exceptional circumstances.

The year of 1966 had started promisingly. Marea Hartman was awarded the MBE, Edith Holland was able to deliver an encouraging financial report to the AGM, and exciting new talent was making itself felt. Southend schoolgirl Ann Wilson set a world age-16 pentathlon best of 4676 when winning an international contest in Holland against Mary Rand no less; Rosemary Stirling (18) improved at 440y and 880y from 58.1 and 2:13.9 to Scottish records of 54.4 and 2:05.4 when finishing fourth both times at the Commonwealth Games; while Lillian Board (17) started to fulfil the prophecy of her LOAC clubmate Mary Rand that she would develop into a great quarter-miler by clocking 54.6 in her first season at the event.

All three progressed during 1967, none more so than Lillian who established herself as a genuine Olympic medal prospect after pulling off an unexpected victory in a USA v British Commonwealth match in Los Angeles. Her 400m time of 52.8 ranked second on the European all-time list behind Ann Packer. Rosemary Stirling, who set a European indoor 440y record of 56.3 a week after capturing the Midland cross country title, collected two world record relay plaques. Teamed up with Pat Lowe and Pam Piercy she helped Britain set new figures at 3x880y with 6:25.2 and 3x800m with 6:20.0. Born in New Zealand, living in England (since 1963) and running for Scotland (her father's country of birth), Rosemary was at 5ft 1in (1.55m) the shortest of all international class 400/800m runners. Still only 17, Ann Wilson topped the British pentathlon year list, but an even more precocious all-rounder bounded onto the scene in the shape of Sue Scott who totalled 4419 for a world age-15 best. Another fast rising schoolgirl of that age was the tall, powerfully built Marilyn Neufville, winner of the WAAA Junior 100y and 150y double .... only three years later she would smash the world 400m record.

An earlier world record, three in fact, came in 1967 from Anne Smith. She may have been banned from international competition that year but she set the home tracks alight with her metronomic front running displays. At the Surrey Championships she ran the fastest mile yet with 4:39.2, made up of quarters of 70.0, 70.4, 70.0 and 68.8, while in the Southern Championships she not only bettered that with 4:37.0 (68.0, 69.8, 69.2, 70.0) but picked up a world record of 4:17.3 at 1500m on the way. Both marks were the first at those distances to be officially ratified by the IAAF. Anne, who was coached by Gordon Pirie, emigrated to New Zealand the following year, returned to Britain in 1986 but died of a cerebral haemorrhage in 1993, aged only 52.

An important decision was taken at the 1967 WAAA AGM when it was agreed by 43 votes to 14 to allow Juniors (girls of 11-15 on September 1-2 in the year of competition) to race at 880y, having previously been restricted to 150y. As WAAA Coaching Secretary Ken Oakley put it: "The athletes created the demand, we are merely legislating for it." Not everyone welcomed the initiative, WAAA Vice-President Vera Searle declaring herself "horrified" but Doris Dixon (14) went on to win the inaugural WAAA title and the event's popularity has never waned.

Another welcome move in 1967 was the organisation of a women's race in conjunction with the men's prestigious International Cross Country Championships at Barry. It was a modest affair, involving teams from England, Scotland,

Wales and Ireland plus two individual entrants from the USA, but it produced an outstanding performance from the American winner, Doris Brown, who finished 37 sec clear of Rita Lincoln who led England to victory in the team race.

Injury prevented Mary Rand, who had been preparing for the pentathlon, being selected for the 1968 Olympics in high altitude Mexico City (she announced her retirement shortly before the Games), and the stars of the British women's team were Lillian Board and Sheila Sherwood (née Parkin), both of whom came back with silver medals.

Sheila opened with a personal best long jump of 6.60m, which held the lead for a minute or two until Romania's Viorica Viscopoleanu landed at 6.82m to break Mary Rand's world record. In the fifth round Sheila reached 6.68m for fourth place on the world all-time list. Next day husband John Sherwood seized the 400m hurdles bronze medal in 49.03 in a race won in the world record time of 48.12 by David Hemery. It was the Sherwoods' exploits that inspired a 12-year-old boy living in their home city of Sheffield to dream of becoming an Olympic athlete himself … his name was Sebastian Coe, and it was Sheila who gave him his first pair of spikes, a gesture Lord Coe has never forgotten. The Sherwoods' son, David, developed into a Yorkshire 200m champion before concentrating on tennis, successfully partnering Andy Murray in the 2005 Davis Cup tie against Israel.

Lillian enjoyed a brilliant build-up towards the Games. She was not only much faster than ever before but her endurance could not be questioned after running 2:02.0 for 800m in the WAAA Championships. She concentrated on the 400m at the Olympics. "Lillian has got to go through the first 200m in 24.5 to win," commented her coach Denis Watts, and that's what she did, spot on, in the Olympic final. She ran the third 100m hard to enter the final straight some four metres ahead, and it was only in the final few strides that the unheralded Colette Besson of France edged past for victory in the European record time of 52.03. In only her third season at the event, still aged 19 and seemingly with years ahead of her, Lillian had run 52.12 to break Ann Packer's UK record and move to fourth on the world all-time list.

Running a blinder in fourth place was Janet Simpson, who despite not having trained specifically for 400m and being troubled by a cold was timed at 52.57 – an extraordinary result for someone who had not run faster than 55.9 prior to 1968. She, Lillian, Anita Neil and Maureen Tranter set a UK 4x100m relay record of 43.78, but only in seventh place. Intrinsically, that was a better performance than the world record breaking 45.0 4x110y by the same foursome the previous month. Earlier in the summer, Tranter, Della James, Simpson and Val Peat set new 4x200m world figures of 1:33.8. In Mexico City none of the sprinters reached the final although both Della (11.36 electrical) and Val (11.39) tied Dorothy Hyman's hand timed UK 100m record of 11.3 in their quarter-finals. Sheila Taylor, ranked only 18th among the entrants with a best of 2:05.5, excelled herself by placing fourth in the 800m in 2:03.81 with Pat Lowe (second coming into the finishing straight) sixth in 2:04.25. There were commendable showings also in the pentathlon by team captain Mary Peters, third after day one but finishing ninth with 4803, and Sue Scott whose score of 4786 in tenth was a world age-17 best. Hampered throughout by injury, Ann Wilson – who had set a world teenage best of 4841 earlier in the season – placed 16th with 4688.

Marea Hartman, the women's manager, had this to say about the team in Mexico City: "Not only did our girls perform admirably in the competition itself, but there was also a tremendous team spirit. They really enjoyed themselves, and after all that's what it's all about, isn't it? It's no good going all that way to be miserable! We were there for six weeks and there was absolutely no trouble whatsoever. Team managers from other countries were coming up to me and saying 'How do you keep your team so cheerful?'"

BRITAIN'S 1968 OLYMPIC TEAM

Over 40 years later it's interesting to reflect on the make-up of the British women's team in Mexico City. The average age of the 20-strong squad was 22, none of course was a professional athlete in those strictly amateur days and all apart from one housewife and mother were either students (one a schoolgirl) or worked for a living. All were white except for Anita Neil.

Della James (age 19; 100m & 4x100m) London Olympiades; born: Southsea; student. She later married 400m hurdles star Alan Pascoe; **Anita Neil** *(18; 100m & 4x100m) London Olympiades; born: Wellingborough; seamstress;* **Val Peat**, *née Wild (21; 100m, 200m & 4x100m)) Dorothy Hyman TC; born: Thurnscoe, nr Rotherham; clothing cutter [Val died in 1997, aged 50];* **Maureen Tranter** *(21; 200m & 4x100m)) Wolverhampton & Bilston; born: Bilston; GPO telephonist;* **Lillian Board** *(19; 200m, 400m & 4x100m) London Olympiades; born: Durban, S Africa; typist; [Lillian died in 1970, aged 22];* **Janet Simpson** *(24; 400m & 4x100m) London Olympiades; born: Barnet; typist. Later married Swiss European 200m champion Philippe Clerc [Janet died in 2010, aged 65];* **Mary Green**, *née Tagg (24; 400m) Norfolk Olympiads; born: Derby; PE teacher. Sister of 1970 International Cross Country champion Mike Tagg, married to sub-3:58 miler Andy Green;* **Pat Lowe** *(25; 800m) Birchfield; born: Leicester; PE teacher. Later married fellow 800m star Dave Cropper;* **Joan Page** *(21; 800m) Cambridge H; born: Woolwich; PE teacher. Later became better known under her married name of Joan Allison;* **Sheila Taylor** *(22; 800m) Coventry Godiva; born: Coventry; civil servant (Ministry of Labour). Later became better known under her married name of Sheila Carey;* **Pat Jones** *(26; 80m hurdles) Birchfield; born: Purley; women's PE officer at Leicester University;* **Pat Pryce**, *née Nutting (26; 80m hurdles) Hillingdon; born: Willesden; housewife & mother;* **Ann Wilson** *(19; 80m hurdles, long jump & pentathlon) Southend AC; born: Southend; civil servant (Customs & Excise);* **Barbara Inkpen** *(18; high jump) Aldershot Farnham & District; born: Farnham; assistant buyer with stud welding company. Later married international walker Carl Lawton;* **Dorothy Shirley** *(29; high jump) Spartan Ladies; born: Manchester; student (later a teacher);* **Maureen Barton** *(20; long jump) Surrey AC; born: Walthamstow; PE student;* **Sheila Sherwood**, *née Parkin (22; long jump) Sheffield United H; born: Sheffield; teacher. Married to John Sherwood (1968 Olympic 400m hurdles bronze medallist);* **Sue Platt** *(28; javelin) London Olympiades; born: Mill*

*Hill; youth worker; **Mary Peters** (29; pentathlon) Spartan Ladies; born: Halewood, nr Liverpool; secretary; **Sue Scott** (17; pentathlon) Birchfield; born: Birmingham; schoolgirl. Later married long jumper and coach Kevin Reeve.*

While in Mexico City the high regard in which Marea Hartman was held internationally was made apparent when she was elected Chairman of the IAAF's Women's Commission. She was a strong influence behind the introduction of several new events. The 1500m and 4x400m relay would be added to the Olympic programme in 1972, with the 80m hurdles replaced by 100m hurdles (2ft 9in) – those changes coming into effect at the 1969 European Championships. The 200m hurdles would be recognised as a standard event, and there would be three new events for the 1970 Commonwealth Games: 1500m, 100m rather than 80m hurdles, and pentathlon. Additionally, the International Cross Country would be run over a longer distance than previously.

Another interesting project of Marea Hartman's was her "Big Girls" campaign. Through her IAAF activities she saw that tall athletes dominated the throwing events, particularly in Europe, and she persuaded the BBC and sections of the press to encourage a search for similar young women in England to try the throws with the aim of being coached to national or even international standard. More than 800 expressed an interest but, as Ken Oakley pointed out, "unfortunately the title seemed to Anglo-Saxon eyes to describe persons both large in girth and weight as well as stature, leading to adverse comments and reluctance to be so labelled." No one progressed to world class standards although some did attain local and national level. One such was Sue Campbell (20), who became the eighth ranked discus thrower in Britain in 1969 with 44.30m. She went on to achieve greater distinction as an England netball international, Chief Executive of the National Coaching Foundation from 1985 to 1995 and Chairman of UK Sport since 2003. In 2008 she was created Baroness Campbell of Loughborough.

Perhaps the best news of 1968 was the reinstatement of Dorothy Hyman. By the time of her retirement following the 1964 Olympics, and still only 23, Dorothy could claim to be the most be-medalled of British athletes. She remains the most successful British female sprinter ever and in 1963 was without doubt the world's number one – but injury dashed her hopes in Tokyo the following year. After retiring to concentrate on coaching she published an autobiography *Sprint To Fame* which, because payment was involved, caused her to be barred from competition under the strict amateur laws of that era. Having made a success of coaching and the Dorothy Hyman Track Club she felt the urge to return to the track and in April 1968 applied to the WAAA to be reinstated. The WAAA Executive Committee informed her she was eligible to race again at club and county level, and at the Yorkshire Championships, in her first race for nearly four years and after only a few weeks of training, she was timed at 11.0 in a 100y race won by one of her protégées, Val Peat, in the UK record equalling time of 10.6. By the following year Dorothy was again Britain's top sprinter but was not eligible to represent Britain in international competition, thus missing the 1969 European Championships in Athens where Anita Neil (100m) and Val Peat (200m) – both well behind Dorothy in the WAAA Championships – gained bronze medals.

The "golden girl" in 1969 was Lillian Board even though her fastest 400m was "only" 53.7 when she scored a deeply satisfying victory over her Olympic conqueror Colette Besson in a match when Britain crushed France 84-48, winning 11 of the 13 events. Another notable winner was Dorothy Shirley who, nine years after her Olympic silver medal, jumped a personal best of 1.74m – a "British differential record" 7cm above her own height.

Lillian went so well at the shorter distances early in the season, including a 52.9 solo anchor when she, Jenny Pawsey, Pauline Attwood and Janet Simpson set a world 4x400m relay record of 3:37.6, that she seriously considered making the 400m her goal at the European Championships. But then she encountered such acute back trouble that all her plans were compromised. The injury affected the nerves in her legs and was more painful the faster she ran, and that convinced her to go for the 800m. The European final was a very fast race and but for the strong wind Vera Nikolic's world record of 2:00.5 could have been in serious danger. However, Lillian was always up with the leaders and, timing her drive to perfection off the last bend, she strode to victory in 2:01.4.

With that triumph behind her she could face the 4x400m relay in a more relaxed frame of mind and she produced the performance for which she is best remembered. On the anchor leg the now co-holder of the world record (at 51.7 in Athens) Besson seemed to be in an unassailable position at 300m but Lillian gradually began to pull back her lactic-drowning rival and overtook her in the final stride of one of the most thrilling races anyone has ever witnessed. Thanks to earlier brilliant team work by Rosemary Stirling (54.2), Pat Lowe (52.1) and Janet Simpson (52.1), Lillian (52.4) anchored the British team to a world record of 3:30.8.

There were three other medals for the British contingent. Anita Neil took bronze in the 100m in 11.8, a time shared in fourth place by Val Peat who finished third over 200m in 23.3, a personal best and only 0.1 outside the UK record of her coach Dorothy Hyman – who, in Val's opinion, "would definitely have been first in both sprints." Anita and Val, along with the latter's DHTC clubmates Denise Ramsden and Sheila Cooper, took third in the relay in 44.3. Worthy of mention also was Rita Ridley in the inaugural 1500m championship, breaking Anne Smith's UK record with 4:15.9 … in seventh place.

*Highlights from each of the WAAA Championships meetings
1960–1969*

1960 (White City)

DESPITE THE ABSENCE through injury of Britain's top Olympic hope, Mary Bignal, and the morgue-like atmosphere of an almost deserted White City, these Championships produced the highest all-round standard yet achieved at this meeting. Dorothy Hyman retained both sprint titles, clocking 11.7 for 100m (all other events apart from the hurdles were staged over yards) and 24.0 for 220y. Fifth in the 100m (12.1) and hurdles (11.5w) and winner of the long jump with 5.68m was Ann Packer, who improbably would find Olympic glory four years later as an 800m runner. Carole Quinton twice equalled the UK all-comers record for the hurdles in the preliminaries with 11.0 but the wind was over the legal limit for the final when she was timed at 10.8. Runner-up in 11.0 was Betty Moore, an Australian who went on to represent Britain and become a world record holder. Front running Dr Roma Ashby finished 4 sec ahead of Diane Charles (née Leather) in a championship record 4:54.2 mile, while Joy Jordan ran a negative split 880y for victory in 2:09.1. Later in the season she would run exactly 3 sec faster for a world record. The mile and a half walk, which replaced the mile event, went to 18-year-old Judy Woodsford in 12:31.2. She wouldn't capture another WAAA title under that name but as Judy Farr she won the event for nine consecutive years from 1962 to 1970. Another prolific title winner was Sue Platt, who set a UK javelin record of 50.83m for the second of eight victories between 1959 and 1969. Sue Allday lifted her fourth shot/discus double with marks of 14.30m and 45.25m, while another superbly consistent and durable competitor, Dorothy Shirley, won the first of five high jump titles over a ten-year period with a personal best equalling leap of 1.67m.

1961 (White City)

IN THE ABSENCE of an injured Dorothy Hyman, Jenny Smart – sixth in the Rome Olympic 100m and still only 18 – succeeded her as double sprint champion with personal best equalling times of 10.7 for 100y and 24.0 for 220y. Later in the summer she equalled Dorothy's UK 100m record of 11.5 and broke her 200m mark with 23.6. At the other end of the age scale, 32-year-old Irish Olympian and hockey legend Maeve Kyle from Ballymena took the 440y title from the outside lane in a personal best of 56.3. Although she was ineligible to represent the UK internationally, Maeve competed for Northern Ireland in the Commonwealth Games and in time became a prominent official in UK as well as Northern Irish athletics. Betty Moore, Australia's gift to British athletics, won her first major title, clocking a wind-assisted 10.8 in the hurdles while the former Mary Bignal (who had recently married Olympic sculler Sidney Rand) long jumped a modest 5.95m for victory. Sue Platt in the javelin (47.88m) was among those who successfully defended titles and later in the season would raise the UK record substantially to a world class 54.45m, roughly the distance she achieved and so unluckily forfeited at the Olympics. Pat Nutting won the inaugural 200m hurdles championship in a best on record 28.3 for this fledgling event which would survive only until 1972.

1962 (White City)

THE ÂTHLETICS WEEKLY report, by the author of this book, described the meeting as "a success in that the standard of performance reached an unprecedented level but a failure, in that first, only a very thin crowd was attracted, and secondly in that the presentation of what could have been one of the most attractive meetings ever staged in this country reached an all-time low. A good deal of hard work, not to mention money, had been put in to make this an occasion worthy of marking the WAAA's 40th anniversary but as a spectacle it fell flat." The fault lay with the policy laid down for the announcing, which was insufficiently informative for those present. In response to the criticism, the chief announcer Vera Searle stated: "There was never any intention to 'present' the meeting. The WAAA happens to run the Championship meeting for the athletes and surely no one will quarrel with that." She claimed the sponsors, Bovril Ltd, were delighted. Thanks to their sponsorship some prominent overseas stars were brought over and, for the first time, the programme included invitation events for men.

Dorothy Hyman bounced back to her Olympic form, equalling the UK record in both the 100y (10.6) and 220y (23.8). In the furlong final, despite it being her sixth fast race in less than five and a half hours, she defeated Jutta Heine, the German who had beaten her for the Olympic 200m silver medal. The 440y set new standards. The previous UK all-comers record was 55.6 but six women clocked that time or faster. Swiftest of all was defending champion Maeve Kyle who won her heat in an Irish record of 54.9 with Pam Piercy second with a UK record of 55.3. Later that day in the final Maeve entered the finishing straight ahead but faded to third in 55.4 as Jean Sorrell (née Dunbar) won in 55.1 ahead of Joy Grieveson (55.3). Joy Jordan set a championship record of 2:08.0 when notching up her fifth successive 880y title and Betty Moore tied the UK hurdles record of 10.7. The following month, in Germany, the Manchester research chemist would equal the world record of 10.5. In the high jump Romania's stork-like Iolanda Balas became the first woman to clear 6 feet (1.83m) on British soil.

1963 (White City)

INCESSANT RAIN FOR five hours made conditions very unpleasant and in the circumstances many of the performances were quite admirable. Yet again the sprints were dominated by Dorothy Hyman, who scored her fourth WAAA double. While those around her floundered, she kept her stride magnificently although her times of 10.9 and 24.3 reflected the state of the track. By the end of the afternoon the surface resembled porridge, to quote Maeve Kyle who entered the finishing straight of the 440y nearly ten yards up before treading water (and oats?) and finishing second to Joy Grieveson's 55.9. With Joy Jordan now retired, the way was clear for Phyllis Perkins (née Green) to recapture the 880y title (2:12.2) she had previously won in 1956. Pat Nutting won both hurdles events, 80m in 11.2 and 200m in 28.9; in fact she was a triple champion as she also won the inaugural 100m hurdles title, held elsewhere, in 14.1. Even Iolanda Balas was brought down to earth by the weather, her 1.70m high jump being her worst result since 1956, and Mary Rand was reduced to a winning long jump of 5.91m. Meanwhile, a big name of the future was beginning to attract attention: South African-born Lillian Board (14), who had been brought home by her English parents at the age of one and had joined London Olympiades as a 12-year-old, won the English Schools Junior long jump and placed second in the WAAA Junior Championships.

1964 (White City)

AS JIMMY GREEN, editor of *Athletics Weekly*, wrote of these Championships: "Undoubtedly the best of all time, both from the point of view of standard of performance, and sales of tickets and programmes. It was a great pity the crowd was not even larger, for the competition was really first class and inspiring in this Olympic year." Mary Rand and Ann Packer, who would emerge as Olympic champions in Tokyo three months later, tuned up nicely with UK records of 6.58m in the long jump and 54.3 for 440y respectively, but it was the brilliance of the sprinting which most caught the eye with Daphne Arden completing a terrific double. The 100y semis paved the way for a mouth-watering final as Dorothy Hyman won the first in a European record equalling 10.6, Mary Rand the second in the same time and Daphne the third in 10.7. In the final Daphne clocked 10.6 ahead of Mary (10.7) and Dorothy (10.8), the last named feeling the effects of a thigh injury in her fifth race of the day. One hour later came the 220y final and here the Birchfield Harrier was totally dominant, equalling the European record and setting new UK figures of 23.6 with Dorothy runner-up in 24.0. Pat Pryce (née Nutting) was in splendid form also, clocking 10.7 for 80m hurdles – which although outside Betty Moore's 10.5 was the fastest ever by a native Briton. She didn't enter for the 200m hurdles, which went to Pat Jones in a best on record 27.9, but did go on to retain her 100m hurdles title (2ft 6in barriers) – contested at Watford – in a UK best of 13.4. Other fine performances included a front running half mile victory by Anne Smith in a personal best of 2:08.0, a 1½ mile walk win by Judy Farr in a championship record of 12:06.8, and 1.73m by the straddle jumper Frances Slaap, who would later raise the UK record to 1.76m. Mary Peters won her first shot title with a modest 14.22m, but in May had retained her pentathlon championship with the formidable UK record score of 4801. In a remarkable year for the all-rounders, Mary Rand recaptured the record with 4815 in June, Peters responded with 4823 in August ... only for Rand to score a breathtaking 5035 for the Olympic silver medal.

1965 (White City)

DISAPPOINTINGLY, EVEN THE prospect of a long jumping rematch between Mary Rand and her Olympic runner-up Irena Kirszenstein (later Szewinska) and a star-studded invitation men's mile featuring New Zealand's Olympic hero Peter Snell failed to lure more than 5000 spectators, little more than a tenth of the White City's capacity. That long jump duel was something special as Mary produced her best mark of the season, 6.40m, but was pressed hard by her 19-year-old rival who closed with 6.37m. Earlier the long striding Pole had become the first foreigner ever to win the 100y title, equalling the European record of 10.6 despite a shaky start. There were championship records by two women named Smith in the middle distance events as Anne won the 880y in 2:07.5 and Joyce the mile in a personal best of 4:53.5 after having run a 5:08.9 heat three hours earlier. It's amusing in view of the longevity of her career to note that Joyce, then 28, stated she would continue competing "at the most two more track seasons."

1966 (White City)

ANNE SMITH FINALLY recorded a time in keeping with her status as the world's leading half miler when she clipped 1.3 sec off the European record with 2:04.2 in winning her third consecutive 880y title. Gordon Pirie's protégée smashed Joy Jordan's UK record of 2:05.9 and her 800m clocking en route of 2:03.2 raised her to seventh on the world all-time list. The standard in the 440y was extraordinary as Lillian Board (17), a prodigious talent in her first season at the event, found a time of 54.6 – a performance which would have merited fourth place in the 1964 Olympic 400m – was insufficient to qualify for the final. Only five Britons had ever run faster, one of them being Rosemary Stirling (18), who followed up her 54.5 semi with 55.1 for third in the final less than two hours later. Deirdre Watkinson won her semi in a personal best of 54.4 but in the final she was shunted back to fourth behind Hilde Slaman of Holland (54.7), Joy Grieveson and Stirling. Daphne Slater (née Arden) flashed to a wind-assisted 10.5 100y, while Janet Simpson took the furlong in 24.1. The mile heralded the emergence of a new star in Rita Lincoln (19), who set a championship record of 4:47.9, third fastest by a Briton … while her twin sister Iris finished fourth in

5:01.2. Mary Rand added to her long list of titles with a 100m hurdles win in 13.7 but fell short in three other events; she was second in the long jump, third in the high jump (won by Dorothy Shirley at 1.70m, her best for five years) and was disqualified for two false starts in her 80m hurdles semi-final.

1967 (White City)

THIS WAS THE last occasion the meeting would be held at the White City, and it was just as well as the attendance on the Saturday was a possible all-time low of 1500. Arguably the most meritorious performance came from a South African who didn't win her event. Anne Smith steamed away with the 880y in 2:04.8 but the runner-up in a national record of 2:07.4 was the remarkable 41-year-old Anne McKenzie! She had started out as a sprinter, aged 11, back in 1936, took up half miling in 1962 and was 37 before she first broke 2:20 for the distance. Another South African star on view was Kesie Cornelissen, who completed a sprint double in 10.5w and 24.0. Joy Jordan ran her fastest mile of 4:55.4 behind Rita Lincoln's 4:51.4, while another runner-up to set a personal best was Mary Green, wife of sub-four minute miler Andy Green and sister of future International Cross Country champion Mike Tagg. She ran 55.3 for 440y, the same time as winner Lillian Board. Pat Jones scored a sprint hurdling double in 11.0 and 13.8 and went on three weeks later to collect the 200m hurdles title in a world best of 27.3 and in between was credited with a British-born 80m best of 10.6. Chris Perera, who had earlier set a world best of 13.7 for the as yet undeveloped 100m hurdles with 2ft 9in barriers, finished only fourth in that event at the Championships. The all-time record of six consecutive WAAA titles, shared by Florence Birchenough (discus, 1923-1928) and Valerie Winn (400m/440y, 1948-1953), was equalled by Judy Farr, winner of the 1½ mile walk in 12:09.2 ... and she would remain champion for another three years! Highlight of the field events from a British viewpoint was the 1.70m high jump by Linda Knowles, who had recently converted from western roll to straddle and who cleared a personal best of 1.74m in an exhibition after the contest had finished. Western roller Dorothy Shirley, who after a gap of seven years had raised her best to 1.73m when winning the Northern title, was second with 1.68m.

1968 (Crystal Palace)

A NEW, MORE intimate venue boasting one of Europe's first all-weather tracks and jumping surfaces, a good sized crowd and consequent "atmosphere", fine weather and the excitement of this being in effect the Olympic team selection trials all contributed to an outstanding Championships. And, to cap it all, there was a brilliant world record for the fans to savour. Two years after she won the European title aged 17, Vera Nikolic of Yugoslavia front ran her way to an 800m time of 2:00.5. The place times were superb also. Lillian Board, still only 19 and a virtual novice over two laps, clocked 2:02.0 to become Britain's second fastest ever behind Ann Packer's 2:01.1; American cross country legend Doris Brown exhibited surprising speed with 2:02.2 and Pat Lowe moved to third on the UK all-time list with 2:02.9. As Crystal Palace has a 400m track the Championships became all-metric again for the first time since 1951. Val Peat, coached by Dorothy Hyman, emulated her mentor as a double sprint winner, taking the 100m in 11.5, after setting a UK all-comers record of 11.4 in her semi, and the 200m in 23.6. In her first serious season at the event, Janet Simpson ran 53.9 for second in the 400m to Holland's Myrna van der Hoeven (53.6). The ever astonishing and youthful looking Maeve Kyle, a couple of months short of her 40th birthday, clocked 55.5 in her heat! There was some admirable hurdling with Pat Pryce victorious over 80m in 10.9 after matching her best of 10.7 in her semi and Chris Perera (18) setting a UK record of 13.5 over 100m. Field event action included a high jump victory by Dorothy Shirley over Barbara Inkpen at a modest 1.68m but Dorothy did scale 1.72m in a jump-off, while Sheila Sherwood (the former Miss Parkin had married 400m hurdler John Sherwood in April) long jumped 6.42m. The East Germans, Margitta Gummel (16.99m) and Karin Illgen (57.23m), shattered the previous championship records for the shot (15.48m) and discus (50.93m), but the javelin title remained at home as Sue Platt – who had raised her UK record to 55.60m earlier in the season

– threw a championship record of 53.26m for her seventh WAAA victory. Judy Farr topped that with track walk title number eight. A new championship event, 3000m, was held separately at Crawley with Carol Firth (later Gould) setting a UK best of 10:06.4. Much later in the year WAAA 1500m champion Rita Lincoln became the first Briton to duck under 10 min, just, with 9:59.6.

1969 (Crystal Palace)

RETURNING TO CHAMPIONSHIP racing after five years, having been reinstated by the WAAA for domestic competition, and in her first meeting on an all-weather track, Dorothy Hyman rolled back the years in glorious style. Her time in the 100m final of 11.9 may have seemed slow but it was into a stiff 2.6m/sec wind and she finished only half a yard behind the fabulous Chi Cheng of Taiwan (Chinese Taipei), who the following year would set world records at 100y, 100m, 200m, 220y and 100m hurdles. Dorothy performed even better in the 200m where, again into the wind, she won by five yards in 23.7 for her first WAAA title since 1963. Runner-up was 16-year-old Marilyn Neufville, who would a few weeks later run Lillian Board close over 400m in a UK age best of 54.4 and then, in her international debut, would win against Finland and Romania in 54.2. The Jamaican born schoolgirl displayed immense promise … but who could have predicted that as soon as the following year she would be a world record breaker? With Chi Cheng also winning the 100m hurdles, the 80m event having now been discontinued, four titles went abroad as Mia Gommers of Holland, who had broken Anne Smith's world mile record with 4:36.8 at Leicester in June, ran away with the 1500m in 4:16.0 and Romania's Olympic champion Lia Manoliu threw the discus 55.58m. However, Vera Nikolic was unable to hold on to the 800m title. She faded to third as Pat Lowe – her spirits soaring after a recent 52.0 400m relay leg – brought off a notable victory in 2:03.3. Sue Platt (49.34m) notched up her eighth and final javelin title, but Judy Farr – unbeaten by a Briton since July 1961 – topped that with her eighth consecutive (ninth in all) walk victory, clocking 12:45.8 for the slightly longer new distance

111

of 2500m ... and she wasn't finished yet. The closest event was the high jump, won on countback at 1.72m by straddle stylist Barbara Inkpen (19) over western roller Dorothy Shirley, ten years her senior and going so close at a personal best of 1.74m, a height she cleared the following month. It was a vintage year for the event as Barbara had already set a UK record of 1.78m, only for Linda Hedmark (née Knowles) to snatch that away with 1.79m. New talent was emerging all the time and two non-championship 100m races held in conjunction with the meeting were won by Intermediate Andrea Lynch (16) and Junior Sonia Lannaman (13), both of whom would develop into sprinters of the highest world class. Another athlete of great promise was the 17-year-old Scottish schoolgirl Moira Walls, equally good at high jump and long jump and winner of the WAAA pentathlon title with 4591 points. Also 17, Sue Scott had earlier set a UK record of 4731 for the event which now started with the 100m (not 80m) hurdles.

UNITED KINGDOM RECORDS AT 1 JANUARY 1970

100y: 10.6 Heather Young 1958, Dorothy Hyman 1962 & 1964, Mary Rand 1964, Daphne Arden 1964, Val Peat 1968 & Maureen Tranter 1968; 100m: 11.3 Hyman 1963, 11.3A Della James (later Pascoe) 1968 & Peat 1968; 200m: 23.2 Hyman 1963; 400m: 52.1A Lillian Board 1968; 800m: 2:01.1 Ann Packer 1964; 1500m: 4:15.9 Rita Ridley 1969; Mile: 4:37.0 Anne Smith 1967; 3000m: 9:54.4 Barbara Banks 1969; 80mH: 10.6 Pat Jones 1967; 100mH: 13.5 Chris Perera 1968; 200mH: 27.3 Pat Jones 1967; HJ: 1.79 Linda Hedmark 1969; LJ: 6.76 Mary Rand 1964; SP: 16.31 Mary Peters 1966; DT: 52.22 Rosemary Payne 1969; JT: 55.60 Sue Platt 1968; Pentathlon: (scored on 1954 tables) 5035 Rand 1964 (80H-10.9, SP-11.05, HJ-1.72, LJ-6.55, 200-24.2); (new format, scored on 1954 tables) 4731 Sue Scott 1969 (100H-14.4, 11.93, 1.60, 5.86, 24.4); 4x100m: 43.7A British Olympic team 1968; 4x400m: 3:30.8 British team 1969; Mile Walk: 7:36.2 Judy Farr 1965; 3000m Walk: 15:28.0 Betty Jenkins 1969; 5000m Walk: 26:27.0 Barbara Fisk 1969. (A = at high altitude).

THE SEVENTIES

CASTING A GIANT shadow over the sport in the 1970s was the tragic death from cancer of Lillian Board at the obscenely young age of 22. Lillian had succeeded her LOAC clubmate Mary Rand as the "golden girl" of British athletics, and as gold medallist at the 1969 European Championships at 800m and 4x400m relay it was her destiny – or so it seemed – that she would go one better than her 400m silver medal in Mexico City and triumph over two laps at the Munich Olympics in 1972. By an ironic twist of fate, she died on Boxing Day of 1970 in a clinic … in Munich.

Shocked by the death of a young lady who I counted as a friend and whose athletics career I had reported on with increasing delight and pride, this is part of the tribute I (Mel Watman) penned in sorrow for *"Athletics Weekly"*. It expressed my feelings at the time, and more than 40 years later the pain and poignancy of her premature passing has lessened but little.

LILLIAN

It has been my sad duty to write many obituary notices but none has caused me so much distress as this one. It still seems unbelievable that Lillian Board, who should have had at least fifty years of life ahead of her, is no longer among us and I feel a sense of deep personal loss that I know will be shared by all readers, whether or not they had the good fortune to have met Lillian.
Lillian's fame will endure as a result of her wonderful athletics career and her incredibly courageous fight against

the illness that was eventually to cut her life so tragically short. Certainly I shall always treasure such magic moments as her thrilling triumphs in Athens and ponder on the bravery of this young woman as she struggled against the unimaginable pain and debilitating effects of her illness. Most of all I shall remember with gratitude Lillian, the friendly and vivacious "girl next door".

Her stunning successes on the track, allied to her very attractive looks and bubbling personality, led to acclaim and publicity of film-star proportions to be thrust on Lillian while still a teenager. It could have turned her head, but it most certainly did not. She remained a thoroughly delightful girl: charming, sincere, gracious. A credit to her parents.

I have fond memories of her in the bar at Crystal Palace after her Sunday morning training sessions … sipping her drink, giggling at Cliff Temple's jokes and hesitantly contributing a few of her own, discussing the challenges ahead. I remember her on the evening of the 4x400m relay in Athens, when she was guest of honour at the "AW" Tour dinner, and how she captivated everyone there. I recall her at numerous social functions, in her element on the dance floor – never more so than when she was energetically doing the Charleston with her father.

Lillian was a good talker, never reluctant to discuss her training, her races, her rivals, her prospects. She was a good listener, too, and had the happy knack of being able to put anyone at ease – from the shyest of young autograph hunters upwards. The Press and broadcasters adored her, partly because she provided such "good copy" but also because she was always so patient and courteous, politely answering the most fatuous of questions at times. Even the most cynical of Fleet Street scribes would melt as, with breathless enthusiasm and with a generous sprinkling of "super" and like expressions, she would talk with engaging candour – invariably patting her hair in place in an agreeably feminine gesture.

At all times I found Lillian modest and generous (not to be confused with condescending) to her opponents. She knew she was a great athlete but she never took anything or anyone for granted. She was always avid for news of overseas rivals like Colette Besson, Kathy Hammond and Vera Nikolic and

*The PRINCESS ROYAL with WAAA Honorary Secretary MAREA HARTMAN at the
1986 WAAA Championships in Birmingham*

MAEVE KYLE, an outstanding quarter miler who has made a major contribution to women's athletics also as an administrator and coach.

MARY RAND during the heptathlon at the 1964 Olympics in Tokyo, where she finished second after winning the long jump with a world record distance

SUE PLATT – so unlucky to lose an Olympic medal in 1960

British medallists at the 1969 European Championships in Athens. Standing, from left: John Whetton. Ron Hill (and son), ROSEMARY STIRLING, Mike Tagg, LILLIAN BOARD, David Hemery, Alan Pascoe, Andy Todd, Ian Stewart, Jim Alder, PAT LOWE, John Sherwood, JANET SIMPSON, Alan Blinston & Paul Nihill. Seated: Lynn Davies and officials MAREA HARTMAN, Arthur Gold, Cecil Dale & BRENDA BEDFORD. On ground: ANITA NEIL, DENISE RAMSDEN, SHEILA COOPER & VAL PEAT

LILLIAN BOARD, who became British athletics' 'golden girl' after the retirement of her London Olympiades clubmate Mary Rand

ROSEMARY PAYNE (now CHRIMES), 1970 Commonwealth discus champion ... and still competing!

SHEILA SHERWOOD
1968 Olympic long jump silver

MARGARET BEACHAM
Set world indoor 1500m record

MARY PETERS, winner of a desperately exciting 1972 Olympic pentathlon contest with a world record score. She was made a Dame in 2000.

RITA RIDLEY
UK record breaker at 1500m

VERONA ELDER
3 x European Indoor 400m winner

Finish of the 1970 Commonwealth Games 800m in Edinburgh: ROSEMARY STIRLING of Scotland (526) wins from PAT LOWE of England and CHERYL PEASLEY of Australia.

Birchfield dance troupe comprising PAT JONES (world record breaker at 200m hurdles), SUE SCOTT (1978 Commonwealth long jump champion as SUE REEVE) and their coach, DORETTE NELSON NEAL

LORNA BOOTHE, winner of the Commonwealth 100m hurdles title in 1978

MARILYN NEUFVILLE
World record breaker at 400m

JUDY VERNON
1974 Commonwealth champion

ANDREA LYNCH
Set a world record for 60m

MARY STEWART
1st 1978 Commonwealth 1500m

JANE COLEBROOK (FINCH)
Set world indoor 800m record

MEG RITCHIE
UK discus record holder since 1977

JOYCE SMITH
First London Marathon winner

CAROL TYSON
World record breaking walker

CHRIS BOXER
1982 Commonwealth 1500m champion

BEV KINCH
UK record holder 1983–2012

DONNA HARTLEY (née MURRAY), the 1978 Commonwealth 400m champion, set UK records at both that distance with 51.28 in 1975 and 200m with 22.75 in 1978

SHIRLEY STRONG followed up her 1982 Commonwealth title at 100m hurdles with an Olympic silver medal two years later

DIANA DAVIES (née ELLIOTT) set a UK high jump record of 1.95m in 1982 which has been equalled but never beaten

JUDY OAKES, who set her first UK shot put record in 1979 and has held the record continuously since 1986, represented the UK on a record 87 occasions

KATHY COOK, seen here at the 1984 Olympics where she placed third in the 400m, has been UK record holder at that distance since 1982 and at 200m since 1980. Her best sprint times: 11.10 100m, 22.10 200m, 49.43 400m

held her British contemporaries in very high esteem. It was totally characteristic that she should be unstinting in her praise of Marilyn Neufville after having been beaten by her in the 1970 Southern Championships at Crystal Palace. That was Lillian for you; a great sportswoman in defeat as well as victory. May her memory and shining example live on for ever.

During Lillian's illness Marea Hartman had been instrumental in setting up the Lillian Board Trust Fund to raise money for her treatment and cancer research, and the public responded magnificently. Prior to her death over 20,000 people had contributed. Marea paid this tribute: "I feel Lillian was a symbol to many for her courage, modesty, integrity and youthfulness. She was probably one of the greatest fighters we have had on the track and she was not only modest in victory but never made excuses when she lost. I do not profess to understand all that has happened to such a fine girl in the last few months, and I never will. But I am glad she lived long enough to realise the love and respect so many people had for her."

Some 2000 people packed St Paul's Cathedral for the Memorial Service on January 21 1971. It was a solemn and poignant occasion as her family, friends, sporting colleagues and members of the general public who had shared in her struggles on and off the track, joined together to pay a final tribute. Among the many British internationals present were several of the women most closely associated with Lillian: her former rivals and relay team-mates. The arrangements for the service were largely organised by Marea Hartman and as I wrote in *Athletics Weekly*: "This may be an appropriate moment to record the appreciation of all in athletics for the part played by the WAAA secretary during these last unhappy months. Organising the Lillian Board Fund, visiting the Ringsberg Clinic, comforting and helping the family … Marea has been a tower of strength throughout, and I would like her to know that her selfless devotion and compassion has not gone unnoticed."

Another exciting season for Lillian had looked in prospect when, in May 1970, she ran a 4:44.6 mile, second on the

UK all-time list, and after clocking 53.6 for second place over 400m at the Southern Championships she said "I'll be disappointed if I do not run 800m this season in under two minutes." On June 13 she anchored a British team comprising Rosemary Stirling, Sheila Carey (née Taylor) and Pat Lowe to a world 4x800m relay record of 8:27.0 but signs that something was wrong came at the WAAA Championships on June 20. Sheila Carey won the 800m in 2:03.6 with Lillian third in 2:05.1. She said she had been suffering from a stomach upset and that "my legs just gave out in the home straight." It would prove to be the last race of her life.

It was the athlete who beat Lillian for that Southern 400m title who turned out to be the brightest star of 1970. Marilyn Neufville had long overshadowed her opponents throughout the age groups. In 1967, at 14, she won the WAAA Junior 100y and 150y double and the following year, ranked fifth among Britain's seniors with 23.9 for 220y, she turned down an invitation to compete for her native Jamaica in the Mexico City Olympics. She explained: "It was a great honour, and I was tempted to accept but now that I have been picked for Britain [for the 1968 European Junior Games] I want to go on representing them. I hope to make the British Olympic team for Munich in 1972." In 1969 the Cambridge Harrier moved up seriously to 400m and gave Lillian a close race (British age-16 record of 54.4 to the winner's 53.9), while in a late season match she made a winning international debut in 54.2.

That was just the start. The South London schoolgirl, in her first season of indoor racing, won the 1970 WAAA title (54.9), equalled the UK record of 54.8 when finishing first in a match against the East Germans, and at the first official European Indoor Championships in Vienna she created a sensation by lifting the gold medal in a world indoor record shattering 53.0. More shocks followed. When winning that Southern title at Crystal Palace she was timed at 52.0, a tenth inside Lillian's UK record and a performance which ranked her fourth fastest ever at the distance. It was widely accepted that she had got away to a "flier" but marks of 52.6 winning the WAAA title, 52.7 and 52.3 attested to her world class form. Nonetheless, few were prepared for the astonishing breakthrough at the

116

Commonwealth Games in Edinburgh. There had already been drama aplenty as, despite having lived (since she was eight), trained, competed and been coached in England and her previous refusal to represent Jamaica, she opted to race in the yellow strip of her native island – a decision which caused a huge controversy within the British athletics community. She won the title by the colossal margin of 2.6 sec in 51.0 (51.02 electronic) to break the official world record by 0.7 sec. It was hailed at the time as one of the greatest exploits in women's athletics history and ten years would pass before any British athlete ran faster. Although she did become Pan-American and Central American & Caribbean champion in 1971 Marilyn underwent Achilles tendon surgery early in 1972 and never ran anywhere near as fast again.

Women from the home countries fared well at those Edinburgh Commonwealth Games. Representing England, Rita Ridley (née Lincoln) won the 1500m in 4:18.8 just 0.2 sec ahead of team-mate Joan Page (later Allison), and Sheila Sherwood took the long jump with a personal best of 6.73m which ranked her equal third on the world all-time list. Scotland's Rosemary Stirling won the 800m in 2:06.2 and 37-year-old Rosemary Payne the discus with 54.46m (her then husband Howard winning the hammer for England the same day), while Mary Peters of Northern Ireland gained a double: the shot with 15.93m and the pentathlon with a huge wind assisted score of 5148. Earlier in the season she had set a UK record of 5031. England's Ann Wilson was second at the Games in the pentathlon with an acceptable UK record of 5037, and was runner-up also in the high jump at 1.70m and the long jump with 6.50m, commenting wistfully: "I am very pleased at getting three silver medals but I would have preferred to have gained one gold." Other English silver medallists were Pat Lowe at 800m, javelin thrower Anne Farquhar and the 4x100m relay team of Anita Neil, Margaret Critchley, Madeleine Cobb (née Weston; her first international medal since 1958) and Val Peat.

Also in 1970 a team of Rosemary Stirling, Georgena Craig, Pat Lowe and Sheila Carey reduced the world 4x800m relay record to 8:25.0 but, sadly, at 29 Dorothy Hyman ran her last race. Disappointed that her appeal for international reinstatement had been rejected by the IAAF, she called it a day after winning the Yorkshire 100m title in 11.5w following a legal 11.5 heat. Happily, though, there were signs of some young sprinters developing impressively. At the first official European Junior Championships in Paris, with Dorette Nelson Neal as team manager, Helen Golden (17) of Scotland won the 200m against a very strong wind in 24.3 after clocking 23.7 in her heat, while Andrea Lynch (17) placed second over 100m. More precocious still was Sonia Lannaman, who competed in the first ever junior women's international match, against West Germany, at Leicester. At 14, the youngest athlete ever to be awarded a British vest, she finished second to Helen Golden in the 200m at that match and ran the first leg for the winning 4x100m relay team.

Right at the beginning of the decade the WAAA made public extracts from minutes of its Executive Meetings with reference to recommendations made in the Byers Report. "We consider this will give a clear indication," wrote Marea Hartman, "of how the WAAA would envisage the UK Coaching Scheme, and the re-constitution of the British Amateur Athletic Board."

Proposed Re-constitution of the BAAB

The WAAA agrees in principle to the re-constitution with the following reservations:

The WAAA will not, in any way, lose any of its domestic powers, will continue to hold its own Championships and retain its domestic autonomy.

We can see no reason to change the name of the BAAB. In our view this is completely unnecessary as the BAAB is respected internationally throughout the world for its integrity and efficiency.

Representation on the newly constituted BAAB will come direct from the WAAA and not from the territories, although the representatives will come from the various territories.

It is obvious that women's athletics in Great Britain have not suffered by remaining amateur and we could not, therefore, agree at any time to our sport becoming professionalised.

Equally we do not consider anyone from outside the sport would be capable of directing athletics in Great Britain.

Proposed UK Coaching Scheme

The WAAA agrees in principle to the scheme as submitted to the BAAB by the UK Coaching Steering Committee, subject to the following:

That the scheme shall be under the control and direction of the BAAB and that the Honorary Secretary of the Coaching Committee or Coaching Administrator (if and when appointed) shall be responsible to the BAAB.

ABSOLUTELY VITAL is the need to consider at all times the role and functions of the club coach who must remain the corner stone of athletics. Neither the regional or event coach must appear to be taking over the personal coaching of the best athletes and leave the club to coach the poorer performers. This problem can be overcome by everyone clearly understanding the difference in function of TEACHER, COACH, ADVISER.

The WAAA will only accept a supervising Chief Officer from within the sport, experienced in the sport, and acceptable to all constituent members of the re-constituted Board.

A new constitution for the BAAB was adopted in 1970, the constituent members being representatives of the AAA, Scottish AAA, Welsh AAA, N Ireland AAA and their female counterparts the WAAA (Dorette Nelson Neal, Phyllis Pope and Vera Searle), Scottish WAAA (Betty Steedman), Welsh WAAA (Florence Watts) and N Ireland WAAA (Maeve Kyle). Marea Hartman was Acting Honorary Treasurer (taking over the following year as Honorary Treasurer), while Brenda Bedford – who worked as a secretary at the AAA/BAAB offices – was one of the two International Athletes' Representatives.

Two athletes stood out during the 1971 indoor season. Sonia Lannaman became at 14 Britain's youngest ever senior national champion, winning the 60m title in 7.5 and later setting a UK 50m best of 6.2. The revelation, though, was Margaret Beacham (née Moir), who was married to international 800m runner Peter Beacham and coached by Joyce Smith's husband, Bryan. The grand-daughter of James

"Gunner" Moir, a British heavyweight boxing champion who unsuccessfully fought for the world title in 1909, Margaret broke the world indoor 1500m record on three occasions: 4:20.5 when winning the WAAA title at Cosford, 4:17.4 on a tight 143m track in East Berlin and 4:17.2 to become European champion in Sofia, defeating the Soviet Union's Lyudmila Bragina, who would the following year in Munich become the inaugural Olympic champion in a world record 4:01.38.

A far-reaching innovation that year was the first area women's league, the Midlands leading the way with three divisions, seniors and juniors. Among the division one winners was Mary Stewart with a UK age-15 1500m best of 4:36.0, while in the second division match a 15-year-old scored a mass of points with victories in the 200m (26.1), high jump (1.52m) and javelin (38.44m). The young lady in question went on to win the WAAA Intermediate title with 42.02m, prompting National Coach Wilf Paish to observe: "I particularly like the look of Theresa Sanderson." Thirteen years later Tessa, coached by Paish, would become Olympic javelin champion! And to think that Tessa, who first picked up a javelin when she was about 12, recalled: "I was so bad I tossed it away with the comment that it was a silly sport for a girl anyway!"

The league system, as with the men, quickly found favour. The Motorway League was formed in 1972; Northern and Southern Leagues were inaugurated in 1973. In 1974 a total of 32 clubs competed in the newly instituted British Athletics League Women's Cup, while in 1975 the UK Women's Athletics League came into existence with four divisions of six clubs.

The WAAA continued to be at the forefront of creating new events for women, although some of the older members of the Executive Committee took a conservative view and spoke against their introduction. However, to quote Ken Oakley, "the WAAA were represented at major explorations of new or modified events. West Germany pushed hard for a longer hurdle event and the European Association staged on behalf of the IAAF a weekend in Bonn in May 1971 experimenting with both spacing of hurdles and distances of 300m and 400m. This culminated in a 400m race with lower hurdles and the men's spacing being won by Britain's Sandra Dyson, setting the first recognised time of 61.1 for this event."

The high point of the 1971 season was the European Championships in Helsinki, where three medals were obtained. In the 800m, won by Yugoslavia's Vera Nikolic in 2:00.0, Pat Lowe finished second in 2:01.7 and Rosemary Stirling third in 2:02.1 – personal bests for all three. The other medal came in the high jump where Barbara Inkpen exceeded all expectations by tying for second place. Barbara ranked only 19th among the entrants with her personal best of 1.80m, but barely three weeks after switching from the straddle to the Fosbury Flop she cleared 1.83m to equal the recently established UK record by Linda Hedmark and then 1.85m to match Canadian Debbie Brill's Commonwealth record. Another UK record fell in the 1500m where Rita Ridley was fourth in 4:12.65.

Barbara Inkpen added a centimetre to her record in 1972 but it was Mary Peters who utilised the Flop to the best advantage that year. In order to recharge her batteries prior to the all-important Olympic season Mary had only one competition outdoors in 1971, but indoors at Cosford in November 1971 she showed her training was going well by high jumping 1.67m, matching her 1964 personal best. Previously just a competent straddle jumper she gradually emerged as a "flopper" of near world-class, and that was the key to her Olympic pentathlon triumph. Indoors in January 1972 she improved to 1.71m but she and her coach "Buster" McShane knew there was far more to come as a figure of 1.78m was listed as her target for Munich, along with 13.4 hurdles, 16.76m shot, 6.20m long jump and 23.9 200m. In her first pentathlon of the year she scored 4630 for a Commonwealth record (5250 on the old scoring tables), and that included a high jump of 1.77m. She raised that to 1.78m in her final pre-Olympic contest, but even she was pleasantly shocked by what transpired at the Games.

From the very first event it was apparent she was in superb form and afraid of nobody. She clocked 13.29 for the hurdles, a UK record on electrical timing; put the shot 16.20m, her best in a pentathlon and only 11cm below her UK record; and ended the first day with an inspired display of high jumping. She experienced a crisis at 1.71m, being nowhere near to clearing, but she managed to solve her run-up problems for the final attempt and kept her gold medal hopes alive by sailing over. She went on to become the only competitor to clear 1.78m and even the predominantly German crowd took the bouncy blonde with the flashing smile and cheery wave to its collective heart despite the fact that with each successful clearance she was widening her points advantage over West Germany's big hope, Heide Rosendahl. Mary responded by clearing 1.80m and 1.82m at the first time of asking! She even went desperately close at 1.84m. Her overnight score of 2969, the highest ever recorded, gave her a handsome lead over the GDR's world record holder Burglinde Pollak (2872) with Rosendahl only fifth on 2668 ... but with her two strongest events to come.

Nearly 80,000 were on hand at 11 am to see the opening event of the second day, the long jump. Mary went close to her modest personal best with 5.98m, but Rosendahl – world record holder for the event – cleared a massive 6.83m to narrow the gap considerably. The scores going into the final event, the 200m, were: 1, Peters 3871; 2, Pollak 3824; 3, Rosendahl 3750. Bearing in mind that Mary's personal best stood at 24.2, compared to 23.1 by Rosendahl and 23.8 by Pollak, it was clear that it was still anybody's title. It would be the ultimate test of nerve as well as speed, and the tension during the race and afterwards as everyone waited for the times to flash up was almost unbearable. Rosendahl had finished about ten metres clear and her time was displayed as a superb 22.96. Hasty consultation of the scoring tables indicated Mary would need to have run 24.18 to win ... but agonising minutes passed by before the other times were made known. At last it was revealed that Pollak had run 23.93, Mary 24.08 ... she had won by ten points, her final score of 4801 being a world record for good measure. Like Mary Rand and Ann Packer before her, she had achieved the ultimate: an Olympic title and world record.

THE WORLD'S GREATEST ALL-ROUNDER

It was not until she was 33, contesting her 45th pentathlon over a 17-year period, that Mary Peters of Spartan Ladies became a household name throughout the British Isles by joining Mary Rand and Ann Packer in the Olympic hall of fame. At the beginning of 1972 she had said: "I'd like to improve my British pentathlon record before the Olympics, and go for a world record in Munich. Taking a break for much of last season has really helped me, and I feel raring to go. I'd like to show that not all the news out of Belfast is bad." How well she succeeded.

Her story is one of perseverance. Overshadowed as a pentathlete by Mary Rand and never quite making world class as a shot putter, her career might well have ended after a disappointing showing at the 1968 Olympics when, hampered by an injured ankle, she placed ninth in the pentathlon after having finished fourth four years earlier. She was already 29 and had she quit then she would have been remembered as a very good and big hearted athlete but not truly a great one.

Instead she took 1969 off in order to regain her zest and, competing at her fourth Commonwealth Games, in 1970, she won gold medals in both the shot and pentathlon, representing Northern Ireland. Although born in Halewood, near Liverpool, on July 6 1939, she had lived in Ulster from the age of 11. Her pentathlon score of 5148 (4515 on the later tables) re-established her among the world's elite after a gap of six years.

Again she passed up competition in 1971 as, with her coach "Buster" McShane, she prepared for Munich. The key to her eventual success was her conversion to the Fosbury Flop, her improvement as a high jumper being worth over 100 points in that one event. Tragically, McShane died in a car crash in April 1973 aged 42, and understandably Mary never rose to such heights again, but she bade a golden farewell to the Commonwealth Games in 1974 with another pentathlon victory. Mary P continued to make valuable contributions to the sport she had graced for so long. She raised a huge amount of money for what became the Mary Peters Track at Queen's University, Belfast (it opened in 1976); she qualified as a senior coach in 1975, was British women's team manager at the 1980 and 1984 Olympics, and from 1996 to 1998 was

President of the British Athletics Federation. In 2000 she was made a Dame for her services to the sport.

That was the only medal for the British women's squad, managed by Marea Hartman, but such was the standard of performance in a Games that was overshadowed by the massacre of Israeli team members by a Palestinian terrorist group that several UK records went almost unnoticed. Rosemary Stirling, ranked no higher than about 30th with her best 800m time for the year of 2:04.4, clocked 2:00.15 to break Ann Packer's celebrated 1964 record ... in seventh place. She also anchored the British team with a 51.8 leg for a 4x400m record of 3:28.74 in fifth place (she was preceded by Verona Bernard 53.1, Janet Simpson 52.0 and Jannette Roscoe 51.8). Rita Ridley's UK 1500m record came in for a battering as Joyce Smith – making her Olympic debut at 34 – ran 4:11.27 in her heat and 4:09.37 in the first semi-final, while Sheila Carey (whose fastest time previously was only 4:16.2) ran out of her skin to clock 4:07.41 in the second semi and wind up fifth in the final in 4:04.81 – way inside the pre-Games world record! Finishing fourth in the high jump, equalling her record of 1.85m, was Barbara Inkpen (who went 1.86m later in the season), while the 4x100m relay squad of Andrea Lynch, Della Pascoe (née James; now married to hurdling star Alan Pascoe), Judy Vernon and Anita Neil clocked 43.71 in seventh place. Worthy of note also was Rosemary Payne, making her first and only Olympic appearance at age 39, who placed 12th in the discus final with 56.50m, having raised her UK record early in the summer to 58.02m. There was no 3000m on the Olympic programme until 1984 but Joyce Smith's UK record of 9:05.8 that year, the world's second fastest ever time, indicated she would have been a strong medal contender had the event been held.

The WAAA celebrated its Golden Jubilee in 1972 and present at the AGM in February were six ladies who in 1922 had been active competitors – daring young women at the time to appear in public in knee-length shorts! They were former WAAA Hon. Secretary Mary Amies (née Atkins), Rose Gillis (née Thompson), Assistant Hon. Secretary Connie Leslie (née

Owen), Edith Peacock (née White), Phyllis Pope (née Wright) and Vice-Chairman Vera Searle (née Palmer). Another nostalgic occasion, a Golden Jubilee Dinner, was held at Goldsmiths' Hall in the City of London in November and those in attendance included two founder members in Florence Millichap (née Birchenough) and Teddy Knowles. The toast to The Queen was proposed by WAAA President Lady Luke, while the toast to the WAAA was proposed by journalist Roy Moor of Polytechnic Harriers with a reply by Vera Searle.

Mary Peters would ensure that 1972 would always shine brightly in the history of British women's athletics but earlier in the year there was another special exploit to savour when Joyce Smith became the first Englishwoman to win the International Cross Country Championship, which had been run on an annual basis since 1967 and would from 1973 be upgraded to become the IAAF World Championship.

For the first time since its foundation in 1922 the WAAA elected a female Chairman at the 1973 AGM. Dick Taylor stepped down after 35 years, to be succeeded by 71-year-old Vera Searle, with Dorette Nelson Neal taking over from Vera as Vice-Chairman. That year Mrs Searle also became Chairman of the newly formed Women's Veterans' AC (for athletes of 35 or over) with Hazel Rider the Secretary/Treasurer. Other founder members included Maureen Smith, Marea Hartman and Jill Lindsay.

There were no outdoor international championships in 1973 and the top exploit of the year was Verona Bernard's enthralling 400m run at the European Indoor Championships in Rotterdam. The 19-year-old was in inspired form, setting personal bests of 53.98 in her heat and 53.35 in her semi-final before blasting to a time of 53.04 (hand time of 53.0) in the final, which equalled Marilyn Neufville's world indoor best. Other stars of the indoor season were Sonia Lannaman, who twice ran a UK record 7.3 for 60m, and Barbara Inkpen, whose 1.86m high jump matched her UK outdoor record height. On the cross country scene, Joyce Smith regained the National title after 13 years and, in second place individually despite an attack of stitch, led England to team victory in the first IAAF International Cross Country Championship. Summer highlights included a 100m gold medal in the European Junior Championships by Sonia Lannaman and UK records in the 200m (23.14 by Helen Golden), 400m (52.1 by Verona Bernard, equalling Lillian Board's mark), mile (4:36.18 by Joan Allison), the new 400m hurdles event (59.87 by Judy Vernon) and high jump (1.87m by the former Miss Inkpen, who by then had married international walker Carl Lawton).

Athletes from the UK collected four titles at the Commonwealth Games in Christchurch, New Zealand, in January 1974. American-born Judy Vernon, who remains to this day heavily involved in coaching and officiating with her international triple jumper husband John Vernon, took the 100m hurdles in 13.45; Barbara Lawton high jumped 1.84m; the England 4x400m team of Sue Pettett, Ruth Kennedy, Jannette Roscoe and Verona Bernard (with a spectacular 50.4 anchor leg) won in 3:29.23; and Mary Peters, in her farewell appearance, produced her highest pentathlon score since Munich with 4455. That was her fifth Commonwealth Games, starting in 1958, and Mary remarked later: "I went through hell thinking about this competition. This is my swan-song but no matter how old and experienced you are you get just as nervous as the first time." The one who got away was Canada's Yvonne Saunders, winner of the 400m in 51.67 ahead of Verona Bernard's UK record of 51.94. Born in Jamaica, she lived in Manchester between 1960 and 1968 (aged 8-16) and as a member of Stretford AC was primarily a high jumper. However, she was lost to British athletics when she emigrated to Canada.

Andrea Lynch, who came away from Christchurch with silver medals in the 100m (11.31) and 4x100m relay, had to settle for second place again at the European Indoor Championships in Gothenburg. Leading almost the entire way, she was pipped on the line by double Olympic champion Renate Stecher of the GDR (7.16), her time of 7.17 smashing her own UK record. Outdoors, she equalled the world record for 60m of 7.2 and proved she was among the top three in the world at 100m. Her 11.1 in Warsaw behind Poland's Irena Szewinska's 10.9 broke her own UK record; she was earlier timed at a wind assisted 10.9 in Lisbon, while at the European Championships in Rome she placed third (11.28 into a headwind) behind Szewinska and Stecher but defeated the East German shortly afterwards in Munich, 11.29 to 11.38. The only other medal at those European Championships – also a bronze – went to evergreen Joyce Smith in the 3000m (8:57.4).

There were other moments to savour during the summer of 1974, UK record breakers including Helen Golden in the 200m (23.0), Donna Murray in the 400m (51.77), Joyce Smith at 3000m (8:55.53), Judy Vernon and Blondelle Thompson in the 100m hurdles (13.0) and Christine Warden (née Howell) in the 400m hurdles (58.0), while Marion Fawkes set new walking marks at 3000m (14:33.50) and 5000m (24:59.2). Interesting to note that Blondelle Thompson, aged 20 when she tied the hurdles record, would in 1976 marry 400m runner Joe Caines, in 1979 give birth to a son, Daniel Caines, who in 2001 would become World Indoor 400m champion, and she herself – as a well established barrister and expert on sport law – would be appointed in 2011 to the Court of Arbitration for Sport in Lausanne.

It was in 1974 that a long-simmering campaign for amalgamation between the AAA and WAAA really took off and became a major topic in the columns of *Athletics Weekly*, the sport's main forum of public discussion. The first step towards a marriage between the AAA and its female counterpart was taken when a proposal at the AAA AGM in November, by journalist and coach Cliff Temple on behalf of Folkestone AC, that the WAAA be approached "with a view to the amalgamation of the two Associations at the earliest possible moment" was approved by a large majority. However, the redoubtable WAAA Chairman, Vera Searle, remarked that half a century ago "the then officers of the AAA told us we would be better off on our own, and so it has proved." She added that the WAAA ("we're a very happy band; we never get any complaints from our international athletes") was not, at the present time, "kindly disposed towards amalgamation" but it would approach the men if it became convinced that its athletes would benefit from such a move.

A Special General Meeting of the WAAA was called in April 1975 and after over two hours of debating the advantages or otherwise of merging with the AAA, Folkestone AC's proposal which sought an "eventual amalgamation between the two Associations" was rejected by 50 votes to 10. Instead the meeting voted 69-0 in favour of setting up a joint committee which would discuss the issue. The successful proposition, tabled by Geoff Clarke, was worded: "This meeting requests the General Committee of the WAAA to invite the General Committee of the AAA to establish as soon as possible a small joint consultative committee with the task of ensuring that arrangements are made as soon as possible to achieve as many joint enterprises and as much joint administration throughout English and Welsh athletics in clubs, districts, counties, areas and at national level as is practicable."

The consultative committee was duly set up and closer co-operation between the two associations over the organisation of officials was discussed, as was the possibility of a common rule book. Ways of raising money together were examined and the two associations were negotiating jointly for sponsorship of the combined 1976 Indoor Championships. It was also agreed to investigate the advantages and disadvantages of combining the outdoor AAA and WAAA Championships.

In the years that followed, men's and women's athletics did become increasingly entwined – but at national level progress was painfully slow and the governing bodies remained totally separate for many more years. Combined AAA and WAAA Championships, the wish of increasing numbers of athletes of both sexes, were staged at last from 1988, but not until 1991 did the two governing bodies actually amalgamate to become the AAA of England.

The other topic aired at the Special General Meeting related to women being permitted to race at much longer distances than previously. In the USA and Germany women had been allowed to compete in marathons for some years but in Britain they could not officially race beyond 6000m. As the women's committee of the IAAF, chaired by Marea Hartman, had been recommending the encouragement of women's marathon running, there appeared to be no obstacle to the WAAA – or rather the Women's CC&RWA, which had been delegated responsibility for road racing – amending its rules accordingly. And so it proved. The WCC&RWA accepted that, for a trial period of a year starting in October 1975, women of 21 or over could race at the marathon; at age 20 they could race up to 15 miles, at 19 a maximum of 10 miles, and at 17/18 up to 7 miles.

The first British marathon in which women were officially sanctioned to compete was the Masters & Maidens Marathon at Guildford on October 19 1975; 12 women finished with Anne Clarke first home in 3:11:54. Just seven days later in Korso (Finland), Margaret Thompson – wife of Commonwealth and European marathon champion Ian Thompson – reduced the record to 3:07:47. Three women broke through the three-hour barrier at Feltham in 1976, Christine Readdy winning in 2:50:55, and Rosemary Cox shaved one second off that at Rugby in 1978. It was in 1979 that the event really began to take off. By year's end Joyce Smith had run 2:36:27 and fifteen Britons broke three hours.

It was all a far cry from the far-sighted yet amusingly conservative prediction, in 1961, of Sir Adolphe Abrahams, the BAAB's Honorary Medical Officer at the time. The brother of Harold Abrahams wrote: "I am bold enough to say that if so minded some girls could tackle the marathon. I would expect a number of young women, who could undertake the necessary training, to achieve something of the order of three and three quarter hours – perhaps even better!" One and a half hours better in the case of Paula Radcliffe!

The 1975 season was fairly low-key but there were some memorable moments. At the European Indoor Championships in Katowice gold medals went to Andrea Lynch with 7.17, equalling her UK 60m record, and Verona Elder (née Bernard) who set new national 400m figures of 52.68. Outdoors, Andrea tied her hand-timed 100m record of 11.1 and smashed the auto-timed best with 11.16. Despite Verona's heroics indoors, it was Donna Murray who shone at 400m during the summer. She lowered the UK record to 51.28 and in the European Cup Final she anchored (in 50.2) the 4x400m relay squad of Jannette Roscoe, Gladys Taylor and Verona to a UK record of 3:26.6.

British women athletes had won at least one medal at every Olympics since they started to participate in 1932, but that proud record came to an end in Montreal in 1976. This proved to be a deeply disappointing Games for the entire British team, with Brendan Foster's bronze in the 10,000m the only medal to be gained. For the women's side it was a disaster, the team ranking 13th based on top eight placings. The one athlete who could have been a legitimate medal contender was Sonia Lannaman, who had lost by 1/100th in the European Indoor Championships 60m in 7.25, set a personal best of 11.23 for 100m not to mention a hand-timed wind-assisted 10.8, and defeated defending Olympic champion Renate Stecher of the GDR and West Germany's Annegret Richter, co-holder of the world record at 10.8. Some thought her chances at 200m were even better after setting a UK record of 22.81 plus a wind-aided 22.6 and 23.0 into a 4m/sec wind on a cold and damp evening in Gateshead. Alas, she had to scratch from both events and the relay in Montreal after sustaining a hamstring injury during relay practice three days before the 100m heats. How galling for her to witness Richter setting a world auto-timed record of 11.01 in her semi-final and winning the Olympic crown in 11.08 ahead of Stecher (11.13). Even without Sonia, the 4x100m team of Wendy Clarke (whose footballer son Justin Hoyte, born in 1984, would play for Arsenal), Denise Ramsden, Sharon Colyear and Andrea Lynch set a UK record of 43.44 in their heat but finished last in the final. The one athlete to come home with happy memories of Montreal was Tessa Sanderson, at 20 the youngest of the javelin finalists. She broke her UK record in qualifying with 57.18m and in the final placed tenth with 57.00m. Olympic glory lay eight years ahead.

Marea Hartman admitted that our athletes were falling ever further behind the East Europeans, who had won 13 of the 14 Olympic titles on offer. They were state sponsored – their only responsibility being to train diligently and bring prestige to their countries. In the case of the East Germans in particular (winners of nine gold medals in Montreal) that training and consequent performance levels were, we now know, enhanced by state-approved doping programmes. By way of contrast, Britain's female athletes remained resolutely amateur. Of the 23 who competed in the 1976 Olympics no fewer than 19 held down jobs, mostly of a clerical/secretarial nature, and their training had to be fitted in before or after working hours. But gradually the strict amateur rules were relaxed, athletes were able to receive sponsorship and other forms of assistance, and during the 1980s a new breed of British athlete – the full-time professional – would begin to emerge.

The revelation of the 1977 indoor season was Jane Colebrook, the 1972 WAAA Junior 200m champion whose first love remained sprinting but who had gradually moved up in distance to such good effect that in December 1976 she succeeded Rosemary Wright (née Stirling) as UK indoor 800m record holder with 2:05.0, a time she reduced to 2:03.1 and then 2:02.5. At the European Indoor Championships in San Sebastian the 19-year-old ran a race reminiscent of Ann Packer at the Tokyo Olympics, even down to the winning time of 2:01.1, which equalled the world indoor record. Among Britons only Rosemary Wright (2:00.2) had ever run faster outdoors. Another great young talent, Mary Stewart, clocked a world indoor record of 4:08.1 for 1500m – the first in her remarkable family to become a world record holder. A few weeks later, having turned 21, she captured the European title in 4:09.4. She thus emulated brothers Ian and Peter, both European Indoor title winners themselves! The family tradition of athletic excellence is now in the hands of Mary's son, Adam Cotton, who in 2011 ran 3:41.33 for 1500m and became European Junior champion.

Outdoors in 1977 Jane Colebrook just missed the UK record with 2:00.6 while Mary Stewart set a UK mile record of 4:36.1, but it was the sprinters who monopolised the headlines. Andrea Lynch, now a student in the USA, clocked the startling time of 10.9 for a hand-timed UK 100m record, but it was Sonia Lannaman who was the dominant figure. Early in the season she defeated the legendary Irena Szewinska over 200m in a wind assisted 22.83, won both sprints at the BAAB's newly established UK Championships, ran inside her UK 200m record figures of 22.81 with a wind-assisted 22.69 and again a week later with a windy 22.71 in the European Cup Semi-Final, beating Olympic champion Bärbel Eckert (later Wöckel). She also won the 100m in an equally wind-blown 10.93. At the European Cup Final in Helsinki she placed second to Marlies Oelsner (later Göhr) over 100m in a legal personal best of 11.22 and to Szewinska over 200m in a near record 22.83, the British team finishing an admirable third overall. At the WAAA Championships she not only gained the double in 11.24 and 23.06 but ran a storming anchor leg for the British team which set a world record of 1:31.57 for the 4x200m relay. Verona Elder led off in 23.8, followed by Donna Hartley (née Murray, having married 400m hurdles star Bill Hartley earlier in the summer) 23.1, Sharon Colyear 22.7 and Sonia 22.0 flat!

The other big star of 1977 proved to be Tessa Sanderson. Many felt she might progress to the magical 60m mark with the javelin, but no one could have foreseen that in the space of a single season she would improve by precisely ten metres, go close to the world record and defeat the seemingly invincible East German double Olympic champion Ruth Fuchs! Her metamorphosis from promising youngster to world beater was completed in Dublin at the European Cup Semi-Final. Fuchs, world record holder at 69.12m, threw a not inconsiderable 64.46m ... but was well beaten by Tessa's astonishing 67.20m which moved her to no 2 on the world all-time list. A fit of pique helped produce this massive breakthrough. She explained: "I brought my own javelins from Britain but they took them away and wouldn't let me use them. I had to use the ones they supplied. After my first throw (60.34m) I was so mad I went right to the back of the banking and made my record throw."

The most prolific record breaker that year was 19-year-old Carol Tyson, an 800m and 1500m competitor at the English Schools Championships who took up race walking in 1974. At 3000m she reduced her record in three stages to 13:40.0 (just 0.4 sec outside the world best), and at 5000m she lowered Marion Fawkes' mark to 23:42.4. Other UK record breakers included Ann Ford (née Yeoman; married to cross country great Bernie Ford) with 8:52.79 for 3000m; Chris Warden with a hand timed 57.6 and Liz Sutherland with an electronic 57.59 for 400m hurdles; Meg Ritchie with a 59.88m discus throw; and Sue Longden (née Wright) who raised her pentathlon figures of 4117 in 1976 – the 800m having replaced the 200m since Mary Peters' day – in three instalments to 4385. Not a record because of a 3.2m/sec aiding wind but Sue Reeve (née Scott) created a stir by long jumping 6.84m, a distance only two women, both East Germans, had ever exceeded.

The WAAA Executive Committee approved the BAAB's UK Championships, a mixed event open only to athletes eligible to represent Great Britain & Northern Ireland. The inaugural meeting at Cwmbran in 1977 proved to be a hit with the athletes, although the WAAA stuck to its guns and failed to heed the views of so many competitors who were in favour of likewise combining the AAA and WAAA Championships.

The increasing use of performance enhancing drugs like anabolic steroids, particularly by female athletes from the Eastern European bloc, was casting a shadow over the sport and it was refreshing that 19-year-old Judy Oakes, whose 16.74m shot put indoors in February 1978 was far in excess of Mary Peters' UK outdoor record, welcomed her first random doping test. Only 1.64m (5ft 4½in) tall, Judy was always the smallest competitor in international events and was eager to show that good results could be achieved without recourse to illegal aids. On a pound for pound basis she was quite outstanding in her event but her long career was blighted by facing opponents who were not only much taller and heavier but in all too many cases were resorting to doping to achieve success.

It was a busy summer for Britain's athletes in 1978. The WAAA Commonwealth Games Trials were staged in June at Birmingham's newly opened Alexander Stadium, the highlight of which was a UK 200m record of 22.75 by Donna Hartley, who went on to capture the Commonwealth Games 400m title in Edmonton, Canada in 51.69 after setting a hand-timed UK record of 51.2 in a warm-up meeting. Those Games in August proved highly successful as other English victories were claimed by Sonia Lannaman (11.27w 100m), Mary Stewart (4:06.34 1500m), Paula Fudge (Ann Ford's twin sister; 9:12.95 3000m), Lorna Boothe (12.98w 100m hurdles), Sue Reeve (6.59m long jump), Tessa Sanderson (61.34m javelin) and both relays (43.70 and 3:27.19) with Hartley timed at 50-dead for her 400m anchor leg to become the latest incarnation of Britain's "golden girl".

Just a few days after the closing in Edmonton most of our top athletes were in action again at the WAAA Championships, Chris Benning setting a UK 3000m record of 8:52.33, and it wasn't too surprising that many of the team under-performed at the European Championships in Prague, which started before August was out. Two silver medals were gained, by Tessa Sanderson (62.40m to become the first British woman ever to win a European throws medal) and the 4x100m team of Bev Goddard, Kathy Smallwood, Sharon Colyear and Sonia Lannaman whose time of 42.72 was a UK record. Such was the standard that despite setting a UK record of 8:48.74 Paula Fudge could finish no higher than eighth in the 3000m. Other national records that summer included a 2:50:54 marathon by Rosemary Cox, 13.08 100m hurdles by Lorna Boothe, a hand-timed 57.0 by Chris Warden and electronic 57.43 by Liz Sutherland in the 400m hurdles, 16.40m shot and 60.80m discus by Meg Ritchie and walking marks of 13:40.0 (3000m) and 49:59.0 (10,000m) by Carol Tyson. In addition, at the IAAF's request, an experimental heptathlon was staged in Birmingham, the events added to the pentathlon being the javelin and 800m. The creation of this event was another WAAA initiative.

The final year of the decade was notable for a plethora of walking records, including world track bests for 10,000m of 48:11.4 by Marion Fawkes and 23:11.2 for 5000m by Carol Tyson. The most exciting developments came in the world of road running. Joyce Smith, aged 41, set UK 10 miles bests of 55:55 in March and 54:13 in October, and in between set the world of marathoning alight. In her debut at the distance, she won the WAAA title at Sandbach in 2:41:37, taking over NINE MINUTES off the previous UK record. Gill Adams "borrowed" the record with 2:41:03 in Eugene, but Joyce regained it when winning at Waldniel in Germany in 2:36:27, a race which attracted over 200 runners from 24 countries, indicating the fast growing and widespread appeal of the marathon for women who, let it not be forgotten, could still not race at anything longer than 1500m at the Olympics during the 1970s. Gill Adams– who later married the distinguished American playwright Israel Horovitz and settled in the

USA – went on to place second to Grete Waitz in New York in 2:38:31 and Joyce ended her season with a third victory, clocking 2:37:48 in Tokyo.

Records tumbled within the stadium too. Kathy Smallwood, helped by the thin air of Mexico City at the World University Games, ran 200m in 22.70, and Chris Boxer had the distinction of being the first to break the 2 minute 800m barrier with 1:59.05 as well as producing a 4:30.20 mile although that was overshadowed by a 1500m time of 4:01.53 by Chris Benning. Other records from 1979 that would still be good enough to make the British team today came in the 400m hurdles (56.06 by Chris Warden) and shot (16.72m by Judy Oakes). Still in its very early days, the heptathlon record was raised to 5357 (5138 on current tables) by Sue Longden. Indoors there was a noteworthy UK 400m record of 51.80 – for second place on the world all-time list – by Verona Elder when capturing her third European title. On the coaching front, the BAAB's Principal National Coaches John Le Masurier (who had guided such talents as Mary Rand, Diane Leather, Sue Platt and Ann Wilson) and Denis Watts (Dorothy Hyman, Ann Packer and Lillian Board among others) retired and Frank Dick became the BAAB's Director of Coaching. His team of National Event Coaches included two women: Margaret Whitbread (javelin), herself a former international and foster mother of Fatima, and Mary Peters (heptathlon), who at year's end was named as manager of the 1980 Olympic women's team.

During the decade, several athletes, officials and coaches were included in the twice-yearly Queen's Honours List. The OBE was awarded to Dorette Nelson Neal in 1976, Marea Hartman in 1978 and Vera Searle in 1979; the MBE to Lillian Board in 1970, Phyllis Pope in 1971, Mary Peters in 1973, Pat Cropper (née Lowe) in 1974, Sheila Sherwood in 1975, Denis Watts in 1976, Sonia Lannaman and Donna Hartley in 1979.

In addition to Lillian Board and "Buster" McShane, other notable personalities who passed away during the seventies included WAAA founder member and multi-record breaker Florence Millichap (née Birchenough) in 1973; 1948 Olympic 80m hurdles silver medallist and AAA Chief Coach Geoff Dyson's wife, Maureen Dyson (née Gardner), and Fred

Housden, First World War hero, international athlete, coach to David Hemery and several women internationals including Pat Pryce (1974); Ruth Taylor, Hon. Secretary of the Northern Counties WAAA 1932-1959 and WAAA Life Vice-President, and pioneering hurdler/high jumper Hilda Hatt (1975); Mary Amies, WAAA Hon. Secretary 1953-1960 and team manager at the 1956 and 1960 Olympics (1976); and in 1978 Kitty Dyer (née Tilley), winner of eight WAAA shot titles outdoors and indoors; prolific early world record breaker Mary Lines; and Dick Taylor, Ruth Taylor's husband and WAAA Chairman for 35 years until 1973.

Highlights from each of the WAAA Championships meetings
1970–1979

1970 (Crystal Palace)

IN RETURNING 4:15.4, Rita Ridley clipped half a second off her UK record in a highly competitive 1500m at these first Championships to be sponsored by Birds Eye Foods. The second British finisher in what was only the fourth 1500m race of her life was Norine Braithwaite – daughter of 1968 Olympic trap shooting champion Bob Braithwaite – whose 4:16.8 equalled the world's best by a teenager. An unwell Lillian Board, in what was to prove her last ever race, finished third in the 800m won by Sheila Carey in 2:03.6, the 400m title going to 17-year-old Marilyn Neufville in a championship record of 52.6. Anita Neil took the 100m in 11.6 but the sprinter who really caught the eye was 14-year-old Sonia Lannaman, who in a Junior 100m held in conjunction was timed at 12.1 into a 2.6m/sec wind. Mary Peters completed an unique hurdles/shot double with marks of 14.0 and 14.85m, while Judy Farr also made history by notching up her ninth consecutive track walk title, setting a championship record of 12:34.0 for the 2500m event in the process. It was a sequence unmatched by any other British champion, male or female. Against all the odds, as she had been unable to train since the previous autumn, was fretting over her terminally ill mother, had hardly competed that year and had missed out on her sleep due to a car breakdown, Dorothy Shirley (1.68m) triumphed in the high jump for the fifth time since her Olympic medal winning year of 1960.

136

1971 (Crystal Palace)

EIGHT OF THE 14 titles on offer went abroad, four of them to Canadians. Stephanie Berto (18) completed a sprint double in 11.42w and 23.54, Abby Hoffman (who became, and remains, a prominent member of the IAAF Council) set a national 800m record of 2:04.04, and Debbie Brill (17), whose distinctive "Brill Bend" technique was developed at around the same time as the "Fosbury Flop", equalled her Commonwealth high jump record of 1.83m. Nevertheless, there was much for the home athletes to celebrate, including three UK records. Rita Ridley clocked 4:14.32 for 1500m; Sharon Colyear (16), who had left school just the previous day, produced a time of 26.68 in the 200m hurdles (a mark which was never bettered as the event was dropped after 1972 to make way for the 400m hurdles); and Joyce Smith not only smashed her month-old 3000m figures of 9:43.8 but also the unofficial world best with 9:23.4. Another good result came in the 400m where Jannette Roscoe (née Champion) won in a personal best of 54.0 with Verona Bernard (18), who hadn't broken 57 sec before 1971, excelling herself with 54.3. The longest ever title winning streak came to a sad end in the 2500m walk when Judy Farr was disqualified just before the bell, leaving Brenda Cook the new champion in 12:39.8 ... the same Brenda Cook who in 1963 had won the WAAA indoor 600 yards title!

1972 (Crystal Palace)

THE MEETING SERVED as Olympic selection trials but many hopefuls came away disappointed. Anita Neil, who had run 11.4 for 100m in California in May, was far from that form and failed to reach the final, while Madeleine Cobb, an international since 1956 who had recently clocked her fastest time of 11.5, had to withdraw injured from the final. In their absence it was Della Pascoe (née James) who took the title, against the wind in very wet conditions, in 11.86 ahead of Sonia Lannaman and Andrea Lynch. Last in the 1500m was an ill Sheila Carey in 4:40.8. Fortunately for her, she won a later run-off race for the third selection place and was picked for Munich, where she surpassed all expectations by finishing fifth in a time (4:04.81) that would have been a world record prior to the final! First British finisher in the WAAA 1500m was Joyce Smith (4:17.60) and thus – 12 years after narrowly missing selection for the 800m in 1960 – she became an Olympian at 34, and awarded the honour of captaining the team. Eliminated in her heat was an 18-year-old Norwegian by the name of Grete Andersen ... who, many years later under her married name of Waitz, would become a marathoning legend. Three titles went to teenagers: Donna Murray (17) the 200m in 23.98, Verona Bernard (19) the 400m in a personal best of 53.20, and Ros Few (17) the high jump with 1.74m from a puddle strewn take-off area. Mary Tracey set an Irish record when winning the 800m in 2:02.98, Betty Jenkins (née Franklin) set a championship record of 12:31.2 in the 2500m walk, and Australia's Pam Ryan (née Kilborn), who had recently equalled the world record of 12.5, found 13.48 sufficed for an easy victory in the 100m hurdles, taking the last ever 200m hurdles title also in 26.82. Pru French must have been happy to become national javelin champion with a throw of 51.00m ... but an even greater sporting thrill awaited her in 1975 when, as Pru Carter, she made a dream debut for the England hockey team by scoring against Wales before 60,000 ecstatic schoolgirls at Wembley.

1973 (Crystal Palace)

AN INNOVATION WAS the awarding of the title 'UK champion' to the top placed Briton in any event not won by a home athlete. Thus Rosemary Wright (née Stirling), third in the 800m in 2:05.05 in a race won again by Ireland's Mary Tracey in 2:03.31, was designated UK champion. That was quite an achievement considering that during the previous three months she had got married, moved house, nursed husband Trevor Wright (the cross country and marathon star) following an Achilles tendon operation and been teaching full-time. The other UK as distinct from WAAA champions were Joyce Smith in the 3000m (9:11.45), behind the 18-year-old Swede Inger Knutsson (9:08.04 for a world junior best), and Barbara Lawton (née Inkpen), who high jumped 1.82m behind Austria's European champion Ilona Gusenbauer (1.85m). Andrea Lynch, fresh from a UK 100m record of 11.2, captured her first title, by a wide margin, in 11.74 against the wind. Sue Howell, younger sister of UK record holder Chris Howell, became the inaugural 400m hurdles champion in 61.41 but the event had yet to catch on as there were only five entries. Another new event was the 3000m walk (replacing the 2500m version), in which Betty Jenkins (35), who won her first WAAA walking title – at a mile – back in 1958, held off the younger generation in 14:59.4. The oldest champion to be crowned was Scotland's 40-year-old Rosemary Payne with an excellent discus throw of 56.40m, easily her longest in several WAAA Championship appearances, for her fifth and final title. She "retired" following the 1974 season, having chalked up a record 50 appearances for Britain since 1963; she went on to become a popular team manager and emerge as a most versatile star of the veterans scene. At the first World Masters Championships in Toronto in 1975, when she was 42, she not only won the discus (52.18m) but also the 100m in a windy 12.3, the high jump at 1.55m and a new event for women, the hammer, with 30.10m! Indeed she has never stopped competing and, as Rosemary Chrimes, was still winning age-group events in her late seventies.

1974 (Crystal Palace)

ONLY SIX TITLES stayed at home. Lesley Kiernan (2:05.12 800m) became at 16 one of the youngest ever champions, a contrast to Joyce Smith who regained the 3000m title (9:07.15) at the age of 36. The other British winners were Lorna Drysdale (13.45 100m hurdles), Val Harrison (1.82m high jump), Wales' Commonwealth Games bronze medallist Ruth Martin-Jones (6.26m long jump) and Marion Fawkes – probably the shortest ever WAAA champion at 1.52m or 4ft 11½in – with a UK 3000m walk record of 14:33.50. The outstanding performance of the meeting was watched by just a few hundred on the Friday evening when Joyce Smith, feeling relaxed as it was only a heat, went after a fast time in the 3000m. She succeeded gloriously, shattering her own UK record of 9:04.31 with a barrier-breaking 8:55.53. Had she not set off quite so fast (4:22

at halfway!) she might have broken the world record of 8:52.8 by the USSR's Lyudmila Bragina. A future marathon rival of Joyce's, Grete Andersen (later Waitz), set a championship and Norwegian record of 4:10.02 in the 1500m, and among several other championship records were sprint times of 11.23 and 23.23w by Raelene Boyle, who was based in Britain all that summer. Andrea Lynch, who had beaten the Australian in their eight previous clashes that season, was second in 11.27 but did not get the credit of being designated UK champion as that idea was dropped after just one year.

1975 (Crystal Palace)

IT HAS LONG been an unpalatable fact that exclusively women's meetings have limited public appeal and on this occasion fewer than 1500 were present on the second day, Saturday. The level of performance was low also. With some of the most successful athletes of recent years either retired or apparently in decline, Britain could claim only two women of undeniable world class stature – Andrea Lynch and Donna Murray – and both outstripped their opposition at these championships. Andrea, who had set impressive UK 100m records of 11.1 (manual) and 11.16 (electrical timing), was slowed by a 2.0m/sec headwind to 11.68 but that was good enough for a winning margin of 0.26 sec, and Donna – who had set a UK record of 51.28 a week earlier – trounced arch-rival Verona Elder (née Bernard) in 51.88. There was a UK record, on electrical timing, in the 400m hurdles when Jannette Roscoe clocked 58.31 although Chris Warden (née Howell) had run a hand-timed 58.0 the previous year. The biggest surprise came in the inaugural 5000m walk championship where 20-year-old Ginney Lovell, who had taken up walking as a schoolgirl as it seemed the easiest event in the Five Star Award scheme, not only beat the likes of Marion Fawkes and Judy Farr but went very close to the UK record with 25:02.8. Tessa Sanderson (19) threw 54.40m to collect the first of her ten javelin titles over a 21-year period! She was on her way to a fabulously successful career, but who noticed the 14-year-old who placed fourth in the WAAA Junior Championship with 34.26m … the future world record breaker, Fatima Whitbread? Two other stars of the future hardly drew attention to themselves either: Judy Oakes (17), who would nail the shot title an amazing 17 times between 1979 and 2000, finished sixth with 13.31m, and 15-year-old Kathy Smallwood (later Cook) wound up sixth in the Intermediate 200m championship in 25.3.

1976 (Crystal Palace)

THESE, THE LAST Championships to be sponsored by Bird's Eye Foods, were a gigantic affair as for the first time all three age categories – Seniors, Intermediates and Juniors – shared the programme of events over the two days. Held three weeks after the team's calamitous showing at the Montreal Olympics, the meeting had a subdued air about it and the only performance of global significance came in the 100m where Andrea Lynch, whose good form had been delayed by injury, set a championship record of 11.22, a mark which would have placed fourth in the Olympic final. The 400m hurdles, an event still in its infancy (it didn't receive Olympic status until 1984), saw Chris Warden reclaim the UK record from Jannette Roscoe with a time of 57.84. Chris, married to 1966 Commonwealth Games 440y hurdles bronze medallist Peter Warden, thus became the second member of her family to win this title as sister Sue Howell was the inaugural champion in 1973. Another UK record fell in the 5000m walk as Marion Fawkes beat Carol Tyson and Judy Farr by a big margin in 24:10.0. Tessa Sanderson, who had broken her UK javelin record with 57.18m at the Olympics, went close with 56.98m. Meanwhile, Fatima Whitbread was making progress, finishing third with 40.40m among the Intermediates.

1977 (Crystal Palace)

SPRINTERS HOGGED THE the limelight as Sonia Lannaman not only won her first senior outdoor titles with times of 11.24 and a championship record of 23.06, but at the end of the Sunsilk sponsored meeting she ran a blistering anchor leg for a world 4x200m relay record of 1:31.57 in which her team-mates were Verona Elder (who had won the 400m in a hand timed 52.3), Donna Hartley and Sharon Colyear. The squad averaged 22.9 per leg, with Sonia taking just 22 flat for her stint. The Junior 100m was notable also as Joanne Gardner won in an age-14 best of 11.89. She played no further part in British athletics but, settled in New York, in 1986 she gave birth to a daughter – Natasha Hastings – who would clock sprint times of 11.40, 22.61 and 49.84 and win an Olympic gold medal in 2008 as a member of the USA 4x400m relay squad. Runner-up to Joanne was the even more precocious Jane Parry who set an age-12 best of 11.92, although it was the slightly built athlete who finished an unnoticed sixth in 12.61 who would go on to much greater things as a senior … 13-year-old Linsey Macdonald. Another Scot, Liz Sutherland – at 30 in her first season at 400m hurdles after a distinguished career in the sprints and 100m hurdles – took the 400m hurdles in 57.93, just missing Chris Warden's UK record of 57.84, a mark she broke the following week when winning against the USSR in 57.59. Chris Boxer took the 800m in a personal best of 2:03.78 for the first of six WAAA titles at 800m or 1500m between then and 1990. Brenda Gibbs high jumped 1.85m to tie the championship record, Brenda Bedford – Britain's most capped international and two weeks short of her 40th birthday – put the shot 15.79m for her sixth title (and tenth time as highest placed Briton), and Tessa Sanderson (59.96m) had almost 11 metres to spare over her closest rival in the javelin, while Fatima Whitbread won the Intermediate title with an age-16 best of 48.28m.

1978 (Crystal Palace)

HIGHLIGHT OF THE meeting, held only four days after the athletes returned from the Commonwealth Games in Canada, was the Commonwealth 3000m record of 8:52.33 by Chris Benning (née Tranter), the 1500m silver medallist in Edmonton. In her first race at the distance that year, and with a previous personal best of 9:19.5, she pulled away from the previous record holder Ann Ford along the finishing straight. Another vastly improved athlete was Joslyn Hoyte in the 400m. She had started the season with a best time of 57.4 and here she beat Verona Elder in 52.66! Kathy Smallwood was a double sprint champion with times into the wind of

11.66 and 23.24. Chris Boxer, the only 1977 champion to win again, took the 800m in a personal best of 2:03.10. One title left the country, Mary Appleby winning the 400m hurdles in an Irish record of 57.46. Two golden oldies participated in the throws: Brenda Bedford, just short of her 41st birthday, finished second in the shot, while placing eighth in the discus was the even more durable Sue Allday, who won her first WAAA title way back in 1952 but at 43 could still throw in excess of 40m. Outside of the Crystal Palace meeting, two new championship events were inaugurated: Carol Tyson set a UK 10,000m track walk record of 49:59.0 in very windy conditions at West London Stadium in March and Margaret Lockley won marathon honours over the tough Isle of Wight course in 2:55:08, the second fastest time by a Briton. There were just eleven runners, only five of whom broke four hours … and no one could have anticipated the huge fields that the then undreamt of London Marathon would attract just three years later.

1979 (Crystal Palace)

CHRIS WARDEN TOOK British women's 400m hurdling a step nearer top world class by breaking her own national record of 56.80 with a cracking 56.06 for the best performance of the meeting. Chris Benning stepped down to 800m and beat some of the event's specialists in 2:01.3, a personal best by over two seconds, while Joslyn Hoyte-Smith retained the 400m title with her best time of 51.90, ranking her third on the UK all-time list behind Donna Hartley and Verona Elder. Two future Olympic medallists, aged 18 at the time, came up with UK junior records: Sue Hearnshaw when winning the long jump with 6.55m and Fatima Whitbread with 56.66m in the javelin behind Tessa Sanderson's 61.82m. Later in the season Fatima improved that record to 58.20m when claiming the European Junior title and Sue progressed to 6.68m for victory in a three-a-side match against the Russian Federal Republic, which resulted in a noteworthy British victory by 156 points to 151. Judy Oakes, with a put of 16.38m, became shot champion for the first time. Astonishingly, she would win another SIXTEEN outdoor titles between 1980 and 2000.

Wee Linsey Macdonald, barely 15 yet destined to become UK 400m record holder the very next summer, scored a 100m/400m double in the Intermediate events. During 1979 she clocked windy sprint times of 11.5 and 23.2, was fourth quickest in the UK at 400m with 52.62 and scored valuable points against Russia in her senior international debut.

UNITED KINGDOM RECORDS AT 1 JANUARY 1980

100m: 10.9 Andrea Lynch 1977 & 11.16 Lynch 1975; 200m: 22.70A Kathy Smallwood (later Cook) 1979; 400m: 51.28 Donna Murray (later Hartley) 1975 & 51.2 Murray 1978; 800m: 1:59.05 Chris Boxer 1979; 1500m: 4:01.53 Chris Benning 1979; Mile: 4:30.20 Boxer 1979; 3000m: 8:48.74 Paula Fudge 1978; Mar: 2:36:27 Joyce Smith 1979; 80mH: 10.6 Pat Jones 1967; 100mH: 13.08 Lorna Boothe 1978 & 13.0 Judy Vernon 1974 & Blondelle Thompson 1974; 200mH: 26.7 Sharon Colyear 1971; 400mH: 56.06 Chris Warden 1979; HJ: 1.87 Barbara Lawton 1973; LJ: 6.76 Mary Rand 1964; SP: 16.72 Judy Oakes 1979 (16.74 indoors 1978); DT: 60.80 Meg Ritchie 1978; JT: 67.20 Tessa Sanderson 1977; Pentathlon: (scored on 1971 tables) 4801 Mary Peters 1972 (100H-13.29, SP-16.20, HJ-1.82, LJ-5.98, 200-24.08); (new format, scored on 1971 tables) 4385 Sue Longden 1977 (100H-13.80, 11.69, 1.74, 6.35, 800-2:16.3); Heptathlon: (scored on 1971 tables) 5357 Longden 1979 (100H-14.3, SP-11.78, HJ-1.71, 200-26.0, LJ-5.70, JT-24.12, 800-2:20.02); 4x100m: 42.72 British team 1978; 4x400m: 3:26.6 British team 1975; Mile Walk: 7:14.4 Marion Fawkes 1979; 3000m Walk: 13:25.2 Carol Tyson 1979; 5000m Walk: 23:11.2 Tyson 1979 (road – 22:51 Fawkes 1979); 10,000m Walk: 48:11.4 Fawkes 1979. (A = at high altitude).

THE EIGHTIES

IT WAS AN eventful decade. The WAAA managed to retain its independence, despite increasing pressure to amalgamate with the AAA, but at last in 1988 – after 66 years of going it alone – the AAA and WAAA held combined outdoor championships. It was a decade of innovation. The London Marathon was inaugurated; the Olympic programme for women was extended to include the 3000m, 10,000m, marathon and 400m hurdles, while the heptathlon replaced the pentathlon; the IAAF introduced long awaited World Championships; and the strict amateur code was finally jettisoned. Two great javelin exponents, Tessa Sanderson and Fatima Whitbread, emerged as global champions, the former achieving the distinction of being the first British Olympic champion in a throwing event (1984) and the latter becoming the first British thrower ever to set a world record (1986). There were world records also by Paula Fudge (1981) and the ever controversial Zola Budd (1985) at 5000m, and by Liz McColgan at 10km on the road (1989).

The decade did not start too auspiciously for even though the Americans, West Germans and other strong teams boycotted the 1980 Moscow Olympics there were few good results for the British women's team. The only medals came in the relays with Heather Hunte (later Oakes), Kathy Smallwood (later Cook), Bev Goddard (later Callender) and Sonia Lannaman clocking the still current UK record of 42.43 for third in the 4x100m, a position occupied also by the 4x400m team (3:27.5) of 16-year-old Scottish schoolgirl Linsey Macdonald, Michelle Probert (later Scutt), Joslyn Hoyte-Smith and Donna Hartley. The biggest disappointment was the javelin where neither

Tessa Sanderson (48.76m) nor Fatima Whitbread (49.74m) came anywhere near making the final. It was the lowest point of Tessa's career. As the third longest thrower of all-time with 69.70m in June, qualifying for the final should have been a formality (58.76m sufficed) and she had expected to finish first or second, but she appeared to suffer from something akin to stage fright and her Olympic bid was over before it had even really started. Altogether it was a disappointing display, particularly compared to the four gold, two silver and two bronze medals won by the British men.

The year was no write-off, though, as UK records were set at 200m, 400m, 5000m, 10,000m, marathon, 100m hurdles, high jump, shot and discus as well as javelin and 4x100m relay. The most prolific record breaker was Meg Ritchie, a Scottish teacher studying at the University of Arizona. From small beginnings – her first try at the discus resulted in a throw of just 87ft (26.52m) – she first exceeded 50m in 1973, 60m in 1978 and in 1980 she raised the record six times, finishing up with 65.96m. The following year she progressed to 67.48m, which remains unapproached by any other Briton.

Meg was also a formidable shot putter and in 1983 led the way over 18m, Angela Littlewood having been the first over 17m in 1980. Meg in 1983 (18.99m) and Venissa Head from Wales in 1984 (18.93m) went close to 19m with unratified marks, and Venissa did reach 19.06m indoors in 1984, but the distinction of achieving the first 19m put outdoors fell appropriately to the long reigning star of the event, Judy Oakes. She reached that distance precisely when winning the 1986 UK title, and carried the record out to its current figure of 19.36m in 1988. Judy won three Commonwealth Games gold medals (1982, 1994 and 1998), collected a record 17 WAAA titles between 1979 and 2000 and was awarded the MBE in 1988 for her services to athletics. In 1980 she had declared her long-term aim was to throw in excess of 60 feet (18.29m) ..."and prove it can be done without artificial aids and without being a monster." Although weighing only 77kg Judy won Britain's Strongest Woman title in 1983 and went on to become a world powerlifting and European weightlifting champion.

146

TESSA SANDERSON uniquely, among British athletes, competed in six Olympics – winning in 1984. She was Commonwealth champion three times and raised the UK record from 56.14m in 1976 to 73.58m in 1983

SUE HEARNSHAW
1984 Olympic bronze medallist

PRISCILLA WELCH
Set UK marathon record at 42

CHRIS BENNING
UK 1500m record breaker

VÉRONIQUE MAROT
Two UK marathon records

Overshadowed by the Zola Budd-Mary Slaney incident, WENDY SLY ran a brilliant race at the 1984 Olympics to take the 3000m silver medal behind Romania's MARICICA PUICA (316)

ZOLA BUDD played a brief, controversial but significant role in British athletics. Winner for England of the 1985 and 1986 World Cross Country titles, she set a world 5000m record in 1985 and a world indoor 3000m record the following year

*JUDY SIMPSON on her way to Commonwealth Games heptathlon gold in 1986.
She set a UK record of 6623 that year, her individual pbs including 13.05 hurdles,
1.92m high jump and a wind assisted 6.56m long jump*

KIRSTY WADE, representing Wales, wins the 800m at the 1986 Commonwealth Games, adding the 1500m title two days later

FATIMA WHITBREAD celebrates her victory at the 1986 European Championships in Stuttgart, having the previous day set a world record of 77.44m in the qualifying round!

DIANE MODAHL
1990 Commonwealth 800m champion

YVONNE MURRAY
1990 European 5000m champion

FIONA MAY
Longest ever UK-born jumper

LORRAINE SHAW
2002 Commonwealth hammer gold

SALLY GUNNELL holds an unique record: she has won Olympic (pictured here), World, European & Commonwealth titles at 400m hurdles, and was a world record breaker with 52.74 in 1993

LIZ McCOLGAN on the way to her World Championships 10,000m victory in Tokyo in 1991. Her daughter EILISH competed in the 2012 Olympic steeplechase

DENISE LEWIS – triumphant against the odds in the Sydney Olympic heptathlon in 2000. She held the UK record from 1996 until 2012

KATHARINE MERRY competing at the 2000 Olympics in Sydney where she finished third over 400m. She would top the world list the next year with 49.59

ASHIA HANSEN, seen retaining her Commonwealth Games triple jump title in Manchester in 2002. She won the European title also that year and was twice World Indoor champion

PAULA RADCLIFFE during her phenomenal world record shattering 2:15:25 marathon in London in 2003. No British man ran faster that year!

KELLY HOLMES always dreamt of winning an Olympic gold medal one day, despite all her setbacks, but even she never envisaged two of them! Her double triumph in 2004 led to her being made a Dame the following year

VERA SEARLE – the Grand Old Lady of British women's athletics. The former world record breaking sprinter was the last President of the WAAA (1981-1991) prior to the merger with the AAA

Another field event on the rise in 1980 was the high jump. Britain's great tradition of Olympic medals in this discipline had not been maintained since Dorothy Shirley's silver in 1960, but the UK record came under continual assault. Moira Maguire, who as Moira Walls had won Scotland a Commonwealth Games bronze ten years earlier, tied Barbara Lawton's 1.87m mark from 1973, but then just six days later Louise Miller took over. She had begun high jumping four years earlier ("I was tall, skinny, asthmatic and couldn't run") and in quick succession in May cleared 1.88m, 1.90m twice, 1.92m and 1.94m. Two years later Diana Elliott jumped 1.95m, and all these years later no Briton has gone higher.

Other events in which UK records of the 1980s remain unbeaten are the 200m, 400m and long jump. Kathy Smallwood, who went on to marry world 4x800m relay record holder Garry Cook in November 1982, defeated Jamaica's Merlene Ottey over 200m in 22.31 in 1980 and the following year amazed herself as much as anyone else by splitting the world's top two 100m runners, Evelyn Ashford (USA) and Marlies Göhr (GDR), in the World Cup with a time of 11.10 which survived as the UK record until 2008. At 200m she progressed to 22.13 for second place to Olympic champion Bärbel Wöckel (GDR) in the 1982 European Championships and 22.10 for fourth place, 1/100th away from bronze, in the 1984 Olympics in Los Angeles. That time remains 0.4 sec quicker than no 2 on the UK all-time list. The 400m record came in for a battering during the decade. Young Linsey Macdonald, all 1.62m (under 5ft 4in) and 42kg (92lb) of her, kicked off with 51.16 when winning the 1980 UK title, while Joslyn Hoyte-Smith (coached by Dorothy Hyman) succeeded her that season with 51.06 and 50.88. Michelle Scutt reduced that to 50.63 in 1982 before Kathy took over with 50.46 later that summer and her stupendous 49.43 for the Olympic bronze medal in Los Angeles. Note that Kathy's times of 22.10 and 49.43 would have been winning marks at the 2011 World Championships!

Mary Rand's UK and former world record long jump of 6.76m from 1964 fell at last to the enigmatic Bev Kinch, who cut the sand at 6.90m at the inaugural IAAF World Championships in 1983. She produced an astonishing series, the shortest of her six jumps being 6.81m, and her longest was a heavily wind assisted 6.93m but such was the standard that she finished fifth. Bev was also a talented sprinter, winning the 1983 World University Games 100m title in 11.13w and the 1984 European Indoor 60m in a UK record 7.16, improving that to 7.13 in 1986. Another fine long jumper was Sue Hearnshaw, whose Olympic bronze medal in 1984 with a wind assisted leap of 6.80m enabled her to go one better than her mother, the former Muriel Pletts, who was fourth in the 4x100m relay at the 1948 Games. Earlier that year she won the European Indoor title with 6.70m and during the summer she registered precisely 7.00m with over-the-limit wind assistance.

That year of 1984 will also be remembered for the controversial appearance in Britain of Zola Budd. A phenomenal waif-like teenage runner in her native South Africa, a country barred from the Olympics because of its apartheid policies, Zola was spirited into the UK in March 1984 by the *Daily Mail* who thought it would be a good circulation booster to get her into the British Olympic team with the possibility of her winning the 3000m in Los Angeles for the glory of Britain ... not to mention the *Daily Mail*. She was granted UK citizenship in record time: just ten days after setting foot on British soil for the first time. The grounds for her eligibility? Her grandfather was British and her South African father had taken up British nationality. Zola was the most talented teenage middle and long distance runner yet seen, for running barefoot as a 17-year-old between January and March 1984 she had covered 800m in 2:00.9, 1500m in 4:01.81, 3000m in 8:37.5 and 5000m in 15:01.83 – that last time would have been a world record had South Africa not been expelled from the IAAF.

Zola, who had been reluctant to leave South Africa in the first place and never really settled into her new and alien environment, lost little time demonstrating how good she was ... demonstrating being the key word as in all her public appearances there were protests directed against this symbol of the hated apartheid regime about which she, a student of politics, consistently refused to comment. Her British track opponents were split. Some welcomed her in the knowledge that racing against her could raise their own standards; others deplored her presence either on political grounds or because she was likely to usurp one of their places on the team for Los Angeles. She clinched Olympic selection, after winning the UK 1500m title in an official World Junior record of 4:04.39, by finishing first in the Olympic 3000m trial in a European Junior record of 8:40.22.

In her last race before the Games she set a world 2000m best of 5:33.15 but in LA she met with disaster. A genuine 3000m gold medal contender, she was involved in a collision which resulted in the USA's World champion Mary Slaney falling, and many in the crowd booed Zola even though the fault lay with the American. A distraught Zola was so traumatised that she went through the motions to finish seventh while, almost unnoticed, Wendy Sly ran the race of her life to grab the silver medal in 8:39.47. Zola, who had the physiological advantage of having been born and resident for most of her life in Bloemfontein with its altitude of over 1400m, enjoyed a brilliant season in 1985. After winning (barefoot) the World cross country title by a 23 sec margin she took over 10 sec from the world 5000m record with 14:48.07. She also set UK records at 1500m (3:59.96), mile (4:17.57) and 3000m (8:28.83). However, in a notorious 3000m race at Crystal Palace, for which she was reputedly paid £90,000 (worth over £213,000 in today's money), she trailed in a distant fourth in 8:45.43 with the winner Mary Slaney (who received £54,000) clocking 8:32.91.

In 1986 she set a world indoor 3000m best of 8:39.79 and successfully defended her World cross country title, again racing barefoot, this time in muddy conditions, winning by 18 sec and leading England to team victory. Her outdoor track season was not so notable. She was selected by the WAAA but ruled ineligible by the Commonwealth Games Federation to represent England at the Games in Edinburgh as she had not fulfilled the requirement of physically residing in that country for six of the past 12 months, and she finished fourth over 3000m at the European Championships (8:38.20), one place behind Yvonne Murray whose 8:37.15 was a Scottish record. That was the end of her international career for

Britain. She did not compete in 1987 and returned to South Africa in 1988. She married Mike Pieterse the following year, and at last spoke out against apartheid in a TV interview. With the new South Africa welcomed back to international athletics she represented that nation at the 1992 Olympics and she remains an active athlete.

Coincidence or not, British women's middle and long distance standards rocketed during the Budd era. Chris Boxer set UK records of 4:00.57 for 1500m and 4:22.64 for the mile in 1984, while Kirsty McDermott produced new records in 1985 at 800m (1:57.42), 1000m (2:33.70) and the mile (4:19.41). Both had been winners at the 1982 Commonwealth Games – Kirsty at 800m (2:01.31) and Chris at 1500m (4:08.28) – and at the 1986 edition Kirsty Wade as she now was scored a double in 2:00.94 and 4:10.91. Born in Scotland, resident in England, Kirsty represented Wales. Two other Scottish-born runners who in the 1980s were well on their way to stardom were Yvonne Murray and Liz Lynch. In 1986 Yvonne set a UK 2000m record of 5:29.58 and finished third over 3000m at the Commonwealth Games (8:55.32) and European Championships (8:37.15). She was European Indoor champion in 1987 (8:46.06), Olympic bronze medallist in 1988 (8:29.02) and in 1989 was a World Cup winner in 8:44.32. Liz became Scotland's darling at the 1986 Commonwealth Games in Edinburgh by winning the 10,000m in a UK record 31:41.42, a time she reduced to 31:19.82 when placing fifth in the 1987 World Championships and 31:06.99 as Liz McColgan in 1988, a time she almost matched when taking the Olympic silver medal in Seoul in 31:08.44. Liz was also second in the 1987 World Cross Country and the 1989 World Indoor 3000m in a UK record 8:34.80 which was inside Budd's previous world mark of 8:39.79. Amazingly, just 15 minutes after the finish of that 3000m in Budapest she lined up for the 1500m, and placed sixth in 4:10.16! Seven days later, in Florida, she set a world road best of 30:38 for 10km. An earlier Olympic runner-up was Wendy Sly in the 1984 3000m but knee surgery in 1985 and 1989 hampered her later career.

Clearly the most successful event for British women's athletics in the 1980s was the javelin with Tessa Sanderson and

Fatima Whitbread between them capturing Olympic, World, European and Commonwealth titles, plus an astonishing world record.

MOSCOW TO LOS ANGELES ... ZERO TO HERO

History was made in Los Angeles in 1984 when Tessa Sanderson's opening throw of 69.56m – an Olympic javelin record – remained unsurpassed throughout the rest of the competition and the 28-year-old member of Wolverhampton & Bilston AC was crowned champion. She thus became the first Briton, male or female, ever to win an Olympic throwing title. This time, four years after weeping in frustration and disappointment when failing to qualify for the final in Moscow, she was able to cry for joy atop the victory rostrum. Beset by so many injury problems, most notably a ruptured Achilles tendon early in 1982 which left her on crutches for four months, she could easily have faded from the scene before realising her true potential, but she persevered during the dark days, fought back and finally landed the biggest prize of all. As her then coach Wilf Paish testified at the time of her Olympic triumph: "the tenacity and toughness of the girl has to be believed."

Theresa Ione Sanderson was born in Jamaica on March 14 1956, moving to England when she was eight. She collected her first national javelin title at the 1971 WAAA Intermediate Championships and two years later set a UK age-17 best of 51.34m. She became UK Junior record holder with 55.04m in 1974 and after breaking Sue Platt's UK record with 56.14m in 1976 she qualified for the Olympic final in Montreal with 57.18m. She first broke through the 60m barrier in June 1977 (60.24m) but at a European Cup Semi-Final in Dublin the following month she shook the world of athletics by not only defeating the East German world record holder and Olympic champion Ruth Fuchs but in the process throwing 67.20m to rank second on the world all-time list. That remained her best until 1980, in the meantime winning the first of three Commonwealth titles and finishing second to Fuchs at the European Championships in 1978.

She progressed to 69.70m in June 1980 and was confident of finishing no worse than second in Moscow, but disastrously failed to qualify for the final. In 1981 she made her mark as a heptathlete, setting a UK record of 6125 as re-scored on the 1985 tables. She was an extraordinary all-rounder for in addition to her javelin exploits she ran 200m in 24.89, clocked 13.46 for 100m hurdles and 60.46 for 400m hurdles, high jumped 1.69m, long jumped 5.98m and put the shot 13.27m. Meanwhile, a domestic rival had developed in the person of Fatima Whitbread, who at the 1983 UK Championships beat Tessa for the first time in 19 meetings. That was just the spur Tessa required and the following weekend she threw a barrier-busting 70.82m and later that June raised the UK record again to 73.58m, the world record now standing at 74.76m. However, it was Fatima who so nearly won the inaugural World title that summer, Tessa placing fourth before undergoing further surgery on both legs a few days later. In 1984 everything clicked into place and Tessa became Britain's first female Olympic champion since Mary Peters 12 years earlier.

Although Tessa continued at the highest level for many more years, uniquely among British athletes competing in a sixth Olympics in 1996, aged 40, she was more often than not outshone by Fatima. Their rivalry became acrimonious at times but, as Tessa put it: "It's nice when we're out there battling it out together. We would never, ever, be the best of friends but we're damn big rivals in athletics and that's the way I like it to be." She was awarded the MBE in 1985 in recognition of her Olympic victory, the OBE in 1998 for her charity work and the CBE in 2004 for services to sport as Vice-Chairman of Sport England. She married former Olympic judo player Densign White in St Paul's Cathedral in 2010.

FATIMA FULFILLED HER MOTHER'S PROPHECY

The first time former javelin international Margaret Whitbread laid eyes on the 13-year-old who would eventually become her fostered daughter she whispered to fellow coach George

Holroyd: "This girl is going to be the greatest javelin thrower the world has seen." It took 12 years for that seemingly far-fetched prophecy to come to pass ... 12 years of blood, sweat and tears, culminating in two fantastic throws at the 1986 European Championships in Stuttgart which made all the hard work, sacrifices and setbacks totally worthwhile.

The motivation to throw the javelin had originated in the classroom. Fatima, born of Cypriot parents in North London on March 3 1961, recalled: "We were read an interesting story about a Greek goddess, Atalanta, who could throw a spear farther than any man could fire an arrow. By sheer coincidence the following lesson was PE and we were introduced to the javelin. I enjoyed both lessons and when I arrived home I asked my mum to let me go training with her." Margaret was only too happy to oblige and thus was born an athletic partnership which would in time make history. Rarely was she absolutely free of injury or illness ... perhaps it was nature's way of telling her that a price must be paid for the tremendous demands she made on her body. That fearsome training regime made the Thurrock Harrier one of the strongest women in Britain, yet one of the fastest too. She was timed at 11.9 for 100m in training and clocked 24.38 for 200m in competition.

It was in 1977 that Fatima first competed against Tessa. Five years older, Tessa won their first 18 clashes but gradually the gap closed. In 1979 Fatima became the first British thrower to win a European Junior title and in 1981 she broke into world class, improving from 60.14m to 65.82m. With Tessa out injured, Fatima became Britain's no 1 in 1982 and the following year she defeated her arch-rival for the first time and improved to 69.54m before a throat infection nearly cost her the chance of competing in the inaugural IAAF World Championships in Helsinki. Her doctor advised her to withdraw but she refused to back out. Only the 12th and last qualifier for the final, she let rip with an opening throw of 69.14m. The world title was hers ... until with her very last throw the favourite, Finland's world record holder Tiina Lillak, topped that with 70.82m.The last British thrower to win a global medal was hammer thrower Malcolm Nokes as long ago as the 1924 Olympics.

The 1984 season proved Tessa's high point but Fatima did improve to 71.86m and despite severe medical problems that summer she managed to place third in the LA Olympics. Restored to full vigour in 1985 she progressed to 72.98m, while her day of days was August 28 1986. In a practically deserted Neckarstadion in Stuttgart for the qualifying round at the European Championships she despatched her spear the undreamed of distance of 77.44m, not only smashing Tessa's UK record of 73.58m but adding over two metres to the world record held by the GDR's Petra Felke. She thus became the first British thrower ever to break a world record. It was no fluke, for in the final next day – despite nursing a shoulder injury – she took the gold medal with 76.32m, the second longest throw in history. Fatima prevailed again at the 1987 World Championships in Rome with another great throw of 76.64m. Once more the by now famous 'Whitbread Wiggle' was in evidence as she celebrated before the TV cameras. She collected the silver medal at the 1988 Olympics in Seoul, but shoulder injuries took their toll and she retired in 1990. She married former British Athletics Promotions Officer Andy Norman in 1997 and gave birth to a son, Ryan, the following year. Norman died in 2007.

The hurdles events yielded several notable achievements during the decade. Shirley Strong led the way over 100m with new UK record times of 13.06 in 1980 and 12.95, 12.91 and 12.87 in 1983. She won the Commonwealth Games title in 1982 and two years later came away from the Olympics with a silver medal, clocking 12.88 behind Benita Fitzgerald-Brown (12.84). Shirley rued a lost opportunity to be crowned champion. She was neck and neck with the American until the final barrier. "At the last hurdle I looked over – it was stupid, I know. I saw her there and it was a struggle from there. I must have lost my concentration." Shirley's successor as Commonwealth champion in 1986 and UK record holder was Sally Gunnell, who ran 12.82 in 1988. Sally, whose coach Bruce Longden also guided Daley Thompson to Olympic glory, proved even better at the 400m hurdles. In her first serious season at the event, 1988, she smashed Sue Morley's 1983 UK record of 56.04 with 55.40 at the WAAA Championships and excelled herself by running 54.03 for fifth place at the Seoul Olympics that year. A fine all-rounder who had set UK age-16 and age-17 heptathlon bests of 5564 and 5680 in 1983/84, Sally broke Verona Elder's UK indoor 400m record with 51.77 in 1988. The following winter she won the European Indoor 400m title in 52.04 ... but it was in the early 1990s that she would achieve true greatness.

The 1980s will be remembered as the decade when women's marathon running really took off. In quick succession inaugural championships were held in 1982 (European), 1983 (World) and 1984 (Olympics) and although there were no British medallists several UK runners were of world class. The first was the ever remarkable Joyce Smith, who lowered her 1979 national record of 2:36:27 to 2:33:32 and 2:30:27 (the fastest to that date in an all-women's race) in 1980. She broke through the 2:30 barrier with 2:29:57 when winning the first London Marathon in 1981 by over seven minutes, a time she cut – as a 44-year-old – to 2:29:43 in London the following year, this time winning by over six minutes. Another amazing veteran, Priscilla Welch, clocked 2:28:54 to finish sixth in the 1984 Olympic race. Sarah Rowell trimmed that to 2:28:06 in 1985 and French-born Véronique Marot (who took 3:42 for her marathon debut in 1979) reduced it to 2:28:04 later in the year. Priscilla, who began as a recreational runner aged 33 and ran 3:26 in her first marathon, recaptured the record with 2:26:51 in 1987, at the age of 42, while Véronique got it back with 2:25:56 when winning in London in 1989. Incidentally, the first marathon to be staged through the heart of London was not the inaugural London Marathon in 1981 but the Avon International Women's Marathon which in August 1980 started at Battersea Park and finished at the Guildhall. The success of that race, which attracted over 200 runners from 27 countries, had much to do with the introduction of the Olympic race four years later.

There was another marathon breakthrough in 1981 when the Women's Cross Country Association, which then controlled road running in England, accepted an invitation from the AAA to hold a national championship in conjunction with the men's event in Rugby. It was another small but significant step towards full integration of men's and women's athletics although it was a low-key beginning as only four women started the race. The indefatigable Glasgow-born physiotherapist Leslie Watson won in 2:49:08 – her fourth sub-2:50 race in six weeks. The previous weekend she had set a world best 50 miles time of 6:02:37 in the USA, and the following weekend she won the tough Isle of Wight Marathon in 2:52:51. A further innovation in 1981 was Brendan Foster's brainchild, the Great North Run half marathon from Newcastle to South Shields. In addition, a national 10 miles road championship was held for the first time.

The marathon had entered the WAAA championship schedule in 1978; the 5000m and 10,000m followed in 1981, Kath Binns having set UK bests of 15:49.6 and 32:57.17 the previous year. That 10,000m mark survived until Scotland's Liz Lynch (later McColgan) won the Commonwealth Games title on home soil in Edinburgh in 1986 with a time of 31:41.42 but the 5000m record didn't last long as Paula Fudge – in her first race at the distance – set the inaugural officially ratified world record of 15:14.51 in Norway in 1981, easily defeating Norway's Ingrid Kristiansen who in 1984 would become the first woman to break 15 minutes. The younger by ten seconds of the former Yeoman twins, Paula already held the UK 3000m record of 8:48.74 from 1978. Uniquely, her sister Ann Ford was a previous holder of that record with 8:52.79 in 1977. In 1982 Paula and Ann finished first and second in the English cross country championship.

Another event which came into being in the 1980s was the heptathlon, which comprised the five pentathlon disciplines plus 200m and javelin. Sue Longden won her fourth and last WAAA pentathlon title in 1980 with a UK record score (with the 800m substituting for the 200m of Mary Peters' day) of 4395. The heptathlon was brought in the following year with Tessa Sanderson displaying her all-round prowess by becoming the first Briton to exceed 6000 points. Her score of 6125 (per the tables used today) included a massive javelin throw of 64.64m, still the world best in a multi-event contest. She was succeeded as UK record holder by another Jamaican born talent in Judy Livermore (later Simpson), who scored (1985 tables) 6259 in 1982, 6347 in 1983 and an outstanding 6623 for the European bronze medal in 1986. On that occasion she clocked 13.05 for 100m hurdles, high jumped a stunning 1.92m, put the shot 14.73m, ran 200m in 25.09, long jumped a wind assisted 6.56m, threw the javelin 40.92m and covered 800m in 2:11.72. Note that four of those marks were superior to those achieved by Jessica Ennis at the 2011 World Championships.

Events were moving fast in the world of athletics. The age of shamateurism was coming to an end, but the lure of legitimate cash payments and other benefits in the case of athletes from capitalist countries and state assistance and privileges for those who brought glory to the communist powers led to a big increase in the use of performance enhancing drugs. Unfortunately the IAAF missed a golden opportunity to try to eradicate this growing menace by going soft on a group of five women athletes from Eastern Europe. Particularly incensed was UK 1500m record holder Chris Benning who, as President of the British Milers' Club, signed a letter in June 1980 addressed to the IAAF protesting about the reinstatement of the five who had been found guilty the previous year of taking anabolic steroids. Chris had previously announced she would not be seeking Olympic selection in view of the fact that three of the athletes benefiting from the IAAF's leniency were likely to be in her event: Natalia Marasescu and Ileana Silai of Romania and Totka Petrova of Bulgaria. "I am completely disillusioned," she said. "These girls have cheated and yet they've been banned for only nine months and can compete in the Olympic Games. The International Federation has let down the athletes in a complete abrogation of their responsibility." IAAF President Adriaan Paulen admitted at the Moscow Olympics that the decision had been a wrong one, but by then the damage had been done.

Vera Searle retired as Chairman of the WAAA at the 1981 AGM. "One must face the fact that I am now in my 80th year," she said. "It has not been an easy decision after 59 years in athletics." Following a distinguished active running career she became Hon. Secretary of the WAAA while still in her twenties and had remained one of the dominant figures in the Association ever since. She was presented with a silver salver from her successor as Chairman, the equally formidable Dorette Nelson Neal, and received the honour of being unanimously elected WAAA President. Margaret Oakley and Marea Hartman (who was also re-elected Hon. Secretary) were named Vice-Chairmen; also re-elected were Edith Holland as Hon. Treasurer, and Connie Leslie and Susan Deaves as Assistant Hon. Secretaries, while the previous President, Lady Luke, accepted the position of Patron.

Alas, Mrs Nelson Neal's spell as Chairman was all too brief as she died in October 1982. "Nelson" was one of the sport's great characters along with being an outstanding official and coach. She was connected with her beloved Birchfield Harriers for 53 years, from the time she joined as a half miler and cross country runner in 1929. She quickly became Birchfield Ladies' Hon. Secretary in the 1930s and was Hon. Secretary of the Midland Counties WAAA for a staggering 51 years from the age of 18. In time she developed into a coach of repute, team manager, judge (at the 1948 Olympics), referee (at WAAA Championships between 1946 and 1975), and filled numerous important offices. She was the inaugural Chairman (1952) and subsequent President of the Women's Cross Country & Race Walking Association, WAAA Vice-Chairman from 1973 to 1980 and ultimately Chairman for the last year or so of her life. She was a driving force behind the UK Women's League and helped design Birmingham's Alexander Stadium, which became the new home of Birchfield Harriers. Her contribution to women's athletics at all levels was simply stupendous, and deservedly she was awarded the OBE in 1976. A few months after her death the new grandstand at Alexander Stadium was named after her.

Nelson's successor as WAAA Chairman was Margaret Oakley. A former sprinter, she became involved as a technical official after marrying Ken Oakley and progressed to the highest level as a field judge, refereeing several internationals and championships. As an administrator, she served as Secretary of the Northern Counties WAAA from 1966 to 1991 and was involved in team management at the 1976 and 1980 Olympics as well as the Edinburgh and Brisbane Commonwealth Games. Her close working relationship with Marea Hartman played a significant role in the steady move towards amalgamation and helped overcome the opposition of older and more sceptical members of the Executive.

Delegates stood in silence at the start of the 1983 WAAA AGM in memory not only of Mrs Nelson Neal but of Assistant Hon. Secretary and 1948 Olympic team manager Connie Leslie who died just a few days before the meeting. Among the most popular of all officials, Mrs Leslie – who joined Middlesex Ladies back in 1924 – had held every office in the Southern Counties WAAA: Treasurer 1943-53, Secretary 1953-61, President 1965-67 and 1979-80.

Other notable figures who passed on during the 1980s included Len Ward, former WAAA Chief Coach (1980); Geoff Dyson, former AAA Chief Coach (1981); Phyllis Pope, a founder member of the Northern Counties WAAA and President for 25 years as well as officiating as a track referee at the 1948 Olympics (1985); Kathleen Dale, née Tiffen, 1936 Olympic 80m hurdles semi-finalist (1986); two world record breaking athletes in Gladys Lunn and Eileen Edwards (1988); and noted women's hurdles coach and Wigmore Ladies founder George Stratford (1989). In addition, Lindley Armitage and his wife Isabel died within a week of each other in 1984. He was the WAAA's Hon. Auditor for over 40 years, she was Secretary of the WAAA Officials Committee, and together they helped organise the Lillian Board Memorial Service for the WAAA at St Paul's Cathedral.

Reverting to the 1983 AGM the main business before the WAAA was a proposal by Swindon AC for one national governing body for men and women, but that was defeated by 50 votes to 41. Mrs Mary Wall of the Swindon club stressed she was not criticising the WAAA or its work but that "pooling the resources and experience of the WAAA with that of the men, we believe, must inevitably bring about a stronger governing body for athletics as a whole." Ken Oakley, Secretary of the WAAA Development & Advisory Panel, warned that by becoming part of a single governing body the voice of women's athletics would be muted, concluding:

"Rejecting this motion is not reactionary. It is plain common sense."

Later that year, in an International Athletes' Club survey of 68 women internationals, 64 were in favour of ending separate governing bodies for men and women. In a postal vote agreed by a Special General Meeting of the WAAA 151 clubs voted in favour and 79 against a proposal that the WAAA establish a working party to seek ways and means of obtaining the Swindon AC's objective of a single governing body for the UK and for that working party to report back with recommendations at a General Meeting of the Association. More than half the clubs contacted did not reply. Marea Hartman's comment was: "I'm disappointed that more clubs have not troubled themselves but it seems to be that the silent majority are satisfied with the way things are."

In February 1984 all clubs affiliated to the WAAA received a questionnaire from the working party and just over a year later the working party's interim report was presented to the WAAA AGM. It considered that "a single UK Governing Body will evolve" although its report then equivocally went on to state "that one UK body does not necessarily mean union between men's and women's national associations." It recommended that each of the four home countries should set up its own working party, and concluded "that athletics in the UK could only be administered by one UK governing body if a constitution could be produced which would be acceptable to each national governing body." Although the previous year the AAA resolved "that the Men's and Women's Associations of England shall be vigorously encouraged to amalgamate", it was clear that the WAAA was at that time far from convinced. However, in 1987 John De'Ath, a retired Air Commodore, was appointed independent Chairman of a joint AAA/WAAA working party which produced an agreed proposal for a joint AAA of England, and in 1989 the concept was approved by the WAAA Executive. The actual marriage would not take place until 1991, although a sign of what would transpire came at the BAAB AGM in December 1989 when Marea Hartman succeeded Ewan Murray to become the Board's first female chairman.

The WAAA may have been cautious in the matter of amalgamation but did more than any other national governing body to widen the range of events open to women. At the 1983 AGM Ken Oakley had pointed out that events such as the 400m hurdles, 3000m, 5000m, 10,000m and marathon had been introduced by the IAAF as a result of proposals which had initially come from the WAAA, and in 1987 it was the WAAA which began investigations into the suitability, feasibility and need for the triple jump, hammer, pole vault and steeplechase. Also to its credit was the WAAA's strict policy concerning doping. The WAAA instituted a comprehensive drug testing programme in 1974 and in 1988 a AAA Drugs Enquiry report noted: "Anyone coming into women's athletics even as a young girl will have been accustomed from the outset to the possibility of being tested at competition. The WAAA took a most creditable leading role in this regard."

The MBE was awarded to five outstanding athletes during the decade: Verona Elder (1983), Joyce Smith (1984), Tessa Sanderson (1985), Kathy Cook (1986) and Judy Oakes (1988).

Highlights from each of the WAAA Championships meetings
1980–1989

1980 (Crystal Palace)

COMPLETING HER SECOND WAAA sprint double, Kathy Smallwood followed up her 11.45 victory in the 100m with a runaway win in the 200m, her margin being a gaping six metres. With no one to press her it was not surprising that the time of 23.14 was considerably slower than the personal best of 22.61 she registered when finishing fifth in the Moscow Olympic final and the magnificent UK record of 22.31 she set on this track the week before the Championships when defeating Jamaica's legend in waiting, Merlene Ottey. Coming so soon after the Games, the Championships provided an opportunity for some of those who under-performed in Moscow to regain some lost pride. Chief among them was Tessa Sanderson, who managed to throw the javelin a mere 48.76m as an Olympic non-qualifier but here reached a solid 64.08m. Ann-Marie Devally produced one of the best marks of the meeting as she high jumped 1.88m for second place on the UK all-time list behind Louise Miller's 1.94m. The biggest breakthrough came from Scotland's Ann Clarkson, who improved in the 800m from 2:04.3 to 2:01.9 for a clearcut win over Jane Finch (née Colebrook). Star of the Intermediate events not surprisingly was Olympic 400m finalist Linsey Macdonald (16) who dropped down in distance for an 11.75/23.89 sprint double, while a name to note in the Junior division was that of 14-year-old Sally Gunnell, long jump winner at 5.56m ... 12 years before her Olympic 400m hurdles triumph.

1981 (Crystal Palace)

FATIMA WHITBREAD ANNEXED her first senior javelin title with a modest throw of 57.74m. So where was Tessa Sanderson? She was busy sprint hurdling, finishing a close second to UK record holder Shirley Strong (13.36) in a remarkable 13.46! Tessa's previous best was 13.72 and she now ranked seventh on the UK all-time list. What an athlete. Not only was she one of the world's greatest javelin throwers but as an all-rounder only two British women could be rated above her: Mary Peters and Mary Rand. Two weeks before the championships Tessa had become the first British heptathlete to exceed 6000 points, setting a Commonwealth record of 6110 (6125 on the present tables). The meeting threw up three championship records: by Joslyn Hoyte-Smith, the UK record holder at 50.88, in the 400m with 51.70; Ann-Marie Cording (née Devally), who incurred no failures up to and including a personal best height of 1.90m; and Meg Ritchie (UK record holder with 65.96m) who, despite suffering from flu, threw the discus 62.22m for a winning margin of almost ten metres. Back from one of the injuries which blighted her career, Sonia Lannaman went close to a sprint double by winning the 200m in 23.14 after finishing a close second to Wendy Hoyte (née Clarke) in an 11.73 100m run into a strong wind. An unnoticed ninth in the 3000m in 9:31.30 was a lanky 16-year-old Scot who would develop into one of Britain's most successful international runners ... Yvonne Murray.

1982 (Crystal Palace)

NO FEWER THAN seven championship records fell on a beautifully warm afternoon. One of them, a 1.92m high jump, won Barbara Simmonds the new sponsor's TSB (Trustee Savings Bank) "Golden Girl" award – a specially designed piece of jewellery for the best performance of the meeting by a British athlete. Barbara enjoyed the competition of her life. After matching her previous best of 1.86m she cleared 1.90m prior to the 1.92m, rising to third on the UK all-time list behind Diana Elliott (1.95m) and Louise Miller (1.94m). The 100m, run into a 1.5m/sec wind, was the closest in WAAA Championships history as just 2/100ths separated first (Wendy Hoyte 11.62) from fifth. Ever injury-prone, Sonia Lannaman – who shared the winning time in second place in the 100m – met with disaster in the 200m. Making up ground in the straight in a bid to retain her title she began hopping in agony and fell to the track, victim of a groin injury. Kathy Smallwood won in 23.00. That was a championship record, as were the 51.05 400m by Michelle Scutt (née Probert), 4:07.28 1500m by Chris Boxer and 17.59m shot put by Judy Oakes. Two Australian visitors also accounted for championship records: Robyn Strong, whose 6.65m long jump supplanted the oldest mark on the books (6.56m by Mary Rand in 1964) and world record holder Sue Cook with 23:03.52 in the 5000m walk. A new event, the 5000m, was dominated by the Joyce sisters, Monica (15:45.26) and Regina, who though born in Sussex and British internationals, later opted to represent the country of their parents' birth, Ireland. Earlier in the year Verona Elder (née Bernard) captured her eighth and final WAAA indoor 400m title in 52.77. The previous year she had struck bronze at the European Indoor Championships, to add to her three gold and a silver. Verona announced her retirement in January 1984 having accumulated the record number of 72 GB international vests and later became a well respected British team manager.

British medallists at the European Championships in Athens were Kathy Smallwood (2nd 200m in a UK record 22.13) and the 4x100m team of Wendy Hoyte, Smallwood, Bev Callender (née Goddard) and Shirley Thomas (2nd in

42.66). In both cases the British women were beaten by East Germans, all or most of whom would have been on a state sponsored drugs programme. The Commonwealth Games in Brisbane produced gold medals for Kirsty McDermott (later Wade) of Wales in the 800m (2:01.31), Chris Boxer in the 1500m (4:08.28), Shirley Strong in the 100m hurdles (12.78w), Judy Oakes in the shot (17.92m), Scotland's Meg Ritchie in the discus (62.98m) and England's 4x100m team of Hoyte, Smallwood, Callender and Sonia Lannaman (43.15).

1983 (Crystal Palace)

THE OBVIOUS RECIPIENT of the "Golden Girl" award was Shirley Strong who, after equalling her own UK 100m hurdles record of 13.06 in her heat, sped to a barrier-breaking 12.95 clocking in the final. It wasn't only her athletic performance which commanded attention; in those days of relatively conservative racing attire she appeared in an eye-catching leotard. Eighth and last in that final (in 13.92) was 16-year-old Sally Gunnell, destined five years later to succeed Shirley as UK record holder, not to mention her ultimate blossoming as a 400m hurdler. That 12.95 was a championship record, and others fell in the long jump (Australia's Robyn Lorraway, née Strong 6.74m), shot (Judy Oakes 17.61m) and javelin (Fatima Whitbread 65.24m). Kathy Cook (née Smallwood) regained the 100m title in 11.26, while Michelle Scutt took the 200m in 23.17. Just missing record status was Shireen Bailey's personal best of 2:00.58 in the 800m, although that was effectively on a par with Vera Nikolic's 1968 manual time of 2:00.5.

The meeting was staged only a week before the start of the inaugural IAAF World Championships in Helsinki where Fatima Whitbread placed second (69.14m) and Tessa Sanderson fourth (64.76m); Kathy Cook finished third in the 200m (22.37) and helped Britain into second place in the 4x100m relay (42.71) alongside Joan Baptiste, Bev Callender and Shirley Thomas; and British records fell to Wendy Sly in the 3000m (8:37.06), Shirley Strong (12.91), Sue Morley (56.04 400m hurdles) and Bev Kinch, whose 6.90m long jump survived until 2012. Such was the standard that their placings were 5th, 5th, 7th and 5th respectively. At year's end, Wendy Sly (née Smith) won the inaugural IAAF World 10km road title in San Diego in 32:23. Earlier in the year she had been the first to defeat Norway's Grete Waitz in a road race, clocking 31:29.

1984 (Crystal Palace)

JUST WEEKS BEFORE she would go on to set long-standing UK records at 400m (49.43) and 200m (22.10) at the Los Angeles Olympics, Kathy Cook picked up the "Golden Girl" award for her sprint double: 100m in 11.44 and 200m in a championship record of 22.77. She must have been run close by Sue Hearnshaw, who not only excelled in her main event, the long jump, with a wind-assisted championship record of 6.79m, backed up by two legal efforts of 6.71m, but set personal bests of 11.66 for third in the 100m and 23.43 for fourth in the 200m. The long jump was notable also for second and third places going to sisters Georgina (with a UK age-17 best of 6.52m) and Joyce (6.40m) Oladapo. Shirley Strong missed her 100m hurdles championship record of 12.95 by 1/100th with Sally Gunnell (17) progressing well to finish second with a UK junior record of 13.30. The throws yielded championship records for Judy Oakes (18.01m shot) and Fatima Whitbread (65.76m) and there was an English discus record of 57.32m by Lynda Whiteley. Shirley would win a silver medal (12.88) at the boycott-affected Olympics, while bronzes were claimed by Kathy in the 400m and 4x100m relay (43.11) in the company of Simmone Jacobs, Bev Callender and Heather Oakes, and by Sue (6.80m) and Fatima (67.14m), but javelin gold medallist Tessa Sanderson (69.56m) and 3000m runner-up Wendy Sly (8:39.47) did not compete at Crystal Palace. A future World champion and Olympic medallist representing Italy, Slough-born Fiona May won the Junior long jump title with 6.07m. However, Olympic glory would still be a full 20 years away for Kelly Holmes (14) who ran a personal best of 4:35.3 when finishing a close second in the English Schools Junior 1500m, a title she had won the previous year.

1985 (Birmingham)

ALTHOUGH TESSA SANDERSON collected the "Golden Girl" award – in the form of an 18ct gold brooch with diamonds valued at £2000 – as a reward for setting a javelin championship record of 66.38m, almost inevitably it was Zola Budd who was the centre of attraction, stirring up yet another controversy. She had been entered only for the 1500m but was allowed at short notice, contrary to previous practice, to switch instead to the 3000m. Chris Boxer was particularly critical of officials for allowing this as she had been anticipating a 1500m race against Zola, but when her clubmate from Aldershot Farnham & District failed to declare for the 1500m Chris opted instead for the 800m, which she won in 2:00.60. Zola took her first WAAA title, setting a championship record of 8:50.50. Much earlier in the year, at the National Cross Country Championships at Birkenhead, Zola had been obstructed by anti-apartheid demonstrators, causing her to drop out. The Track & Field Championships, with TSB trebling its sponsorship to £20,000, were staged for the first time at the Alexander Stadium and attracted a record entry of 957. After being beaten in the 100m by Heather Oakes, née Hunte (11.37w), Kathy Cook won the 200m in 23.39 and UK record holder Diana Davies (née Elliott) high jumped 1.89m.

1986 (Birmingham)

A COUPLE OF months in advance of her staggering world record at the European Championships, Fatima Whitbread threw the javelin 66.56m and then 69.02m to smash Tessa Sanderson's championship record of 66.38m ... but it still didn't earn her the "Golden Girl" award. That went instead to 20-year-old Zola Budd who, in very windy conditions, took the 1500m in a championship record of 4:01.93, winning by some 50m from a field which included Yvonne Murray and Wendy Sly. Commenting for television, Chris Boxer estimated that run was worth 3:58 on a windless day. Chris herself finished only fifth in defence of her 800m title which passed to 19-year-old Diane Edwards (later Modahl) with a front running 2:04.26. Another fast improving talent was Paula Dunn, who cut her fastest 100m time from 11.55 to 11.34. Kathy Cook contested the 400m for the first time at these championships, winning in a wind-affected 53.50. Sally Gunnell (13.13w) won her first senior 100m hurdles title, while Judy Oakes set a championship record of 18.70m in the shot. Crowned Olympic heptathlon champion 14 years later, 13-year-old Denise Lewis failed to make the final of the Junior Girls' 75m hurdles but finished sixth in the long jump with 5.09m. Presentations on the first day were made by Princess Anne, later the Princess Royal.

English winners at the boycott-affected Commonwealth Games in Edinburgh were Heather Oakes (11.20w 100m), Sally Gunnell (13.29 100m hurdles), Joyce Oladapo (6.43m long jump), Tessa Sanderson (69.80m javelin), Judy Simpson (6282 heptathlon) and the 4x100m squad of Paula Dunn, Kathy Cook, Joan Baptiste and Oakes (43.39). Kirsty Wade completed an 800m/1500m (2:00.94/4:10.91) double for Wales and Liz Lynch won the 10,000m for Scotland in 31:41.42. At the European Championships in Stuttgart, Fatima Whitbread won the javelin with 76.32m after setting a world record of 77.44m in the qualifying round, and there were bronze medals for Yvonne Murray in the 3000m (8:37.15) and Judy Simpson in the heptathlon (UK record of 6623).

1987 (Birmingham)

THE ONE WORLD class performance came from "Golden Girl" award winner Fatima Whitbread. In accumulating her sixth senior title, the world javelin record holder took just two throws: the first landed at 72.96m, smashing her own championship record; the second travelled 72.50m. After achieving the 42nd and 43rd 70m-plus throws of her career, Fatima directed her attention to the garden-party atmosphere of the meeting. "I support the WAAA Championships year in, year out," she remarked, "but perhaps they should speculate more on what the athletes need. Today was a lovely family occasion, but there were less than a thousand paying spectators and they're not getting value for money – nor are the sponsors. I would like to see the AAA and WAAA Championships amalgamated as soon as possible. The atmosphere today was nil and in these circumstances it's hard for the girls to be motivated to produce the world class performances they need four weeks before the

World Championships. We need men and women competing together to draw the best out of each other." Her views reflected those of many in the sport and indeed this proved to be the last time that the AAA and WAAA Championships would be held separately.

The only other championship record in the senior events came in the 5000m walk where Lisa Langford, who broke the UK record earlier in the year with 22:19.04, clocked 22:35.04. Earlier in the season she had posted a UK 10km road record of 45:42. In the shot Judy Oakes' eighth victory (18.44m) equalled the most WAAA titles ever won in a single event. Sally Gunnell retained her sprint hurdles title and but for a hesitant start would surely have become only the second Briton to break 13 sec; spectating Shirley Strong, now retired, was the first. As it was, Sally had to settle for equalling her personal best of 13.01. Of the new crop of champions perhaps the most surprising was Olympic silver medallist Wendy Sly, now coached by Seb Coe's father Peter ... not because her 3000m victory in 9:04.83 was unexpected but in that it was her first WAAA track title. Long, leggy Donna Fraser (14) became the Junior Girls 200m champion in a windy 24.59 after finishing fourth in the 100m, one place behind the precocious 12-year-old Katharine Merry, who that season ran 100m in 12.1, high jumped 1.69m and long jumped a windy 5.55m. Thirteen years later Katharine would place third and Donna fourth in the Olympic 400m final, both clocking inside 49.8.

1988 (Birmingham)

COMBINED AT LAST! The Kodak AAA Championships and TSB WAAA Championships shared the stage at the Alexander Stadium in a three-day meeting (including Sunday, a first for the WAAA) which served as the Olympic Trials with the first two in each event automatically selected for Seoul subject to having acquired the requisite qualifying standard. Star of the show was Sally Gunnell. In this, her first serious season at the event, she smashed the UK 400m hurdles record with 55.40 and next day held on to her 100m hurdles title in 13.02. Sally would improve that 400m hurdles record three more times that summer, culminating in 54.03 for fifth place in the

Olympic final, while in Zürich she would break Shirley Strong's UK 100m hurdles record with 12.82. Earlier in the year she had set a UK indoor 400m record of 51.77. Assured of their selection, Liz McColgan and Fatima Whitbread– who would finish second in the 10,000m (31:08.44) and javelin (70.32m) respectively in Seoul – did not compete, but Yvonne Murray (destined to take bronze at 3000m in an outstanding 8:29.02) took the opportunity to tune up with a casual 8:47.34 victory. Chris Cahill (née Boxer), who finished just outside the medals in Seoul with fourth place in the 1500m with 4:00.64, won in 4:08.26 ahead of Shireen Bailey and Kirsty Wade, the latter having taken the 800m title the previous day in 2:01.52. Judy Oakes (18.76m shot) notched up a record ninth title and there was a classy long jump duel between Australia's London-based Nicole Boegman (final round 6.82m) and World Junior champion Fiona May (6.79m), at 19 the youngest woman in the Olympic team. Two of the Junior Girls champions would blossom into world class athletes: Katharine Merry, still only 13, took the 100m in 12.04 (she would later run a UK age best of 11.85) and Joanne Davis completed an 800m (2:12.94) and 1500m (4:30.23) double. Who? You would know her better as Jo Pavey! Earlier, at the English Schools Championships, Jo had won the Junior Girls 1500m in a UK age-14 best of 4:27.9 with one Paula Radcliffe a distant eighth in 4:41.0. Meanwhile, 15-year-old Denise Lewis was progressing nicely, winning the WAAA Intermediate heptathlon with 4915 points and long jumping over 6m.

1989 (Birmingham)

HELD IN CONJUNCTION with the 100th edition of the Kodak AAA Championships, the second mixed meeting saw the 100m champion for the previous three years, Paula Dunn, go one better by not only retaining that title in 11.32w but also taking the 200m in 23.43. Linda Keough reduced her personal best from 51.65 to 51.09 for an excellent 400m victory, chased home by Jenny Stoute (down from 52.28 to 51.53). Diane Edwards (later Modahl) – who would strike gold at the Commonwealth Games early in 1990 in 2:00.25 – won the 800m in 2:01.24. Alison Wyeth, a member of the IAAF staff then based in London, had a busy weekend. First she won the 3000m in 9:11.12 and then placed second to Bev Nicholson (4:09.34) over 1500m. Sally Gunnell concentrated just on the sprint hurdles (13.26), defeating Kay Morley (13.35), but it was the Welsh athlete who came out on top at the Commonwealth Games in 12.91. Nicole Boegman and Fiona May clashed again in the long jump, the Australian winning, 6.74m to 6.62m, while Tessa Sanderson, whose only valid throw travelled just 58.64m, became WAAA champion again 14 years after her first senior title. She would go on to throw much further (65.72m) at the Commonwealth Games, where another English winner was Myrtle Augee (18.48m) who, in Judy Oakes' absence, took the WAAA shot title with a throw of 17.51m. A triple jump championship was added to the programme, Evette Finkin becoming the first title winner. Betty Sworowski, winner of the 5000m walk in 22:30.59, set UK records during the season at that distance (22:02.06) as well as at 3000m (12:59.1) and 10,000m (46:36.1). Lisa Langford, who finished second, also broke UK records that year, clocking 22:09 and then 22:01 for 5km on the road.

UNITED KINGDOM RECORDS AT 1 JANUARY 1990

100m: 11.10 Kathy Cook 1981; 200m: 22.10 Cook 1984; 400m: 49.43 Cook 1984; 800m: 1:57.42 Kirsty Wade 1985; 1500m: 3:59.96 Zola Budd 1985; Mile: 4:17.57 Budd 1985; 3000m: 8:28.83 Budd 1985; 5000m: 14:48.07 Budd 1985; 10,000m: 31:06.99 Liz McColgan 1988 (30:39 road 1989); Half Mar: 69:56 Susan Tooby 1988; Mar: 2:25:56 Véronique Marot 1989; 100mH: 12.82 Sally Gunnell 1988; 400mH: 54.03 Gunnell 1988; HJ: 1.95 Diana Davies 1982; LJ: 6.90 Bev Kinch 1983; TJ: 13.15 Evette Finikin 1987; SP: 19.36 Judy Oakes 1988; DT: 67.48 Meg Ritchie 1981; JT: 77.44 Fatima Whitbread 1986; Heptathlon: (scored on 1984 tables) 6623 Judy Simpson 1986 (100H-13.05, HJ-1.92, SP-14.73, 200-25.09, LJ-6.56w, JT-40.92, 800-2:11.72); 4x100m: 42.43 British team 1980; 4x400m: 3:25.51 British team 1984; 3000m Walk: 12:59.1 Betty Sworowski 1989; 5000m Walk: 22:02.06 Sworowski 1989 (22:01 road Lisa Langford 1989); 10,000m Walk: 46:36.1 Sworowski 1989 (45:42 road Langford 1987); 20km Walk: 1:40:45 Irene Bateman 1983.

THE NINETIES

AFTER NEARLY SEVENTY years of proudly and defiantly going it alone, the Women's AAA finally faced up to the sport's practicalities and merged with the AAA. For decades the WAAA, Scottish WAAA, Welsh WAAA and Northern Ireland WAAA had been unique in world athletics as women-only governing bodies; in every other country there was one organisation dealing with men and women. The WAAA pioneers of the 1920s, led by such strong personalities as Vera Searle, had jealously guarded the organisation's independence, but in truth the WAAA could never have flourished without the input of men at every level in administration, coaching, officiating and in medical matters. The vast majority of female athletes themselves wished to belong to mixed clubs and compete in mixed meetings, yet it was only in 1988 that the WAAA consented to holding their outdoor national championships alongside the AAA's. That was a landmark and the pressure for complete amalgamation could not be resisted for much longer.

It was part of a huge change in the administration of British athletics. A key date was March 17 1991 when consecutive Extraordinary General Meetings of the BAAB, AAA and Women's AAA at Birmingham University transformed the situation. The BAAB, founded in 1932 and affiliated to the IAAF as the governing association (men and women) for the UK, decided by 220 votes to none to replace itself by the British Athletic Federation (BAF). The AAA voted 835-39 and the WAAA 80-0 in favour of BAF's creation ... 23 years after the Byers Commission had recommended a unified governing body. At the same time, the AAA and WAAA, after co-existing since 1922, finally merged to form what would be known initially as the AAA of England, with Her Majesty The Queen as Patron.

The final WAAA Executive meeting was held in Birmingham on September 8 1991, the principal officers present including Margaret Oakley (Chairman), Marea Hartman (Hon. Secretary), Edith Holland (Hon. Treasurer), Ken Oakley (Development & Advisory Panel Secretary), Pat Green (Standards Secretary) and Vera Duerdin of the Women's Cross Country & Road Running Association. Miss Holland stated that the WAAA had assets of about £112,000 less any liabilities. The final balance sheet, as at October 31 1991, showed net assets of £87,541.

It was on October 1 1991 that the AAA of England officially came into being. On the same day the WAAA ceased its activities and transferred its funds to the new body and four days later, at the AAA of England's first Council meeting, Marea Hartman was elected President, with David Cropper as Chairman, Derek Johnson as Hon. Secretary and Geoff Clarke as Hon. Treasurer. The new Association would be responsible for the co-ordination and development of athletics in England in conjunction with the Regional Associations.

BAF, whose Patron was the Duke of Edinburgh (previously President of the BAAB), also officially began life on October 1 1991, bringing together for the first time all the clubs of the UK under a single umbrella organisation with every affiliated club and athletic body in the UK entitled to attend and vote on major constitutional matters and the election of officers. The inaugural Chief Executive was Malcolm Jones and the first honorary officers were Arthur McAllister as President, Dr Bill Evans as Chairman, Dave Bedford as Secretary and John Lister as Treasurer.

Women occupied some key positions in the new Federation. Norma Blaine became an elected member of the Management Board, while Beryl Randle – a record breaking walker in the 1950s – was appointed Secretary of the Race Walking Commission. Joan Allison and former sprint international Jill Lindsay were among the eight 1992 Olympic team selectors. Norma Blaine was also Chairman of the BAF Women's Advisory

Group, formed to promote and help resolve "special women's issues", with former international high jumper Gwenda Ward its Secretary, although she resigned in 1995. Pat Green was Secretary of the Junior International Track & Field Committee, former UK shot record holder Angela Littlewood was the Development Officer for the South of England, and the long-time WAAA National Coaching Secretary Ken Oakley became Chairman of the Development Committee. However, there was a severe imbalance in certain areas as the GB Coaching Team for 1995 included only one woman (Judy Vernon, sprint hurdles) among 42 names. That year there was but one woman on the 14-strong BAF Management Board and the Council of 65 included 13 women. In 1995 there were two females (Judy Vernon and another former hurdles star, Christine Warden) among 38 National Event Coaches. In 1996 Vera Duerdin, for many years Britain's women's cross country team manager, was elected Secretary of BAF's Road Running Commission.

BAF's responsibilities included the co-ordination and disciplinary procedures of all doping matters, and this proved to be a monumental burden, contributing to its financial ruin. A number of high profile doping positives rocked British athletics during the 1990s, the most costly being that attributed to Diane Modahl.

Diane Edwards, as she was then, was Commonwealth 800m champion in 1990, the year she set an English record of 1:58.65. A cousin of world boxing champion Chris Eubank, she married Vicente Modahl in 1992 and ran well in the following year's World Championships to place fourth in 1:59.42. Her world collapsed around her two months after her 800m victory helped Britain finish second in the 1994 European Cup, the team thus qualifying for the IAAF World Cup. Out in Canada in August to defend her Commonwealth title, she was informed by team manager Susan Deaves that she had tested positive following a race in Portugal in June. In a shocked state, Diane was sent home, protesting her innocence. However, in December 1994 the BAF Disciplinary Committee came to the unanimous decision that a doping offence had been committed and announced she would serve a four-year ban, ending in June 1998.

The first British woman to fail a drugs test, Diane and her husband fought for the restoration of her good name and she was eventually cleared in July 1995 by a BAF Appeals Panel who concluded there was reasonable doubt over the Portuguese laboratory's findings. The Panel stated: "There is a possibility that the cause of the testosterone-to-epitestosterone ratio in her urine [a startling level of 42:1, seven times the allowable ratio] was not that testosterone had been administered, but that the samples had been degraded owing to their being stored in unrefrigerated conditions and that bacteriological action had resulted in an increase in the amount of testosterone in the samples."

There was further joy for Diane when she gave birth to a daughter in October 1995, and the IAAF reinstated her in March 1996, conceding that the test was unreliable. She resumed racing in May 1996 and made the Olympic team but a hamstring injury forced her to drop out in her heat. Her last big international race was at the 1998 Commonwealth Games where she placed third (1:58.81) behind two runners from Mozambique, a country which had joined the Commonwealth only three years earlier. Diane launched High Court proceedings against BAF early in 1996, seeking £480,000 for loss of earnings and other fees incurred while suspended – later rising to £1 million to include punitive damages. The action was contested by BAF whose own legal expenses led in part to the body's acute financial problems which resulted in BAF going into administration in October 1997. The High Court in London eventually ruled against her claim in December 2000.

During its six years of existence BAF, despite launching many useful initiatives, appeared to be constantly in a state of crisis, a situation not helped by various power struggles within the Federation. Malcolm Jones resigned as Chief Executive in 1993, to be replaced by Professor Peter Radford, the former world record holder at 200m and 220 yards, as Executive Chairman. At the 1994 AGM Dave Bedford was ousted as Hon. Secretary by Matt Frazer with Ken Rickhuss becoming Chairman. Also that year Frank Dick resigned as Director of Coaching following a reduction in the development budget and Andy Norman was dismissed as Director of Promotions in the wake of the suicide of noted journalist and coach Cliff Temple. Mary Peters succeeded Arthur McAllister as President at the 1996 AGM, where John Lister stood down as Hon. Treasurer. With the AAA of England declining to bail out the financially ailing BAF its future looked bleak, the accounts showing a deficit of £324,000 in 1996, and there was a further shock when Peter Radford announced his resignation in January 1997. In July 1997 former world 5000m record holder Dave Moorcroft was appointed the new Chief Executive ... but within days of his beginning work in October he had to announce the devastating news that BAF had been placed in the hands of the administrators after declaring a substantial cash shortfall which included payments of £860,000 yet to be made to athletes who had competed in BAF meetings.

An interim body, UK Athletics 98, was set up with £300,000 of funding from the UK Sports Council to act as agents for the administrators managing the affairs of BAF, while a steering group, chaired by Sir Chris Chataway (the former world 5000m record holder), identified the needs of a new governing body. In May 1998 UK Athletics 98 was able to announce that agreement had been reached with the administrators of BAF over the ownership of the sport's commercial rights and with the AAA of England to ensure that the AAA Championships would be held as a combined UK Trials event for at least the next four years. It was also revealed that Fast Track, a new company formed by former European and Commonwealth 400m hurdles champion Alan Pascoe, had been appointed to stage televised events and seek sponsors for British athletics. In July 1998 the AAA of England announced its backing for the new proposals.

A brochure entitled "A new future for athletics in the UK" was distributed to more than 1600 affiliated athletic clubs and associations, setting out the structure and aims of the new organisation, and later in the year UK Athletics 98 received an overwhelming vote of confidence following the most extensive review conducted by any sport within Britain with 97% of the clubs which took part voting in favour of the proposals. Clubs were invited also to vote for President of the new governing body with 1968 Olympic 400m hurdles champion David Hemery the winner. As the year ended, Dave Moorcroft was appointed Chief Executive Officer of UK Athletics, which came into existence in January 1999. The future looked bright with a lucrative BBC television contract worth £17.5 million over four years and increasing lottery funding for top athletes. That summer CGU Insurance (which merged with Norwich Union in 2000) and UKA announced a new four year £10 million sponsorship package, which not only provided title sponsorship for all the major British meetings (including the AAA Championships) but included investment in a broad range of grassroots and development initiatives. Meanwhile the AAA of England retained its healthy financial situation, the accounts presented to the AGM in February 1999 indicating a surplus of £1,150,945.

The decade saw the sport at the elite level become openly professional at last. The trust fund arrangement was disbanded and athletes via their agents could be paid whatever they could earn in prize money, bonuses, sponsorship, advertising and promotional deals. There was big money available. In 1999, for example, Kenya's Joyce Chepchumba collected a total of $230,000 for winning the London Marathon in a world best for a women-only race (plus a substantial appearance fee); and Wilson Kipketer of Denmark and Gabriela Szabo of Romania shared a million dollar jackpot in the IAAF's Golden League. On a more modest level, it was announced in 1997 that 196 British athletes of a certain standard would share in £2.6 million of subsistence grants via Performance Athlete Services (PAS) from the government's Lottery Sports Fund.

During the 1990s two British women athletes reached the dizzy heights of becoming true global champions.

The first, at the 1991 World Championships in Tokyo, was Liz McColgan, who front-ran her way to 10,000m victory in 31:14.31. It was Liz at her uncompromising best. In hot and humid conditions she flung down the gauntlet right from the start with an opening kilometre of 3:02.95 and gradually the field of 25 fell by the wayside. Before halfway (15:34.15) even such formidable rivals as Ingrid Kristiansen of Norway and Lynn Jennings (USA) were out of contention. Just one athlete doggedly held on, 20-year-old Derartu Tulu who was then on the threshold of one of the most successful careers in distance running history. With 3000m to go the Ethiopian briefly got past Liz in order to slow it down and make it a sprint finish, but the canny Scot was having none of that and eventually Tulu faded to eighth place.

One year later Sally Gunnell became Olympic 400m hurdles champion, and here is how she described that experience when interviewed by the author of this book for *Athletics Today* a few weeks after her triumph in Barcelona:

"I had a certain amount of confidence beforehand, and was talking about medals, but as I went through the heats and semis that's when I realised I could win. I was lucky; I had the easier semi for sure, had a good run [53.78] and was given the best lane [three with Sandra Farmer-Patrick of USA in four] for the final. I was really quite calm for the final. I was quite surprised; I thought I would be a nervous wreck. The race that I ran was one of the races that I had been running in my mind, so it just went to plan. I ran fifteens to hurdle six, changed down at seven and then sixteens home. It was the first time I had ever managed that.

"I remember going down the back straight thinking 'okay, I haven't lost too much on Sandra, I'm in a good position.' Then my next thought was coming off the eighth hurdle, being level almost and realising that a lot of people had said to me that if I could be up there at the eighth hurdle it was mine on the way home. That gave me a lot of positive thought and I just concentrated so hard down the home straight. I ran very conservatively at the beginning just to keep my energy for the last part of the race. So many people went off so fast and that's why, apart from Sandra [53.69] and I [53.23], the times were very slow. They all hammered it out.

"I really stretched for the last hurdle. Last year I had a negative thought at that stage, but this time I was so determined and had run it so often in my mind that I was going to get there. I was still running scared, waiting for Sandra to come up, but I was just as determined that she wasn't going to be able to. Technically, it was my best race. All the way around that lap of honour I just couldn't believe I had done it. It was like being in a dream world."

Both McColgan (32:23.56) and Gunnell (55.38) had started the decade on a high note, winning at the Commonwealth Games in Auckland early in 1990 along with Diane Edwards in the 800m (2:00.25), Kay Morley in the 100m hurdles (Welsh record of 12.91), Myrtle Augee in the shot (18.48m), Tessa Sanderson in the javelin (65.72m) and the England 4x400m relay team of Angela Piggford, Jenny Stoute, Gunnell and Linda Keough (3:28.08), but the European Championships in Split later that year yielded only one gold medallist: Yvonne Murray at 3000m (8:43.06). Yvonne was among the medal favourites at 3000m at the 1991 World Championships and launched her strike with over a lap to go, only to crumble in the closing stages and finish a distressed tenth. She suffered a similar fate at the following year's Olympics, fading from first to eighth in the last 600m, but better days for the Scot were ahead. A superb front running display in Toronto in 1993 saw her become the first British woman to win a World Indoor title, clocking 8:50.55 for a 12 sec winning margin. In 1994 she finished second to Ireland's Sonia O'Sullivan in the European Championships (8:36.48), overtaken with 200m remaining, and went on to succeed Liz McColgan as Commonwealth 10,000m champion (31:56.97) in only her second race at the distance. Yvonne ended her distinguished track career in 1999 with gold medals to her name from the European Championships (indoors and out), World Indoors and Commonwealth Games, plus Olympic bronze.

THE WORLD'S BEST AT 10,000 METRES

When Liz McColgan ground down the opposition to win the 1991 World 10,000m title Brendan Foster described it as "the greatest performance by a male or female British athlete in the history of long distance running." That run proved to be the summit of her career, but she made several other ascents to the upper slopes of athletic greatness including an Olympic silver medal, a World half marathon championship, two Commonwealth titles, a world indoor record, world bests on the road and marathon victories in London and New York.

CHRISTINE OHURUOGU has good reason to smile ... she has just won the 2008 Olympic 400m, the first Briton to triumph in that event since Eric Liddell back in 1924.

JOICE MADUAKA, aged 35, wins her final national 100m title in 2009, 11 years after her first

TASHA DANVERS provided one of the major surprises of the 2008 Olympics in Beijing by taking the bronze medal in the 400m hurdles with her fastest ever time of 53.84

*KELLY SOTHERTON makes a good start to the heptathlon at the 2006
Commonwealth Games in Melbourne. She won the contest with 6396 points*

NICOLA SANDERS was a brilliant winner of the 2007 European Indoor 400m title in Birmingham, clocking 50.02, and later that year was second in the World Championships in 49.65

GOLDIE SAYERS, the national javelin champion for the past ten years running and throwing better than ever in 2012

JO JACKSON has rewritten the UK record book in walking and here she strides towards the Commonwealth Games 20km title in Delhi in 2010

LISA DOBRISKEY during the 2009 World Championships 1500m in Berlin where she finished an exultant if frustrated runner-up, just 1/100th of a second behind the winner

JO PAVEY winning the UK 10,000m title in 2010 – 22 years after becoming WAAA 800m and 1500m champion in the Junior Girls category!

HELEN CLITHEROE was aged 37 when she produced the finest victory of her long career, lifting the 2011 European Indoor 3000m title in Paris

Pole vaulter HOLLY BLEASDALE has made a rapid advance to elite world class status. She improved from 4.35m in 2010 to UK records and world age-19 bests of 4.70m and 4.71m (indoors) in 2011, while in 2012 she moved up to 4.87m indoors

HANNAH ENGLAND was as shocked (delightedly so) as anyone when she grabbed the 1500m silver medal at the 2011 World Championships in Daegu

JENNY MEADOWS in action at the 2009 World Championships in Berlin where she captured the bronze medal at 800m in her best time of 1:57.93

JESSICA ENNIS was one of the stars of the British athletics team at the 2012 Olympics. Here she celebrates a clearance of 1.86 in the high jump on her way to a British record total of 6955

PERRI SHAKES-DRAYTON, winner of an unprecedented 400m and 400m hurdles double at the 2011 UK Championships

TIFFANY PORTER, here winning the silver medal at 60m hurdles at the 2012 World Indoor Championships, had become UK record holder for 100m hurdles the previous year with 12.56

JODIE WILLIAMS – one of Britain's brightest ever prospects – was World Youth 100m & 200m champion in 2009, World Junior 100m champion in 2010, European Junior 100m & 200m champion in 2011

Liz Lynch didn't exactly set the world alight as a youngster. The skinny girl from Dundee, where she was born on May 24 1964, had best times of 4:25.9 for 1500m and 9:34.5 for 3000m as a junior, but after three years on athletic scholarships in the USA she was ready for an international breakthrough. That came at the 1986 Commonwealth Games in Edinburgh where she won the 10,000m in the Commonwealth record time of 31:41.42. A member of Dundee Hawkhill Harriers, Liz finished second in the 1987 World Cross Country Championship, yet demonstrated great speed to clock 4:01.38 for 1500m, while at that year's World Championships – despite her feet being severely blistered – she lowered the Commonwealth record to 31:19.82 in fifth place. She married Northern Ireland steeplechase record holder Peter McColgan in October 1987.

Her ambition to become Olympic 10,000m champion in Seoul started to look more realistic when, in July 1988, she improved her Commonwealth record to 31:06.99. With 13 laps to go in the Olympic final, Liz took the lead, intent on burning off the opposition. With her body stooped, elbows working furiously, she ploughed on remorselessly and with a kilometre left only one woman – the USSR's Olga Bondarenko – remained in contention. It was with 200m remaining that Bondarenko launched her kick and in the space of that final half lap she drew 20m clear with Liz a gallant second in 31:08.44. "Next time it will definitely be gold," she declared. She was as good as her word, for she did indeed strike gold in the next global 10,000m championship, but that was three years away in Tokyo. There were other notable happenings on the way. At the 1989 World Indoor Championships she smashed the world indoor 3000m record with 8:34.80, but still got beaten into second place. One week later she posted the world's fastest road 10km time of 30:38. In January 1990 she retained her Commonwealth 10,000m title and in November 1990 she gave birth to daughter Eilish, who would in 2011 become Scottish steeplechase record holder. Just 119 days after becoming a mother she finished third in the World Cross Country Championship, followed by a UK half marathon best of 69:15 and a Commonwealth 10,000m record of 30:57.07. Everything came together brilliantly in Tokyo, and a couple of months later she lined up for the 1991 New York Marathon. The previous weekend she had sharpened up with a world 5km road best of 14:57 and she swept to victory in 2:27:32, at that time easily the fastest ever debut marathon.

She made a terrific start to Olympic year by winning the 1992 Tokyo Half Marathon in a world best of 67:11 and setting a world indoor 5000m record of 15:03.17, but at the Barcelona Games she struggled to finish fifth in 31:26.11. Medical tests revealed she had been suffering from anaemia for the past six months. After taking iron tablets she regained top form to become World half marathon champion. Injuries took an increasing toll for the remainder of her career, but in 1996 she won the London Marathon in 2:27:54. It looked as though she would prevail again in the 1997 edition, but Kenya's Joyce Chepchumba nipped past in the last few strides with Liz running her fastest ever time of 2:26:52. As well as giving birth to three sons she continued to race spasmodically and, in her 40th year (2004), she won Scottish titles at cross country and indoor 3000m!

SALLY GUNNELL WON EVERY HONOUR

It was touch and go whether Sally Gunnell, born in Chigwell (Essex) on July 29 1966, took up athletics seriously at all. At school she was equally into gymnastics and it was only when a friend plumped for athletics that she decided to follow suit. At 11 she joined Essex Ladies and it was as a long jumper that she achieved her first successes: she was WAAA and English Schools Junior champion in 1980. Her development was swift and in 1983 she set a UK age-16 heptathlon best of 5564. She improved to 5680, for an age-17 best in 1984, but by then the 100m hurdles was her strongest event. She set a UK junior record of 13.30 and two years later was crowned Commonwealth champion.

Coach Bruce Longden realised Sally wasn't ever going to be a world beater at 100m hurdles and persuaded her to try a low-key 400m hurdles race in 1987. Although she hadn't trained

*for it she won in 59.9 and the following summer she became
a top class exponent. Indoors she broke Verona Elder's UK
400m record with 51.77 while outdoors her results included
UK records in both hurdling events: 12.82 and 55.00. At the
Seoul Olympics she improved to 54.03 in fifth place. Sally
won the 1989 European Indoor 400m title in 52.04 and the
1990 Commonwealth Games saw her come away with two
golds and a silver. She won her speciality event in 55.38, kept
her hand in as a sprint hurdler by finishing second (13.12)
and ran third leg for the victorious England 4x400m relay
team.*

*Within the space of four days in 1991 she twice broke her UK
record with victories in Monaco (53.78) and Zürich (53.62),
and at the World Championships in Tokyo she came so very
close to snatching the title. Tatyana Ledovskaya of Belarus
scraped home in 53.11 while Sally's Commonwealth record
time of 53.16 was the third quickest ever. Later she was
timed at a spectacular 49.46 for the third leg in the 4x400m
relay, the team finishing fourth with a UK record of 3:22.01.
The build-up towards the Barcelona Olympics of 1992 did
not go as smoothly as hoped, but after a good run in the
semis (53.78) she realised she could win the gold medal –
which she achieved in a time of 53.23 after a great duel
with the Jamaican-born American, Sandra Farmer-Patrick.
A bronze medal in the 4x400m relay followed, and, as if
all that was not enough excitement for one year, Sally was
married two months later to 1:48.40 800m runner Jon Bigg.
In 1993 she created further history by becoming world
record holder. She went undefeated up to and including the
World Championships in Stuttgart, where she was involved
in another titanic battle with Farmer-Patrick. Victory went
to Sally, 52.74 to 52.79, with both inside the world record.
Again there was another medal to come in the relay, where
Sally ran 49.90 on the anchor leg, and she was voted world
female athlete of the year.*

*More honours came her way in 1994 with victories in the
Goodwill Games (53.51), European Championships (53.33),
Commonwealth Games (54.51) and World Cup (54.80). She
thus joined Daley Thompson and Linford Christie as the*

only athletes to complete the grand slam of titles: Olympic, World, European and Commonwealth. She was busy in relays, too, clocking her fastest ever split of 49.45 in the Europeans and anchoring England and Britain to victory in the Commonwealth Games and World Cup respectively.

At 28 she felt she could still improve, but her medal winning days were now at an end. Although in 1996 she ran 54.65 to win the AAA hurdles title she pulled up injured in Lausanne and broke down again in her Olympic semi in Atlanta. Sally's final season of 1997 was also thwarted by injury but she retired with a strong claim to being considered the most successful British woman athlete of all time.

Another major player during the 1990s, but one who would reach a fabulous peak in the following decade, was Kelly Holmes. A former English Schools 1500m champion and junior international who quit the sport when she joined the Army at 17, she was motivated to make a comeback after watching an old schoolgirl rival, Lisa York, running in the 1992 Olympics. Her return to the track in 1993 was nothing short of sensational. Corporal Holmes won the AAA 800m title and broke Diane Modahl's English record with 1:58.64 when narrowly failing to reach the final of the World Championships. In 1994 she revealed her qualities also over 1500m, defeating Yvonne Murray in an epic and very fast AAA final in 4:01.41, and won her first major medal – silver – at the European Championships (4:19.30), clocking around 57 sec for the last lap. Her finishing speed was evident also at that year's Commonwealth Games where a 59.6 final lap brought her victory in 4:08.86.

Now promoted to sergeant, she enjoyed another great season in 1995, lowering the English record to 1:57.56 when winning the AAA title, creating a Commonwealth 1000m record of 2:32.82 and bagging two medals at the World Championships: silver in the 1500m (4:03.04) followed by bronze in the 800m where her time of 1:56.95 was a Commonwealth record. She reduced that to 1:56.21 when finishing second to Maria Mutola of Mozambique at the IAAF Grand Prix Final. Injuries ruined her medal chances at the 1996 Olympics but despite suffering from a hairline fracture of the lower left leg she courageously placed fourth in the 800m (1:58.81) and led for three laps of the 1500m before the pain overwhelmed her and she dropped to 11th in 4:07.46. She was even more unfortunate in 1997. After setting a Commonwealth record of 3:58.07, featuring a 59.69 last lap, she was favourite for the World title but again she was jinxed by serious injury and ended up walking in tears to the finish line in her heat. It was not until 2000 that she was able to reclaim her place among the world's elite.

Another working her way towards future Olympic glory was heptathlete Denise Lewis. She made a dramatic entry into world class at the 1994 Commonwealth Games. Lying third after the first day, she rocketed into the lead thanks to a monumental javelin throw of 53.68m (her previous best was 48.58m!) and held on in the 800m to win the title with 6325 points – 256 more than her previous highest score. That ranked her a distant second on the UK all-time list behind Birchfield clubmate Judy Simpson's 6623 in 1986, but in Götzis in 1996 she took over as UK record holder with 6645. She threw the javelin only 47.86m on that occasion but her prowess with the spear brought her an Olympic medal later that summer in Atlanta. Only eighth after five events, a timely personal best of 54.82m took her up to third, and her final score of 6489 was good enough for bronze. She set a Commonwealth record of 6736 in 1997 and claimed the silver medal at that year's World Championships with 6654, while in 1998 she became European champion (6559) and retained her Commonwealth Games laurels (6513). She maintained her formidable consistency by winning another World Championships silver medal in 1999 (6724) ... but even better was still to come.

It was a good decade also for the 4x400m relay team with victories for England at the 1990 and 1994 Commonwealth Games and silver in 1998. Bronze medals for the British squad were obtained at the 1990 European Championships (3:24.78), 1992 Olympics (3:24.23), 1993 World Championships (3:23.41) and 1997 Europeans (3:25.66), while a UK record of 3:22.01 was established when finishing fourth in the 1991 World Championships. Fastest splits were 49.45 and 49.46 by Sally

Gunnell, 49.71 by Linda Keough, 50.1 by Phylis Smith and 50.2 by the 1991 European Junior champion Donna Fraser. On the individual plane, Phylis was the highest achiever with eighth place in the 1992 Olympic final after clocking 50.40 in her semi, for second to Kathy Cook on the UK all-time list, and a bronze medal in the 1994 Europeans. Allison Curbishley won the European Under-23 (50.85) and World University Games (50.84) titles in 1997 and set a Scottish record of 50.71 for second place at the 1998 Commonwealth Games, but a persistent knee injury prevented her from fulfilling her potential at 400m and 400m hurdles. Meanwhile, Katharine Merry, so precocious and versatile that in 1987 she topped the UK Under-13 lists in eight events and first represented Britain when she was 13, was maturing nicely. She became European Junior 200m champion in 1993, completed a AAA sprint double the next year and took the 1999 AAA 400m title in a championship record of 50.62, thus becoming only the third athlete, after Nellie Halstead and Kathy Cook, to win titles at all three distances. Later in the season she moved to second on the UK all-time list with a 50.21 clocking in her semi at the World Championships, finishing fifth in the final in 50.52.

Although Liz McColgan continued to be a major force throughout the 1990s, her UK 10,000m record would eventually be demolished by Paula Radcliffe, who first made a name for herself internationally as a schoolgirl by winning the World Junior Cross Country title on a snow-covered Boston course in 1992. She finished five seconds ahead of Wang Junxia, the Chinese who just the following year would set stunning (and, in the eyes of many, unbelievable) world records of 8:06.11 for 3000m and 29:31.78 for 10,000m, times still unapproached nearly 20 years later. Paula's progress was far more measured and credible. At the 1993 World Championships, aged 19, she clocked a 3000m personal best of 8:40.40 in seventh place; in 1995 she finished fifth in the World Championships 5000m, as she did also in the 1996 Olympics, the year she became UK record holder with 14:46.76. She placed a close second to Derartu Tulu in the 1997 World Cross Country, while in that year's World Championships she was fourth at 5000m after leading at the bell. Paula moved up successfully to 10,000m in 1998, setting a UK record of 30:48.58 as well as clocking a world best 24:54 for 5 miles on the road, and ending the year as European cross country champion. Her steady progression continued in 1999. She posted Commonwealth records of 8:27.40 for 3000m, 14:43.54 for 5000m and 30:27.13 for 10,000m, the latter when finishing second to Ethiopia's Gete Wami at the World Championships after having led most of the way in 30°C+ heat. She also lowered her world best for 5 miles to 24:47. Her sensational marathon career was still for the future.

There were other distance performers of note. Jill Hunter followed her silver medal in the 1990 Commonwealth Games 10,000m with world road bests of 51:41 for 10 miles and 1:24:26 for 25km as well as an English 10,000m record of 31:07.88 the year after. Andrea Wallace, who had only taken up running three years earlier, was silver medallist, one second behind the winner, in the 1991 World 15km championship, and 6ft (1.83m) tall Marian Sutton won the prestigious Chicago Marathon in 1996 and 1997. Notable also was the exploit of 42-year-old Sandra Brown who in 1991 set a world best of 4:50:51 for the 50km walk, finishing eighth in the men's RWA national championship. Sandra was still winning national titles at 100 miles in 2011 at age 62!

No athlete had more of a rollercoaster of an international career than triple jumper Ashia Hansen. The UK record holder since 1994, she failed to reach the final at that year's European Championships, indoors or out, and at the 1995 World Championships, while she came last or almost last at the 1996 European Indoors, 1999 World Championships and 2000 Olympics, and didn't even get to the World Championships of 2003 and 2005 or the 2004 Olympics. A failed international athlete, right? Wrong, because the same athlete proved herself one of the world's greatest exponents of the event with victories in the 1998 European Indoors (with a spectacular world indoor record of 15.16m), 1998 Commonwealth Games (14.32m), 1999 World Indoors (15.02m),. 2002 Commonwealth Games (14.86m) and Europeans (wind assisted 15.00m) and 2003 World Indoors (15.01m). Who knows what more she would have achieved but for a seemingly endless series of injuries.

Born in the USA, adopted at the age of three months by a British woman and her Ghanaian husband, Ashia came to Britain from Ghana when she was eight. As a schoolgirl athlete she started off, without success, as an 800m/1500m runner before switching to the sprints, high jump and long jump (she was a junior international in 1989) before discovering that the triple jump was her forte, although her best distance in her first year at the event, 1990, was hardly earth-shattering at 10.84m. She surpassed 12m in 1991, 13m in 1992, 14m in 1994 and – coached by former UK record holder Aston Moore – 15m in 1997 when she jumped 15.15m to become the first woman to rank among the British men's top twenty in a standard "Olympic" event.

Ironically, a British-born jumper achieved even greater distinction than Ashia ... but her senior medals were won wearing Italy's national colours. Representing Britain, Fiona May was the 1987 European Junior and 1988 World Junior long jump champion but it wasn't until she had opted for Italy (she married Gianni Iapachino, that country's national pole vault record holder, in 1993) that she really made her mark. She became World champion in 1995, Olympic silver medallist in 1996 (behind the recently reinstated drugs offender, Chioma Ajunwa of Nigeria, who in 2002 was banned for life after failing another doping test), World Indoor champion in 1997 and was second in the 1999 World Championships, overtaken by a final round effort from Spain's Niurka Montalvo that Fiona insisted was a foul. However, she won back the World title in 2001. Fiona's legal personal best of 7.11m in 1998 is far beyond Shara Proctor's UK record of 6.95m, while her 14.65m triple jump that year is also – remembering Ashia Hansen's place of birth – easily the longest by a British-born athlete. The one that got away ...

The decade saw the death of so many distinguished figures in the history of British women's athletics, including the two most influential and long serving officials in Marea Hartman and Vera Searle.

Made a Dame in the New Year's Honours List of 1994 for her services to the sport, Marea died of cancer in August of that year, aged 74. John Rodda, in his obituary for *The*

Guardian, wrote: "There are those who believe she held on to office too long and stood up for what ultimately was the losing cause of trying to keep women's athletics separate from the men's. Certainly the development of women's track and field suffered in Britain from this insularity and the struggle for change through the seventies and eighties became wearying. Marea Hartman eventually turned into a supporter of the new way forward, and the sport recognised her long and unstinting contribution by making her the first President of the AAA of England. She had a jolly, florid personality and her permanent smile had a way of winning points at the negotiating table. In team management, she was a firm but gentle disciplinarian."

The Times' appreciation included this paragraph describing her qualities as team manager: "It has been remarked of her that her personality was a cross between 'that of a favourite great aunt and the Queen Mother'. Certainly, the range of qualities implied by both these descriptions was necessary to maintain discipline among teams of young women competing – as well as enjoying themselves – in often exotic climates, far from home. One moment she might find herself having to be severe to a young charge who had become addicted to nights on the tiles to the extent that her performance on the track or in the field was threatened. At another she might well have to produce a large handkerchief to stem floods of tears – the result perhaps of homesickness or a broken heart."

Sir Arthur Gold paid this tribute in *The Independent*: "Marea Hartman was one of the longest serving and most influential people in athletics, an internationally respected figure, and Chairman for 13 years of the Women's Commission of the IAAF. And all her work for the sport was carried out in a purely honorary capacity, without remuneration. As Honorary Secretary of the WAAA, she was effectively the Honorary Chief Executive for women's athletics in the whole of Britain, her duties including the organising of the annual WAAA Championships, both indoors and out. As Honorary Treasurer of the BAAB, she found sponsors for BAAB international meetings and organised fund-raising. We served together on the BAAB and I found her support as a council member invaluable; she always emphasised the importance of correct behaviour in athletics, and campaigned against the use of performance-enhancing drugs. She took a Corinthian approach to the present-day professional aura of sport. For her, sport remained a recreation rather than a source of income. Marea was a white-haired, smiling figure and was known throughout the athletics world for her taste for Campari and soda, her favourite drink. She was too sick to attend the Commonwealth Games in Canada ... but was as alert and as concerned as ever at all that was going on in the sport she loved, and to which she gave so much."

Vera Searle, whose favourite tipple was a daily pint of Guinness (not to mention cigar!), lived to a much greater age. She was 97 when she passed away in September 1998. Seventy years earlier she led the British boycott of the Amsterdam Olympics, the first to feature women's athletics. "We strongly object to the mixing up of men and women in the Olympic Games or at any other meeting," she proclaimed. "If this actually happened it would kill our movement, and we should be absorbed by the men as in other countries. In England we have nothing to do with the AAA; we are entirely a separate body."

Pat Green, then Chairman of the North of England AA, wrote of her: "Vera Searle was the very foundation of women's athletics in this country. She represented Great Britain in the 1920s and held the world record for 250m. Vera, along with Marea Hartman and Nelson Neal, was the hub of the WAAA in the 50s, 60s, 70s and 80s. Vera was an indomitable character and the world of women's athletics has much to thank her for."

Maureen Smith, the 1958 WAAA mile champion and a long serving official who became President of the English Cross Country Association, made reference to Vera being "one of the six founder members of the original Women's Vets [Maureen being one of the others], encouraging women to return to the sport after marriage or babies, knowing that when she married she had to train and sometimes compete in secret because it was thought not ladylike. She was, of course, one of the great leaders of the Women's Cross Country Association. Vera loved her sport and was a track referee, giving lectures and encouraging us to put something back into our sport by taking up officiating. She backed women's athletics to the hilt and did not believe the amalgamation of women's athletics would work." Vera Duerdin recalled that Mrs Searle was always there to give advice. "I was immensely grateful to her for the invaluable help she was able to give from her vast knowledge and experience. No time was ever the wrong time to ask questions and the answers were always in the best interest of women's athletics."

Other notable figures who died during the decade included celebrated coach and TV commentator Ron Pickering (husband of the former Jean Desforges), the much loved officials Mabel Cotton and Tallie Swallow, pioneering sprinter Baroness (Elaine) Burton and the world record breaking Nellie Halstead in 1991; miling great Anne Smith in 1993; journalist, coach and persistent amalgamation campaigner Cliff Temple in 1994; 1922 WAAA 100 yards champion Nora Callebout in 1995, aged 99; long jump record breaker Muriel Cornell and coach/author George Pallett in 1996; sprint star Val Peat, UK shot and discus record breaker Bevis Shergold and successful high jump coach Ron Murray in 1997; *Athletics Weekly* founder and long-time editor Jimmy Green in 1998; pre-war Olympian Violet Webb (Janet Simpson's mother) and the first 5ft high jumper Phyllis Green in 1999. That year also saw the tragic death of 24-year-old Sophia Smith, an 11.49/23.57 sprinter who had finished third at 200m in the 1993 European Junior Championships.

In addition to Marea Hartman being made a Dame in the 1994 New Year's Honours List, others to receive awards during the decade were: (CBE): Mary Peters 1990; (OBE): Joan Allison 1995, Tessa Sanderson 1998 & Sally Gunnell 1998; (MBE): Yvonne Murray 1991, Liz McColgan 1992, Edith Holland (WAAA Hon. Treasurer for 28 years) 1992, Kelly Holmes 1998 & Denise Lewis 1999.

The award to Joan Allison (née Page) was not so much for her achievements on the track (1970 and 1974 Commonwealth Games 1500m silver medallist and UK mile record breaker) as for her admirable work in team management. After Marea Hartman had bowed out as team leader in 1978 the BAAB decided on a policy of appointing relatively recently retired internationals as manager of the British women's squad, a move which proved very popular with the active athletes. The 1972 Olympic pentathlon champion Mary Peters was the women's team manager at the 1980 and 1984 Olympics; Pam Piercy, fourth in the 1966 European Championships 800m, took over in 1985 (with Joan Allison as her assistant) and managed the women at the 1988 Olympics; and she in turn was succeeded by Joan, who was in charge at the 1990 Europeans and 1991 World Championships as well as working full-time as General Administrator of the International Athletes' Club. She was such a success that after the tragically early death of Les Jones in March 1992 she was promoted by BAF to manage the entire British athletics team at the Barcelona Olympics, an historic breakthrough.

Interviewed by Gwenda Ward, Joan said: "The job has changed beyond recognition since I took part in the 1968 and 1972 Olympics. Then we hardly saw management, now we are with an athlete from the moment they wake on competition day, which in Split [1990 Europeans] for instance often had to be 5.30 am." In April 1992, after her new appointment as overall manager, she remarked: "It is an important step forward for women in the sport that I've been given this position and I'll continue to fight for them as I have done in the past." In an interview with Bob Frank in *Athletics Weekly* in August 1993, shortly after her final engagement, the World Championships, she explained: "I think my strength is relating to and understanding athletes; my empathy with the athletes having been one myself. It's knowing when to talk and when to stand back."

Joan's assistant, from 1989, was Verona Elder, three times European Indoor 400m champion in the 1970s with 71 GB appearances to her name, a record subsequently surpassed by Judy Oakes. Verona was appointed women's team manager in 1992 and took over as overall team manager in 1994, continuing through to the 1996 Olympics. She in turn was succeeded by 1978 Commonwealth Games 100m hurdles champion Lorna Boothe.

*Highlights from each of the AAA/WAAA Championships
meetings 1990–1999*

1990 (Birmingham)

THREE OF THE "golden oldies" of British athletics added to their haul of titles at the Panasonic AAA/WAAA Championships. Judy Oakes (18.63m), who had set an indoor championship best of 18.55m when chalking up her 20th WAAA title, made it 21 – her tenth victory outdoors. In the process she soundly beat Myrtle Augee (17.91m), who at the Commonwealth Games in Auckland at the start of the year had, for the first time in her career, defeated Judy, 18.48m to 18.43m. Tessa Sanderson, whose 65.72m javelin victory in Auckland was supposedly her final competition, threw a modest 58.42m for her eighth title since 1975, while Chris Cahill (née Boxer) became 1500m champion (4:12.54) again, 13 years after her first WAAA 800m win. Apart from Tessa, the only athlete to retain her title in Birmingham was Betty Sworowski, who despite the hot weather broke her championship record in the 5000m walk with 22:23.35. This was another notable year for the walkers with UK records being set by Betty (12:49.16 3000m and 21:50 road 5km), Lisa Langford (21:57.68 5000m) and Julie Drake (45:53.9 10,000m). Bidding for a record fifth consecutive 100m title, Paula Thomas (née Dunn) had to settle for second to Stephanie Douglas (11.38w). Unnoticed in seventh place, in 11.71, was a 17-year-old Australian by the name of Cathy Freeman. Ten years later she would deliver a nation's Olympic dream. The most surprising winner was Lesley-Ann Skeete (13.03) in the 100m hurdles, who finished 0.02 ahead of Wales' Commonwealth champion, Yorkshire-born Kay Morley. Youngest winner was Welsh-born Lea Haggett (18), who high jumped 1.88m – a height she would replicate a week later for a bronze medal in the World Junior Championships where London schoolgirl Diane Smith became, at 15, one of the youngest ever champions. She clocked a personal best and championship record of 23.10 for 200m but her career was a brief one. Beset by medical problems, she retired the next year.

Official History of the WAAA

1991 (Birmingham)

THE FASTEST WOMAN ever to compete in the Championships, former 100m world record holder and 1984 Olympic champion Evelyn Ashford (USA), broke Andrea Lynch's championship record with 11.19 in her semi and reduced that to 11.15 in the final, three metres clear of the first British finisher, defending champion Stephanie Douglas ... who this time won the 200m in 23.37. Another American winner was Maicel Malone, with 50.89 in the 400m. That was a championship record, as were Yvonne Murray's 8:46.47 3000m and Evette Finikin's UK triple jump record of 13.46m. In fifth place, 7cm below her personal best of 12.68m, was a 19-year-old novice at the event of whom much more would be heard ... Ashia Hansen. Another 19-year-old with quite a future, Denise Lewis, placed 14th in the long jump (5.83m), won by Fiona May with 6.58m. Denise was rather more successful at the European Junior Championships where she placed fifth in the heptathlon with a score of 5476. At those Championships in Thessaloniki, Donna Fraser won the 400m in 52.54, Keri Maddox the 100m hurdles in 13.39 and Yinka Idowu the long jump with 6.60m. The WAAA sprint hurdles title reverted to Sally Gunnell in 13.02, and in her absence the 400m hurdles was won for a second year by Gowry Retchakan, a former Sri Lanka international (though born in London), whose time of 55.67 had only ever been surpassed among British athletes by Gunnell. Judy Oakes collected her 11th outdoor shot title with a distance of 18.24m. At the end of the season she announced her retirement but, happily, she had second thoughts and would continue to dominate British shot putting for many more years. By the time she did retire for good at age 41 she had won 17 WAAA/AAA outdoor titles between 1979 and 2000 and was a record breaker indoors too with 18 championship victories between 1977 and 2000.

Earlier in the year, at the final AAA/WAAA Indoor Championships to be held at RAF Cosford, the much appreciated but somewhat geographically remote venue since 1965, the star performer was Swiss-born Debbie Marti, who back in 1984 had high jumped 1.89m for a UK junior record at

192

16 to qualify for the Olympic team, only to be passed over on the grounds that she was too young. She was unable to progress for several years after contracting the ME virus, and came close to retiring, but at Cosford she cleared a resounding 1.94m to equal Diana Davies' UK indoor record. From 1992 until 2001 the meeting would be held each year in Birmingham's magnificently equipped National Indoor Arena.

1992 (Birmingham)

DESIGNATED THE AAA of England Championships, following the amalgamation of the AAA and WAAA, and incorporating the British Olympic Trials, this was a meeting full of suspense as athletes strove for selection for the Barcelona Games. Among those who succeeded was Tessa Sanderson, whose 63.26m throw was over eight metres better than her nearest British rival. She collected her ninth javelin title and qualified for her fifth Olympics, a British "record". She would go on to place fourth in Barcelona with 63.58m. Sally Gunnell, destined to become Olympic 400m hurdles champion a little over a month later, confined herself to the 100m hurdles, winning in 13.13. Britain's only other medal winners at the Games were the third placed 4x400m team of Phylis Smith, Sandra Douglas, Jenny Stoute and Gunnell. In Birmingham the first three named won their places by finishing third (51.36), fourth (51.83) and sixth (52.50) respectively in a final which featured four Australians and was won by Cathy Freeman in 51.14. Vera Nikolic's 1968 championship (and former world) 800m record fell at last to Diane Edwards (who became Mrs Modahl later that summer) with 2:00.41. Eliminated in her heat, in 2:06.1, was one Kelly Holmes. The best in-depth race was the 1500m where Yvonne Murray won in 4:05.87 ahead of Kirsty Wade (4:06.07) and Liz McColgan (4:07.68). National cross country champion Lisa York took the 3000m in 8:50.18 with World Junior cross country champion Paula Radcliffe – looking for a time of around 9:20 – smashing her personal best by 26 sec with 8:57.23 in fourth place. Later in the season Paula improved to 8:51.78 for fourth in the World Junior Championships. Other than in the 800m, the only other championship record was Vicky Lupton's 22:12.21 in the 5000m walk.

1993 (Birmingham)

INCORPORATING THE WORLD Championships Trials, the meeting featured one reigning Olympic champion in Sally Gunnell, who snatched her seventh and final 100m hurdles title in 13.08, and three future gold medallists in Australia's Cathy Freeman, whose 22.71 200m broke Kathy Cook's 1984 championship record; Kelly Holmes, winner of the 800m in 2:02.69; and Denise Lewis, third in the long jump. Another great star of the future, Ashia Hansen, had less pleasant memories as she was stretchered off after sustaining a leg injury in the triple jump, in which she placed third with 13.16m. She had earlier suffered misfortune at the Indoor Championships when an injury led her to fail to register a valid mark, Rachel Kirby (the indoor 200m champion in 1988) winning with a UK best of 13.52m. Two events made their bow as AAA championship events: Kate Staples, well known from her TV appearances as a Gladiator, won the pole vault with a modest 3.20m clearance, and the inaugural hammer champion was Australian junior Debbie Sosimenko with 56.86m. In second place was Esther Augee, who held the UK best with 56.76m but managed only 52.22m on this occasion. She was the elder sister of shot winner Myrtle. Third in the hammer with 51.76m was the woman who would in time become Britain's first world class exponent ... Lorraine Shaw. At this stage of her career the former Irish international was more adept with the discus, which she had thrown over 50m.

1994 (Sheffield)

COMMONWEALTH AND CHAMPIONSHIP records fell to Kate Staples (3.65m pole vault) and Michelle Griffith (14.08m triple jump) but the undoubted highlight of this KP-sponsored meeting, which incorporated Trials for the European Championships and Commonwealth Games, was the 1500m scrap between Kelly Holmes and Yvonne Murray. They fought stride for stride through 400m in 63.86, 800m in 2:08.44 and 1200m in 3:13.49 before Kelly prevailed by just 3/100ths in 4:01.41, breaking Zola Budd's 1986 championship record and unapproached at this meeting or its later equivalent since. Kelly, who had not run faster than 4:17.3 prior to 1994, shattered her personal best of 4:07.7 in a race against men in the Army Championships four days earlier, while Yvonne just missed her best of 4:01.20 dating from 1987. Both would go on to claim silver medals at the European Championships (at 1500m and 3000m respectively) and strike gold at the Commonwealth Games, Kelly at 1500m and Yvonne at 10,000m. Despite a dreadful start, Katharine Merry (19) won the 100m in a windy 11.27, her fastest ever time, and completed a sprint double with a personal best 200m time of 22.85. However, the top British sprinter of the year would prove to be 29-year-old Paula Thomas. Only fifth in the 100m and third in the 200m, she went on to finish third in the Commonwealth Games 100m (11.23) after clocking 11.15 in her semi for second place on the UK all-time list and fourth over 200m in another personal best of 22.69. There was a surprise in the 100m hurdles where slow starting Sally Gunnell couldn't quite catch 34-year-old international heptathlete Clova Court whose time of 13.04 was a personal best to set alongside such other sparkling marks as 23.57 for 200m and a javelin throw of 55.30m. No surprise at all was that Judy Oakes (36) reclaimed the shot title (18.38m), returning after a "retirement" of two and a half years. That was a UK veterans record, which she extended to 18.68m the following month, and at the Commonwealth Games she bagged another gold. Lorraine Shaw threw the hammer 59.58m, which would have been a UK record had she not registered 59.92m early in the season. Two youngsters who would develop into Olympic medallists many years later were starting to make an impression. Kelly Sotherton (17), who in 1992 had placed third in the AAA Under-17 long jump and fourth in the English Schools Intermediate 300m, switched events again to finish third in the English Schools Senior triple jump; while Tasha Danvers (16), coached by Judy Vernon, won both the English Schools Intermediate and AAA Under-17 300m hurdles titles for the second year running.

1995 (Birmingham)

AGAIN SGT KELLY Holmes was the star turn. Steaming through 200m in 28.67, 400m in 58.35 and 600m in 87.20, she left her nearest pursuer nearly five seconds behind as she set an English and championship 800m record of 1:57.56, so close to Kirsty Wade's UK figures of 1:57.42 – a record Kelly would lower first to 1:56.95 and then 1:56.21 later in the summer. In fifth place Paula Radcliffe clocked a lifetime best of 2:05.22. Another championship record fell in the hammer, Australian Debbie Sosimenko's distance of 65.24m being also a Commonwealth record, which she reclaimed from Lorraine Shaw who had thrown 64.90m the previous month. A routine shot put of 17.75m was enough to give Judy Oakes a two metre winning margin and a record 13th WAAA outdoor title. Other victories by athletes in their thirties were gained by Paula Thomas (11.48, her fifth 100m title since 1986), Yvonne Murray (4:11.47 1500m), Alison Wyeth (15:39.14 5000m) and Gowry Retchakan (57.18 400m hurdles, her fifth title in six years). Joice Maduaka, at 21, opened her championship medal account with bronze in the 200m won by Catherine Murphy (19) in a personal best of 23.40. Joice's final national medal – her 34th – would come in 2011 when she won the UK indoor 200m title! Melanie Neef, daughter of German-born Rangers goalkeeper Gerry Neef, retained her 400m title in 51.63. One of the best races was the 5000m walk, in which Lisa Langford (22:20.03) shook off Vicky Lupton (22:23.80) only over the final 300m, but it was Vicky who went on to set two UK records later in the season with an unratified 21:52.38 for 5000m and 45:18.8 for 10,000m. Interesting to note that among the also-rans in the 1500m heats were two 21-year-olds in Helen Pattinson (8th in 4:31.56) and Joanne Davis (7th in 4:36.10) – still gracing the international scene today as Helen Clitheroe and Jo Pavey.

1996 (Birmingham)

WITH OLYMPIC SELECTION at stake, the Securicor AAA Championships – at the request of the athletes themselves

– were restricted to competitors eligible to represent Britain, and attracted a capacity crowd of around 15,000 on the last of the three days of competition. For the third year running, it was Kelly Holmes who provided the highlight of the women's events. In the 800m she led through splits of 28.17, 58.64 and 88.62 for an unchallenged victory in 1:57.84. An emotional runner-up in 1:59.87 was Diane Modahl, contesting her first championship race since her reinstatement, and the pair took a joint lap of honour before an appreciative crowd. Next day, Kelly was back for the 1500m final, which she won by a country mile in 4:08.14 to complete the first such double since Diane Leather in 1957. Unhappily, injury would end her dreams of Olympic glory in Atlanta. Paula Radcliffe, who would finish fifth over 5000m in her Olympic debut, had almost 20 seconds to spare as she won her first AAA track title in 15:28.46. About a lap behind in ninth place was Mara Myers, who would become national cross country champion in 1998 and, under her married name of Mara Yamauchi, develop in 2009 into Britain's second fastest ever marathoner.

The closest race was the 100m hurdles with Angie Thorp the winner by 1/100th over 1993 European Junior champion Diane Allahgreen in 13.26, the slow time explained by a 2.3m/sec headwind. Angie later displayed her true worth by breaking Sally Gunnell's UK record with 12.80 in her Olympic semi-final. As for Sally, she won the 400m hurdles in a championship record of 54.65, raising hopes of a successful Olympic defence, but injury prevented her from even reaching the final in Atlanta. Vicky Lupton (23:04.57) regained the 5000m walk title, her 43-year-old mum, Brenda, finishing fourth! Top field event action included a world age 40 javelin best of 62.88m by Tessa Sanderson, claiming her tenth and final title over a 21-year period. She had only returned to competition the previous month after retiring in 1992 and she thus made her record sixth Olympic team. She improved her world veterans record to 64.06m but in Atlanta she fell short of qualifying for the final. Another evergreen, Judy Oakes (38), won the shot with 18.65m, and there were championship records by Ashia Hansen (14.25m triple jump), who would go on to place fourth in the inaugural Olympic event, and Debbie Marti with a 1.94m high jump. Denise Lewis, who turned out to be Britain's only female medallist in Atlanta with bronze in the heptathlon, won the long jump with 6.55m and finished third in the 100m hurdles.

1997 (Birmingham)

ALTHOUGH THE DOOMED British Athletic Federation controversially organised a separate British Championships meeting in July which included the selection trials for the World Championships, the AAA defiantly staged its View From-sponsored Championships in late August. That came after events in Athens where again Denise Lewis was Britain's sole female medallist with second place in the heptathlon although Paula Radcliffe went close with fourth in the 5000m after leading at the bell. With many of the leading lights opting to sit it out, this meeting – 75 years after the first WAAA championship events were staged – was a low-key occasion and there were very few top class performances. Pick of the bunch was the 1.90m high jump by Debbie Marti, who went close to succeeding at the UK record height of 1.96m. In February she had cleared 1.95m for a UK indoor record. The most prolific record breaker of the summer was Janine Whitlock; a vault of 3.80m sufficed for the title but she improved during the year to 4.23m. Meanwhile, Judy Oakes continued on her merry way, a shot put of 17.89m bringing her a 15th outdoor AAA title ... and there were more to come.

1998 (Birmingham)

NORMAL SERVICE WAS resumed at the Bupa AAA Championships, incorporating selection trials for the European Championships and Commonwealth Games. Denise Lewis, destined to win heptathlon gold medals at both those meetings, tuned up with a long jump victory (6.44m) plus fourth in the high jump (1.82m) and fifth in the 100m hurdles (13.73) and javelin (51.28m). Disappointingly, Denise (6559) would be the only individual female medallist at the Europeans in Budapest although Donna Fraser, Vicki Jamison, AAA 200m winner in 23.46 Katharine Merry and

400m champion in 50.92 Allison Curbishley did finish third in the 4x400m relay in 3:25.66, Katharine credited with a 50.4 split. Joice Maduaka won her first 100m title in 11.40 and Diane Modahl her last 800m championship in 2:02.73; Tasha Danvers (56.27), aged 20, and 38-year-old Gowry Retchakan (56.57) finished one-two in the 400m hurdles; Judy Oakes, now 40, continued her shot domination (17.82m); Shelley Drew threw the discus 60.82m for an English record; and Lisa Kehler (née Langford) was second in the 5000m walk to Ireland's Gillian O'Sullivan (21:52.68) with a UK record of 22:01.53. Lorraine Shaw, who had only resumed training in January following surgery to remove a disc from her back, won the hammer with 60.71m.

The Commonwealth Games in Kuala Lumpur proved a much happier hunting ground than Budapest for British athletes. In addition to Denise Lewis (6513) there were victories for Jo Wise (6.63m long jump), Ashia Hansen (14.32m triple jump) and Judy Oakes, whose 18.83m was her longest for two years. Silver medals were won by Allison Curbishley with a Scottish 400m record of 50.71, Kelly Holmes (4:06.10 1500m), Andrea Whitcombe (15:56.85 5000m), Gowry Retchakan (55.25 for a UK veterans record), Jo Jennings (1.91m high jump), Lorraine Shaw (62.66m hammer), Karen Martin (57.82m javelin) and the England 4x400m team (3:29.28), while bronze went to Donna Fraser (51.01 400m plus a 50.2 relay anchor), Diane Modahl (1:58.81 800m) and Lisa Kehler, whose 45:03 was a UK 10km road walk record.

1999 (Birmingham)

AS FAR AS most people were concerned, 1999 was the last year of the 20th century and these CGU World Trials & AAA Championships brought the millennium to a satisfactory close. Joice Maduaka completed the sprint double which had so narrowly eluded her the previous year, her times being 11.37 and 22.83. Katharine Merry, the last to accomplish that double in 1994, had now realised – under the coaching of Linford Christie – that her forte was the 400m and she won that title with a championship record of 50.62. Another easy winner was Kelly Holmes in the 800m (1:59.86), but the

1500m was a hotly contested race in which newly married Hayley Tullett (née Parry) from Wales ran 4:08.06 to hold off Helen Pattinson whose 4:08.71 was a personal best. Keri Maddox was only 2/100ths outside the championship record with her 12.97 100m hurdles although the following wind was just over the limit at 2.3m/sec. The previous day she had clocked her fastest time of 55.55 for second in the 400m hurdles behind Sinead Dudgeon's Scottish record of 55.24, with Tasha Danvers third in her best of 55.69. There were two championship records in the field: Janine Whitlock, fifth in the 200m in 23.30, pole vaulted 4.25m, while Kirsty Morrison threw the javelin 55.70m. That was a long way short of Fatima Whitbread's massive 72.96m from 1987 but the specification of the implement had been altered from April 1, with a change in the centre of gravity to avoid flat landings, and all previous records were scrapped. At season's end Karen Martin, second at the championships with 55.55m, was named inaugural UK record holder with 59.50m.

The World Championships in Seville yielded two silver medals: for Paula Radcliffe, whose time of 30:27.13 in the 10,000m was a Commonwealth record, and for the ever dependable Denise Lewis with a heptathlon score of 6724. In a semi-final Katharine Merry improved her 400m time to 50.21, second only to Kathy Cook in British annals, and went on to finish fifth in the final in 50.52, and fifth was the position also of Jo Wise with her 6.75m long jump. Meanwhile, a 13-year-old schoolgirl from Sheffield was just beginning to draw attention to herself. A month after high jumping 1.64m Jessica Ennis cleared 1.61m at the AAA Under-15 Championships in her home city, placing second on countback behind Ireland's Michelle Doherty. We shall hear a lot more about this young lady in the next chapter!

UNITED KINGDOM RECORDS AT 1 JANUARY 2000
100m: 11.10 Kathy Cook 1981; 200m: 22.10 Cook 1984; 400m: 49.43 Cook 1984; 800m: 1:56.21 Kelly Holmes 1995; 1500m: 3:58.07 Holmes 1997; Mile: 4:17.57 Zola Budd 1985; 3000m: 8:27.40 Paula Radcliffe 1999; 5000m: 14:43.54 Radcliffe 1999; 10,000m: 30:27.13 Radcliffe 1999; Half Mar:

67:11 Liz McColgan 1992; Mar: 2:25:56 Véronique Marot 1989; 2000mSC: 6:40.95 Tara Krzywicki 1999; 100mH: 12.80 Angie Thorp 1996; 400mH: 52.74 Sally Gunnell 1993; HJ: 1.95 Diana Davies 1982 (1.95 indoors Debbie Marti 1997); PV: 4.31 Janine Whitlock 1998; LJ: 6.90 Bev Kinch 1983; TJ: 15.15 Ashia Hansen 1997 (15.16 indoors 1998); SP: 19.36 Judy Oakes 1988; DT: 67.48 Meg Ritchie 1981; HT: 67.10 Lorraine Shaw 1999; JT: (new specification) 59.50 Karen Martin 1999; (old specification) 77.44 Fatima Whitbread 1986; Heptathlon: 6736 Denise Lewis 1997 (100H-13.32, HJ-1.82, SP-14.33, 200-24.10, LJ-6.77w, JT-52.30, 800-2:16.70); 4x100m: 42.43 British team 1980; 4x400m: 3:22.01 British team 1991; 3000m Walk: 12:49.16 Betty Sworowski 1990; 5000m Walk: 21:52.4 Vicky Lupton 1995 (21:36 road Lupton 1992); 10,000m Walk: 45:18.8 Lupton 1995 (45:03 road Kehler 1998); 20km Walk: 1:37:44 Lupton 1999; 50km Walk: 4:50:51 Sandra Brown 1991.

THE TWENTY-FIRST CENTURY

THE FIRST DECADE of this century brought, at the highest level, more success to UK women's athletics than any previous comparable period. To recap, there were two Olympic gold medals in the 1960s (for Mary Rand and Ann Packer) and one apiece in the 1970s (Mary Peters), 1980s (Tessa Sanderson) and 1990s (Sally Gunnell). Yet in the space of a few years that total of five Olympic victories almost doubled thanks to Denise Lewis in the heptathlon (2000), Kelly Holmes in the 800m and 1500m (2004) and Christine Ohuruogu at 400m (2008). World titles by Christine, Paula Radcliffe and Jessica Ennis added to the euphoria, as did Paula's 2:15:25 marathon - considered by many to be the most outstanding of all women's world records.

Fourteen years after her first significant title, the English Schools Junior long jump as a 13-year-old, Denise Lewis became Olympic heptathlon champion in Sydney. As the reigning European and Commonwealth champion and runner-up in the 1997 and 1999 World Championships, Denise was clearly a gold medal contender, all the more so after setting a Commonwealth record of 6831 points in July, the second highest score in 2000 after the 6842 by France's World champion Eunice Barber. Her individual marks were 13.13 hurdles, 1.84m high jump, 15.07m shot, 24.01w 200m, 6.69m long jump, 49.42m javelin throw and 2:12.20 800m. She was in the shape of her life ... only to receive an immense blow to her Olympic hopes seven weeks before the Games when she injured her left Achilles tendon. It took intensive physiotherapy to get her to the point where, only ten days before leaving for Sydney, she was able to start running again.

At the Olympics Denise was heartened by clocking a creditable 13.23 in the opening event, but was way below par in the high jump. A 1.87m performer at her best, she made a seemingly disastrous decision to pass at 1.78m after clearing 1.75m and then proceeded to fail three times at 1.81m. "My heart sank, and I realised I had probably just kissed goodbye to the gold medal", was how she described that moment in her book, *Personal Best*. She dipped to eighth place overall, but the shot transformed the situation. Denise (15.55m) threw it over four metres further than Barber and following a 24.34 200m she found herself in third place after day one with Barber (who retired injured during the opening event of the second day) a distant seventh. But Denise was having serious problems too with her Achilles tendon. She managed a decent 6.48m leap, taking her into second place overall, before feeling such intense pain that she could hardly walk. She very nearly didn't make it to the javelin. After taking painkillers she managed to throw 50.19m to take the lead for the first time and, declining another injection, pluckily toughed it out in the 800m, doing enough with her time of 2:16.83 to ensure victory with 6584 points.

INJURIES COULD NOT STOP DENISE LEWIS

Although she was never a world record breaking all-rounder like Daley Thompson or Mary Peters, Denise Lewis thoroughly deserved her heptathlon gold medal in Sydney in 2000 as she struggled bravely against injuries which came so close to shattering her Olympic dream. Her career was one of long-term consistency at the highest level.

Denise , born in West Bromwich on August 27 1972 (a few days before Mary Peters' Olympic pentathlon victory), was only nine when she joined the local Wolverhampton & Bilston club. At 15 she joined Birchfield and began to be coached by Darrell Bunn, the man who would steer her to top world class.

It was in 1988, just turned 16, that she entered her first heptathlon. It was the Midland Championship, she won and had found her forte. Injuries held her back for a time but in 1994 she made a breakthrough at the Commonwealth Games, not only winning but improving her best score from 6069 to 6325. It was the javelin which made all the difference. With a previous best of 48.58m she couldn't believe it when the spear touched down at a colossal 53.68m!

In 1996 she joined the world elite, setting a UK record of 6645 in Götzis. The statuesque Syrian, Ghada Shouaa, captured the Olympic title in Atlanta while Denise was so despondent after a modest long jump which left her in eighth place overall that she was tempted to drop out. However, a timely personal best of 54.82m with the javelin moved her all the way up to third and she clung on to the bronze medal with 6489.

She continued to improve in 1997, setting a Commonwealth record of 6736 in Götzis and claiming a silver medal (6654) in the World Championships. Now coached by Charles van Commenee, she became the world's number one in 1998, winning both of the year's major titles: European with 6559 and Commonwealth with 6513. A calf injury early in 1999 severely hampered her preparation for the World Championships but she recovered in time to score 6724 for second place.

The year ended in surgery for Denise; she was on crutches for four weeks and had ten weeks of rehabilitation. Nevertheless she scored a Commonwealth record 6831 in Talence, indicating she was in great shape as the 2000 Olympics approached ... until injury struck again. Only eighth in Sydney after the second event, the high jump, she moved to third after the shot and second after the long jump ... but was in such pain she could hardly walk. Thanks to her prowess with the javelin she took the lead before the 800m and ran out the winner with 6584.

Although keen to carry on and defend her title in Athens in 2004, her glory days were effectively over. Irritable Bowel Syndrome, which had continually plagued her for ten years, led to her withdrawing on the eve of the 2001 World Championships. She gave birth to her first child in April 2002, came back in 2003 to place fifth in the World

Championships but dropped out during the Athens Olympics and retired. She subsequently became even better known to the general public when she became a star of Strictly Come Dancing in 2004, and today is part of the BBC TV's athletics presentation team.

There were two other medals for British athletes in Sydney: bronze by Katharine Merry in the 400m and by Kelly Holmes in the 800m. Katharine finally fulfilled the potential she had displayed from her earliest days in the sport (she set a world age-12 200m best of 25.4 in 1987), although it wasn't until 1998 that she moved up seriously to the 400m. She progressed to 50.05 in July 2000, second only to Kathy Cook on the UK all-time list, and at the Games clocked 49.72 behind Australian icon Cathy Freeman (49.11) and Jamaica's Lorraine Graham (49.58). Katharine had to work hard for her medal, as finishing fast only 7/100ths behind was the improbably long-legged figure of team-mate Donna Fraser. Donna had been beavering away at the 400m ever since 1988, her best time being 50.85 in 1998 ... until she ran 50.77 in her quarter-final, 50.21 in her semi and an inspired 49.79 in the final. Katharine would go on to top the world year list in 2001 with 49.59 before injuries hampered her career to such an extent that she finally gave up in 2005. Donna, who underwent Achilles tendon surgery in 2002 and 2003, never again broke 51 seconds for the distance although she did win the AAA 200m/400m in 2005 and, at age 36, the same double indoors in 2009.

Kelly produced one of the most astonishing sights of the Sydney Olympics. So short of training was she after her latest round of injuries that making the Olympic team had for most of the year seemed a forlorn hope and her season's best of 2:00.35 was far behind the sub-1:57.4 clockings of Maria Mutola, Stephanie Graf and the top two Russians. Yet it was Kelly, taking everyone by surprise with an early strike, who entered the finishing straight well clear of the field ... even she couldn't believe it! Mutola of Mozambique and Austria's Graf did steam past in the final 50m to take gold (1:56.15) and silver (1:56.64) but Kelly hung on to third place in a remarkable 1:56.80. "I'm in shock," she exclaimed. "Six weeks ago I didn't think I'd even be here. What I have done tops every other single medal. To run my second ever fastest time is incredible. This is my gold medal." But even she could not have imagined that four years hence she would actually win not one but two of the real thing!

The team's other two main medal prospects experienced only frustration in Sydney. Injury problems meant that Ashia Hansen was unable to compete all summer and after a nervy qualifying round – jumping 14.29m after two fouls – she met with disaster in the final. Again she opened with two no jumps and then proceeded to take off so far behind the board with her third 'safety' jump that she registered a mere 13.44m for 11th place. Lacking the finishing powers of her main rivals in the 10,000m, Paula Radcliffe (who had married 3:34.76 1500m runner Gary Lough in April) attempted to make the pace so fast that the opposition would fall back exhausted before the last lap was reached. At the previous year's World Championships she had burned off everyone except Ethiopia's Gete Wami, clocking a Commonwealth record of 30:27.13. This time she ran 30:26.97 ... and yet came fourth. Paula gave it all she had, reaching halfway in a scorching 15:05.70, but approaching the bell she dropped from first to fourth and while her weary last lap took close to 70 sec Derartu Tulu of Ethiopia (the 1992 champion) sped round in a stunning 60.26 for victory in 30:17.49 some 30m ahead of Wami and Portugal's defending champion Fernanda Ribeiro. Barely three weeks later Paula gained some consolation by winning the Great North Run half marathon in a European best of 67:07 and followed that with the World half marathon title in Mexico in 69:07 for her first senior global title. Incidentally the Scottish-born Olympic gold medallist in the modern pentathlon, Dr Stephanie Cook, was an accomplished athlete, having placed seventh in the 1997 national cross country championship.

Paula Radcliffe was the star turn in 2001. Ever since winning the World Junior cross country title in 1992, Paula had yearned for victory in the senior 8km championship. On three occasions she had come so close to the major prize, finishing second in 1997 and 1998, third in 1999. At last, she realised her dream in Ostend. It was a fight to the finish between Paula and the 1999 champion Gete Wami, with the distinctively head-nodding Briton actually outsprinting the diminutive Ethiopian this time. Next day, in the 4km race, the tables were turned and Paula collected the silver medal in a close finish. Paula went on to win the European Challenge 10,000m in 30:55.80, the world's fastest for the year, and set a Commonwealth 3000m record of 8:26.97. It was looking good for the World Championships 10,000m in Edmonton, Alberta, but in a slow race at 2000ft altitude she finished fourth behind three Ethiopians in 31:50.06. However, she ended the year in style, posting a Commonwealth 5000m record of 14:32.44, equalling Liz McColgan's world road 5km best of 14:57 and retaining her World half marathon title with a European record of 66:47, clocking 63:26 at 20km en route for a world record.

There were other international successes in 2001. Jade Johnson (6.52m) won the European Under-23 long jump, Vernicha James (22.93) the European Junior 200m, Aileen Wilson the World Youth high jump with 1.87m, and Abi Oyepitan (11.42 100m) and Tasha Danvers (54.94 400m hurdles) struck gold in the World University Games. Susan Jones equalled the UK high jump record of 1.95m when unexpectedly winning at the European Cup, and UK records were set by former Welsh international footballer Tara Krzywicki with 9:52.71 for the 3000m steeplechase, Janine Whitlock with a 4.40m pole vault and Lorraine Shaw with a hammer throw of 68.15m, her 15th national record.

Enter Paula Radcliffe, prospective marathoner. Excitement ran high as she completed her preparations for the 2002 London Marathon with another deeply satisfying victory in the World 8km Cross Country. The date of Paula's momentous marathon debut was April 14 2002. The conventional wisdom was that she would stay with more experienced runners until 20-22 miles before making a move if still feeling comfortable. But that's not Paula's style. Before halfway (71:04) she was on her own, and her second half was just awesome. She covered it in 67:52 and her final time of 2:18:56 was hailed as the fastest ever in a women-only race and broke every other record in the book except for the world and Commonwealth best of 2:18:47 by Kenya's Christine Ndereba.

In July she embarked upon her track season; just three races, each one a gem. First she set a Commonwealth 3000m record of 8:22.20 ... fabulous speed for someone who had been training for the marathon. Next came the Commonwealth Games 5000m in Manchester, where she not only won her first international track title but came within 3.33 sec of the world mark with a Commonwealth record of 14:31.42. Better still was her continental record of 30:01.09 nine days later when winning the European 10,000m title in Munich, the second fastest ever behind Wang Junxia's controversial world record. She quickly dropped all opposition and reached 5000m in 14:57.65, easily the fastest ever halfway split. There was more to come. Tuning up for the Chicago Marathon she set a European 10km road best of 30:38 and in the Windy City on October 13 she smashed the world record with 2:17:18, leaving Ndereba over two minutes adrift. Paula set a devilish pace from the outset. She reached halfway, with Ndereba for company, in 69:05 – only to cover the second half even faster in 68:13. Not surprisingly, Paula won every athlete of the year award going. No longer was she the plucky loser; now she was a superlative winner.

The second most successful athlete of 2002 was Ashia Hansen, who came away with two shining gold medals that summer. In each case victory was won at the final gasp. With the penultimate jump at the Commonwealth Games Francoise Mbango from Cameroon soared to an African record of 14.82m, her demeanour suggesting she felt the competition was over. That in turn fired up Ashia even more for her final attempt and she bounced out to 14.86m. Even better was to follow ten days later at the European Championships. The challenge this time came from Finland's Heli Koivula, who had opened with a wind assisted 14.83m. For Ashia, a distant second with 14.60m, it was all down to her final attempt and she responded gloriously. She broke the sand at exactly 15 metres (with 3.1m/sec wind assistance), and became the first British woman to win a European jumping title since Thelma Hopkins (high jump) and Jean Pickering (long jump) in 1954.

Others to win at Manchester's splendidly organised Commonwealth Games were Kelly Holmes (4:05.99 1500m) and Lorraine Shaw (66.83m hammer), while at the European Championships there was a silver medal in the long jump for Jade Johnson (6.73m) and bronze for Lee McConnell (400m in a personal best 51.02 plus a 49.90 relay anchor) and Kelly Holmes (1:59.83 800m). Worthy of celebration also was the World Junior 200m victory (22.93) in Kingston, Jamaica by Vernicha James. Her defeated rivals included the Americans Sanya Richards and Allyson Felix, both of whom would reach the supreme heights. Vernicha, on the other hand, would never run as fast again and quit the sport at an early age ... in contrast to the gangling 15-year-old Jamaican who took the men's race in 20.61, someone by the name of Usain Bolt.

Paula began 2003 as she finished 2002 ... breaking world records. Racing 10km in Puerto Rico she ran 30:21 on a hilly course in warm, humid and windy conditions. "I'm in way better shape than before London last year," she claimed, having been covering up to 140 miles a week in high altitude Albuquerque, and so it proved. Theoretically, world records should be progressively harder to beat as an event develops, yet Paula's stunning run in London on April 13 2003 represented the biggest single improvement for 20 years. Her astonishing time was 2:15:25. The pace she set was unprecedented; her third mile was covered in 4:57 and she flashed past 10km in 32:01, 10 miles in 51:48, halfway in 68:02, 30km in 1:36:36 and 20 miles in 1:43:33. No British man ran the marathon faster that year!

Frustratingly, a combination of a shin injury and bronchitis caused her to sit out the entire 2003 track season. Again, though, Paula produced a strong finish to the year. A week apart, she set world bests at 5km (14:51) in London's Hyde Park and at half marathon (65:40) in the Great North Run from Newcastle to South Shields. On the way she passed 15km in 46:41, 10 miles in 50:01 and 20km in 62:21 but because of the downhill nature of the point to point course none of those times could be officially accepted. Two weeks later she won her third World half marathon title in 67:35, and to round off the year nicely she claimed a second European cross country title, leading Britain to team victory.

Ashia Hansen enjoyed another momentous success when the 2003 World Indoors were staged in Birmingham. Suffering from a heel injury she could only compete in the qualifying round after being injected with an anaesthetic, and even then she was in pain while jumping 14.61m. In the final she opened promisingly with 14.77m but Francoise Mbango concluded the first round with an African record of 14.88m.

In round 5 everything came together for Ashia ... a splendid winning effort of 15.01m, a distance only she and Russia's Iolanda Chen had ever bettered indoors. It was all too good to last and sure enough, due to a seemingly unending series of injuries, that proved to be Ashia's last international championship appearance.

PAULA: IN A CLASS OF HER OWN

No other British athlete has pushed out the frontiers of performance in the way that Paula Radcliffe has in the marathon or been so far ahead of the world's second best in their event. Her time of 2:15:25 in the 2003 London Marathon was a truly phenomenal achievement. No woman in the world, other than herself, has yet run faster than 2:18:20 ... a gap representing around 900 metres of road. Her record time is over seven minutes quicker than Emil Zátopek's when he famously won the 1952 Olympic title. Like Jim Peters half a century earlier, Paula has revolutionised the marathon; unlike him she has a global title (the 2005 World championship) to her name besides being a fabulous track and cross country runner.

Her career started modestly. At the 1986 English Girls Cross Country Championships, aged 12 (she was born near Northwich in Cheshire on December 17 1973), she finished 299th, but a year later she placed fourth in the same race, with her Bedford club winning the team title which pleased her coaches, Alex and Rosemary Stanton, even more. Her first individual national cross country title came as an Intermediate in 1991 and just a year later she created a sensation by becoming World Junior champion. In 1996 she succeeded Zola Budd as UK 5000m record holder and graduated from Loughborough University with first class honours in Modern European Studies.

For the next three years Paula's uncompromising front running carried her to records galore, including world bests on the road, but time and again she was outsprinted in her most important track and cross country races. It was at the end of 2000 that the tide began to turn and the good loser became a winner at the highest level. She captured the World half marathon title and in 2001 she finally realised her dream – at the eighth attempt – of winning the senior version of the World Cross Country. She was disappointed by her fourth place in the 10,000m at the World Championships that year but in 2002 she carried all before her. After retaining her World cross country title she made a fabulous marathon debut in London, clocking the world's second fastest ever time of 2:18:56; demonstrated she had lost none of her track speed by setting a Commonwealth 3000m record of 8:22.22 and followed that with brilliant victories at the Commonwealth Games (Commonwealth record of 14:31.42) and European Championships (European record of 30:01.09); and ended the year with a world record 2:17:18 in the Chicago Marathon. In April 2003 she wowed the world of athletics even more with her stunning 2:15:25 in London for the biggest single improvement in the world record for 20 years.

Other triumphs would follow, including a third London win and the coveted World title in 2005 (becoming the first British marathoner to win a global championship), and three New York City victories between 2004 and 2008, but injuries and illness played havoc with her preparations all too often and she was unable to do herself justice in her two Olympic marathons. She had hoped a third chance would await her in London 2012, at the age of 38, but it was not to be. A foot injury forced her to withdraw.

That year of 2003 was a topsy-turvy one for Kelly Holmes. She trained with Maria Mutola at altitude in South Africa and embarked upon her first indoor season since her schooldays. An early dividend was a UK indoor 800m record of 1:59.21, while at the World Indoor Championships in Birmingham she astounded herself by clocking a UK 1500m record of 4:02.66 for a silver medal behind Regina Jacobs (4:01.67), the 39-year-old American who would three months later fail a drugs test. Full of hope that the summer would see her crowned World 1500m champion, she returned to South Africa, only to sustain a very painful injury to the left knee. Over-compensating for that, she proceeded to cause damage to her right calf. It was all very disheartening and later, in the Pyrenees training base of Font Romeu, everything just got too much for Kelly. She had unsuccessfully tried jogging and, as she revealed in her book, *Black, White & Gold*: "After one particularly frustrating day I suddenly felt as if I couldn't cope any longer. I stood in the bathroom, locked the door and stared in the mirror, feeling utterly miserable. I was crying uncontrollably. There was a pair of nail scissors on a shelf. To this day, I don't know what made me do this, but I picked them up, opened them and started to cut my left arm with one of the blades. One cut for every day that I had been injured."

From the pit of despair, hope returned as gradually the leg responded to treatment. She would be able to compete in the Paris World Championships after all ... but decided to concentrate on the 800m. It proved a wise decision. In a slow final the training companions finished one-two. Kelly led into the straight but Mutola was always in command and slipped past to win in 1:59.89, covering the last 200m in 27.57, with Kelly showing 2:00.18. Britain's other medallist in Paris was Hayley Tullett from Wales, who finished third in the superb time of 3:59.95 to rank second on the UK all-time list for 1500m behind Kelly. Later in their careers the two women who beat her, Süreyya Ayhan of Turkey and Russia's Tatyana Tomashova, were banned for doping offences.

And so to 2004, the year in which Kelly's long-held dream of becoming an Olympic gold medallist became a reality. What's more, she proved lightning can strike twice!

Of course, even in her *annus mirabilis*, not everything ran smoothly and her season leading up to the Athens Olympics was curiously uneven. She won all three of her 800m races, including a record seventh AAA title at the distance , but only two of her six races at 1500m which she had always considered her stronger event. Consequently, Kelly found herself facing a dilemma. Should she run the 800m first and thus probably have three races in her legs before embarking upon the heats of the 1500m, or should she put all her eggs in one basket and simply opt for the 1500m? In fact, Kelly's mind was made up when a particularly good speed session at the Olympic team's holding camp in Cyprus convinced her she was ready to run a great 800m.

In Athens she clocked the quickest semi-final time of 1:57.98, her best for three years. It was looking promising and in the final she ran the most tactically astute race of her long career. Content to run near the back (57.6) while Jearl Miles Clark (USA) blazed through the first lap in 56.37, she followed Mutola as she clawed her way towards the front along the back straight. Into the final stretch it was Miles Clark, Mutola and Holmes.

"Suddenly I was side by side with Maria," she reflected. "I've never beaten her in a major race and normally in that situation I would buckle but there was something magical about this race. I just had to win it." The two women slogged it out and until a few strides from the finish Mutola was still just in front, but out in lane 3 Kelly was even more resolute than her opponent, the most bemedalled female 800m runner in history, and Kelly crossed the line first in 1:56.38, her fastest since setting the UK record nine years earlier. Her 200m segments of 28.7, 28.9, 29.2 and 29.6 proved the value of even pace running. Her look of disbelief, turning to wonderment and delight when she realised she had indeed won, will forever remain in the memory.

Kelly was back next day to finish second in her 1500m heat in 4:05.58; two days after that she placed second in her semi in 4:04.77. Having discovered her most effective way of racing, she ran with assurance in both those races, holding back until the finishing straight, and that's how she ran – and won – the final too, five days after her 800m triumph. At the bell Kelly was lurking in eighth place; with 200m to go she was up to fifth and by the time Russia's Tatyana Yevdokimova led into the finishing straight the Briton was second and no power on earth was going to deprive her of a second golden moment. Running inside 60 sec for her last lap, she moved into the lead 60m from the finish, looked round to assess the danger, and held on grimly. Her winning time of 3:57.90 broke her 1997 UK record. Kelly also went into the record books as, at 34, the oldest man or woman to have won either title and she became the only British woman to win two Olympic gold medals. Ever since, she has become one of Britain's most recognisable and feted citizens, and in the 2005 New Year Honours she became the first active athlete to be made a Dame – or be knighted for that matter.

DREAM COMES TRUE FOR KELLY HOLMES

Previously unknown outside her native Kent, 13-year-old Kelly Holmes (born at Pembury on April 19 1970) was the unexpected winner of the Junior Girls 1500m at the 1983 English Schools Championships, and so began an Olympic dream which would finally come true all of 21 years later. The following year she watched the Los Angeles Olympics on TV and Seb Coe became her hero. "He was an aggressive runner who didn't give up and his determination was obvious. I identified with that even then."

In 1987 she became English Schools Senior 1500m champion and represented Britain at junior level but, once she left school, athletics ceased to be a priority. She joined the Army at 17 and put her military career first, and it was only at the urging of the Army's star athlete, Kriss Akabusi, that she resumed training in 1989, but her times were mediocre. The turning point was when she watched the 1992 Olympics on TV and recognised Lisa York running in the 3000m – an athlete she had often raced during their schooldays. "It dawned on me," Kelly reflected in her autobiography, "if she could make it to the Olympics, then maybe I could too."

She began to train seriously again and took British athletics by storm in 1993. Short but well muscled after working hard on her upper body strength, she was a revelation at 800m, setting an English record of 1:58.64. The following year she burst forth as a world class 1500m runner, taking a silver medal at the European Championships and winning at the Commonwealth Games in her first serious season at the event. Medals of other denominations would continue to come her way but, her career constantly interrupted by injuries and illness, that would remain the only gold for eight often frustrating years.

Her Olympic hopes in 1996 were dashed when just prior to the Games she developed a hairline fracture in her lower left leg. Injections helped numb the pain and it was remarkable that she should finish fourth in the 800m. Next year she was favourite for the World 1500m title but broke down in her heat with a torn Achilles tendon. Further serious setbacks followed but almost miraculously she finished third in the 2000 Olympic 800m. What, one wondered, was she capable of if only she ever had a full year of injury-free training and racing? We and she found out in 2004. At the Athens Olympics she not only won the 800m in 1:56.38, her fastest for nine years, but came back to take the 1500m in the UK record time of 3:57.90! As she wrote: "The feeling was indescribable. I had achieved my lifetime's dream twice over. It had taken years of dedication, commitment, focus, emotional struggle and pain but now I had done it. I was double Olympic champion. And yes, it was worth all the wait."

In 2005 she was made a Dame and since her retirement from the track that year she has done wonderful work mentoring several of Britain's most promising young middle distance runners through her "On Camp With Kelly" scheme and she is currently President of Commonwealth Games England.

Britain's other individual medallist in Athens was heptathlete Kelly Sotherton, the finest athlete ever to have been born on the Isle of Wight (current population: 140,000). It had been a long ascent to reach the heights as an all-rounder. She had contested her first heptathlon in 1994, winning the English Schools title aged 17, but did not hit 6000 points until 2003. It all started to click in 2004 when she placed second in the classic Götzis (Austria) event, improving from 6059 to 6406 to move to third on the UK all-time list behind Birchfield clubmates Denise Lewis (with whom she trained under Charles van Commenee) and Judy Simpson. In the process she set five individual personal bests, including a respectable javelin throw of 40.81m to prove – in the light of future events – that there was a time when she was quite accomplished at that discipline. At the Olympics she progressed to 6424 in third place, producing personal bests in the high jump, 200m and 800m. There was one other British medallist in Athens with an athletics background: Sarah Winckless. The AAA under-17 discus champion in 1990, who threw 53.16m in 1994, gave up the sport to concentrate on rowing and won a bronze medal in the double sculls. Abi Oyepitan reached the 200m final, her heat time of 22.50 being the fastest by a Briton for 20 years; Christine Ohuruogu provided a glimpse of what was to come by clocking 50.50 in her 400m heat; and another classy personal best was a 6.80m long jump by Jade Johnson.

How unlucky was Paula Radcliffe at those Olympics. She was in fantastic form in June, setting a Commonwealth 5000m record of 14:29.11 and a UK all-comers record and 2004 world leading mark of 30:17.15 at 10,000m in windy conditions. But then she ran into problems and was in such a bad way before she even started the marathon that had it been any competition other than the Olympics she would have withdrawn. As Paula explained in the *Daily Telegraph* the problem was that anti-inflammatories used in the treatment of a leg injury shortly before the Games upset her bowel so that she was unable to absorb enough energy and nutrients. "My fuel tank was very low before I began the race. This meant I had to break down body tissue for fuel while I was running. Had I pushed further I would have damaged my body further. As it is, tests showed my liver was struggling to cope and I lost a lot of weight." She was one of 16 competitors who failed to complete that merciless course in a race conducted in extreme heat. As for dropping out during the 10,000m five days later, she said: "I don't have any regrets about trying. At least I won't always be wondering if I could have raced it. My legs were just unable to recover from the trauma." For the record, Mizuki Noguchi of Japan won the marathon in 2:26:20, Xing Huina of China the 10,000m in 30:24.36.

Much of what was written about Paula's excruciating experience in Athens by certain British sports columnists (the ones who know nothing about athletics but feel qualified once every four years to pontificate on Olympic competition) was an absolute disgrace. To accuse Paula of all people of being a quitter, of dropping out when the going got too tough or the prospect of a medal had disappeared, would be laughable if the comments had not been so hurtful, damaging and ignorant. Nobody in athletics can surpass Paula for sheer guts and determination, and the fact that she was unable to complete either the marathon or 10,000m was because her body would not permit her to.

Typically, Paula bounced back magnificently in her next race with a hard fought victory in the 2004 New York City Marathon in 2:23:10 and her rehabilitation was completed at the 2005 London Marathon. This race saw her back to her sparkling best as she won by a full mile in 2:17:42, her – and the world's – third fastest ever time and a world best for a women-only race. Undecided for a while as to which event to run at the World Championships, she eventually opted for both although the marathon was the main goal. She was disappointed with her 10,000m (ninth in 30:42.75) but was able to start the marathon, eight days later, mentally and physically ready for the challenge. Leading from the start, she pulled clear of her nearest pursuer at 27km to win in 2:20:57, easily the fastest ever time in a global championship race, and becoming the first Briton of either sex to win a world or Olympic marathon title.

The only other medal winners in Helsinki were the 4x400m team of Lee McConnell 51.4, Donna Fraser 51.0, Nicola Sanders 50.80 and Christine Ohuruogu 51.27, who placed third in 3:24.44. Kelly Sotherton was third after five events of the heptathlon but a poor javelin throw of 33.09m proved costly and she wound up fifth with 6325. With Denise Lewis now retired, Kelly was clearly the UK's top all-rounder, having improved her best score to 6547 in Götzis, but coming up fast was Jess Ennis, nine years her junior at 19. She won the European Junior title with a UK junior record of 5891 and scored higher still with 5910 for third place in the World University Games.

Only one UK record was broken in 2006, national cross country champion Lizzie Hall clocking 9:48.51 for the steeplechase, and with Paula Radcliffe undergoing foot surgery in April and then becoming pregnant (her daughter Isla was born in January 2007), it was a year when the highest world ranked British athletes were Becky Lyne in the 800m and Kelly Sotherton in the heptathlon, both rated no 7 in the annual merit rankings compiled by *Athletics International*. However, one former athlete who did shine at global level was Shelley Rudman of Swindon Harriers, seventh in the 1997 English Schools 300m hurdles, who won a silver medal at the Winter Olympics in the skeleton bob.

There were three victories to celebrate at the 2006 Commonwealth Games in Melbourne in March. Christine Ohuruogu took the 400m in a personal best 50.28, Lisa Dobriskey the 1500m in 4:06.21 and Kelly Sotherton the heptathlon with 6396, but none was able to reproduce that form in the European Championships in Gothenburg in August. Lisa was eliminated in her heat and Kelly's score of 6290 gained her only seventh place, while Christine was dropped from the team as she had missed three mandatory drug tests, resulting in a one-year ban.

The only European medallists were Becky Lyne in the 800m (third in 1:58.45) and the 4x100m team of Anyika Onuora, Emma Ania, Emily Freeman and Joice Maduaka (second in 43.51). Jo Pavey was fourth in the 5000m (15:01.41) to add to her Commonwealth Games silver medal (14:59.08), while Jess Ennis followed up her bronze in Melbourne (6269) with 6287 for eighth in Gothenburg, both personal best scores. Worthy of note was Mara Yamauchi, who became Britain's second fastest ever marathoner when clocking 2:25:13 for sixth place in London. As Mara Myers she was national cross country champion in 1998 and now, married to a Japanese, she was taking unpaid leave from her work as a Foreign & Commonwealth Office diplomat in Tokyo to concentrate on her racing career.

The 2007 season was much brighter, six athletes merit ranked among the world's top four in their events, with a pair of 400m runners at the forefront. Nicola Sanders was the first to hit the headlines with her astonishing display at the European Indoor Championships in Birmingham. Six metres clear at 200m, reached in a sizzling 23.31 (which remains her personal best indoors or out!), she passed 300m in an unofficial UK indoor best of 36.0 and had almost a second to spare at the finish in the Commonwealth record time of 50.02. Only three Britons had ever run faster outdoors. It took former 400m hurdler Nicola a while to rediscover that form outdoors, clocking a best of 50.97 prior to the World Championships in Osaka ... but in Japan she timed her peak to perfection with a 49.77 semi-final victory and 49.65 in the final two days later. The problem was she wasn't even the top British finisher in that final! Nicola finished as silver medallist, the gold going to Christine Ohuruogu in 49.61.

It was an extraordinary scenario. Christine's suspension came to an end on August 5. Two days later the British team selectors showed faith in her by picking her for Osaka. On August 11 she lined up for her first race for 13 months, winning a 400m heat at the Scottish Championships in a modest 53.09; next day she won the 200m in 23.71w but scratched from the 400m final in order to catch her flight to Osaka. There, on August 16, she clocked a startling 50.56 at a warm-up meeting, close to her personal best of 50.28. At the World Championships Christine won her heat on August 26 in 50.46 and semi next day in 50.16. The final on August 29 – just 18 days after that tentative 53.09 in Glasgow – was the stuff of dreams for the British supporters. The Jamaican favourite, Novlene Williams, blasted away and held the lead ahead of Russia's Natalya Antyukh, Ohuruogu and Sanders at the 300m mark. With 50m to run Nicola was third and her team-mate fourth but they found another gear to surge past Antyukh and close on Williams. For a second or two it looked as though Nicola was the more likely to catch the flagging Jamaican but then Christine's superior strength came into play and both Britons produced a dip finish while Williams stayed upright. It was only the second British one-two in World Championships history, Colin Jackson and Tony Jarrett in the 1993 110m hurdles being the first.

There were bronze medals also for Christine and Nicola in the 4x400m relay, the team placing third in the UK record time of 3:20.04. Christine led off in 50.6, followed by Marilyn Okoro (50.9) and Lee McConnell (49.79), with Nicola anchoring with a great split of 48.76 which displaced Sally Gunnell's 49.45 as the fastest ever by a Briton. Donna Fraser, who ran in the heats, also received a medal.

Another success story in Osaka occurred in the heptathlon. Carolina Klüft of Sweden (7032) and Ukraine's Lyudmila Blonska (6832) – who the following year was banned for life for a second doping offence – finished far ahead but Kelly Sotherton and Jess Ennis performed well to take third and fourth. Kelly's score of 6510 was her second highest but again she was let down by an ineffectual javelin throw of 31.90m. Jess got away to a brilliant start, "winning" the hurdles with a personal best 12.97, followed by a 1.89m high jump. A disappointing shot (11.93m), which dropped her to sixth overall, was redeemed by a superb personal best 200m of 23.15, and at the end of day one she was fourth and Kelly (personal bests of 13.21 in the hurdles and 23.40 in the 200m) third. Kelly started well on day two with a personal best equalling 6.68m long jump, while Jess was frustrated to jump 6.33m with almost 20cm to spare on the board. Jess made up ground on Kelly in the javelin with a personal best of 38.07m and was just ahead of her in the 800m in 2:11.39. Her score of 6469 was a personal best. In an earlier heptathlon Jess had high jumped 1.95m, which equalled the UK record.

Two other events yielded UK records during the summer of 2007: Hatti Dean clocked 9:38.56 for the steeplechase and Goldie Sayers threw the javelin 65.05m. There was an indoor 3000m record (8:31.50) by Jo Pavey, who had the misfortune to be pipped for the bronze medal at 10,000m in the World Championships by Kara Goucher. The following month the American won the Great North Run in 66:57 ahead of Paula Radcliffe (67:53) in her first race for 21 months following maternity and injury. Paula then went on to win the New York Marathon in 2:23:09.

Of the young talent on display in 2007 no one was more promising than Asha Philip (16), winner of the World Youth title in 11.46 to become the first British female ever to win a global 100m championship. Her best time was 11.37. But later that year, at the World Trampolining Championships (where she was defending her under-17 'double-mini' title), she suffered a severe knee injury. She was out of action for the next two seasons, made a tentative comeback in 2010, came close to regaining top form with 11.47 in 2011, and early in 2012 she clocked the excellent 60m time of 7.24. An exciting future beckons once more.

That Christine Ohuruogu was a championship performer par excellence was confirmed at the Beijing Olympics in 2008. Already the Commonwealth and World 400m champion, she rose splendidly to the biggest occasion of all. Again she timed her peak to perfection as her fastest for the season coming into the Games was 50.80 when winning ahead of Nicola Sanders (51.27) at the London Grand Prix. Nicola, whose career since her great exploits in Osaka would be blighted by persistent injury, failed to make the Olympic final (fourth in her semi in 50.71) but Christine produced her second fastest ever time of 49.62.

She ran with cool judgement. She was in fourth place entering the final straight, at which point the American favourite Sanya Richards held a four metre lead over two Russians, but as they started to flail so Christine sailed through serenely to victory. "If you are going to beat me, you have to fight me very hard. My coach Lloyd Cowan has always said to me that the race is going to be won in the last 50m. If you can just keep your cool, keep your composure for the last 50m, that's when people start dying and he knows that I don't start dying – that's how I run and it works for me. It's not about who's fastest or strongest, it's about greatest will."

TWICE A GLOBAL ONE-LAP CHAMPION

Godfrey Brown in 1936, Ann Packer in 1964 and Lillian Board in 1968 had all come achingly close to victory, but no British athlete had succeeded in winning a global title at 400m since Eric Liddell at the 1924 Olympics until Christine Ohuruogu triumphed unexpectedly at the 2007 World Championships ... and then did the same again at the following year's Olympics!

The turning point for Christine, born close to the Olympic Stadium in East London of Nigerian parents on May 17 1984, came when she placed third in the 2003 European Junior Championships. An England under-17 & 19 netball international, the Newham & Essex Beagles club member realised that athletics was the sport for her and began training in earnest. Swift and spectacular results materialised. In 2004 she by-passed the 54 and 53 sec barriers by improving at one fell swoop from 54.21 to 52.20 and then – even more remarkably – avoided the sub-52 milestone when she took the AAA title in 50.98. She ended that season with 50.50 in her Olympic heat before being eliminated in the semis.

Her first senior international medal came at the 2004 Olympics when she won bronze in the 4x400m relay. It was in 2006 that she landed her first major title. She won at the Commonwealth Games in a personal best 50.28 and expectations ran high that she could add the European title. However, she was withdrawn from the team, having missed three drug tests between October 2005 and July 2006. The Court of Arbitration for Sport rejected her appeal against her one-year suspension but noted there was no suggestion of her taking drugs; it was a case of a "busy young athlete being forgetful." It was a salutary lesson to be more organised in future but it was most unfair that certain sections of the press chose to draw and perpetuate totally unwarranted conclusions.

During her suspension Christine continued to train in the hope that the selectors would show faith in her, which they did, and she repaid them handsomely. Two days after her ban ended she was picked for Osaka and before the month of August 2007 was out she was crowned World champion. Again she surpassed herself on the big occasion by clocking 49.61. A bronze medal followed in the relay.

Her superb pace judgement came into play on the biggest stage of all the following year in Beijing. Her best time that summer was an unremarkable 50.80 which ranked her ninth among the Olympic entrants, but once more she peaked just right, winning her semi in 50.14 and the final in 49.62. As she commented afterwards: "I know I can perform well when

*I need to. I may not have a good season but, like at the World
Championships, that's what I train all year for. It's not luck.
I worked damn hard for this."*

*Injuries have taken their toll since then and although
she has improved her best 200m time to 22.85 she has
struggled to remain among the world elite at 400m. She
placed fifth at the 2009 World Championships in 50.21
while her fastest times in 2010 and 2011 were 50.88 and
50.85 respectively. However, she ran a spectacular leg for the
victorious British 4x400m relay team at the 2012 World
Indoor Championships and once again timed her peak well
to take the Olympic silver medal in London in 49.70.*

The other great Olympic success story was Tasha Danvers,
who snatched a totally unexpected bronze medal in the 400m
hurdles, her time of 53.84 bettered among British performers
only by Sally Gunnell. That she was given the opportunity
to run the race of her life was due to the insight of the team
selectors who picked her – knowing about her struggle to get
racing fit again after Achilles tendon and hamstring injuries –
even though she had been well beaten by young Perri Shakes-
Drayton in the Olympic Trials. Her fastest that season prior to
the Games was merely 55.91 but in the rounds she progressed
to 55.19 and 54.31, setting her up well for the final.

A frustrating fourth place was the fate which befell Kelly
Sotherton, Goldie Sayers and Lisa Dobriskey, all of whom
performed with the utmost credit. Kelly at least already had
a medal that year, having finished a very close second to Tia
Hellebaut (4852 to 4867) in the World Indoor pentathlon
championship. Kelly outscored the Belgian in four of the
five events but the high jump (1.99m to 1.81m) made all the
difference. The previous year, at the European Indoors, Kelly
had lost to Sweden's Carolina Klüft by 17 points with a UK
record score of 4927.

In Beijing Kelly scored 6517, her second highest total. She
was third after the first day, clocking personal bests of 13.18
in the hurdles and 23.39 in the 200m but below expectations
in the high jump and shot. She dropped to fifth after a
disappointing long jump of 6.33m (she leapt 6.79m the

previous month) and a 37.66m javelin throw didn't help her position, but she finished with a flourish, running her fastest 800m time of 2:07.34. That wasn't the end of her exertions as she clocked a brilliant 50.4 for her third leg in the 4x400m relay as the team placed fifth in 3:22.68 with Nicola Sanders offering a glimpse of her old form by anchoring in 49.54. Much had been expected of Jess Ennis in 2008 but after lying second on day one in Götzis she had to withdraw. A scan revealed stress fractures to the right ankle, and her Olympic dream was over.

Four athletes set national records in 2008, the most unanticipated being Montell Douglas, who broke the oldest individual record: Kathy Cook's 11.10 100m from 1981. Montell, whose previous best was 11.28, was timed at Loughborough at a staggering wind-assisted 10.95 in her heat and then credited with a legal 11.05 (2.0m/sec wind) in the final. Was it a flash in the pan? Montell's next best time in 2008 was 11.27 and she didn't get beyond the quarter-finals in Beijing. During the four subsequent seasons her fastest was 11.39.

The other record breakers were Helen Clitheroe with 9:29.14 in her Olympic steeplechase heat; Jo Jackson with walking records which included 1:31:33 for 20km, a time which placed her 22nd in Beijing but was bettered by only one British man that year; and Goldie Sayers, whose javelin throw of 65.75m fell only 38cm short of the bronze medal in Beijing. Lisa Dobriskey was equally close to standing on the podium. Finishing faster than anybody after being boxed in when the strike for home began, she missed a bronze medal by a stride's length in clocking 4:02.10. Others to perform with distinction in Beijing included Jeanette Kwakye, who followed up her silver medal over 60m at the World Indoors (setting a UK record of 7.08) with sixth in the Olympic 100m in 11.14 for third spot on the UK all-time list, and Mara Yamauchi – who had previously gained her first ever marathon victory in Osaka in 2:25:10 – finished sixth in 2:27:29. Paula Radcliffe pluckily completed the race in 23rd place (2:32:38), suffering acute leg problems arising from the stress fracture to the left thigh which had so severely curtailed her preparations. As in 2004 she bounced back with victory in November's New York City Marathon

(2:23:56), a week after running a UK 10 miles best of 51:11. Mara Yamauchi, already the UK's second quickest marathoner, ended her year by finishing third in Tokyo in 2:25:03.

Britain's athlete of the year for 2009 was undoubtedly Jess Ennis. Out injured since May 31 2008, she returned to heptathlon competition just under a year later. The aim was merely to reach the World Championships qualifying standard of 6100 points ... but she won with a resounding personal best score of 6587. She compiled her highest first day score of 4003 with 12.98 hurdles, 1.90m high jump, 13.19m shot and 23.49 200m, and on day two she long jumped 6.16m, followed by 42.70m in the javelin and a personal best 800m of 2:09.88. Her run-up towards the World Championships was faultless. She set personal bests of 11.68 for 100m, 12.81 for the hurdles (just 0.01 outside the UK record), 6.43m long jump, 13.72m shot and 46.47m javelin, and kept her hand in well with 200m in 23.39 and 1.91m high jump.

She was ready for something exceptional in Berlin, and she didn't disappoint. Starting with her two strongest individual events (like Daley Thompson), she capitalised by clocking 12.93 for the hurdles, her fastest in a heptathlon, and clearing a season's best of 1.92m for a lead of 181 points. In the shot, after two poor attempts, she displayed a Daleyesque ability to produce a brilliant effort under intense pressure ... in her case a lifetime best of 14.14m. A season's 200m best of 23.25 brought her first day total to 4124 – a figure bettered ever only by world record holder Jackie Joyner-Kersee and European record holder Carolina Klüft – and a colossal overnight lead of 307 points. She kept most of that advantage on a second day which saw her long jump 6.29m, throw the javelin 43.54m and cover 800m in 2:12.22 . Her final score of 6731 was the third highest ever by a Briton behind Denise Lewis's 6831 and 6736 and she finished 238 points clear. Ukraine's Olympic champion Natalya Dobrynska placed fourth and Beijing bronze medallist Tatyana Chernova of Russia was eighth.

Jess's success owes much to the skill of Toni Minichiello, her coach since she was 13. Toni's former wife, Nicola Minichiello (née Gautier), also became a global champion in 2009. The former international heptathlete, who scored 5784 in 2001, linked up with Scottish 6.43m long jumper Gillian Cooke to win the World two-woman bobsleigh title.

Two others came away from Berlin with medals. A delighted Lisa Dobriskey was second in the 1500m in 4:03.75, although it must have been tantalising to be within 1/100th of a second of the winner, Maryam Jamal, a former Ethiopian representing Bahrain. It was a remarkable result for Lisa who, because of injury, wasn't fit enough to contest the selection trials. She later crashed through the four minute barrier with 3:59.50 to rank second to Kelly Holmes on the UK all-time list. Jenny Meadows' accurate pace judgement helped win her the 800m bronze medal. Her husband and coach, Trevor Painter, set her a target of 57.5 at 400m ... and she hit halfway in 57.4 in seventh place. Still only sixth entering the final straight she finished strongly in 1:57.93, promoting her to third on the UK all-time list behind Kelly Holmes and Kirsty Wade.

There were only two UK record breakers in 2009. One was pole vaulter Kate Dennison, who set nine new marks indoors and out, ending up with 4.60m. Kate, born in South Africa, was brought to Britain at age four and was a former gymnast of promise, fourth in the national under-12 championship. The other was walker Jo Jackson whose records included 20km in 1:31:16, a time she would improve to 1:30:41 the following year. Jodie Williams succeeded Asha Philip as World Youth 100m champion (11.39), taking the 200m also in 23.08, while Katarina Johnson-Thompson won the heptathlon with 5750. European Under-23 titles were won by Perri Shakes-Drayton (55.26 400m hurdles), Eden Francis (57.29m discus) and the 4x100m team (43.89). Other notable achievements included Mara Yamauchi's second place in the London Marathon in her best time of 2:23:12 and Hayley Yelling, coming out of retirement, winning her second European cross country title.

Jess Ennis continued to dominate the world multi-events scene in 2010. She started the indoor season by beating World champion Lolo Jones (USA) with a UK 60m hurdles record of 7.95, together with an indoor high jump best of 1.94m, while at the World Indoor Championships in Doha she won the pentathlon with 4937 points. That broke Carolina Klüft's championship record and replaced Kelly Sotherton in third place on the world all-time list. Her individual marks were 8.04, 1.90m, 14.01m, 6.44m (personal best) and 2:12.55, finishing well clear of Dobrynska (4851) and Chernova (4762). Outdoors in Götzis she produced her second highest heptathlon score thus far as despite awful weather conditions she totalled 6689 (4119 first day) to win by 117 points from Chernova. Her marks: 12.89, 1.91m, 14.25m (personal best), 23.31, 6.13m, 43.40m and 2:11.19. She was better still at the European Championships in Barcelona, amassing 6823 (4080 first day) to miss Denise Lewis's Commonwealth record by just eight points. Her series: 12.95, 1.89m, 14.05m, 23.21, 6.43m, 46.71m (personal best) and 2:10.18. She needed that strong second day as Dobrynska finished only 45 points adrift.

Jess did not contest the late season Commonwealth Games in Delhi, the gold medal going to Louise Hazel with her highest score of 6156. The only other Commonwealth champions were Jo Jackson in the 20km walk (1:34:22) and the England 4x100m relay team (44.19). In addition to Jess's gold, there were three bronze medals at the Europeans: Jenny Meadows (who had placed second in the World Indoors 800m in a UK record 1:58.43) ran 1:59.39, Perri Shakes-Drayton 54.18 in the 400m hurdles and the 4x400m team clocked 3:24.32 with Perri producing a splendid anchor split of 49.60. There was a highly commendable effort also by Hatti Dean in the steeplechase, finishing an unexpectedly high fourth and so close to a bronze medal with her personal best time of 9:30.19.

Other honours were gained during 2010 in the younger age groups, boding well for the future. Jodie Williams, still only 16, became World Junior 100m champion in 11.40 prior to finishing second in the 200m (23.19), which extraordinarily was her first ever defeat after 151 victories between 60 and 400m. Earlier in the season she had set European Youth (under-17) records in both events with 11.24 and 22.79. The other World Junior gold medallist was Sophie Hitchon. A former ballerina, capable of running 100m in 12.1, Sophie won the hammer with a UK junior record of 66.01m. Laura Samuel placed second in the triple jump with a UK junior record of 13.75m and Holly Bleasdale – who had earlier vaulted 4.35m for a national junior record – found 4.15m sufficed for third place. Another young athlete making waves was national cross country champion Steph Twell. Before she was 21 she had run 800m in 2:02.59, 1500m in 4:02.70, road 10km in 32:26 and half marathon in 71:56 as well as winning a World Junior 1500m title and three European Junior cross country championships. In the weeks following her 21st birthday she improved to 4:02.54, ran 3000m in 8:42.75 and 5000m in 14:54.08 and at the Commonwealth Games, representing Scotland – her mother's country of birth – she took the 1500m bronze medal.

JESS MAINTAINS OLYMPIC TRADITION?

Mary Peters and Denise Lewis have been crowned Olympic multi-event champions ... and in those glorious London Olympics Jessica Ennis followed suit. Promoted as "The Face" of the Games, Jess ran out the heptathlon winner by a massive 306 points with the Commonwealth record score of 6955.

Born in that Yorkshire city on January 28 1986, Jess joined the local City of Sheffield AC and from the age of 13 has had the good fortune to be coached by Toni Minichiello. Although it quickly became apparent that the high jump was her strongest individual event, despite being quite short (she stopped growing at 1.64m or just under 5ft 5in), he appreciated her all-round ability and willingness to explore new events. She contested her first pentathlon in 1999, placing fourth in the national under-15 championship, and her first AAA titles came in 2000 when she became pentathlon and high jump champion in that age group. She contested her first heptathlons in 2001, gaining a junior international vest, and her progress continued relentlessly.

Her international championship blooding came at the 2003 World Youth Championships, where she was a clear leader after five events but because of a weak javelin she ended up fifth. There was a similar scenario at the 2004 World Juniors, again leading on the first day but winding up eighth. The tide turned at the 2005 European Juniors where she retained her advantage throughout and set a UK junior record of 5891. Only just turned 20, she scored 6269 for third place in the 2006 Commonwealth Games and her next big breakthrough came in May 2007 when she won an international competition with 6388 which included a 1.95m high jump, a full foot (31cm) above her own head, to equal the UK record. Later that season she won at the European Cup with 6399 and placed fourth in the World Championships with 6469.

Everything was shaping up well for the 2008 Olympics, including personal bests in her two weakest events of 13.52m (shot) and 43.08m (javelin), when she suffered a triple stress fracture to her right ankle. Her season was over and during her rehabilitation she had to re-learn the long jump, taking off from the other (left) foot. Her comeback in 2009 was sensational, winning with 6587 in Italy in May and becoming World champion in Berlin in August with 6731 – finishing a massive 238 points clear. She enjoyed another wonderful campaign in 2010, taking the World Indoor pentathlon title with a UK record 4937, winning the Götzis classic with 6689 and capturing the European title with her best score thus far of 6823.

She came close to that with a 6790 victory in Götzis in May 2011 but despite setting personal bests in the shot, long jump and 800m she had to settle for second (6751) to Russia's Tatyana Chernova (6880) in the World Championships in Daegu. She was second again at the 2012 World Indoor Championships in Istanbul despite a UK record score of 4965 but struck brilliant form in the summer with victories at Götzis and the Olympics with Commonwealth record scores of 6906 and 6955. Her individual personal bests of 12.54 100m hurdles (UK record), 1.95m high jump (equalling UK record), 14.79m shot, 22.83 200m, 6.51m long jump, 47.49m javelin and 2:07.81 800m add up to no fewer than 7128 points.

Jess Ennis continued as Britain's top female athlete in 2011 but was run close by Hannah England, the surprise package of the World Championships in Daegu. An ankle injury cost

Jess seven weeks of training and caused her to withdraw from the European Indoor Championships but she was in fine form in Götzis with a score of 6790 which included personal bests in the 200m (23.11) and 800m (2:08.46). Left far behind was runner-up Tatyana Chernova, the statuesque Russian scoring 6539. Prior to Daegu, Jess clocked 12.79 for the hurdles, which would have been a UK record earlier in the year, only American-born Tiffany Porter (née Ofili), now eligible to represent Britain, ran 12.60 and 12.56. At the World Championships Jess "beat" Chernova in five of the seven events but – conceding no fewer than 251 points in the javelin (39.95m to 52.95m) – the Russian won the title with 6880 to Jess's 6751. At the end of day one Jess held a 4078-3927 advantage and after long jumping a personal best of 6.51m (6.66m from take-off to landing) she was still 118 points ahead with her best ever five-event score of 5088 but the javelin situation made all the difference even though Jess finished off with her fastest ever 800m time of 2:07.81.

Britain's other silver medallist in Daegu was, to everyone's astonishment, Hannah England, who had only just scraped through to the 1500m final. It was a bizarre race, marred by the fall of one of the favourites, and Hannah and another outsider, Jennifer Simpson (USA), took full advantage as more fancied runners wilted along the finishing straight. Hannah, moving from seventh to second, clocked 4:05.68. Earlier in the season she had improved her personal best to 4:01.89. Hannah's exploit made up somewhat for the disappointment of Jenny Meadows (1:59.07 semi) failing to reach the 800m final and the disqualification for a false start in her 400m heat of Christine Ohuruogu. Most frustrated of all may have been Tiffany Porter who, after her UK record 12.56 for the second quickest time in the semis of the 100m hurdles, realised she was capable of a medal. She looked almost certain to go sub-12.50 and possibly finish second or third when she hit the ninth hurdle and was thrown out of position for the final barrier. She still clocked 12.63 for fourth but it was a lost opportunity for the former American who in her GB team debut at the European Indoors had finished second in a photo finish with the UK 60m hurdles record time of 7.80. There were two British winners in Paris as Helen Clitheroe captured her first major international title at 37 and Jenny Meadows, second in the 800m in 2:00.50, was promoted to champion due to a drugs disqualification. Having earlier in the winter been "gobsmacked" by clocking a big 3000m pb of 8:39.81, Helen took the gold medal with a dip finish in 8:56.66.

The 2011 season produced some other golden moments, but by much younger athletes. Jodie Williams won the sprint double at the European Junior Championships in 11.18 (UK junior record) and 22.94; Desiree Henry (23.25 200m) and Louisa James (57.13m hammer) were victorious at the World Youth Championships, and Holly Bleasdale not only won the European under-23 pole vault title with 4.55m but became UK record holder with 4.70m, adding a centimetre to that indoors in December ... before clearing a remarkable 4.87m (and attempting a world indoor record of 5.01m) in January 2012! That 4.87m is the highest ever by any 20-year-old and at time of writing ranked her third on the world all-time list indoors or out.

The Olympic Games in London was obviously the major target for Britain's elite athletes in 2012 but several hit top form for the World Indoor Championships in Istanbul in March and no fewer than six medals were gained – our best ever showing at these championships. Holly Bleasdale (4.70m pole vault) and Anguilla-born Shara Proctor (UK indoor long jump record of 6.89m) finished third in their events, while Jess Ennis, who broke her UK pentathlon record with 4965 points, and Tiffany Porter (7.94 60m hurdles) won silver. One of the two gold medals achieved went, somewhat improbably, to the 39-year-old triple jumper Yamilé Aldama. A native of Cuba, who she represented between 1996 and 2000, she moved to London with her British husband in 2001 and had hoped to compete for Britain at the 2004 Olympics. Unable to receive a UK passport in time, she accepted an invitation to represent Sudan, which she did until 2010. She finally became a UK citizen that year and in 2011 as a member of the British team placed fifth in the World Championships. Yamilé, whose personal best of 15.29m back in 2003 ranks her fifth on the world all-time list, produced an astonishing performance in Istanbul by leaping 14.82m, her longest jump since 2005, and a world "masters" (35 and over) best. The other British triumph came in the 4x400m relay, surely the most thrilling race at this distance since the 1969 GB v France classic at the European Championships in Athens. A back to form Christine Ohuruogu propelled the team into the lead on the third leg after sound work by American-born Shana Cox and Nicola Sanders, and Perri Shakes-Drayton on the anchor held on – just – against the individual 400m champion Sanya Richards-Ross (USA) to ensure a famous British victory in 3:28.76. It was an auspicious start to a very special Olympic year. (see page 247 for an Olympic year update).

The England Athletics Hall of Fame was instituted in 2008 and women athletes to be inducted during the first four years have been Sally Gunnell, Ann Packer, Mary Rand, Dorothy Tyler, Kelly Holmes, Kathy Cook, Dorothy Hyman, Denise Lewis and Jean Pickering, while Paula Radcliffe was voted athlete of the decade, 2000-2010. Liz McColgan and Yvonne Murray have been inducted into the Scottish Sports Hall of Fame and Kirsty Wade was similarly recognised in Wales.

Honoured by The Queen since the year 2000: Dame: Mary Peters 2000 (for services to sport and to the community in Northern Ireland), Kelly Holmes 2005 & Tanni Grey-Thompson (now Baroness Grey-Thompson) 2005 (multi Paralympic champion; for services to disabled sport); CBE: Tessa Sanderson 2004 (Vice-Chairman Sport England); OBE: Judy Oakes 2000, Denise Lewis 2001, Maeve Kyle 2008, Zahara Hyde Peters 2010 (former UKA Head of Athletic Development & WAAA indoor 3000m champion 1999/2000); MBE: Freda Clarke 2000 (managed England teams at six successive Commonwealth Games), Dr Stephanie Cook 2001 (2000 Olympic modern pentathlon champion; 7th in 1997 national cross country), Paula Radcliffe 2002, Dorothy Tyler 2002 (at age 81), George Bunner 2002 (for services to athletics for young people), Ashia Hansen 2003, Wilf Paish 2005, Christine Ohuruogu 2009, Myrtle Augee 2009 (for her work as a senior officer at Pentonville Prison), Jean Pickering 2010, Norma Blaine 2011, Jessica Ennis 2011.

Sadly, many distinguished personalities from women's athletics passed away during the first years of this century. In 2000: 95-year-old Edith Peacock (née White), 2nd in the 1926 Women's World Games 100 yards hurdles and a founder member of Manor Park Ladies (later Essex Ladies); and Margaret Elgie, who represented Wales on the BAAB & BAF and helped form the Athletic Association of Wales. In 2001: 96-year-old Ruth Christmas, who set her first British 800m record in 1929 and an unofficial world best for the mile in 1932. In 2002: Sir Arthur Gold, former President of the AAA of England and European Athletic Association. In 2003: Denise Ramsden, a protégée of Dorothy Hyman who won a bronze medal in the 1969 European 4x100m, aged 17. In 2005: 92-year-old Audrey Brown (Court), silver medallist in the 1936 Olympic 4x100m; Denis Watts, coach to Dorothy Hyman, Ann Packer and Lillian Board among many others; and Dr Carol Tyson, world record breaking walker. In 2006: Dave Arnold, the coach who guided Kelly Holmes to many of her triumphs; and Eric Cowe, the foremost women's athletics historian. In 2007: Bertha Crowther, 1950 European pentathlon and Empire Games high jump silver medallist. In 2009: 101-year-old Marjorie Harris (née Okell), WAAA high jump champion in 1929 and 1931 and a WAAA Life Vice-President. In 2010: Wilf Paish, who coached Tessa Sanderson to Olympic javelin gold; Janet Clerc (née Simpson), Olympic 4x100m bronze medallist in 1964 and member of the world record breaking 4x400m team at the 1969 European Championships; and Janet Ruff, England hockey international who set a world 440y record in 1956. In 2012: Margaret Oakley, WAAA Chairman 1983-1991 and Sally Gunnell's coach Bruce Longden.

What of the governing bodies during these early years of the 21st century? There were many fundamental changes, full details of which can be found in the companion volume to this book, *The Official History of the AAA* (1880-2010). Briefly, the British Athletic Federation (BAF), which began life in 1991, did not survive. It went into administration and was eventually succeeded in 1999 as the supreme governing body by UK Athletics (UKA), while in 2006 England Athletics replaced the AAA of England as that country's ruling body. The AAA of

England, which had come into existence in 1991 when the AAA and Women's AAA merged, reverted in 2007 to the historic title of AAA but with its status and functions reduced, and the last time the AAA was incorporated into the name of the national championships was in 2006. Nevertheless, the AAA still has a valuable contribution to make, as explained by former UK 800m record holder Chris Carter, who became AAA Chairman in 2009.

"Since the formation of the AAA in 1880 athletics worldwide has gone through numerous changes in all aspects of communication, organisation, specification, coaching and attitudes. The AAA underwent a fundamental change when it ceased to be the governing body for the sport in England after more than 125 years. There were many outside reasons for this change but not least was that all outside sources of funding were withdrawn which meant the Association was unable to continue in the same way. However painful the loss of governing body status was, the Association has remained positive and is committed to ensure the Association's influence and finances are used as effectively as possible to support the clubs and athletes in England.

"The Association is determined to play its part within athletics in the years up to and beyond the 2012 London Olympics, arguably the greatest sporting festival in the country since 1948. Our contribution to developing initiatives for younger athletes, illustrated by the successful Tom Pink Relay programme, is specifically designed to meet the important objective of stimulating and encouraging interest in athletics. It also serves to keep our younger athletes in the sport longer, thus ensuring many will stay to ensure a thriving and successful sport at the highest level. The transitional period is now over and the Amateur Athletic Association is committed to going forward in partnerships with other like-minded athletic bodies for the common good of athletics in England."

The AAA is responsible for the preservation of the historic trophies that have been entrusted to the Association over the years as part of the sport's heritage. Work has been done by Jack Miller and Philip Andrew of the British Athletics Supporters Club who have photographed and researched the collection.

A selection of AAA and WAAA trophies are now presented each year at the England Athletics Senior Championships.

Sportshall Athletics, created by George Bunner (AAA of England Chairman 2004-2007) in 1976, introduced such names as Denise Lewis, Kelly Sotherton and Jade Johnson to the joys of the sport and it continues to thrive. Another imaginative initiative developed by George Bunner has been the AAA's International Simultaneous Marathon Relay, now known as the World Marathon Challenge, promoted by Save The Children and linked to the United Nations. This event sees enthusiastic teams of around 30 boys and girls from School Year 8 race the marathon distance against the clock and other teams from around the world in a continuous track relay of 200m legs. The AAA Charity for the Young each year awards grants to around 200 young athletes to provide assistance for sports expenses and equipment. Another area in which the AAA is making a difference is support for the English Cross Country Association and the English Road Running Association by providing medals for their championships and grants towards the development of area cross country relays.

The Women's AAA no longer exists as a separate entity, but within the AAA and England Athletics the function of providing competition and coaching for female athletes of all ages and abilities continues.

Highlights from each of the AAA or UK Championships meetings
2000–2012

2000 (Birmingham)

LABELLED THE NORWICH Union Olympic Trials & AAA Championships, the meeting attracted everyone with aspirations of competing in Sydney. The first two finishers in each event would automatically be chosen for the Games, subject to having achieved the 'A' qualifying standard, with a third team place where appropriate being awarded at the selectors' discretion. Struggling somewhat in the closing stages, Kelly Holmes won the 800m in 2:02.08. She would also be picked for the 1500m, an event she didn't contest in Birmingham and which was won by Hayley Tullett by a wide margin in 4:06.44. Dr Lisa Kehler picked up a $5000 bonus for setting a UK record of 45:09.57 in the 10,000m walk, not bad going for someone who had announced her retirement after the 1992 Olympics due to incurring so many stress fractures (pelvis, ribs, feet) and who had undergone an emergency Caesarean giving birth to a son in September 1999. There were championship records by newly married Paula Radcliffe (15:05.48 5000m just two days after a great 8:28.85 3000m in Zürich), Lorraine Shaw (66.85m hammer) and Kelly Morgan (58.45m with the "new" javelin). Donna Fraser, showing the benefits of training with Cathy Freeman, went close to her best time as she took the 400m in 50.94. Katharine Merry, who had lowered her personal best to 50.05 when winning over a star-studded field in Nice the previous month, was a non-starter while recovering from injury niggles, and also absent with physical problems was Denise Lewis who had set a magnificent Commonwealth heptathlon record of 6831 in Talence. Jo Jennings cleared 1.89m to win the high jump for the third year running. In third place, with a personal best of 1.86m (which she raised to 1.88m a week later), was Lee McConnell ... the Scot who would become 400m champion in 2002, 2008 and 2010. Judy Oakes (42), who had earlier notched up her 18th indoor shot title (18.30m), bowed out with her 17th AAA outdoor victory (17.91m) and was rewarded with a standing ovation from the crowd as she took a well deserved lap of honour. Judy, who represented the UK on a record 87 occasions, was presented with an award by her coach Mike Winch, no mean shot putter himself. Meanwhile, 14-year-old Jessica Ennis won all three major under-15 high jump championships she contested: AAA Indoor, English Schools and AAA, raising her personal best during the year from 1.64m to 1.71m.

2001 (Birmingham)

HIGHLIGHT OF THE Norwich Union World Trials & AAA Championships was Janine Whitlock's pole vault clearance of 4.40m, her 33rd UK record indoors or out – winning, as a bonus, a Rover car. That brought her a fifth consecutive title and it was also a championship record, as was Lorraine

Shaw's hammer throw of 66.97m. There were two encouraging comebacks following injury: five years after she last won the title Ashia Hansen triple jumped 14.09m, and Kelly Holmes notched up her sixth 800m championship in 2:02.61. In fourth place was Allison Curbishley, who had just moved up to this distance and was now being coached by Steve Cram. Allison went on to clock 2:03.30 a week later and appeared to have a bright future at this event, but injuries – which had already blighted her career at 400m and caused her to give up the 400m hurdles – struck again and she didn't race again after 2001. Another jinxed athlete was Katharine Merry, who at least had the satisfaction of being an Olympic medallist. She was in tremendous form indoors, setting a UK record of 50.53, and in Athens in June she clocked a cracking 49.59, second only to Kathy Cook's 1984 UK record of 49.43 and a time which remained the world's fastest of the year. A virus caused her to pull out of the AAA Championships and then an Achilles tendon injury led to her withdrawal from the World Championships. Her excellent chance of being crowned a global champion had gone – the world title in Edmonton, Canada going to Amy Mbacke Thiam of Senegal in 49.86. The AAA 400m was won in an outdoor personal best of 52.27 by Lesley Owusu ahead of Donna Fraser and ex-high jumper Lee McConnell. In fifth place was Catherine Murphy, who at the Indoor Championships had become the first woman to win a 400/200m double, setting Welsh indoor records at each distance of 52.31 and 23.35.

2002 (Birmingham)

EVER SINCE TESSA Sanderson and Fatima Whitbread retired, the women's javelin had been a depressed area in British athletics ... until the flowering of Kelly Morgan. Two days before her 22nd birthday in June, she added over four metres to her previous best by throwing the world class distance of 63.03m, a UK record with the revised javelin specification, and now the following month at the Norwich Union European Trials and AAA Championships she extended that to 63.87m and 64.87m, which were also championship records. Kelly unfortunately never got near those distances again, victim of a persistent throwing shoulder injury. Her subsequent best was 58.98m in 2004, and it was left to Goldie Sayers (second in Birmingham with 56.96m) to fly the flag in later years. Triple jumper Yamilé Aldama, fourth in the 2000 Olympics representing Cuba, was permitted to compete as she was now a member of the Shaftesbury Barnet club, having moved to London in November 2001 and married a Scot, Andrew Dodds. Her presence proved a great stimulus for Ashia Hansen, whose championship record of 14.25m was broken three times, first by herself in the third round with 14.29m and then by Aldama with a fourth round 14.40m before Ashia reclaimed the property with a final round 14.50m. Aldama was at the time seeking UK citizenship in the hope of competing for Britain at the next Olympics but the authorities refused to expedite the process and she opted instead for Sudan of all places. She reached a peak in 2003 with a massive jump of 15.29m and it was only in 2011 that she was in a position to represent Britain, making a notable if belated debut at the age of 39 by placing fifth in the World Championships. Quite unexpectedly, she was crowned World Indoor champion in 2012.

Lisa Kehler set a UK and championship record of 21:42.51 in the 5000m walk, 14 years after her first title as Lisa Langford, and there was an inaugural mark of 6:31.77 in the 2000m steeplechase by Tara Krzywicki. Janine Whitlock, who had vaulted an overall UK best of 4.44m indoors, won with 4.35m but was subsequently stripped of the title (which went instead to German-born Irie Hill at 4.15m) as she had tested positive in a drugs test held the previous month and was banned for two years. Lee McConnell won the 400m in a personal best of 51.59, Susan Jones narrowly failed to clear the UK record height of 1.96m after winning with 1.92m, and Myrtle Augee – whose strongwoman exploits outside the shot put ring included a world powerlifting title and a bench-press world record of 137.5kg – picked up her fifth shot title since 1989.

2003 (Birmingham)

AS A CONSEQUENCE of the non-appearance for a variety of reasons of such potential World Championships medallists as Kelly Holmes, Jo Pavey, Paula Radcliffe and Ashia Hansen, there was only one performance of the highest world class at the Norwich Union Trials & AAA Championships. Ex-Cuban triple jumper Yamilé Aldama, who ranked third on the world all-time list with 15.29m, smashed Hansen's championship record with 14.98m. The revelation of the meeting was Abi Oyepitan. Well beaten by Joice Maduaka over 100m (11.31 to 11.54), she ran away with the 200m – at which her personal best was only 23.52 before this season – in 22.95. The 2000m steeplechase was staged for the second and last time before being replaced by the 3000m event and Tara Krzywicki improved her UK record to 6:28.07. With Kelly Morgan out of action all year, Goldie Sayers took the opportunity to open her account with a throw of 56.29m ... the first of ten successive national javelin titles (at time of writing). Approaching the end of her career, 35-year-old Lorraine Shaw – who had earlier raised her UK hammer record to 68.93m – captured the sixth of her seven AAA titles with a throw of precisely three metres less. Sharing the unwanted distinction of being the unluckiest athlete of the meeting were the defending 400m and 400m hurdles champions, Lee McConnell and Tasha Danvers, both of whom injured themselves warming up. Now 17, Jessica Ennis was an inconspicuous sixth in the 100m hurdles, but she was already starting to make a name for herself as an all-rounder. At the World Youth Championships she finished fifth in the heptathlon with 5311 points after having led by 100 points after five events before being dragged down by a poor javelin throw of 25.52m. Another athlete on the move was Christine Ohuruogu who, from the inside lane, placed third in the European Junior 400m in a personal best of 54.21

2004 (Manchester)

THE NORWICH UNION Olympic Trials & AAA Championships were staged at the Manchester Regional Arena, constructed around what was the warm-up track for the 2002 Commonwealth Games. Held in chilly, wet and windy conditions, the meeting was notable on the women's side for the exciting emergence of 20-year-old Christine Ohuruogu. She improved all the way from 54.21 to 52.20 in June and now, a month later, she was AAA champion in 50.98, overtaking the favoured Lee McConnell with a sensational finish. She would later progress to 50.50 at the Olympics. Kelly Holmes won a negative split 800m (60.86/58.53) in 1:59.39 for a record seventh victory in this event, finishing well clear of World Indoor bronze medallist Jo Fenn (née Mersh), a talented singer and songwriter off the track. Also claiming a seventh and final title was hammer thrower Lorraine Shaw (68.11m), while Goldie Sayers retained her javelin crown with a personal best of 60.85m. Tina Brown won the inaugural 3000m steeplechase championship in 10:13.19. The two busiest competitors were Kelly Sotherton and Denise Lewis. Kelly was second in the long jump (6.61m) to Jade Johnson's 6.72m and also contested the high jump (1.74m), shot (personal best of 13.68m) and javelin (38.51m), and Denise popped up in the 100m hurdles (13.82), long jump (5.97m), shot (15.09m) and javelin, where she set a personal best of 51.48m with the "new" javelin, but it was an alarming sight to see her hobble off after three rounds of the long jump and she was destined to be a non-finisher in the Olympic heptathlon, in which Kelly took the bronze medal.

2005 (Manchester)

WHILE THERE WERE several encouraging marks by up-and-coming athletes at the Norwich Union World Championships Trials & AAA Championships, the standout performance came from 32-year-old Donna Fraser, who had won her first WAAA title, the under-15 200m, way back in 1987. After reaching the summit of her career by placing fourth in the 2000 Olympics in 49.79 she was beset with Achilles tendon and hip injuries but she was determined not to give up and her reward was a sparkling double – the first at 200m/400m since Winnie Jordan in 1945. On the first day Donna, whose great rival Katharine Merry had just announced her retirement, clocked 52.07 in her 400m heat, and next day – after 200m preliminaries in 23.21 and 23.61 – she won the final in 51.27 (with Christine Ohuruogu, also returning from injury, second in 52.28) followed 90 minutes later by a 23.36 victory into a headwind. Destined two years later to place second to Christine in the World Championships in 49.65, Nicola Sanders also produced an eye-catching performance. Although she was the European Junior bronze medallist in 1999 her best 400m hurdles time prior to 2005 was only 58.28, but then she progressed rapidly to 56.39 before smoothly handling the challenge of Lee McConnell (now trying this event after specialising in the high jump and flat 400m) in 55.61. It was a lean year for UK records, the only new marks coming in the steeplechase by Tina Brown, winner of the title in 10:01.57 but later running 9:48.57 (Jo Ankier having earlier recorded 9:51.1 and 9:50.10), and in the pole vault where Janine Whitlock was back after a two-year drugs ban. She raised her record to 4.46m before the Championships, won the AAA with a modest 4.20m, and subsequently cleared 4.47m for her 39th UK record indoors and out. Susan Jones (1.86m) chalked up her fifth consecutive high jump victory and Sarah Claxton dipped under 13 sec legally for the first time when clocking 12.96 to retain the 100m hurdles title. Third in that race in a personal best of 13.26 was 19-year-old Jessica Ennis.

2006 (Manchester)

THE FULL UNWIELDY title of the meeting was the Norwich Union European Trials Incorporating the UK Championships and AAA of England Championships and, sadly, this was the last occasion on which the AAA would feature in the name of the senior national track and field championships. From an international standpoint the top performance was Nicola Sanders' 50.74 400m. Having decided to pass up the 400m hurdles for the summer (in March she was fourth in the Commonwealth Games in her best time of 55.32), Nicola ran easily her best ever flat race outdoors as she stormed to a 20m winning margin. Although she had run 50.72 at the AAA Indoor Championships earlier in the year, her previous best on a 400m track was 51.47. Christine Ohuruogu returned from injury with a cautious run-out over 200m, finishing fifth in 24.10 as Joice Maduaka – running better than ever at 32 – completed the double in 23.24 after winning the 100m in a personal best of 11.23. On the comeback trail was Ashia Hansen. Although finishing way behind her American training companion Tiombe Hurd (14.15m), she was relieved to jump

13.65m in her first competition for two years following several knee operations which had threatened to end her career. Alas, it was effectively the end of the road for Ashia who continued to be beset by injuries and never again approached 14m. Kelly Sotherton contested four events (13.33 hurdles, 1.82m high jump, 6.51m long jump and outdoor shot personal best of 13.97m), while Jessica Ennis also jumped 1.82m and ran a personal best 13.19 in the hurdles. Considering the shade temperature was 28°C there were excellent runs by Jo Pavey in the 5000m (15:07.38) and Hatti Dean in the steeplechase (championship record of 9:52.04). The 800m was won by Becky Lyne in 2:00.31 (she was Britain's fastest that year with 1:58.20 but her subsequent career was ruined by injury), and there was an upset in the 1500m where Commonwealth champion Lisa Dobriskey was beaten by defending title holder Helen Clitheroe (née Pattinson), 4:09.64 to 4:10.36. Deirdre Ryan's winning high jump of 1.92m was an Irish record.

2007 (Manchester)

NO LONGER INCORPORATING the historic AAA name, the Norwich Union World Trials & UK Championships produced mainly moderate marks, only Goldie Sayers' 63.02m javelin throw measuring up to world class, but the blustery conditions all weekend at a venue which was at the mercy of the elements conspired to downgrade many worthy performances. Goldie believed she would have broken her UK record of 65.05m from earlier that season given a tailwind rather than the prevailing crosswind. Britain's two outstanding heptathletes fared well too. Jessica Ennis became the first since Thelma Hopkins in 1957 to complete a hurdles and high jump double, clocking 13.25 into a strong wind and following with a clearance at 1.87m before attempting to add a centimetre to the UK record of 1.95m which she had equalled during a heptathlon in May. Kelly Sotherton placed fourth (13.51) and second (1.80m), and next day she narrowly beat Jade Johnson in the long jump with 6.53m and was seventh in the shot with 13.62m. Nicola Sanders' 400m time of 51.33 was impressive in the circumstances, having lost training time while recovering from an Achilles tendon injury. She had been the sensation of the indoor season, having won the UK championship in Sheffield in 50.60 and then the European title in Birmingham with a UK record of 50.02. Hatti Dean, who had lowered the UK steeplechase record in three instalments to 9:38.56, opted instead for the 1500m and left the way clear for victory in 9:47.49 by 33-year-old Helen Clitheroe, three times the 1500m champion and in her first season at the event. Jeanette Kwakye added her name to the list of sprint double winners, her times of 11.59 and 23.66 slowed by strong headwinds, and Jo Pavey – who had won the 10,000m title a month earlier in a personal best of 31:26.94 – completed her double with a 15:17.77 5000m.

2008 (Birmingham)

AFTER FOUR YEARS in Manchester's Sports City, what was this time styled as the Aviva [Norwich Union's new name] National Championships (incorporating Team GB Selection Trials) returned to the more suitable Alexander Stadium. All eyes were on Britain's brightest Olympic hope in the women's events, Christine Ohuruogu. She had displayed much improved basic speed, clocking 11.35 for 100m and 22.94 for 200m, and she chose to race at 200m as her Olympic selection at 400m was already guaranteed. She didn't manage to beat Emily Freeman (22.92) but, closing fast at the end, she wasn't far behind with 22.99, her second fastest ever time. With Nicola Sanders absent, resting a quadriceps strain, the 400m title went to Lee McConnell in 52.31. Also missing were an ill Jenny Meadows in the 800m and an injured Hatti Dean in the steeplechase, those titles going to Marilyn Okoro in 1:59.81 and Helen Clitheroe, whose time of 9:36.98 broke Hatti's UK record. Another UK record came in the 5000m walk where, competing with the men, Jo Jackson finished second in 21:30.75. Jeanette Kwakye, a close runner-up in the World Indoor 60m in a UK record 7.08, took the 100m crown in a personal best 11.26 almost a metre clear of Montell Douglas. Less expected was the 400m hurdles result, with Perri Shakes-Drayton (19) clocking her fastest time of 56.09 ahead of Tasha Danvers (57.00). However, the Olympic selectors opted for the vastly more experienced Danvers, and their faith was justified when she rose to the occasion in Beijing with a time of 53.84 and a bronze medal. Jo Pavey duplicated her 5000m/10,000m double of the previous year, while Jo Duncan – seven years older at 41 – regained the shot title after an interval of five years.

2009 (Birmingham)

THE OUTSTANDING PERFORMANCE of the Aviva World Trials & UK Championships came not from a British athlete but from an Ethiopian guest. Permitted to enter the 10,000m in a bid for World Championships selection, World 5000m champion and record holder Meseret Defar needed to run around 30:48 to stake her claim but right from the outset it was clear she was after something much quicker. Despite heavy rain on a cool and windy evening, she reached halfway in 15:05.66 and covered the last 5000m in 14:53.54 to finish in 29:59.20, shattering Paula Radcliffe's UK all-comers record of 30:17.15. Kate Dennison raised her UK pole vault record to 4.57m (the classic 15 feet). That was a championship record, as were Jo Jackson's 21:21.67 in the 5000m walk – a mixed event in which she finished way ahead of all of the men – and the 12.87 100m hurdles by Jessica Ennis, who also won the high jump at 1.91m. Joice Maduaka's winning 100m time of 11.52 into a 1m/sec wind was nothing special but hers was a record sixth title at an event she first won in 1998, while Goldie Sayers – off a short run-up following back injury – threw the javelin 55.33m for her seventh consecutive victory. Building up for the defence of her World title, Christine Ohuruogu took the 400m in 51.26, which was not as fast as she might have hoped but she was not at 100% due to a lingering virus. Runner-up Perri Shakes-Drayton, the previous year's 400m hurdles champion, improved from 52.98 to 51.81. The following weekend she clocked a personal best of 55.26 to win the European Under-23 hurdles title in Kaunas. Also crowned champion there was Eden Francis in the discus with 57.29m, while the victorious 4x100m relay team in 43.89 included Lucy Sargent, daughter of former UK pentathlon record holder Ann Wilson.

2010 (Birmingham)

DISAPPOINTINGLY, JESS ENNIS (ill) and Christine Ohuruogu (injured) were absent from the Aviva European Trials and UK Championships, Jenny Meadows scratched as a precaution from the 800m final because of a tight calf, and sprint sensation Jodie Williams sensibly by-passed the meeting on the advice of her coach, former Commonwealth 200m co-champion Mike McFarlane, in order to concentrate on the World Junior Championships. In Jodie's absence Laura Turner (11.41) and Joice Maduaka (11.42) fought out a close 100m, with Laura completing the double in 23.66. The most bizarre event was the 1500m, won by Hannah England over Celia Taylor and Lisa Dobriskey in an incredibly slow 4:33.23 ... but with her final 400m covered in an incredibly swift 56.77! Barbara Parker, a former UK record holder, was only just outside her best with a 9:37.7 steeplechase victory against Hatti Dean (9:40.69), who was just getting back after injury and would go so close to a medal at the European Championships. Another who would improve dramatically in Barcelona was Perri Shakes-Drayton, winner of the 400m hurdles in 56.93 but destined to run 54.18 for third place in the Europeans. Two UK junior records went by the board: Laura Samuel won the triple jump with 13.52m and Holly Bleasdale vaulted 4.35m behind Kate Dennison (4.45m). Later in the month the inaugural England Senior Championships were staged in Gateshead, the results being of a generally modest standard.

2011 (Birmingham)

THE BRIGHTEST STAR of the Aviva UK Trials & Championships was someone who didn't need to be there, her place in Daegu assured as defending World heptathon champion. Jess Ennis displayed superb form as she totalled 4746 points for the five individual events she contested. She put the shot 14.25m to equal her outdoor personal best, won the high jump at 1.89m, was second to ex-American Tiffany Porter (championship record of 12.76) in the hurdles with 12.96, placed third in the long jump with 6.44m and threw the javelin 42.93m. She would go on to finish second in Daegu with 6751 points, a position occupied also by Hannah England in the 1500m, the winner in Birmingham in 4:07.05 in a close finish with Lisa Dobriskey. Perri Shakes-Drayton completed an unprecedented double by winning both the 400m (51.52) and 400m hurdles (55.52), while Goldie Sayers also made history by notching up her ninth consecutive javelin title (60.57m) – matching Judy Farr's sequence in the 3000m walk 1962-1970. However, she would need to win again in 2012 to equal Tessa Sanderson's ten victories in this event, spread between 1975 and 1996. Jenny Meadows won the 800m (2:02.28), which wasn't a surprise ... what was is the realisation that this was her first senior outdoor national title although she did win the under-20 400m 11 years earlier. There was a changing of the guard in the pole vault as Holly Bleasdale cleared 4.56m to defeat Kate Dennison (4.40m). Earlier in the month Holly had experienced a massive breakthrough in a German meeting. First she equalled Kate's UK record of 4.60 and then raised it to 4.65 and 4.70. She also won the European Under-23 title (4.55m), a meeting in which Sophie Hitchon had placed third with a UK hammer record of 69.59m. She went on to win the UK title with 67.69m. The UK Indoor Championships in Sheffield threw up sprint winners at either end of their careers. Jodie Williams (17) took the 60m in 7.24 while Joice Maduaka (37) won the 200m in 23.63 for her 18th national sprint title (nine indoors and nine outdoors) and her 34th medal between 1995 and 2011. Only Judy Oakes has bettered those figures with 35 titles and 40 medals.

2012 (Birmingham)

COLD, WINDY WEATHER adversely affected performances in several events at the Aviva Olympic Trials & UK Championships but the conditions did not prevent two UK records being established by Holly Bleasdale and Shara Proctor, two of the stars of the indoor season. Holly cleared 4.71m to add a centimetre to her outdoor pole vault mark, while Shara – watched by two former holders of the record in Jean Pickering and Mary Rand – long jumped 6.95m to break Bev Kinch's 1983 figures. Christine Ohuruogu scored a wide victory in the 400m (51.89), while Perri Shakes-Drayton, the previous holder of that title, opted instead for the 400m hurdles, where she won for the third year running after a close struggle with Eilidh Child, 55.45 to 55.53. Jessica Ennis easily beat Tiffany Porter in the 100m hurdles (12.92) as well as winning the high jump (1.89m), but was disappointed with her sixth place in the long jump with 6.27m. Earlier in the season, when setting a magnificent Commonwealth heptathlon record of 6906 when winning in Götzis, she had tied her personal best of 6.51m as well as setting lifetime bests in the 200m (22.88) and javelin (47.11m). Destined three weeks later to raise her UK record to 66.17m at Crystal Palace, Goldie Sayers notched up her tenth consecutive javelin title (58.45m), while an earlier UK record breaker in Sophie Hitchon (71.61m) took the hammer with 69.79m. Another to set a UK record in 2012, Barbara Parker (9:24.24 steeplechase), ran instead in the 5000m, placing second to Jo Pavey (15:54.18). Jo went on to gain a silver medal, at 38, in the European 10,000m championship in Helsinki (31:49.03), as did UK 800m title winner in 2:01.72, Lynsey Sharp, who improved to 2:00.52. She is the daughter of 1982 European 200m silver medallist Cameron Sharp and the former Carol Lightfoot, who ran 2:02.91 for 800m that year. One other athlete to single out: Katarina Johnson-Thompson, who had earlier smashed Jessica Ennis's UK junior heptathlon record with 6248 points, leapt a wind-aided 6.81m to win the World Junior long jump gold medal in Barcelona.

GOLD AND SILVER AT LONDON OLYMPICS

The pressure on Jessica Ennis, as the "poster girl" of London 2012, was enormous but she came through with flying colours. Inspired by a hugely enthusiastic and supportive capacity crowd of 80,000 for the first morning session of athletics, Jess made a phenomenal start to the heptathlon by clocking 12.54 for 100m hurdles. That was not only a UK record but the fastest ever in a heptathlon and a time which would have won the individual gold medal at the Beijing Olympics! Her high jump of 1.86m was a disappointment but she ended the first day with a reasonable shot put of 14.28m and a sparkling personal best of 22.83 in the 200m for her highest score of 4158 and a comfortable lead of 184 points. World champion Tatyana Chernova, seen as her main rival, was languishing in tenth place 309 points behind. Jess's opening long jump was poor but she recovered well to register 6.48m, only 3cm below her best ever, and a personal best javelin throw of 47.49m gave her an unassailable lead of 188 points going into the final event, the 800m. She could have taken it easy but that's not in Jess's nature and she won a hotly contested race in 2:08.65 for a final score of 6955 and an enormous victory margin of 306 points. Jess (26) will no doubt go on to further triumphs but already her successor is apparent. Katarina Johnson-Thompson (19), winner earlier in the summer of the World Junior long jump title, posted four individual personal bests to finish a meritorious 15th (she was third after the hurdles and high jump!) with a UK junior record of 6267 as compared to Jess's best at that age of 5910. The British team's other medallist was defending 400m champion Christine Ohuruogu. Hitting peak form at just the right time, Christine improved upon her season's best of 50.42 with 50.22 in her semi-final and 49.70 in the final in which she stormed through from sixth to a fast closing second to Sanya Richards-Ross of the USA (49.56) along the finishing straight. Other British athletes to place in the top eight were Jo Pavey (7th) and Julia Bleasdale (8th), the leading Europeans in both the 5000m and 10,000m; Holly Bleasdale, equal sixth in the pole vault; Yamilé Aldama, fifth in the triple jump; and the fifth placed 4x400m team of Shana Cox, Lee McConnell, Perri Shakes-Drayton and Christine Ohuruogu. Sophie Hitchon broke her own UK hammer record when qualifying with 71.98m before placing 12th in the final.

UNITED KINGDOM RECORDS AT 12 AUGUST 2012

100m: 11.05 Montell Douglas 2008; 200m: 22.10 Cook 1984; 400m: 49.43 Cook 1984; 800m: 1:56.21 Kelly Holmes 1995; 1500m: 3:57.90 Holmes 2004; Mile: 4:17.57 Zola Budd 1985; 3000m: 8:22.20 Paula Radcliffe 2002; 5000m: 14:29.11 Radcliffe 2004; 10,000m: 30:01.09

Radcliffe 2002; Half Mar: 65:40 Radcliffe 2003; Mar: 2:15:25 Radcliffe 2003; 3000mSC: 9:24.24 Barbara Parker 2012; 100mH: 12.54 Jessica Ennis 2012; 400mH: 52.74 Sally Gunnell 1993; HJ: 1.95 Diana Davies 1982, Susan Jones 2001 & Jessica Ennis 2007 (1.95 indoors Debbie Marti 1997); PV: 4.71 Holly Bleasdale 2012 (4.87 indoors 2012); LJ: 6.95 Shara Proctor 2012; TJ: 15.15 Ashia Hansen 1997 (15.16 indoors 1998); SP: 19.36 Judy Oakes 1988; DT: 67.48 Meg Ritchie 1981; HT: 71.98 Sophie Hitchon 2012; JT: (current specification) 66.17 Goldie Sayers 2012; (old specification) 77.44 Fatima Whitbread 1986; Heptathlon: 6955 Jessica Ennis 2012 (100H-12.54, HJ-1.86, SP-14.28, 200-22.83, LJ-6.48, JT-47.49, 800-2:08.65); 4x100m: 42.43 British team 1980; 4x400m: 3:20.04 British team 2007; 3000m Walk: 12:22.62 Jo Jackson 2009; 5000m Walk: 20:46.58 Jackson 2009; 10,000m Walk: 45:09.57 Lisa Kehler 2000 (43:52 road Jackson 2010); 20km Walk: 1:30:41 Jackson 2010; 50km Walk: 4:50:51 Sandra Brown 1991.

BRITISH WOMEN'S HONOURS LIST

THIS LIST FEATURES nearly 200 British female athletes who achieved particular international distinction between 1920 and the present day. Criteria for inclusion: placing in first three in the Olympics, World Championships (including cross country since it became an IAAF event in 1973) and World Indoor Championships; winner in individual events only in European Championships, European Indoor Games/Championships, Empire/Commonwealth Games, International (pre-IAAF) & European Cross Country Championships, and World Race Walking Cup, plus world record setters in the more commonly contested or significant events. * = record not ratified by IAAF and/or FSFI (Women's World Federation; marks set between 1921 and 1934). Abbreviations used: Oly = Olympic Games; World = World Championships; World/Eur Ind = World/European Indoor Championships; Int/World/Eur CC = International/World/European Cross Country; Eur = European Championships; CG = Commonwealth Games.

ALDAMA Yamilé: 1 2012 World Ind TJ
ALEXANDER Sheila: see under LERWILL
ALLDAY Sue: 1 1958 CG DT
ARDEN Daphne: 3 1964 Oly 4x100; world record – 4x110y (45.2 – 1963)
ARMITAGE Heather: see under YOUNG
ATTWOOD Pauline: World record – 4x400 (3:37.6 – 1969)
AUGEE Myrtle: 1 1990 CG SP

BALL Valerie: World records – 880y (2:14.5 – 1952), 4x220y (1:43.4 – 1951), 3x800m/3x880y (7:07.8 – 1949)
BAPTISTE Joan: 2 1983 World 4x100
BARTHOLOMEW Phyllis: 1 1934 CG LJ
BEACHAM Margaret: 1 1971 Eur Ind 1500; world indoor records – 1500

(4:20.5*, 4:17.4* & 4:17.2* – 1971)
BELASCO Joan: World record – HJ (1.575* & 1.625* – 1920)
BELL Chris: see under PERERA
BERNARD Verona: see under ELDER
BIGNAL Mary: see under RAND
BLEASDALE Holly: 3 2012 World Ind PV
BOARD Lillian: 2 1968 Oly 400, 1 1969 Eur 800 (1 4x400); world records –
4x110y (45.0 – 1968), 4x400 (3:37.6 & 3:30.8 – 1969), 4x800 (8:27.0 – 1970)
BOOTHE Lorna: 1 1978 CG 100H
BORN Doris: World record – 3x800m/3x880y (7:07.8 – 1949)
BOXER Chris: 1 1982 CG 1500
BRADFORD Carole: 3 1984 World 10k road, 3 1985 World 15k
BRIAN Margaret: World record – 4x220y (1:41.4 – 1951)
BRIGHTWELL Ann: see under PACKER
BROWN Audrey: 2 1936 Oly 4x100
BUDD Zola: 1 1985 & 1986 World CC; world records – 2000 (5:33.15* –
1984), 5000 (14:48.07 – 1985); world indoor record – 3000 (8:39.79 – 1986)
BURKE Barbara (GBR/S Africa): 2 1936 Oly 4x100; world records – 100y
(11.0 – 1935), 220y (24.8 – 1935), 80mH (11.6 – 1937)

CAHILL Chris: see under BOXER
CALLEBOUT Nora: World record – 4x100m/4x110y (51.4/51.8 – 1922)
CALLENDER Bev: (4x100) 3 1980 Oly, 2 1983 World, 2 1984 Oly
CAREY Sheila: World records – 4x800 (8:27.0 & 8:25.0 – 1970)
CAST Alice: World records – 200 (27.8 – 1922), 4x200m/4x220y (1:53.0 – 1921)
CAWLEY Shirley: 3 1952 Oly LJ
CHARLES Diane: see under LEATHER
CHEESEMAN Sylvia: 3 1952 Oly 4x100; world records – 4x200 (1:39.7 –
1952), 4x220y (1:43.9, 1:43.4 & 1:41.4 – 1951)
CHRISTMAS Ruth: World record – 1M (5:27.5* – 1932)
CLITHEROE Helen: 1 2011 Eur Ind 3000
COBB Madeleine: World records – 4x110y (45.3 – 1958, 45.2 – 1963)
COLEBROOK Jane: see under FINCH
COLYEAR Sharon: World record – 4x200 (1:31.6 – 1977)
COOK Kathy: 3 1980 Oly 4x100, 3 1983 World 200 (2 4x100), 3 1984 Oly
400 (3 4x100)
CORNELL Muriel: World records – 80mH (12.2* – 1930), LJ (5.48 & 5.57*
– 1926, 5.57 – 1927)
COX Shana: 1 2012 World Ind 4x400
CRAIG Georgena: World record – 4x800 (8:25.0 – 1970)
CRITCHLEY Muriel: World record – 3x880y (7:00.6 – 1952)
CROPPER Pat: see under LOWE

DANVERS Natasha: 3 2008 Oly 400H
DESFORGES Jean: 3 1952 Oly 4x100, 1 1954 Eur LJ
DISLEY Sylvia: see under CHEESEMAN
DOBRISKEY Lisa: 1 2006 CG 1500, 2 2009 World 1500
DOUGLAS Sandra: 3 1992 Oly 4x400
DRYDEN Joan: World record – 3x880y (7:00.6 – 1952)
DYSON Maureen: see under GARDNER
DYSON Sandra: World record – 400H (61.1* – 1971)

EDWARDS Eileen: World records – 100y (11.3* – 1924), 200 (26.0 –
1926, 25.4 – 1927), 200m/220y (26.2 – 1924, 25.8* – 1926 & 1927),
400m/440y (60.8 – 1924), 4x100m/4x110y (50.2* & 49.8 – 1926),
4x200m/4x220y (1:51.6/1:52.4 – 1923)
ELDER Verona: 1 1973, 1975 & 1979 Eur Ind 400; world record – 4x200
(1:31.6 – 1977)
ELIOTT-LYNN Sophie: World record – HJ (1.47 – 1922)
ELLIOTT Gladys: World records – 200m/220y (26.8* – 1924),
4x200m/4x220y (1:51.6/1:52.4 – 1923)
ENGLAND Hannah: 2 2011 World 1500
ENNIS Jessica: 1 2009 World Hep, 1 2010 World Ind Pen, 1 2010 Eur
Hep, 2 2011 World Hep, 2 2012 World Ind Pen, 1 2012 Oly Hep

FAWKES Marion: 1 1979 World Walk Cup 5k; world records – 10,000
(48:37.6* & 48:11.4* – 1979)
FENN Jo: 3 2004 World Ind 800
FINCH Jane: (800) 1 1977 Eur Ind, 2 1985 World Ind; world indoor record
– 800 (2:01.12* – 1977)
FORSTER Evelyne: World record – 1M (5:15.3* – 1939)
FOSTER Barbara: World record – 4x220y (1:41.4 – 1951)
FOULDS June: see under PAUL
FRASER Donna: 3 2004 Oly 4x400, 3 2005 World 4x400
FUDGE Paula: 1 1978 CG 3000; world record – 5000 (15:14.51 – 1981);
world indoor record – 3000 (8:56.4* – 1981)

GARDNER Maureen: 2 1948 Oly 80mH
GARRITT Eileen: World record – 3x800m/3x880y (7:07.8 – 1949)
GARTON Agnes: World record – 4x200m/4x220y (1:53.0 – 1921)
GODDARD Bev: see under CALLENDER
GODDARD Tracy: 3 1993 World 4x400
GREEN Phyllis (1): World records – HJ (1.52 – 1925, 1.55 – 1926, 1.58* – 1927)
GREEN Phyllis (2): see under PERKINS

GREENWOOD Dora: World record – HJ (1.65* – 1933)
GREIG Dale: World best – Mar (3:27:45 – 1964)
GUNN Muriel: See under CORNELL
GUNNELL Sally: 1 1986 CG 100H, 1 1989 Eur Ind 400, 1 1990 CG 400H, 2 1991 World 400H, 1 1992 Oly 400H (3 4x400), 1 1993 World 400H (3 4x400), 1 1994 CG & Eur 400H; world record – 400H (52.74 – 1993)

HALL Dorothy: see under MANLEY
HALL Olive: World record – 880y (2:17.4 – 1936)
HALL Phyllis: World record – 800m/880y (2:43.0* – 1922)
HALSTEAD Nellie: 3 1932 Oly 4x100; world records – 100y (11.0* – 1931), 220y (25.2* – 1930), 400m/440y (58.8* – 1931, 58.8* & 56.8* – 1932), 800 (2:15.6* – 1935)
HAMPTON Shirley: World records – 4x200 (1:39.7 – 1952), 4x220y (1:39.9 – 1953)
HANSEN Ashia: (TJ) 2 1997 World Ind, 1 1998 Eur Ind, 1 1998 CG, 1 1999 World Ind, 1 2002 CG & Eur, 1 2003 World Ind; world indoor record – (15.16 – 1998)
HARDING Enid: World records – 880y (2:14.4* – 1952), 1M (5:09.8* – 1953)
HARTLEY Donna: 1 1978 CG 400, 3 1980 Oly 4x400; world record – 4x200 (1:31.6 – 1977)
HATT Hilda: World record – 4x100m/4x110y (51.8 – 1921)
HAYNES Florence: World records – 440y (60.8* – 1928), 4x100m/4x110y (50.2* & 49.8 – 1926)
HAZEL Louise: 1 2010 CG Hep
HEARNSHAW Sue: (LJ) 1 1984 Eur Ind, 3 1984 Oly
HICKS Nelly: World record – 800m/880y (2:45.0 – 1922)
HISCOCK Eileen: 3 1932 Oly 4x100, 1 1934 CG 100y & 220y, 2 1936 Oly 4x100; world records – 100y (11.0* – 1931), 220y (25.0* – 1934)
HISCOX Molly: World record – 440y (55.6 – 1958)
HOLMES Kelly: 1 1994 CG 1500, 2 1995 World 1500 (3 800), 3 2000 Oly 800, 1 2002 CG 1500, 2 2003 World Ind 1500, 2 2003 World 800, 1 2004 Oly 800 & 1500
HOPKINS Thelma: (HJ) 1 1954 CG & Eur, 2= 1956 Oly; world record (1.74 – 1956)
HOSKIN Sheila: 1 1958 CG LJ; world record – 4x100 (45.2* – 1956)
HOYTE-SMITH Joslyn: 3 1980 Oly 4x400
HUNTE Heather: see under OAKES
HYMAN Dorothy: 2 1960 Oly 100 (3 200), 1 1962 Eur 100, 1 1962 CG 100y & 220y, 3 1964 Oly 4x100; world records – 4x110y (45.3 – 1958, 45.2 – 1963)
INKPEN Barbara: see under LAWTON

JACKSON Jo: 1 2010 CG 20km Walk
JACOBS Simmone: 3 1984 Oly 4x100
JAMES Della: World record – 4x200 (1:33.8 – 1968)
JOHNSON Ann: World records – 4x200 (1:39.7 – 1952), 4x220y (1:39.9 – 1953)
JOHNSON Ethel: World record – 100y (11.0* – 1932)
JONES Pat: World record – 200H (27.3* – 1967)
JORDAN Joy: World record – 880y (2:06.1 – 1960)

KEOUGH Linda: 3 1993 World 4x400
KINCH Bev: 1 1984 Eur Ind 60
KING Marion: World records – 220y (25.8* – 1928), 440y (60.6* & 59.2* – 1929)
KWAKYE Jeanette: 2 2008 World Ind 60

LANE Gladys: World record – 800m/880y (2:24.8* – 1925)
LANNAMAN Sonia: 1 1978 CG 100, 3 1980 Oly 4x100; world record – 4x200 (1:31.6 – 1977)
LAWTON Barbara: 1 1974 CG HJ
LEACH Daisy: World record – 4x100m/4x110y (51/4/51.8 – 1922)
LEATHER Diane: World records – 440y (56.6* – 1954), 880y (2:09.0 – 1954), 1500 (4:30.0* & 4:29.7* – 1957), 1M (5:02.6* – 1953, 5:00.2* & 4:59.6* – 1954, 4:50.8* & 4:45.0* – 1955), 3x880y (6:49.0 – 1953, 6:46.0 – 1954)
LERWILL Sheila: (HJ) 1 1950 Eur, 2 1952 Oly; world record (1.72 – 1951)
LEWIS Denise: (Hep) 1 1994 CG, 3 1996 Oly, 2 1997 World, 1 1998 Eur & CG, 2 1999 World, 1 2000 Oly
LINES Mary: World records – 60m (7.8* – 1922), 100y (11.8 – 1921, 11.6 – 1922), 100m (12.8 – 1922), 200m/220y (26.8 – 1922), 400m/440y (64.4 – 1922, 62.4 – 1923), 800m/880y (2:26.6 – 1922), 4x100m/4x110y (51.4/51.8 – 1922), 4x200m/4x220y (1:53.0 – 1921, 1:51.6/1:52.4 – 1923)
LOCK Betty: World record – 60m (7.4* – 1938)
LOWE Pat: World records – 4x400 (3:30.8 – 1969), 3x800 (6:20.0 – 1967), 3x880y (6:25.2 – 1967), 4x800 (8:27.0 & 8:25.0 – 1970)
LOWMAN Ivy: World record – HJ (1.47* – 1923)
LUNN Gladys: 1 1934 CG 880y & JT; world records – 880y (2:18.2* – 1930), 1000 (3:04.4 – 1931, 3:00.6 – 1934), 1M (5:24.0* & 5:23.0* – 1936, 5:20.8* & 5:17.0* – 1937)
LYNCH Andrea: 1 1975 Eur Ind 60; world record – 60 (7.2 – 1974)

MACDONALD Linsey: 3 1980 Oly 4x400
MANLEY Dorothy: 2 1948 Oly 100; world record – 4x220y (1:41.4 – 1951)
McCOLGAN Liz: 1 1986 CG 10,000, 2 1987 World CC, 2 1988 Oly

10,000, 2 1989 World Ind 3000, 1 1990 CG 10,000, 3 1991 World CC, 1
1991 World 10,000, 1 1992 World Half Mar; world indoor record – 5000
(15:03.17 – 1992); world road bests – 5k (14:57 – 1991), 10k (30:38 –
1989), Half Mar (67:11 – 1992)
McCONNELL Lee: 3 2004 Oly 4x400, 3 2005 World 4x400, 3 2007
World 4x400
McDERMOTT Kirsty: see under WADE
MEADOWS Jenny: 3 2009 World 800, 2 2010 World Ind 800, 1 2011 Eur
Ind 800
MERRY Katharine: 3 2000 Oly 400
MODAHL Diane: 1 1990 CG 800
MOORE Betty (GBR/AUS): World record – 80H (10.5 – 1962)
MORLEY Kay: 1 1990 CG 100H
MURPHY Catherine: 3 2004 Oly 4x400
MURRAY Yvonne: 1 1987 Eur Ind 3000, 3 1988 Oly 3000, 1 1990 Eur
5000, 1 1993 World Ind 3000, 1 1994 CG 10,000

NEIL Anita: World record – 4x110y (45.0- 1968)
NEUFVILLE Marilyn: 1 1970 Eur Ind 400; world indoor record – 400
(53.01* – 1970); later representing Jamaica: 1st 1970 CG 400; world
record – 400 (51.02 – 1970)
NEWBOULT Jean: World record – 4x220y (1:39.9 – 1953)
NUTTING Pat: World records – 100H (14.3* – 1966), 200H (28.3* – 1961)

OAKES Heather: 3 1980 & 1984 Oly 4x100, 2 1985 World Ind 60,
1 1986 CG 100
OAKES Judy: 1 1982, 1994 & 1998 CG SP
ODAM Dorothy: see under TYLER
OHURUOGU Christine: 3 2004 Oly 4x400, 3 2005 World 4x400, 1 2006
CG 400, 1 2007 World 400 (3 4x400), 1 2008 Oly 400, 1 2012 World Ind
4x400, 2 2012 Oly 400
OKORO Marilyn: 3 2007 World 4x400
OLADAPO Joyce: 1 1986 CG LJ
OLIVER Anne: World records – 1M (5:11.0* – 1952, 5:08.0* – 1953),
3x880y (6:46.0 – 1954)
OLNEY Violet: 2 1936 Oly 4x100

PACKER Ann: 1 1964 Oly 800 (2 400); world record – 800 (2:01.1 – 1964)
PALMER Vera: World record – 4x200m/4x220y (1:51.6/1:52.4 – 1923)
PARLETT Dorothy: see under MANLEY
PASCOE Della: see under JAMES
PASHLEY Anne: 2 1956 Oly 4x100; world records – 4x100 (45.2* – 1956),
4x220y (1:39.9 – 1953)

PAUL June: (4x100) 3 1952 Oly, 2 1956 Oly; world records – 4x100 (45.2* – 1956), 4x110y (45.3 – 1958), 4x200 (1:39.7 – 1952), 4x220y (1:43.9 & 1:43.4 – 1951)

PAWSEY Jenny: World record – 4x400 (3:37.6 – 1969)

PAYNE Rosemary: 1 1970 CG DT

PEAT Val: World record – 4x200 (1:33.8 – 1968)

PERERA Chris: World record – 100H (13.7* – 1967)

PERKINS Phyllis: World records – 1500 (4:35.4* – 1956), 3x880y (7:00.6 – 1952)

PETERS Mary: 1 1970 CG SP & Pen, 1 1972 Oly Pen, 1 1974 CG Pen; world record – Pen (4801 – 1972); world indoor record – 60H (8.5* – 1970)

PICKERING Jean: see under DESFORGES

PIERCY Pam: World records – 3x800 (6:20.0 – 1967), 3x880y (6:25.2 – 1967)

PIRIE Shirley: see under HAMPTON

PLATT Sue: 1 1962 CG JT

PORTER Gwendoline: 3 1932 Oly 4x100

PORTER Muriel: World record – 4x100/4x110y (51.4/51.8 – 1922)

PORTER Tiffany: 2 2012 World Ind 60H

POTTER Edna: World record – 220y (25.8* – 1928)

PROBERT Michelle: 3 1980 Oly 4x400

PROCTOR Shara: 3 2012 World Ind LJ

PRYCE Pat: see under NUTTING

QUINTON Carole: 2 1960 Oly 80mH

RADCLIFFE Paula: 2 1997 World CC, 2 1998 World 8k CC, 1 1998 Eur CC, 3 1999 World 8k CC, 2 1999 World 10,000, 1 2000 World Half Mar, 1 2001 World 8k CC (2 4k CC), 1 2001 World Half Mar, 1 2002 World 8k CC, 1 2002 CG 5000, 1 2002 Eur 10,000, 1 2003 World Half Mar, 1 2003 Eur CC, 1 2005 World Mar; world road records – 10k (30:21 – 2003), 20k (63:26 – 2001), Mar (2:17:18 – 2002, 2:15:25 – 2003); world road bests include – 5k (14:51 – 2003), 8k (24:38 – 1999), 5M (24:47 – 1999), 10M (50:01 – 2003), 15k (46:41 – 2003), Half Mar (65:40 – 2003)

RAND Mary: 1 1964 Oly LJ (2 Pen, 3 4x100), 1 1966 CG LJ; world records – LJ (6.76 – 1964), 4x110y (45.2 – 1963); world indoor record – LJ (6.35* – 1965)

REEVE Sue: 1 1978 CG LJ

RIDLEY Rita: 1 1970 CG 1500, 3 1974 World CC

RITCHIE Meg: 1 1982 CG DT

ROBINS Valerie: World records – 4x220y (1:43.9 & 1:43.4 – 1951)

RUFF Janet: World record – 440y (56.5* – 1956)

SANDERS Nicola: 3 2005 World 4x400, 1 2007 Eur Ind 400, 2 2007

World 400 (3 4x400), 1 2012 World Ind 4x400
SANDERSON Tessa: (JT) 1 1978 CG, 1 1984 Oly, 1 1986 & 1990 CG
SCOULER Doris: World records – 4x100m/4x110y (50.2* & 49.8 – 1926)
SCRIVENS Jean: 2 1956 Oly 4x100; world record – 4x100 (45.2* – 1956)
SEARLE Vera: see under PALMER
SHAKES-DRAYTON Perri: 1 2012 World Ind 4x400
SHAW Lorraine: 1 2002 CG HT
SHERWOOD Sheila: (LJ) 2 1968 Oly, 1 1970 CG
SHIRLEY Dorothy: 2= 1960 Oly HJ
SIMPSON Janet: 3 1964 Oly 4x100; world records – 4x110y (45.0 –
1968), 4x200 (1:33.8 – 1968), 4x400 (3:37.6 & 3:30.8 – 1969); world
best – 500m (1:11.7 – 1968)
SIMPSON Judy: 1 1986 CG Hep
SLATER Daphne: see under ARDEN
SLEMON Chris: World record – 3x880y (6:49.0 – 1953)
SLY Wendy: 1 1983 World 10k road, 2 1984 Oly 3000
SMALLEY Norah: World records – 3x880y (6:49.0 – 1953, 6:46.0 – 1954)
SMITH Anne: World records – 1500 (4:17.3* – 1967), 1M (4:39.2* &
4:37.0 – 1967)
SMITH Joyce: 1 1972 Int CC, 2 1973 World CC; world record – 3000
(9:23.4* – 1971)
SMITH Phylis: (4x400) 3 1992 Oly, 3 1993 World
SOTHERTON Kelly: (Hep) 3 2004 Oly, 1 2006 CG, 3 2007 World; 2 2008
World Ind Pen
STEWART Mary: (1500) 1 1977 Eur Ind, 1 1978 CG; world indoor record
(4:08.1* – 1977)
STIRLING Rosemary: 1 1970 CG 800; world records – 4x400 (3:30.8 –
1969), 3x800 (6:20.0 – 1967), 3x880y (6:25.2 – 1967), 4x800 (8:27.0 &
8:25.0 – 1970)
STONE Anne: World record – 440y (59.2* – 1929)
STOUTE Jennifer: 3 1992 Oly 4x400
STRONG Shirley: (100H) 1 1982 CG, 2 1984 Oly

THOMAS Shirley: 2 1983 World 4x100
THOMPSON Rose: World records – 100y (11.4 – 1922), 4x100m/4x110y
(50.2* & 49.8 – 1926), 4x200m/4x220y (1:51.6/1:52.4 – 1923)
TOOBY Angela: 2 1998 World CC
TRANTER Maureen: World records – 4x110y (45.0 – 1968), 4x200 (1:33.8
– 1968)
TRICKEY Edith: World records – 880y (2:26.6* & 2:24.0* – 1925), 1000
(3:08.2 – 1924)
TULLETT Hayley: 3 2003 World 1500

TURNER Bettie: World record – 4x220y (1:43.9 – 1951)
TYLER Dorothy: (HJ) 2 1936 Oly, 1 1938 CG, 2 1948 Oly, 1 1950 CG;
world records – (1.65* – 1936, 1.66 – 1939)
TYSON Carol: World records – 3000 Walk (13:25.2* – 1979), 5000
(23:11.2* – 1979)

VERNON Judy: 1 1974 CG 100H; world record – 400H (60.4* – 1973)

WADE Kirsty: 1 1982 CG 800, 1 1986 CG 800 & 1500
WALKER Ivy: World records – 100y (11.0* – 1930), 220y (25.4* – 1930)
WALLACE Andrea: 2 1991 World 15k
WEBB Violet: 3 1932 Oly 4x100
WESTON Madeleine: see under COBB
WHITBREAD Fatima: (JT) 2 1983 World, 3 1984 Oly, 1 1986 Eur, 1 1987
World, 2 1988 Oly; world record – (77.44 – 1986)
WILLIAMSON Audrey: 2 1948 Oly 200
WINN Valerie: see under BALL
WISE Jo: 1 1998 CG LJ
WRIGHT Daisy: World record – 4x200m/4x220y (1:53.0 – 1921)
WRIGHT Rosemary: see under STIRLING

YELLING Hayley: 1 2009 Eur CC
YOUNG Heather: 3 1952 Oly 4x100, 2 1956 Oly 4x100, 1 1958 Eur 100;
world record – 4x110y (45.3 – 1958)

OFFICERS OF THE WAAA

President

1922–1925 Lord Hawke
1926–1929 Harry Barclay
1930–1937 Lord Decies
1938–1948 Lady Bailey
1949–1951 Countess of Derby
1952–1964 Lady Reed
1965–1981 Lady Luke
1981–1991 Vera Searle
After merger with AAA:
1991–1994 Dame Marea Hartman
1995–2000 Sir Arthur Gold
2000–2004 Lord (Sebastian) Coe
2004–2011 Sir Rodney Walker

Hon. Secretary

1922–1925 J. M. Thompson
1926–1928 Major W. B. Marchant
1929 Mrs L Goold
1930–1933 Vera Searle
1934–1945 Muriel Cornell
1946–1952 Winifred Hughes
1953–1960 Mary Amies
1960–1991 Marea Hartman
After merger with AAA:
1991–1993 Derek Johnson
1993–2000 Roy Mitchell
2004–   Walter Nicholls

Hon. Treasurer

1922–1928 Major W. B. Marchant
1929–1930 Mrs N. E. Coates
1931–1933 Muriel Cornell
1934–1949 Mrs C. Palmer
1950–1959 Marea Hartman

1960–1963 Hazel Rider
1964–1991 Edith Holland
After merger with AAA:
1991–2001 Geoff Clarke
2001–2005 Keith Atkins
2006   Graham Jessop
2007–2008 Richard Float
2008–2009 Graham Jessop
2010–   Martin Etchells

Chairman

1938–1973 Richard Taylor
1973–1981 Vera Searle
1981–1982 Dorette Nelson Neal
1983–1991 Margaret Oakley
After merger with AAA:
1991–2004 David Cropper
2004–2007 George Bunner
2007–2008 Graham Jessop
2009–   Chris Carter

Awards of Honour

AAA Award of Honour plaques are presented to any person approved by General Committee in recognition of outstanding service to Amateur Athletics and the AAA. The most recent recipients are: 2004: Marianne Lingen, E. Sutters; 2007: G. Clarke, K. A. Oakley.

Founder Life Vice-Presidents (AAA of England, 1991)

R. J. Barrow; Miss N. Blaine MBE; Mrs F. M. Clarke MBE; Wg. Cdr. D. C. Davies OBE; Miss E. M. Holland MBE; Mrs J. Lindsay; Mrs M. M. Oakley; B. E. Willis OBE; G. A. Wright.

Life Vice-Presidents

D. Adams; G. Clarke; D. Cropper OBE; Mrs S. Deaves; Mrs J. Febery; Mrs P. M. Green; E. Nash; K. A. Oakley.

Management Board (2012)

C. Carter – Chairman; W. Nicholls – Honorary Secretary; M. Etchells – Treasurer; A. G. Bunner MBE – Events Director; R. H. Float – Director; I. Byett – Director (Cross Country); E. C. Butcher – Director (Road Running); M. Neighbour – Regional Director; G. Durbin – Regional Director; B. Heywood – Regional Director; Ms F. P. Ratchford – Director.

WAAA CHAMPIONS

SENIOR WOMEN

WAAA title winners from 1922 to 1991 inclusive; AAA or AAA of England champions from 1992 to 2006 inclusive; UK champions from 2007 to 2012. England Senior Championships were instituted in 2010 and winners are listed below the UK champions for that year, 2011 and 2012.
(Where the WAAA title was won by an overseas athlete, the highest placed UK athlete is shown in brackets)

Venues: 1922 various venues; 1923 Bromley; 1924 London/Woolwich; 1925–1926 London/Stamford Bridge; 1927 Reading; 1928–1932 Stamford Bridge; 1933 London/White City; 1934 London/Herne Hill; 1935–1939 White City; 1945 London/Tooting Bec; 1946 White City; 1947–1948 London/Chiswick; 1949–1957 White City; 1958–1959 Motspur Park; 1960–1967 White City; 1968–1984 London/Crystal Palace; 1985–1993 & 1995–2003 Birmingham; 1994 Sheffield; 2004–2006 Manchester; (UK Championships) 2007 Manchester; 2008–2012 Birmingham; (England Senior Championships) 2010 Gateshead; 2011 Bedford; 2012 Birmingham.

60 METRES

(Event instituted in 1935; discontinued after 1950)

1935	Audrey Wade	8.0
1936	Betty Lock	7.6
1937	Betty Lock	7.8
1938	Betty Lock	7.6
1939	Betty Lock	7.6
1946	Irene Stretton	8.1
1947	Irene Royse (Stretton)	7.9
1948	Doris Batter	9.1
1949	Doris Batter	7.7
1950	Isobella Shivas	7.8

100 METRES

(Event instituted in 1922 at 100 yards; y = 100 yards)

1922	Nora Callebout	12.2y
1923	Mary Lines	12.0y
1924	Eileen Edwards	11.3wy

262

WAAA Champions

1925	Rose Thompson	11.8y
1926	Florence Haynes	12.0y
1927	Eileen Edwards	11.4yw
1928	Muriel Gunn	11.6y
1929	Ivy Walker	11.4y
1930	Eileen Hiscock	11.4y
1931	Nellie Halstead	11.4y
1932	Ethel Johnson	11.1y
1933	Eileen Hiscock	12.2
1934	Eileen Hiscock	12.2
1935	Eileen Hiscock	12.2
1936	Barbara Burke SAF	12.3
	(2, Eileen Hiscock)	
1937	Winnie Jeffrey	12.2
1938	Betty Lock	12.2
1939	Betty Lock	12.2
1945	Winnie Jordan (Jeffrey)	12.8
1946	Maureen Gardner	12.6
1947	Winnie Jordan	12.1
1948	Winnie Jordan	12.6
1949	Sylvia Cheeseman	12.1
1950	June Foulds	12.6
1951	June Foulds	12.3
1952	Heather Armitage	10.9yw
1953	Anne Pashley	11.0y
1954	Anne Pashley	11.1y
1955	Margaret Francis	10.8yw
1956	June Paul (Foulds)	10.6yw
1957	Heather Young (Armitage)	10.9y
1958	Madeleine Weston	10.6yw
1959	Dorothy Hyman	10.8y
1960	Dorothy Hyman	11.7
1961	Jenny Smart	10.7y
1962	Dorothy Hyman	10.6y
1963	Dorothy Hyman	10.9y
1964	Daphne Arden	10.6y
1965	Irena Kirszenstein POL	10.68y
	(2, Jill Hall 10.77)	
1966	Daphne Slater (Arden)	10.5yw
1967	Johanna Cornelissen RSA	10.5yw
	(3, Della James 10.7)	
1968	Val Peat	11.5
1969	Chi Cheng TPE	11.87
	(2, Dorothy Hyman 11.92)	
1970	Anita Neil	11.6
1971	Stephanie Berto CAN	11.42w
	(2, Anita Neil 11.51)	
1972	Della Pascoe (James)	11.86
1973	Andrea Lynch	11.74

1974	Raelene Boyle AUS	11.23
	(2, Andrea Lynch 11.27)	
1975	Andrea Lynch	11.68
1976	Andrea Lynch	11.22
1977	Sonia Lannaman	11.24
1978	Kathy Smallwood	11.66
1979	Heather Hunte	11.58
1980	Kathy Smallwood	11.45
1981	Wendy Hoyte	11.73
1982	Wendy Hoyte	11.62
1983	Kathy Cook (Smallwood)	11.26
1984	Kathy Cook	11.44
1985	Heather Oakes (Hunte)	11.37w
1986	Paula Dunn	11.34
1987	Paula Dunn	11.28
1988	Paula Dunn	11.26
1989	Paula Dunn	11.32w
1990	Stephanie Douglas	11.38w
1991	Evelyn Ashford USA	11.15
	(3, Stephanie Douglas 11.44)	
1992	Melinda Gainsford AUS	11.38
	(3, Stephanie Douglas 11.45)	
1993	Bev Kinch	11.44
1994	Katharine Merry	11.27w
1995	Paula Thomas (Dunn)	11.48
1996	Stephanie Douglas	11.55
1997	Evadnie McKenzie JAM	11.63
	(2, Donna Fraser 11.74)	
1998	Joice Maduaka	11.40
1999	Joice Maduaka	11.37
2000	Marcia Richardson	11.41
2001	Sarah Wilhelmy	11.41w
2002	Joice Maduaka	11.31
2003	Joice Maduaka	11.31
2004	Abi Oyepitan	11.54
2005	Laura Turner	11.55
2006	Joice Maduaka	11.23
2007	Jeanette Kwakye	11.59
2008	Jeanette Kwakye	11.26
2009	Joice Maduaka	11.52
2010	Laura Turner	11.41
	Amy Foster	11.52w
2011	Jeanette Kwakye	11.23
	Laura Turner	11.23
2012	Ashleigh Nelson	11.50
	Louise Bloor	11.69

Most titles won: 6 Joice Maduaka 1998, 1999, 2002, 2003, 2006, 2009. Most medals: 12 Maduaka

200 METRES

(Event instituted in 1922 at 220 yards; y = 220 yards)

Year	Champion	Time
1922	Mary Lines	26.8y
1923	Eileen Edwards	27.0y
1924	Eileen Edwards	27.6y
1925	Vera Palmer (later Searle)	26.8y
1926	Vera Palmer	26.8y
1927	Eileen Edwards	25.8y
1928	Kinue Hitomi JPN	26.2y
	(2, Ivy Walker – 3 yards back)	
1929	Winifred Weldon	26.4y
1930	Nellie Halstead	25.2y
1931	Nellie Halstead	25.5y
1932	Nellie Halstead	25.6y
1933	Eileen Hiscock	25.8
1934	Nellie Halstead	25.6
1935	Eileen Hiscock	25.3
1936	Barbara Burke SAF	25.2
	(2, Eileen Hiscock 25.4e)	
1937	Lily Chalmers	24.9
1938	Dorothy Saunders	25.0
1939	Lily Chalmers	25.6
1945	Winnie Jordan	26.7
1946	Sylvia Cheeseman	25.7
1947	Sylvia Cheeseman	25.0
1948	Sylvia Cheeseman	25.7
1949	Sylvia Cheeseman	25.4
1950	Dorothy Hall (later Manley)	25.2
1951	Sylvia Cheeseman	25.0
1952	Sylvia Cheeseman	25.0y
1953	Ann Johnson	25.0y
1954	Ann Johnson	25.2y
1955	Jean Scrivens	24.9y
1956	June Paul	23.8yw
1957	Heather Young	24.2y
1958	Heather Young	24.5y
1959	Dorothy Hyman	24.5y
1960	Dorothy Hyman	24.0y
1961	Jenny Smart	24.0y
1962	Dorothy Hyman	23.8y
1963	Dorothy Hyman	24.3y
1964	Daphne Arden	23.6y
1965	Janet Simpson	24.06yw
1966	Janet Simpson	24.1y
1967	Johanna Cornelissen RSA	24.0y
	(2, Maureen Tranter 24.1)	
1968	Val Peat	23.6
1969	Dorothy Hyman	23.7

1970	Margaret Critchley	23.8
1971	Stephanie Berto CAN	23.54
	(2, Margaret Critchley 23.78)	
1972	Donna Murray	23.98
1973	Helen Golden	24.26
1974	Raelene Boyle AUS	23.23w
	(2, Helen Golden 23.63)	
1975	Helen Golden	24.17
1976	Denise Ramsden	23.48
1977	Sonia Lannaman	23.06
1978	Kathy Smallwood	23.24
1979	Kathy Smallwood	23.39
1980	Kathy Smallwood	23.14
1981	Sonia Lannaman	23.14
1982	Kathy Smallwood	23.00
1983	Michelle Scutt	23.17
1984	Kathy Cook (Smallwood)	22.77
1985	Kathy Cook	23.39
1986	Simmone Jacobs	23.34w
1987	Joan Baptiste	23.24w
1988	Simmone Jacobs	23.37
1989	Paula Dunn	23.43
1990	Jenny Stoute	23.07
1991	Stephanie Douglas	23.37
1992	Melinda Gainsford AUS	23.04
	(3, Sallyanne Short 23.24)	
1993	Cathy Freeman AUS	22.71
	(3, Simmone Jacobs 23.49)	
1994	Katharine Merry	22.85
1995	Catherine Murphy	23.40
1996	Simmone Jacobs	23.11
1997	Sharon Tunaley	23.91
1998	Katharine Merry	23.46
1999	Joice Maduaka	22.83
2000	Sarah Wilhelmy	23.39
2001	Sarah Reilly IRL	23.42
	(2, Shani Anderson 23.43)	
2002	Shani Anderson	23.03w
2003	Abi Oyepitan	22.95
2004	Joice Maduaka	23.16
2005	Donna Fraser	23.36
2006	Joice Maduaka	23.24
2007	Jeanette Kwakye	23.66
2008	Emily Freeman	22.92
2009	Emily Freeman	22.92
2010	Laura Turner	23.66
	Bernice Wilson	23.83
2011	Anyika Onuora	23.26
	Laura Turner	23.47w

2012	Margaret Adeoye	23.11
	Sophie Papps	23.75

Most titles won: 6 Sylvia Cheeseman (later Disley) 1946–1949, 1951, 1952 & Kathy Cook (Smallwood) 1978–1980, 1982, 1984, 1985. Most medals: 9 Joice Maduaka

400 METRES

(Event instituted in 1922 at 440 yards; y = 440 yards)

1922	Mary Lines	64.4y
1923	Mary Lines	62.4y
1924	Vera Palmer (later Searle)	65.2y
1925	Vera Palmer	61.4y
1926	Vera Palmer	61.8y
1927	Dorothy Proctor	62.4y
1928	Florence Haynes	60.8y
1929	Marion King	59.2y
1930	Elsie Wright	59.8y
1931	Nellie Halstead	58.8y
1932	Nellie Halstead	56.8y
1933	Nellie Halstead	58.8
1934	Violet Branch	60.0
1935	Olive Hall	61.9
1936	Olive Hall	58.6
1937	Nellie Halstead	60.1
1938	Olive Hall	60.0
1939	Lily Chalmers	59.5
1945	Winnie Jordan	61.8y
1946	Margaret Walker	59.3
1947	Joan Upton	61.6
1948	Valerie Ball	60.8
1949	Valerie Ball	59.4
1950	Valerie Ball	57.5
1951	Valerie Ball	58.2
1952	Valerie Ball	59.3y
1953	Valerie Winn (Ball)	57.6y
1954	Gloria Goldsborough	57.1y
1955	Janet Ruff	56.9y
1956	Janet Ruff	56.5y
1957	Janet Ruff	56.4y
1958	Shirley Pirie	56.4y
1959	Margaret Pickerell	55.9y
1960	Pam Piercy	57.2y
1961	Maeve Kyle IRL	56.3y
	(2, Jean Dunbar 56.9)	
1962	Jean Sorrell (Dunbar)	55.1y
1963	Joy Grieveson	55.9y
1964	Ann Packer	54.3y
1965	Joy Grieveson	55.11y
1966	Hilde Slaman NED	54.7y

	(2, Joy Grieveson 54.9)	
1967	Lillian Board	55.3y
1968	Myrna van der Hoeven NED	53.6
	(2, Janet Simpson 53.9)	
1969	Jenny Pawsey	54.3
1970	Marilyn Neufville	52.6
1971	Jannette Roscoe	53.93
1972	Verona Bernard	53.20
1973	Jannette Roscoe	53.78
1974	Yvonne Saunders CAN	51.90
	(2, Donna Murray 52.58)	
1975	Donna Murray	51.88
1976	Verona Elder (Bernard)	52.08
1977	Verona Elder	52.3
1978	Joslyn Hoyte	52.66
1979	Joslyn Hoyte-Smith (Hoyte)	51.90
1980	Michelle Probert	51.94
1981	Joslyn Hoyte-Smith	51.70
1982	Michelle Scutt (Probert)	51.05
1983	Denise Boyd AUS	51.62
	(2, Joslyn Hoyte-Smith 52.98)	
1984	Tracy Lawton	52.74
1985	Maree Chapman AUS	51.51
	(2, Linda Keough 52.52)	
1986	Kathy Cook	53.50
1987	Linda Keough	53.17
1988	Linda Keough	51.65
1989	Linda Keough	51.09
1990	Lillie Leatherwood USA	51.62
	(2, Linda Keough 51.77)	
1991	Maicel Malone USA	50.89
	(2, Lorraine Hanson 51.88)	
1992	Cathy Freeman AUS	51.14
	(3, Phylis Smith 51.36)	
1993	Phylis Smith	52.15
1994	Melanie Neef	52.56
1995	Melanie Neef	51.63
1996	Phylis Smith	51.74
1997	Lorraine Hanson	53.45
1998	Allison Curbishley	50.92
1999	Katharine Merry	50.62
2000	Donna Fraser	50.94
2001	Lesley Owusu	52.27
2002	Lee McConnell	51.59
2003	Helen Karagounis	52.51
2004	Christine Ohuruogu	50.98
2005	Donna Fraser	51.27
2006	Nicola Sanders	50.74
2007	Nicola Sanders	51.33

2008	Lee McConnell	52.31
2009	Christine Ohuruogu	51.26
2010	Lee McConnell	51.55
	Kelly Massey	53.34
2011	Perri Shakes-Drayton	51.52
	Nadine Okyere	53.08
2012	Christine Ohuruogu	51.89
	Emma Pullen	54.79

Most titles won: 6 Valerie Winn (Ball) 1948–1953. Most medals: 10 Verona Elder (Bernard)

800 METRES

(Event instituted in 1922 at 880 yards; y = 880 yards)

1922	Mary Lines	2:26.6y
1923	Edith Trickey	2:40.2y
1924	Edith Trickey	2:30.4y
1925	Edith Trickey	2:26.6y
1926	Edith Trickey	2:28.0y
1927	Edith Trickey	2:32.4y
1928	Ivy Barber	2:27.6y
1929	Violet Streater	2:25.8y
1930	Gladys Lunn	2:18.2y
1931	Gladys Lunn	2:22.4y
1932	Gladys Lunn	2:20.4y
1933	Ruth Christmas	2:23.0
1934	Gladys Lunn	2:18.3
1935	Nellie Halstead	2:15.6
1936	Olive Hall	2:20.2
1937	Gladys Lunn	2:18.5
1938	Nellie Halstead	2:20.4
1939	Olive Hall	2:21.0
1945	Phyllis Richards	2:26.7y
1946	Phyllis Richards	2:21.0
1947	Nellie Batson	2:23.1
1948	Nellie Batson	2:20.3
1949	Hazel Spears	2:19.4
1950	Margaret Hume	2:20.5
1951	Nellie Batson	2:18.4
1952	Margaret Taylor	2:17.5y
1953	Anne Oliver	2:15.0y
1954	Diane Leather	2:09.0y
1955	Diane Leather	2:09.7y
1956	Phyllis Perkins (Green)	2:13.2y
1957	Diane Leather	2:09.4y
1958	Joy Jordan	2:13.3y
1959	Joy Jordan	2:09.5y
1960	Joy Jordan	2:09.1y
1961	Joy Jordan	2:11.0y
1962	Joy Jordan	2:08.0y

1963	Phyllis Perkins	2:12.2y
1964	Anne Smith	2:08.0y
1965	Anne Smith	2:07.5y
1966	Anne Smith	2:04.2y
1967	Anne Smith	2:04.8y
1968	Vera Nikolic YUG	2:00.5
	(2, Lillian Board 2:02.0)	
1969	Pat Lowe	2:03.3
1970	Sheila Carey	2:03.6
1971	Abby Hoffman CAN	2:04.04
	(2, Rosemary Stirling 2:04.30)	
1972	Mary Tracey IRL	2:02.98
	(2, Pat Cropper (Lowe) 2:03.68)	
1973	Mary Tracey IRL	2:03.31
	(3, Rosemary Wright (Stirling) 2:05.05)	
1974	Lesley Kiernan	2:05.12
1975	Angela Creamer	2:05.14
1976	Angela Creamer	2:04.61
1977	Chris Boxer	2:03.78
1978	Chris Boxer	2:03.10
1979	Chris Benning	2:01.24
1980	Anne Clarkson	2:01.89
1981	Anne Clarkson	2:03.92
1982	Terri Cater AUS	2:01.54
	(3, Lorraine Baker 2:01.86)	
1983	Shireen Bailey	2:00.58
1984	Heather Barralet AUS	2:02.37
	(2, Chris Boxer 2:02.66)	
1985	Chris Boxer	2:00.60
1986	Diane Edwards	2:04.26
1987	Diane Edwards	2:03.59
1988	Kirsty Wade	2:01.52
1989	Diane Edwards	2:01.24
1990	Ann Williams	2:03.45
1991	Paula Fryer	2:02.19
1992	Diane Edwards	2:00.41
1993	Kelly Holmes	2:02.69
1994	Diane Modahl (Edwards)	2:01.35
1995	Kelly Holmes	1:57.56
1996	Kelly Holmes	1:57.84
1997	Amanda Crowe	2:04.66
1998	Diane Modahl	2:02.73
1999	Kelly Holmes	1:59.86
2000	Kelly Holmes	2:02.08
2001	Kelly Holmes	2:02.61
2002	Susan Scott	2:03.89
2003	Lucy Vaughan	2:03.70
2004	Kelly Holmes	1:59.39
2005	Susan Scott	2:02.97

2006	Becky Lyne	2:00.31
2007	Jemma Simpson	2:00.91
2008	Marilyn Okoro	1:59.81
2009	Jemma Simpson	2:01.16
2010	Jemma Simpson	2:01.50
	Stacey Smith	2:04.48
2011	Jenny Meadows	2:02.28
	Karen Harewood	2:06.07
2012	Lynsey Sharp	2:01.72
	Jenny Welsh	2:09.24

Most titles won: 7 Kelly Holmes 1993, 1995, 1996, 1999–2001, 2004. Most medals: 7 Phyllis Perkins (Green), Diane Modahl (Edwards) & Holmes

1500 METRES

(Event instituted in 1936 at 1 mile; y = mile)

1936	Gladys Lunn	5:23.0y
1937	Gladys Lunn	5:17.0y
1938	Doris Harris	5:29.4y
1939	Evelyne Forster	5:15.3y
1945	Pat Sandall	5:40.2y
1946	Brenda Harris	5:33.6y
1947	Nellie Batson	5:37.6y
1948	Nellie Batson	5:31.8y
1949	Eileen Garritt	5:20.0y
1950	Joyce Heath	5:25.8y
1951	Hazel Needham	5:23.4y
1952	Anne Oliver	5:11.0y
1953	Enid Harding	5:09.8y
1954	Phyllis Green	5:09.6y
1955	Phyllis Perkins (Green)	5:05.2y
1956	Diane Leather	5:01.0y
1957	Diane Leather	4:55.3y
1958	Maureen Smith	5:02.6y
1959	Joan Briggs	5:02.2y
1960	Roma Ashby	4:54.2y
1961	Roma Ashby	5:01.8y
1962	Joan Beretta AUS	4:57.0y
	(2, Madeline Ibbotson 5:00.4)	
1963	Pam Davies	5:10.8y
1964	Alison Leggett	4:56.0y
1965	Joyce Smith (Byatt)	4:53.46y
1966	Rita Lincoln	4:47.9y
1967	Rita Lincoln	4:51.4y
1968	Rita Lincoln	4:25.3
1969	Mia Gommers NED	4:16.0
	(2, Rita Ridley (Lincoln) 4:25.4)	
1970	Rita Ridley	4:15.4
1971	Rita Ridley	4:14.32
1972	Ellen Tittel FRG	4:17.15

	(2, Joyce Smith 4:17.60)	
1973	Joan Allison	4:15.82
1974	Grete Andersen/Waitz NOR	4:10.02
	(5, Chris Tranter (Benning) 4:23.2)	
1975	Mary Stewart	4:14.73
1976	Penny Yule	4:15.11
1977	Penny Yule	4:12.71
1978	Cherry Hanson	4:11.62
1979	Mary Stewart	4:14.78
1980	Gillian Dainty	4:14.02
1981	Gillian Dainty	4:12.26
1982	Chris Boxer	4:07.28
1983	Gillian Green (Dainty)	4:12.53
1984	Chris Benning	4:07.27
1985	Julie Laughton	4:15.08
1986	Zola Budd	4:01.93
1987	Bev Nicholson	4:14.28
1988	Chris Cahill (Boxer)	4:08.26
1989	Bev Nicholson	4:09.34
1990	Chris Cahill	4:12.54
1991	Ann Williams	4:08.93
1992	Yvonne Murray	4:05.87
1993	Alison Wyeth	4:11.03
1994	Kelly Holmes	4:01.41
1995	Yvonne Murray	4:11.47
1996	Kelly Holmes	4:08.14
1997	Dianne Henaghan	4:16.19
1998	Lynn Gibson	4:12.72
1999	Hayley Tullett	4:08.06
2000	Hayley Tullett	4:06.44
2001	Helen Pattinson	4:14.49
2002	Kelly Holmes	4:06.02
2003	Hayley Tullett	4:08.12
2004	Hayley Tullett	4:07.24
2005	Helen Clitheroe (Pattinson)	4:08.29
2006	Helen Clitheroe	4:09.64
2007	Katrina Wootton	4:09.57
2008	Lisa Dobriskey	4:15.84
2009	Charlene Thomas	4:09.18
2010	Hannah England	4:33.23
	Stevie Stockton	4:20.93
2011	Hannah England	4:07.05
	Celia Taylor	4:45.33
2012	Laura Weightman	4:18.83
	Kate Avery	4:20.0

Most titles won: 5 Rita Ridley (Lincoln) 1966–1968, 1970, 1971. Most medals: 9 Helen Clitheroe (Pattinson)

3000 METRES

(Event instituted in 1968; discontinued after 1999)

1968	Carol Firth	10:06.4
1969	Ann O'Brien IRL	9:47.6
	(2, Barbara Banks 9:54.4)	
1970	Ann O'Brien IRL	9:34.4
	(3, Barbara Banks 9:56.0)	
1971	Joyce Smith	9:23.40
1972	Paula Yeoman	9:30.70
1973	Inger Knutsson SWE	9:08.04
	(2, Joyce Smith 9:11.45)	
1974	Joyce Smith	9:07.15
1975	Mary Purcell IRL	9:08.00
	(2, Christine Haskett 9:18.32)	
1976	Mary Purcell IRL	9:07.98
	(2, Thelwyn Bateman 9:35.77)	
1977	Carol Gould (Firth)	9:20.71
1978	Chris Benning	8:52.33
1979	Deirdre Nagle IRL	9:13.24
	(2, Kath Binns 9:13.34)	
1980	Regina Joyce	9:13.82
1981	Cathie Twomey USA	9:05.39
	(2, Val Rowe 9:05.99)	
1982	Debbie Peel	9:04.79
1983	Debbie Peel	9:11.34
1984	Debbie Peel	9:15.0
1985	Zola Budd	8:50.50
1986	Chris Benning	9:05.13
1987	Wendy Sly	9:04.83
1988	Yvonne Murray	8:47.34
1989	Alison Wyeth	9:11.12
1990	Yvonne Murray	8:48.21
1991	Yvonne Murray	8:46.47
1992	Lisa York	8:50.18
1993	Yvonne Murray	8:52.28
1994	Sonia McGeorge	9:03.80
1995	Sarah Bentley	9:27.12
1996	Debbie Gunning	9:26.46
1997	Debbie Sullivan	9:34.30
1998	Amanda Parkinson	9:34.74
1999	Jilly Ingman	9:28.21

Most titles won: 4 Yvonne Murray 1988, 1990, 1991, 1993

5000 METRES

(Event instituted in 1981)

1981	Kath Binns	16:23.35
1982	Monica Joyce IRL	15:45.26
	(3, Julie Asgill 16:50.77)	

1983	Paula Fudge (Yeoman)	16:23.06
1984	Shireen Samy	16:10.10
1985	Monica Joyce IRL	16:16.58
	(2, Alison Hollington 16:19.97)	
1986	Marina Samy	16:22.36
1987	Cathy Newman	16:14.62
1988	Jane Shields	16:04.34
1989	Sue Crehan	16:18.55
1990	Sally Ellis	16:45.54
1991	Amanda Wright	16:50.62
1992	Amanda Wright	16:04.51
1993	Suzanne Rigg	15:57.67
1994	Shireen Barbour	16:06.49
1995	Alison Wyeth	15:39.14
1996	Paula Radcliffe	15:28.46
1997	Andrea Whitcombe	16:07.26
1998	Andrea Whitcombe	15:43.03
1999	Hayley Haining	15:56.59
2000	Paula Radcliffe	15:05.48
2001	Jo Pavey	15:15.98
2002	Hayley Yelling	16:11.23
2003	Hayley Yelling	15:53.20
2004	Catherine Berry	15:45.28
2005	Hayley Yelling	15:45.67
2006	Jo Pavey	15:07.38
2007	Jo Pavey	15:17.77
2008	Jo Pavey	15:12.55
2009	Freya Murray	15:45.07
2010	Freya Murray	15:48.75
	Charlotte Purdue	16:01.71
2011	Julia Bleasdale	15:49.02
	Justina Heslop	15:58.54
2012	Jo Pavey	15:54.18
	Jess Coulson	16:45.6

Most titles won: 5 Jo Pavey 2001, 2006–2008, 2012. Most medals: 6 Hayley Yelling & Pavey

10,000 METRES

(Event instituted in 1981)

1981	Kath Binns	33:56.3
1982	Margaret Boddy	39:15.75
1983	Barbara-Ann King	35:19.86
1984	Priscilla Welch	34:00.5
1985	Sue Crehan	33:53.3
1986	Jill Clarke	33:27.69
1987	Sue Crehan	33:22.28
1988	Angela Tooby	33:13.95
1989	Jill Hunter	33:01.6
1990	Andrea Wallace	32:51.17

1991	Silva Vivod YUG	33:04.60
	(3, Annette Bell 33:46.62)	
1992	Andrea Wallace	32:21.61
1993	Vikki McPherson	33:49.29
1994	Zara Hyde	33:23.25
1995	Jill Hunter	32:26.12
1996	Louise Watson	33:21.46
1998	Tara Krzywicki	34:37.04
1999	Bev Jenkins	33:58.81
2000	Elana Meyer RSA	31:41.1
	(2, Birhan Dagne 32:30.4 – 1, WAAA)	
2001	Irene Limika KEN	32:42.79
	(2, Penny Thackray 33:25.74 – 1, WAAA)	
2002	Sonia O'Sullivan IRL	31:33.19
	(4, Hayley Yelling 33:07.52 – 1, WAAA)	
2003	Aniko Kalovics HUN	31:40.31
	(3, Hayley Yelling 32:02.09 – 1, WAAA)	
2004	Kathy Butler	31:36.90
2005	Kathy Butler	31:46.53
2006	Hayley Yelling	32:38.24
2007	Jo Pavey	31:26.94
2008	Jo Pavey	31:46.90
2009	Meseret Defar ETH	29:59.20
	(5, Claire Hallissey 33:10.73 – 1, UK)	
2010	Jo Pavey	31:51.91
2011	Werknesh Kidane ETH	31:08.92
	(3, Sonia Samuels 33:50.72 – 1, UK)	
2012	Werknesh Kidane ETH	31:28.19
	(2, Caryl Jones 32:52.53, – 1, UK)	

Most titles won: 3 Hayley Yelling 2002, 2003, 2006 & Jo Pavey 2007, 2008, 2010. Most medals: 6 Yelling

3000 METRES STEEPLECHASE

(Event instituted in 2002 at 2000m; 3000m since 2004)

2002	Tara Krzywicki	6:31.77
2003	Tara Krzywicki	6:28.07
2004	Tina Brown	10:13.19
2005	Tina Brown	10:01.57
2006	Hatti Dean	9:52.04
2007	Helen Clitheroe	9:47.49
2008	Helen Clitheroe	9:36.98
2009	Helen Clitheroe	9:48.24
2010	Barbara Parker	9:37.77
	Tina Brown	10:11.19
2011	Lennie Waite	10:03.18
	Emma Raven	10:28.60
2012	Eilish McColgan	9:56.89
	Carolyn Boosey	10:59.51

Most titles won (AAA/UK): 3 Helen Clitheroe 2007–2009. Most medals: 5 Jo Ankier

80 METRES HURDLES
(Event instituted in 1922 at 120 yards; two championships in 1927 at 75m and 100 yards; 100 yards in 1928; 80m 1929–1968)

1922	Daisy Wright	20.4
1923	Mary Lines	18.8
1924	Mary Lines	18.4w
1925	Hilda Hatt	19.0
1926	Hilda Hatt	18.2
1927	Hilda Hatt	12.6w
	Muriel Gunn	14.6w
1928	Marjorie Clark SAF	13.8
	(2, Hilda Hatt – 2 ft back)	
1929	Hilda Hatt	12.4
1930	Muriel Cornell (Gunn)	12.4
1931	Elsie Green	12.0
1932	Elsie Green	12.2
1933	Elsie Green	12.0
1934	Elsie Green	12.0
1935	Elsie Green	12.3
1936	Barbara Burke SAF	11.9
	(2, Violet Webb)	
1937	Barbara Burke SAF	12.1
	(2, Kay Tiffen)	
1938	Kate Robertson	12.2
1939	Kate Robertson	12.4
1945	Zoe Hancock	13.6
1946	Bertha Crowther	12.8
1947	Maureen Gardner	11.5w
1948	Maureen Gardner	12.0
1949	Jean Desforges	11.9
1950	Maureen Dyson (Gardner)	11.6
1951	Maureen Dyson	11.7
1952	Jean Desforges	11.4
1953	Jean Desforges	11.5
1954	Jean Desforges	11.4
1955	Margaret Francis	11.3
1956	Pam Elliott	11.1w
1957	Thelma Hopkins	11.4
1958	Carole Quinton	10.9w
1959	Mary Bignal	11.3
1960	Carole Quinton	10.8w
1961	Betty Moore	10.8w
1962	Betty Moore	10.7
1963	Pat Nutting	11.2
1964	Pat Pryce (Nutting)	10.7
1965	Pat Jones	11.28
1966	Danuta Straszynska POL	10.9w
	(2, Pat Pryce 11.0)	

| 1967 | Pat Jones | 11.0 |
| 1968 | Pat Pryce | 10.9 |

Most titles won: 5 Elsie Green 1931–1935

100 METRES HURDLES

(Event instituted in 1963 over 2ft 6in hurdles; over 2ft 9in hurdles since 1967)

1963	Pat Nutting	14.1
1964	Pat Pryce (Nutting)	13.4
1965	Pat Jones	13.8w
1966	Mary Rand (Bignal)	13.7
1967	Pat Jones	13.8
1968	Chris Perera	13.5
1969	Chi Cheng TPE	13.52
	(4, Chris Perera 14.3)	
1970	Mary Peters	14.0
1971	Valeria Bufanu ROU	13.52w
	(2, Sheila Garnett 13.91)	
1972	Pam Ryan AUS	13.48
	(2, Judy Vernon 13.86)	
1973	Judy Vernon	14.03
1974	Lorna Drysdale	13.45
1975	Liz Damman CAN	13.93
	(2, Lorna Boothe 14.00)	
1976	Sharon Colyear	13.47w
1977	Lorna Boothe	13.48
1978	Sharon Colyear	13.51
1979	Shirley Strong	13.67
1980	Shirley Strong	13.57
1981	Shirley Strong	13.36
1982	Shirley Strong	13.27
1983	Shirley Strong	12.95
1984	Shirley Strong	12.96
1985	Glynis Nunn AUS	13.27
	(2, Kim Hagger 13.35)	
1986	Sally Gunnell	13.13w
1987	Sally Gunnell	13.01
1988	Sally Gunnell	13.02
1989	Sally Gunnell	13.26
1990	Lesley-Ann Skeete	13.03
1991	Sally Gunnell	13.02
1992	Sally Gunnell	13.13
1993	Sally Gunnell	13.08
1994	Clova Court	13.06
1995	Melani Wilkins	13.34
1996	Angie Thorp	13.26
1997	Angie Thorp	13.56
1998	Keri Maddox	13.20
1999	Keri Maddox	12.97w
2000	Diane Allahgreen	13.24

2001	Diane Allahgreen	13.11
2002	Diane Allahgreen	13.00
2003	Rachel King	13.07
2004	Sarah Claxton	13.21
2005	Sarah Claxton	12.96
2006	Sarah Claxton	13.19w
2007	Jessica Ennis	13.25
2008	Sarah Claxton	13.12
2009	Jessica Ennis	12.87
2010	Louise Hazel	13.32
	Zara Hohn	13.57
2011	Tiffany Porter	12.76
	Angelita Broadbelt-Blake	13.12w
2012	Jessica Ennis	12.92
	Serita Solomon	13.62

Most titles won: 7 Sally Gunnell 1986–1989, 1991–1993. Most medals: 9 Gunnell

200 METRES HURDLES

(Event instituted in 1961; discontinued after 1972)

1961	Pat Nutting	28.3
1962	Pat Nutting	28.9
1963	Pat Nutting	28.9
1964	Pat Jones	27.9
1965	Sue Mills	28.14w
1966	Pat Jones	27.7
1967	Pat Jones	27.3
1968	Chris Perera	27.8
1969	Sue Hayward	28.5
1970	Chris Bell (Perera)	27.4
1971	Sharon Colyear	26.68
1972	Pam Ryan AUS	26.82
	(3, Julie Wood 29.87)	

Most titles won: 3 Pat Nutting (later Pryce) 1961–1963 & Pat Jones 1964, 1966, 1967

400 METRES HURDLES

(Event instituted in 1973)

1973	Sue Howell	61.41
1974	Hybre de Lange RSA	58.41
	(2, Linda Robinson 62.47)	
1975	Jannette Roscoe	58.31
1976	Chris Warden	57.84
1977	Liz Sutherland	57.93
1978	Mary Appleby IRL	57.46
	(2, Liz Sutherland 58.36)	
1979	Chris Warden	56.06
1980	Sue Morley	58.76
1981	Chris Warden	56.75
1982	Sue Morley	57.31

1983	Yvette Wray	57.82
1984	Gladys Taylor	56.78
1985	Yvette Wray	57.86
1986	Yvette Wray	59.11
1987	Sally Fleming AUS	57.62
	(2, Elaine McLaughlin 58.69)	
1988	Sally Gunnell	55.40
1989	Wendy Cearns	56.05
1990	Gowry Retchakan	57.14
1991	Gowry Retchakan	55.67
1992	Gowry Retchakan	55.04
1993	Jacqui Parker	58.14
1994	Gowry Retchakan	57.08
1995	Gowry Retchakan	57.18
1996	Sally Gunnell	54.65
1997	Keri Maddox	57.69
1998	Tasha Danvers	56.27
1999	Sinead Dudgeon	55.24
2000	Keri Maddox	55.22
2001	Sinead Dudgeon	56.37
2002	Tasha Danvers	56.14
2003	Liz Fairs	57.06
2004	Katie Jones	58.26
2005	Nicola Sanders	55.61
2006	Tasha Danvers	55.58
2007	Tasha Danvers	55.43
2008	Perri Shakes-Drayton	56.09
2009	Nusrat Ceesay	57.13
2010	Perri Shakes-Drayton	56.93
	Hannah Douglas	58.51
2011	Perri Shakes-Drayton	55.52
	Emily Parker	58.04
2012	Perri Shakes-Drayton	55.45
	Emily Bonnett	59.15

Most titles won: 5 Gowry Retchakan 1990–1992, 1994, 1995, Most medals: 7 Retchakan & Tasha Danvers

HIGH JUMP

(Event instituted in 1922)

1922	Sylvia Stone	1.38
1923	Hilda Hatt	1.45
1924	Sophie Ellott-Lynn	1.45
1925	Phyllis Green	1.52
1926	Phyllis Green	1.47
1927	Phyllis Green	1.58
1928	Marjorie Clark SAF	1.52
	(2, Marjorie Okell 1.47)	
1929	Marjorie Okell	1.47
1930	Carolina Gisolf NED	1.57

(2, Mary Milne 1.55)

1931	Marjorie Okell	1.50
1932	Mary Milne	1.55
1933	Mary Milne	1.50
1934	Gretel Bergmann GER	1.55

(2, Mary Milne 1.52)

1935	Mary Milne	1.55
1936	Dorothy Odam	1.53
1937	Dorothy Odam	1.63
1938	Dorothy Odam	1.57
1939	Dorothy Odam	1.65
1945	Dora Gardner	1.52
1946	Dora Gardner	1.55
1947	Gladys Young	1.55
1948	Dorothy Tyler (Odam)	1.62
1949	Dorothy Tyler	1.60
1950	Sheila Alexander	1.62
1951	Sheila Lerwill (Alexander)	1.72
1952	Dorothy Tyler	1.65
1953	Sheila Lerwill	1.65
1954	Sheila Lerwill	1.65
1955	Thelma Hopkins	1.65
1956	Dorothy Tyler	1.60
1957	Thelma Hopkins	1.65
1958	Mary Bignal	1.65
1959	Nel Zwier NED	1.65

(2, Mary Bignal 1.62)

1960	Dorothy Shirley	1.67
1961	Dorothy Shirley	1.70
1962	Iolanda Balas ROU	1.83

(2, Frances Slaap 1.70)

1963	Iolanda Balas ROU	1.70

(2=, Susan Dennler & Linda Knowles 1.60)

1964	Frances Slaap	1.73
1965	Frances Slaap	1.70
1966	Dorothy Shirley	1.70
1967	Linda Knowles	1.70
1968	Dorothy Shirley	1.68
1969	Barbara Inkpen	1.72
1970	Dorothy Shirley	1.68
1971	Debbie Brill CAN	1.83

(4, Barbara Inkpen 1.73)

1972	Ros Few	1.74
1973	Ilona Gusenbauer AUT	1.85

(2, Barbara Lawton (Inkpen) 1.82)

1974	Val Harrison	1.82
1975	Denise Brown	1.75
1976	Denise Brown	1.79
1977	Brenda Gibbs	1.85

1978	Carol Mathers	1.76
1979	Barbara Simmonds	1.81
1980	Ann-Marie Devally	1.88
1981	Ann-Marie Cording (Devally)	1.90
1982	Barbara Simmonds	1.92
1983	Gillian Evans	1.91
1984	Diana Elliott	1.86
1985	Diana Davies (Elliott)	1.89
1986	Diana Davies	1.80
1987	Hanne Haugland NOR	1.88
	(2, Sharon McPeake 1.85)	
1988	Janet Boyle	1.91
1989	Diana Davies	1.85
1990	Lea Haggett	1.88
1991	Debbie Marti	1.88
1992	Lea Haggett	1.89
1993	Debbie Marti	1.86
1994	Julia Bennett	1.89
1995	Lea Haggett	1.85
1996	Debbie Marti	1.94
1997	Debbie Marti	1.90
1998	Jo Jennings	1.88
1999	Jo Jennings	1.87
2000	Jo Jennings	1.89
2001	Susan Jones	1.91
2002	Susan Jones	1.92
2003	Susan Jones	1.86
2004	Susan Jones	1.89
2005	Susan Jones	1.86
2006	Deirdre Ryan IRL	1.92
	(2, Julie Crane 1.86)	
2007	Jessica Ennis	1.87
2008	Stephanie Pywell	1.88
2009	Jessica Ennis	1.91
2010	Stephanie Pywell	1.84
	Vikki Hubbard	1.84
2011	Jessica Ennis	1.89
	Moe Sasegbon	1.74
2012	Jessica Ennis	1.89
	Isobel Pooley	1.82

Most titles won: 8 Dorothy Tyler (Odam) 1936–1939, 1948, 1949, 1952, 1956.
Most medals: 15 Tyler (Odam)

POLE VAULT

(Event instituted in 1993)

1993	Kate Staples	3.20
1994	Kate Staples	3.65
1995	Melissa Price USA	3.70
	(2, Kate Staples 3.50)	

1996	Kate Staples	3.80
1997	Janine Whitlock	3.80
1998	Janine Whitlock	4.10
1999	Janine Whitlock	4.25
2000	Janine Whitlock	4.10
2001	Janine Whitlock	4.40
2002	Irie Hill	4.15
2003	Tracey Bloomfield	4.15
2004	Zoe Brown	4.15
2005	Janine Whitlock	4.20
2006	Ellie Spain	4.21
2007	Kate Dennison	4.20
2008	Emma Lyons	4.12
2009	Kate Dennison	4.57
2010	Kate Dennison	4.45
	Emma Lyons	4.05
2011	Holly Bleasdale	4.56
	Steph Smith	3.60
2012	Holly Bleasdale	4.71
	Abigail Haywood	3.82

Most titles won: 6 Janine Whitlock 1997–2001, 2005. Most medals: 7 Whitlock

LONG JUMP

(Event instituted in 1923)

1923	Mary Lines	4.86
1924	Mary Lines	5.17w?
1925	Hilda Hatt	4.90
1926	Phyllis Green	5.03
1927	Muriel Gunn	5.41w
1928	Muriel Gunn	5.68
1929	Muriel Cornell (Gunn)	5.77
1930	Muriel Cornell	5.63
1931	Muriel Cornell	5.51
1932	Phyllis Bartholomew	5.69
1933	Phyllis Bartholomew	5.40
1934	Phyllis Bartholomew	5.55
1935	Ethel Raby	5.50
1936	Ethel Raby	5.45
1937	Ethel Raby	5.79
1938	Ethel Raby	5.40
1939	Ethel Raby	5.64
1945	Kathleen Duffy	4.76
1946	Ethel Raby	5.05
1947	Kathleen Duffy	5.26
1948	Joan Shepherd	5.70
1949	Margaret Erskine	5.37
1950	Margaret Erskine	5.45
1951	Dorothy Tyler	5.58
1952	Shirley Cawley	5.61

1953	Jean Desforges	5.76
1954	Jean Desforges	5.83
1955	Thelma Hopkins	5.76
1956	Sheila Hoskin	5.65
1957	Christina Persighetti	5.87
1958	Sheila Hoskin	5.96
1959	Mary Bignal	6.04
1960	Ann Packer	5.68
1961	Mary Rand (Bignal)	5.95
1962	Joke Bijleveld NED	6.21
	(3, Sheila Parkin 5.98)	
1963	Mary Rand	5.91
1964	Mary Rand	6.58
1965	Mary Rand	6.40
1966	Berit Berthelsen NOR	6.30
	(2, Mary Rand 6.13)	
1967	Berit Berthelsen NOR	6.47
	(2, Ann Wilson 6.13)	
1968	Sheila Sherwood (Parkin)	6.42
1969	Sheila Sherwood	6.23
1970	Ingrid Mickler FRG	6.50
	(2, Ann Wilson 6.32)	
1971	Sheila Sherwood	6.52
1972	Sheila Sherwood	6.37
1973	Myra Nimmo	6.33w
1974	Ruth Martin-Jones	6.26
1975	Myra Nimmo	6.30
1976	Sue Reeve	6.28
1977	Sue Reeve	6.31
1978	Jill Davies	6.19
1979	Sue Hearnshaw	6.55
1980	Sue Reeve	6.55
1981	Allison Manley	6.27
1982	Robyn Strong AUS	6.65
	(2, Sue Hearnshaw 6.26)	
1983	Robyn Lorraway (Strong) AUS	6.74
	(2, Joyce Oladapo 6.52)	
1984	Sue Hearnshaw	6.78w
1985	Joyce Oladapo	6.56
1986	Mary Berkeley	6.35
1987	Mary Berkeley	6.52
1988	Nicole Boegman AUS	6.82
	(2, Fiona May 6.79)	
1989	Nicole Boegman AUS	6.74
	(2, Fiona May 6.62)	
1990	Fiona May	6.66
1991	Fiona May	6.58
1992	Fiona May	6.70
1993	Nicole Boegman AUS	6.50

	(2, Jo Wise 6.26)	
1994	Yinka Idowu	6.58w
1995	Nicole Boegman AUS	6.50
	(2, Denise Lewis 6.42)	
1996	Denise Lewis	6.55
1997	Andrea Coore	6.22
1998	Denise Lewis	6.44
1999	Jo Wise	6.62
2000	Jo Wise	6.44
2001	Ann Danson	6.15
2002	Jade Johnson	6.52
2003	Jade Johnson	6.49
2004	Jade Johnson	6.72
2005	Kelly Sotherton	6.48
2006	Kelly Sotherton	6.51
2007	Kelly Sotherton	6.53
2008	Jade Johnson	6.30
2009	Phyllis Agbo	6.42w
2010	Jade Johnson	6.48w
	Amy Harris	6.16
2011	Shara Proctor	6.65
	Amy Woodman	6.25
2012	Shara Proctor	6.95
	Amy Woodman	6.17

Most titles won: 6 Ethel Raby 1935–1939, 1946. Most medals: 8 Jade Johnson

TRIPLE JUMP

(Event instituted in 1989)

1989	Evette Finikin	12.27
1990	Evette Finikin	12.49w
1991	Evette Finikin	13.46
1992	Rachel Kirby	13.09
1993	Lene Espegren NOR	13.43
	(2, Rachel Kirby 13.41)	
1994	Michelle Griffith	14.08
1995	Michelle Griffith	13.43
1996	Ashia Hansen	14.25
1997	Kate Evans	12.58
1998	Connie Henry	13.90
1999	Michelle Griffith	13.41
2000	Michelle Griffith	13.67
2001	Ashia Hansen	14.09
2002	Ashia Hansen	14.50
2003	Yamilé Aldama CUB	14.98
	(3, Rebecca White 12.78)	
2004	Michelle Griffith	13.43
2005	Tanesiha Scanlon IRL	13.30
	(2, Nadia Williams 12.95)	
2006	Tiombé Hurd USA	14.15

	(2, Ashia Hansen 13.65)	
2007	Nadia Williams	13.58
2008	Nadia Williams	13.35w
2009	Nadia Williams	13.67
2010	Laura Samuel	13.52
	Nadia Williams	13.54w
2011	Laura Samuel	13.67
	Nadia Williams	13.94w
2012	Laura Samuel	13.73
	Nadia Williams	13.71

Most titles won: 5 Michelle Griffith 1994, 1995, 1999, 2000, 2004. Most medals: 8 Griffith

8lb SHOT

(Event instituted in 1923; from 1923 to 1929 event comprised both hands aggregate with 8lb SHOT)

1923	Florence Birchenough	16.16
1924	Florence Birchenough	16.17
1925	Mary Weston [later Mark Weston]	17.69
1926	Florence Birchenough	16.58
1927	Florence Birchenough	17.20
1928	Mary Weston	18.89
1929	Mary Weston	19.04
1930	Elsie Otway	8.87
1931	Irene Phillips	9.69
1932	Irene Phillips	9.00
1933	Gerda de Kock NED	10.26
	(3, Kitty Tilley 9.68)	
1934	Kitty Tilley	10.04
1935	Kitty Tilley	10.08
1936	Bernice Steyl SAF	10.74
	(2, Kitty Tilley 10.32)	
1937	Kitty Tilley	10.59
1938	Bevis Reid	11.60
1939	Bevis Reid	11.42
1945	Kitty Dyer (Tilley)	9.39
1946	Kitty Dyer	10.20
1947	Bevis Reid	11.03
1948	Bevis Reid	12.34
1949	Bevis Reid	12.36
1950	Joan Linsell	11.07
1951	Bevis Shergold (Reid)	11.78
1952	Joan Linsell	12.10
1953	Joan Linsell	12.11
1954	Suzanne Allday	12.52
1955	Jo Page	11.90
1956	Suzanne Allday	13.39
1957	Jo Cook (Page)	12.60
1958	Suzanne Allday	14.15

1959	Suzanne Allday	13.19
1960	Suzanne Allday	14.30
1961	Suzanne Allday	13.73
1962	Suzanne Allday	13.88
1963	Marlene Klein FRG	15.48
	(2, Suzanne Allday 14.81)	
1964	Mary Peters	14.22
1965	Gertrud Schäfer FRG	14.81
	(2, Mary Peters 14.06)	
1966	Brenda Bedford	14.52
1967	Brenda Bedford	15.18
1968	Margitta Gummel GDR	16.99
	(3, Brenda Bedford 14.71)	
1969	Brenda Bedford	15.22
1970	Mary Peters	14.85
1971	Jean Roberts AUS	15.81
	(2, Brenda Bedford 14.93)	
1972	Jean Roberts AUS	15.34
	(2, Brenda Bedford 14.72)	
1973	Brenda Bedford	14.82
1974	Jane Haist CAN	15.03
	(2, Brenda Bedford 14.65)	
1975	Brenda Bedford	14.89
1976	Janis Kerr	15.88
1977	Brenda Bedford	15.79
1978	Angela Littlewood	15.97
1979	Judy Oakes	16.38
1980	Judy Oakes	16.85
1981	Angela Littlewood	16.26
1982	Judy Oakes	17.59
1983	Judy Oakes	17.61
1984	Judy Oakes	18.01
1985	Judy Oakes	17.57
1986	Judy Oakes	18.70
1987	Judy Oakes	18.44
1988	Judy Oakes	18.76
1989	Myrtle Augee	17.51
1990	Judy Oakes	18.63
1991	Judy Oakes	18.24
1992	Myrtle Augee	17.29
1993	Myrtle Augee	17.24
1994	Judy Oakes	18.38
1995	Judy Oakes	17.75
1996	Judy Oakes	18.65
1997	Judy Oakes	17.89
1998	Judy Oakes	17.82
1999	Myrtle Augee	17.32
2000	Judy Oakes	17.91
2001	Jo Duncan	16.84

2002	Myrtle Augee	16.16
2003	Jo Duncan	16.19
2004	Julie Dunkley	16.03
2005	Julie Dunkley	16.14
2006	Julie Dunkley	16.08
2007	Eva Massey	16.63
2008	Jo Duncan	15.99
2009	Eden Francis	16.33
2010	Eden Francis	16.02
	Eleanor Gatrell	16.17
2011	Eden Francis	16.73
	Eden Francis	16.53
2012	Eden Francis	16.13
	Rachel Wallader	15.30

Most titles won: 17 Judy Oakes 1979, 1980, 1982–1988, 1990, 1991, 1994–1998, 2000. Most medals: 19 Oakes

DISCUS (1kg)

(Event instituted in 1923)

1923	Florence Birchenough	24.03
1924	Florence Birchenough	25.83
1925	Florence Birchenough	27.18
1926	Florence Birchenough	27.92
1927	Florence Birchenough	28.57
1928	Florence Birchenough	27.92
1929	Mary Weston [later Mark Weston]	30.50
1930	Louise Fawcett	29.30
1931	Irene Phillips	29.78
1932	Ada Holland	30.86
1933	Ada Holland	33.22
1934	Irene Phillips	30.99
1935	Ada Holland	30.94
1936	Irene Phillips	30.81
1937	Irene Phillips	32.61
1938	Bevis Reid	35.42
1939	Bevis Reid	33.85
1945	Kitty Dyer	30.38
1946	Margaret Lasbrey SAF	28.34
	(2, Doris Endruweit 28.04)	
1947	Margaret Lucas	36.40
1948	Bevis Reid	36.74
1949	Bevis Reid	36.96
1950	Joyce Smith	33.02
1951	Bevis Shergold (Reid)	39.88
1952	Suzanne Farmer	39.33
1953	Suzanne Farmer	40.01
1954	Maya Giri	39.42
1955	Maya Giri	41.68
1956	Suzanne Allday (Farmer)	47.02

1957	Sylvia Needham	40.22
1958	Suzanne Allday	47.70
1959	Suzanne Allday	45.21
1960	Suzanne Allday	45.25
1961	Suzanne Allday	45.29
1962	Loes Boling NED	47.27
	(2, Suzanne Allday 46.09)	
1963	Lia Manoliu ROU	49.40
	(2, Suzanne Allday 44.39)	
1964	Kriemhild Limberg FRG	50.93
	(2, Rosemary Payne 46.24)	
1965	Elivia Ballotta ITA	50.56
	(3, Rosemary Payne 48.04)	
1966	Rosemary Payne	49.89
1967	Rosemary Payne	46.66
1968	Karin Illgen GDR	57.23
	(4, Rosemary Payne 47.20)	
1969	Lia Manoliu ROU	55.58
	(2, Rosemary Payne 49.58)	
1970	Rosemary Payne	52.58
1971	Liesel Westermann FRG	58.44
	(3, Rosemary Payne 52.60)	
1972	Rosemary Payne	53.78
1973	Rosemary Payne	56.40
1974	Jane Haist CAN	56.38
	(2, Rosemary Payne 51.70)	
1975	Meg Ritchie	53.12
1976	Janet Thompson	51.38
1977	Meg Ritchie	53.98
1978	Janet Thompson	49.80
1979	Janet Thompson	53.56
1980	Lesley Mallin	51.24
1981	Meg Ritchie	62.22
1982	Janette Picton	51.06
1983	Lynda Whiteley	53.88
1984	Lynda Whiteley	57.32
1985	Julia Avis	50.82
1986	Kathryn Farr	51.20
1987	Ellen Mulvihill	52.16
1988	Jackie McKernan	51.80
1989	Janette Picton	53.22
1990	Lisa-Marie Vizaniari AUS	57.22
	(2, Jackie McKernan 55.48)	
1991	Jackie McKernan	57.76
1992	Jackie McKernan	54.48
1993	Daniela Costian AUS	61.58
	(2, Tracy Axten 54.40)	
1994	Jackie McKernan	56.94
1995	Lisa-Marie Vizaniari AUS	61.98

	(2, Jackie McKernan 58.88)	
1996	Jackie McKernan	54.12
1997	Jackie McKernan	56.00
1998	Shelley Drew	60.82
1999	Shelley Drew	55.16
2000	Shelley Drew	59.03
2001	Shelley Drew	57.22
2002	Philippa Roles	56.32
2003	Shelley Newman (Drew)	58.16
2004	Philippa Roles	58.57
2005	Philippa Roles	57.01
2006	Claire Smithson	56.15
2007	Philippa Roles	57.83
2008	Emma Carpenter	57.26
2009	Philippa Roles	57.57
2010	Jade Nicholls	57.81
	Sarah Henton	48.73
2011	Jade Nicholls	56.19
	Jade Nicholls	53.99
2012	Eden Francis	53.09
	Jade Nicholls	54.84

Most titles won: 7 Suzanne Allday (Farmer) 1952, 1953, 1956, 1958–1961. Most medals: 13 Philippa Roles

HAMMER (4kg)

(Event instituted in 1993)

1993	Debbie Sosimenko AUS	56.86
	(2, Esther Augee 52.22)	
1994	Lorraine Shaw	59.58
1995	Debbie Sosimenko AUS	65.24
	(3, Lorraine Shaw 56.26)	
1996	Lyn Sprules	54.16
1997	Lyn Sprules	61.18
1998	Lorraine Shaw	60.71
1999	Lyn Sprules	62.62
2000	Lorraine Shaw	66.85
2001	Lorraine Shaw	66.97
2002	Lorraine Shaw	64.97
2003	Lorraine Shaw	65.93
2004	Lorraine Shaw	68.11
2005	Shirley Webb	66.60
2006	Eileen O'Keeffe IRL	65.62
	(2, Shirley Webb 63.57)	
2007	Zoe Derham	64.99
2008	Zoe Derham	67.27
2009	Zoe Derham	67.94
2010	Zoe Derham	66.11
	Zoe Derham	64.26
2011	Sophie Hitchon	67.69

	Sarah Holt	64.49
2012	Sophie Hitchon	69.79
	Sarah Holt	68.50

Most titles won: 7 Lorraine Shaw 1994, 1998, 2000–2004. Most medals: 11 Shaw

JAVELIN (600gm)

(Event instituted in 1923; from 1923 to 1927 event comprised both hands aggregate with 800gm javelin; 600gm from 1928; new specification model introduced in 1999)

1923	Sophie Eliott-Lynn	35.76
1924	Sophie Eliott-Lynn	52.78
1925	Ivy Wilson	47.73
1926	Louise Fawcett	49.18
1927	E Willis	41.35
1928	Kinue Hitomi JPN	35.97
	(2, Mary Weston 29.70)	
1929	Mary Weston [later Mark Weston] 25.91	
1930	Leni Rombout NED	32.44
	(2, Nellie Purvey 28.45)	
1931	Louise Fawcett	29.26
1932	Edith Halstead [later Edwin Halstead] 32.86	
1933	Gerda de Kock NED	36.11
	(2, Edith Halstead 35.22)	
1934	Edith Halstead	31.05
1935	Ruth Caro GER/ARG	34.52
1936	Kathleen Connal	35.99
1937	Gladys Lunn	32.97
1938	Kathleen Connal	34.68
1939	Kathleen Connal	34.98
1945	Gladys Clarke	31.72
1946	Margaret Lasbrey SAF	34.44
	(2, Doris Endruweit 26.36)	
1947	Milena Taiblová TCH	31.50
	(3, Doris Chandler 28.76)	
1948	Bevis Reid	31.10
1949	Ellen Allen	31.62
1950	Diane Coates	39.02
1951	Diane Coates	38.04
1952	Diane Coates	45.30
1953	Anne Collins	36.56
1954	Ann Dukes	39.55
1955	Diane Coates	41.78
1956	Doris Orphall	40.82
1957	Averil Williams	40.23
1958	Averil Williams	43.48
1959	Sue Platt	49.04
1960	Sue Platt	50.83
1961	Sue Platt	47.88

1962	Sue Platt	50.72
1963	Anneliese Gerhards FRG	50.30
	(3, Rosemary Morgan 46.19)	
1964	Anneliese Gerhards FRG	51.82
	(2, Sue Platt 49.25)	
1965	Ameli Koloska FRG	53.16
	(2, Averil Williams 43.09)	
1966	Sue Platt	45.19
1967	Sue Platt	49.15
1968	Sue Platt	53.26
1969	Sue Platt	49.34
1970	Ameli Koloska FRG	54.12
	(2, Angela King 46.70)	
1971	Inger Lise Fallo NOR	47.68
	(2, Jan Baker 46.18)	
1972	Pru French	51.00
1973	Sharon Corbett	53.88
1974	Eva Janko AUT	61.56
	(2, Sharon Corbett 51.98)	
1975	Tessa Sanderson	54.40
1976	Tessa Sanderson	56.98
1977	Tessa Sanderson	59.96
1978	Anne Farquhar	49.20
1979	Tessa Sanderson	61.82
1980	Tessa Sanderson	64.08
1981	Fatima Whitbread	57.74
1982	Fatima Whitbread	63.00
1983	Fatima Whitbread	65.24
1984	Fatima Whitbread	65.76
1985	Tessa Sanderson	66.38
1986	Fatima Whitbread	69.02
1987	Fatima Whitbread	72.96
1988	Sharon Gibson	57.32
1989	Tessa Sanderson	58.64
1990	Tessa Sanderson	58.42
1991	Sharon Gibson	57.34
1992	Tessa Sanderson	63.26
1993	Shelley Holroyd	60.10
1994	Shelley Holroyd	57.08
1995	Lorna Jackson	55.48
1996	Tessa Sanderson	62.88
1997	Karen Martin	50.38
1998	Lorna Jackson	57.89
1999	Kirsty Morrison	55.70
2000	Kelly Morgan	58.45
2001	Karen Martin	54.82
2002	Kelly Morgan	64.87
2003	Goldie Sayers	56.29
2004	Goldie Sayers	60.85

2005	Goldie Sayers	57.99
2006	Goldie Sayers	58.81
2007	Goldie Sayers	63.02
2008	Goldie Sayers	62.62
2009	Goldie Sayers	55.33
2010	Goldie Sayers	58.60
	Laura Whittingham	54.52
2011	Goldie Sayers	60.57
	Tesni Ward	49.51
2012	Goldie Sayers	58.95
	Izzy Jeffs	46.71

Most titles won: 10 Tessa Sanderson 1975–1977, 1979, 1980, 1985, 1989, 1990, 1992, 1996 & Goldie Sayers 2003–2012. Most medals: 11 Sanderson, Sharon Gibson & Sayers

PENTATHLON/HEPTATHLON

(Pentathlon instituted in 1949; heptathlon in 1981; point scores shown are per tables then in use)

1949	Bertha Crowther	327
1950	Bertha Crowther	2949
1951	Dorothy Tyler	3224
1952	Sheila Sewell	2544
1953	Jean Desforges	3221
1954	Jean Desforges	3170
1955	Margaret Rowley	3943
1956	Margaret Rowley	3812
1957	Margaret Rowley	4183
1958	Janet Gaunt	3887
1959	Mary Bignal	4679
1960	Mary Bignal	4568
1961	Carole Hamby	3986
1962	Mary Peters	4190
1963	Mary Peters	4385
1964	Mary Peters	4801
1965	Mary Peters	4413
1966	Mary Peters	4625
1967	Janet Oldall	3965
1968	Mary Peters	4723
1969	Moira Walls	4591
1970	Mary Peters	4841
1971	Janet Honour (Oldall)	4571
1972	Ann Wilson	4292
1973	Mary Peters	4429
1974	Ann Wilson	4248
1975	Sue Wright	4196
1976	Sue Longden (Wright)	4337
1977	Sue Longden	4152
1978	Yvette Wray	4140
1979	Marcia Marriott	3897

1980	Sue Longden	4395
1981	Kathy Warren	5674
1982	Judy Livermore	5895
1983	Judy Livermore	5940
1984	Sarah Owen	5150
1985	Ann Turnbull AUS	5289
	(2, Charmaine Johnson 5177w)	
1986	Terry Genge NZL	5547
	(2, Marcia Marriott 5538)	
1987	Anne Brit Skjaeveland NOR	5358
	(2, Charmaine Johnson 5136w)	
1988	Joanne Mulliner	5728
1989	Kim Hagger	6126
1990	Joanne Mulliner	5679w
1991	Clova Court	5875
1992	Clova Court	5846
1993	Clova Court	5957
1994	Vikki Schofield	5587
1995	Emma Beales	5524
1996	Kerry Jury	5703
1997	Clova Court	5712
1998	Clova Court	5639
1999	Katherine Livesey	4851
2000	Julie Hollman	5560
2001	Laura Redmond	5068
2002	Caroline Pearce	5108
2003	Fiona Harrison	5517
2004	Caroline Pearce	5253
2005	Kate Brewington	5041
2006	Katia Lannon	5071
2007	Phyllis Agbo	5471
2008	Julie Hollman	5941
2009	Catherine Holdsworth	5421
2010	Dominique Blaize	5671
2011	Gemma Weetman	5379
2012	Joanne Rowland	5381

Most titles won: 8 Mary Peters 1962–1966, 1968, 1970, 1973.

TRACK WALK (880y–3000m)

(Event instituted in 1923 at 880 yards; 1 mile (y) from 1928 to 1932; 1600m 1933–1939; mile 1945; 1600m 1946–1951; mile 1952–1958; 1.5 miles 1959–1968; 2500m 1969–1972; 3000m 1973–1974)

1923	Edith Trickey	4:35.0
1924	Edith Trickey	4:17.4
1925	Florence Faulkner	4:15.0
1926	Daisy Crossley	4:06.0
1927	M F Hegarty	3:54.2
1928	Lucy Howes	8:27.4y
1929	Lucy Howes	8:16.0y

1930	Connie Mason	8:14.4y
1931	Connie Mason	7:45.6y
1932	Connie Mason	7:47.8y
1933	Jeanne Probekk	7:51.2
1934	Jeanne Probekk	7:38.2
1935	Jessie Howes	7:57.8
1936	Jessie Howes	8:14.2
1937	F Pengelly	8:36.5
1938	Evelyn Webb	8:39.0
1939	F Pengelly	8:19.9
1945	Diana Riddington	8:42.8y
1946	Doris Hart (later Mann)	8:38.6
1947	Diana Riddington	8:36.4
1948	Joyce Heath	8:17.8
1949	Joyce Heath	8:25.0
1950	Joyce Heath	8:17.0
1951	Joyce Heath	7:50.0
1952	Beryl Day	7:58.2y
1953	Beryl Randle (Day)	7:48.2y
1954	Beryl Randle	7:38.4y
1955	Beryl Randle	7:59.4y
1956	Dilys Williams	7:47.6y
1957	Gillian Williams	8:08.4y
1958	Betty Franklin	8:09.4y
1959	Betty Franklin	12:56.4
1960	Judy Woodsford	12:31.2
1961	Sheila Jennings	12:18.4
1962	Judy Farr (Woodsford)	12:20.0
1963	Judy Farr	12:26.4
1964	Judy Farr	12:06.8
1965	Judy Farr	12:14.2
1966	Judy Farr	12:09.2
1967	Judy Farr	12:09.2
1968	Judy Farr	12:39.0
1969	Judy Farr	12:45.8
1970	Judy Farr	12:34.0
1971	Brenda Cook	12:39.8
1972	Betty Jenkins (Franklin)	12:31.2
1973	Betty Jenkins	14:59.4
1974	Marion Fawkes	14:33.50

Most titles won: 10 Judy Farr (Woodsford) 1960, 1962–1970

5000 METRES TRACK WALK
(Event instituted in 1975)

1975	Ginney Lovell	25:02.8
1976	Marion Fawkes	24:10.0
1977	Marion Fawkes	24:50.6
1978	Carol Tyson	24:08.2
1979	Marion Fawkes	23:31.5

1980	Irene Bateman	24:09.0
1981	Carol Tyson	23:12.55
1982	Sue Cook AUS	23:03.52
	(2, Irene Bateman 24:34.92)	
1983	Ann Peel CAN	24:26.04
	(2, Jill Barrett 25:20.73)	
1984	Jill Barrett	23:51.63
1985	Ginney Birch (Lovell)	23:53.47
1986	Helen Elleker	24:27.17
1987	Lisa Langford	22:35.04
1988	Betty Sworowski	24:24.32
1989	Betty Sworowski	22:30.59
1990	Betty Sworowski	22:23.35
1991	Betty Sworowski	22:29.04
1992	Vicky Lupton	22:12.21
1993	Vicky Lupton	22:34.50
1994	Verity Snook	23:22.52
1995	Lisa Langford	22:20.03
1996	Vicky Lupton	23:04.57
1997	Olive Loughnane IRL	24:09.18
	(2, Catherine Charnock 23:42.92)	
1998	Gillian O'Sullivan IRL	21:52.68
	(2, Lisa Kehler (Langford) 22:01.53)	
1999	Vicky Lupton	23:37.47
2001	Niobe Menéndez	23:46.30
2002	Lisa Kehler	21:42.51
2003	Lisa Kehler	23:10.15
2004	Niobe Menéndez	23:53.75
2005	Jo Jackson	23:34.12
2006	Ann Loughnane IRL	22:54.97
	(2, Jo Jackson 23:27.56)	
2007	Jo Jackson	22:03.65
2008	Jo Jackson	21:30.75
2009	Jo Jackson	21:21.67
2010	Jo Jackson	21:52.95
2011	Jo Jackson	21:42.32
2012	Jo Jackson	21:45.98

Most titles won: 7 Jo Jackson 2005, 2007–2012

10,000 METRES TRACK WALK

(Event instituted in 1978; discontinued after 2000)

1978	Carol Tyson	49:59.0
1979	Marion Fawkes	48:37.6
1980	Carol Tyson	49:30.4
1981	Irene Bateman	49:54.3
1982	Irene Bateman	48:57.6
1983	Irene Bateman	48:52.5
1984	Helen Elleker	49:52.3
1985	Helen Elleker	51:22.3

1986	Helen Elleker	49:21.8
1987	Sarah Brown	51:48.7
1988	Betty Sworowski	50:12.0
1989	Lisa Langford & Betty Sworowski	47:15.0
1990	Vicky Lupton	48:12.2
1991	Betty Sworowski	46:23.08
1993	Verity Larby	47:10.07
1994	Verity Snook (Larby)	48:05.0
1995	Vicky Lupton	45:18.8
1996	Vicky Lupton	49:15.0
1997	Catherine Charnock	54:33.6
1998	Pam Phillips	64:08.9
2000	Lisa Kehler (Langford)	45:09.57

Most titles won: 3 Irene Bateman 1981–1983, Helen Elleker 1984–1986, Betty Sworowski 1988, 1989, 1991 & Vicky Lupton 1990, 1995, 1996

4x100 METRES RELAY

(Event instituted in 1949 at 4x100m; y = 4x110y; discontinued after 1986)

1949	Spartan Ladies	
1950	Spartan Ladies	49.4
1951	Spartan Ladies	49.5
1952	London Olympiades	50.2y
1953	Essex Ladies	48.2y
1954	Selsonia Ladies	48.2y
1956	Spartan Ladies	48.2y
1957	Spartan Ladies	47.7y
1958	Spartan Ladies	47.8y
1959	Spartan Ladies	47.6y
1960	City of Stoke	47.5y
1962	Selsonia Ladies	47.7y
1963	Selsonia Ladies	47.9y
1964	Hickleton Main	46.6
1965	London Olympiades	46.61
1966	Birchfield	47.2y
1967	London Olympiades	46.9y
1968	London Olympiades	45.5
1969	Dorothy Hyman Track Club	45.0
1970	Edinburgh Southern	45.2
1971	London Olympiades	46.0
1972	London Olympiades	47.4
1973	London Olympiades	46.8
1974	Stretford	45.37
1975	Mitcham	45.85
1976	Essex Ladies	48.61
1977	Selsonia Ladies	47.5
1978	Selsonia Ladies	45.7
1979	Selsonia Ladies	46.7
1980	Selsonia Ladies	46.5
1981	Borough of Hounslow	44.85

1982	Herne Hill	48.15
1983	Stretford	46.35
1984	Bromley Ladies	47.2
1985	Radley Ladies	46.9
1986	Stretford	46.79

4x200 METRES RELAY

(Event instituted in 1958 at 4x220y; y = 4x220y; discontinued after 1986)

1958	Spartan Ladies	1:41.3y
1961	London Olympiades	1:43.8y
1964	London Olympiades	1:38.3y
1965	Birchfield	1:42.3y
1966	Birchfield	1:39.4y
1967	London Olympiades	1:43.0y
1968	London Olympiades	1:37.7
1969	London Olympiades	1:40.9
1970	Edinburgh Southern	1:36.7
1971	Stretford	1:36.5
1972	London Olympiades	1:42.3
1973	London Olympiades	1:39.2
1974	Stretford	1:36.00
1975	Stretford	1:37.76
1976	Essex Ladies	1:41.62
1977	Wolverhampton & Bilston	1:39.6
1978	Sale	1:37.6
1979	Selsonia Ladies	1:37.8
1980	Wigmore Ladies	1:39.8
1981	Borough of Hounslow	1:35.46
1982	City of Hull	1:38.98
1983	Stretford	1:39.98
1984	Bromley Ladies	1:38.2
1985	Radley Ladies	1:40.8
1986	Stretford	1:39.61

660 YARDS MEDLEY RELAY

(Event instituted in 1922; 4x220 yards that year; discontinued after 1960)

1922	London Olympiades	1:56.6
1923	London Olympiades	1:22.6
1924	London Olympiades	1:21.6
1925	Manor Park Ladies	1:19.4
1926	London Olympiades	1:19.4
1927	Middlesex Ladies	1:18.6
1928	London Olympiades	1:17.2
1929	Manor Park Ladies	1:17.6
1930	London Olympiades	1:18.2
1931	London Olympiades	1:18.0
1932	London Olympiades	1:16.6
1933	London Olympiades	1:16.8

1934	London Olympiades	1:16.6
1935	London Olympiades	
1936	Mitcham	1:18.4
1937	London Olympiades	1:18.0
1938	Mitcham	1:17.2
1939	Essex Ladies	1:17.6
1945	Birchfield	1:20.4
1946	Spartan Ladies	1:21.5
1947	Spartan Ladies	1:18.7
1948	Spartan Ladies	1:17.4
1949	Spartan Ladies	1:15.8
1950	Essex Ladies	1:14.6
1951	Essex Ladies	1:17.2
1952	Spartan Ladies	1:14.9
1953	Spartan Ladies	
1954	Essex Ladies	
1955	Birchfield	
1956	Spartan Ladies	
1957	Birchfield	1:16.9
1958	Spartan Ladies	
1959	Spartan Ladies	
1960	Spartan Ladies	

4x400 METRES RELAY

(Event instituted in 1969; discontinued after 1982)

1969	Edinburgh Southern	3:46.4
1970	Edinburgh Southern	3:44.1
1971	Clonliffe (Ireland)	3:49.1
	(2, Bury & Radcliffe 3:50.2)	
1972	Wolverhampton & Bilston	3:40.6
1973	Wolverhampton & Bilston	3:44.72
1974	London Olympiades	3:52.9
1975	Essex Ladies	3:50.0
1976	Birchfield	3:52.64
1977	Birchfield	3:50.1
1978	Birchfield	3:47.8
1979	Birchfield	3:52.7
1980	Birchfield	3:44.5
1981	Pitreavie	3:41.20
1982	City of Hull	3:45.3

1600 METRES MEDLEY RELAY

(Event instituted in 1953 at Mile Medley; changed to 1600m Medley in 1968; discontinued after 1978)

1953	Spartan Ladies	4:12.7
1954	Birchfield	4:01.8
1955	Birchfield	4:04.8
1956	Ilford	4:03.0
1957	Birchfield	4:00.3

1959	Spartan Ladies	4:03.8
1960	Spartan Ladies	4:15.6
1961	Spartan Ladies	
1962	London Olympiades	4:10.3
1963	London Olympiades	4:15.9
1964	Bury & Radcliffe	4:05.4
1965	Birchfield	4:04.4
1966	Birchfield	3:59.4
1967	Birchfield	4:02.1
1968	Birchfield	3:54.3
1969	Bristol	4:03.5
1970	Wolverhampton & Bilston	4:00.9
1971	Coventry Godiva	3:56.5
1972	Airedale & Spen Valley	3:58.6
1973	Wolverhampton & Bilston	3:55.15
1974	Birchfield	4:10.6
1975	London Olympiades	4:01.2
1976	Birchfield	4:00.20
1977	Stretford	4:02.4
1978	Sale	3:55.9

4x800 METRES RELAY

(Event instituted in 1958 at 3 x 880y; changed to 3x800m in 1968 and 4x800m from 1969; discontinued after 1986)

1958	Highgate	7:01.2
1959	Spartan Ladies	6:59.8
1960	Mitcham	6:59.8
1961	Spartan Ladies	
1962	Mitcham	6:58.6
1963	Mitcham	6:42.4
1964	Bilston Town	6:52.5
1965	Bilston Town	6:51.4
1966	Bilston Town	6:45.0
1967	Bury & Radcliffe	6:48.6
1968	Coventry Godiva	6:39.0
1969	Cambridge Harriers	9:06.4
1970	Barnet & District	8:58.0
1971	Clonliffe (Ireland)	8:48.8
	(2, Barnet & District 8:49.8)	
1972	Airedale & Spen Valley	9:13.4
1973	Cambridge Harriers	8:44.6
1974	Derby Ladies	9:45.0
1975	Cambridge Harriers	8:41.0
1976	Verlea	9:24.01
1977	Birchfield	9:03.6
1978	Leeds City	8:58.4
1979	Birchfield	8:45.3
1980	Sale	8:50.29
1981	Sale	8:49.91

1982	Sale	8:52.34
1983	Coventry Godiva	8:52.88
1984	Coventry Godiva	9:07.1
1985	Bournemouth	9:18.6
1986	Stretford	9:07.44

ROAD WALKING

(Event instituted in 1933; distance varied until 1977 when standardised at 5 kilometres; 10 kilometres event added from 1981; 15 kilometres staged from 1988 to 1992. RWA Championships: 10 miles from 1993 to 1998; 20 kilometres instituted in 1993, 50 kilometres in 2005 and long distance, varying between 100 miles and 24 hours, in 1993)

1933	Jeanne Probekk	25:56
1934	Jessie Howes	22:47
1935	Jessie Howes	26:22
1936	Edith Littlefair (Trickey)	27:15
1937	Doris Harris	29:00
1938	Doris Harris	25:48
1939	F Pengelly	33:32
1946	Doris Mann (Hart)	22:28
1947	Joyce Heath	21:29
1948	Joyce Heath	20:49
1949	Joyce Heath	22:03
1950	Joyce Heath	23:18
1951	Leila Deas	21:07
1953	Dilys Williams	17:09
1954	Dilys Williams (2 races)	20:59/17:49
1956	Dilys Williams (2 races)	20:42/18:39
1957	Gillian Williams	23:58
1958	Pat Myatt	34:55
1959	Beryl Randle	35:48
1960	Sheila Jennings	36:01
1961	Sheila Jennings	34:30
1962	Judy Farr	32:55
1963	Judy Farr	39:33
1964	Judy Farr	35:51
1965	Judy Farr	33:35
1966	Sheila Jennings	28:15
1967	Betty Jenkins	35:21
1968	Judy Farr	34:05
1969	Betty Jenkins	32:57
1970	Judy Farr	34:02
1971	Betty Jenkins	33:50
1972	Betty Jenkins	33:51
1973	Marion Fawkes	31:55
1974	Marion Fawkes	27:25
1975	Judy Farr	32:12
1976	Judy Farr	29:24

5 KILOMETRES ROAD WALK

1977	Carol Tyson	24:02
1978	Carol Tyson	24:08
1979	Elaine Cox	22:30*
1980	Carol Tyson	23:05
1981	Irene Bateman	25:00
1982	Irene Bateman	24:09
1983	Irene Bateman	23:28
1984	Jill Barrett	23:38
1985	Janice McCaffrey CAN	23:12
	(2, Ginney Birch 23:21)	
1986	Bev Allen	23:29
1987	Lisa Langford	23:07
1988	Betty Sworowski	23:43
1989	Julie Drake	24:04
1990	Lisa Langford	22:24
1991	Vicky Lupton	22:50
1992	Sylvia Black	25:18^
1993	Joanne Pope	25:13
1994	Melanie Wright	24:27
1995	Lisa Langford	23:00
1996	Vicky Lupton	23:05
1997	Lisa Kehler (Langford)	23:20
1998	Kim Braznell	24:45
1999	Catherine Charnock	23:09
2000	Niobe Menéndez	24:19
2001	Sharon Tonks	24:51
2002	Lisa Kehler	22:20
2003	Katie Stones	26:49
2004	Rebecca Mersh	26:09

* course about 500m short; ^ course over distance

10 KILOMETRES ROAD WALK

1981	Irene Bateman	48:47
1982	Irene Bateman	51:18
1983	Ginney Birch	51:48
1984	Ginney Birch	50:25
1985	Susan Ashforth	53:08
1986	Helen Elleker	49:27
1987	Lisa Langford	46:37
1988	Julie Drake	49:26
1989	Betty Sworowski	45:30*
1990	Betty Sworowski	46:40
1991	Betty Sworowski	47:23
1992	Vicky Lupton	46:04
1993	Verity Larby	47:51
1994	Karen Smith	48:30
1995	Vicky Lupton	47:44

1996	Vicky Lupton	47:48
1997	Sylvia Black	49:39
1998	Lisa Kehler (Langford)	47:10
1999	Catherine Charnock	47:51
2000	Sharon Tonks	52:00
2001	Niobe Menéndez	49:19
2002	Estlé Viljoen RSA	49:06
	(2, Sharon Tonks 52:07)	
2003	Lisa Kehler	49:44
2004	Sophie Hales	54:37
2005	Jo Jackson	48:37
2006	Jo Jackson	51:24
2007	Jo Jackson	47:49
2008	Jo Jackson	45:20
2009	Jo Jackson	46:23
2010	Jo Jackson	45:31
2011	Jo Jackson	44:59
2012	Heather Lewis	49.51

* course short by 31 metres

15 KILOMETRES ROAD WALK

1988	Betty Sworowski	1:19:03
1989	Vicky Lupton	1:22:00
1990	Betty Sworowski	1:12:36
1991	Vicky Lupton & Betty Sworowski	1:12:32
1992	Melanie Brookes	1:16:17

10 MILES ROAD WALK

1993	Vicky Lupton	1:21:19
1994	Cath Reader	1:30:37
1995	Vicky Lupton	1:21:23
1996	Vicky Lupton	1:22:11
1997	Vicky Lupton	1:25:11
1998	Vicky Lupton	1:21:15
2008	Anne Belchambers	1:37:37
2009	Lisa Kehler	1:22:27
2010	Lisa Kehler	1:23:14
2011	Neringa Aidietyte LTU	1:16:19
	(2, Lisa Kehler 1:24:38)	
2012	Heather Lewis	1:25:03

20 KILOMETRES ROAD WALK

1993	Elaine Callanin	1:45:11
1994	Vicky Lupton	1:44:48
1995	Vicky Lupton	1:42:47
1996	Vicky Lupton	1:46:43
1997	Sylvia Black	1:45:48
1998	Vicky Lupton	1:44:35
1999	Niobe Menéndez	1:40:12

2000	Lisa Kehler	1:39:28
2001	Sheila Bull	2:18:53
2002	Lisa Kehler	1:43:08
2003	Jo Hesketh	1:47:50
2004	Niobe Menéndez	1:50:59
2005	Katie Stones	1:46:48
2006	Jo Jackson	1:43:37
2007	Jo Jackson	1:38:34
2008	Diane Bradley	1:57:18
2009	Jo Jackson	1:35:57
2010	Jo Jackson	1:39:14
2011	Jo Jackson	1:31:50
2012	Neringa Aidietyte LTU	1:38:21
	(2, Rebecca Collins 1:57:34)	

50 KILOMETRES ROAD WALK

2005	Maureen Noel	6:02:53
2006	Cath Duhig	6:07:51
2007	Maureen Noel	5:52:02
2008	Marie Jackson	5:57:32
2009	Maureen Noel	6:07:26
2010	Maureen Noel	5:49:55
2011	Maureen Noel	5:55:31

LONG DISTANCE ROAD WALK

1993	Lillian Millen (100M road)	20:13:15
1994	Sandra Brown (100M road)	19:09:17
1995	Sandra Brown (100M road)	21:37:21
1997	Sandra Brown (100M track)	19:27:15
1999	Sandra Brown (100M road)	20:01:49
2000	Sandra Brown (24hr road)	183.458km
2001	Sandra Brown (100M road)	20:36:45
2002	Sandra Brown (24hr track)	186.324km
2003	Sandra Brown (100M road)	20:27:25
2004	Sandra Brown (100M road)	19:17:28
2005	Sandra Brown (100M road)	19:25:07
2006	Sandra Brown (100M road)	19:28:38
2007	Cath Duhig (100M road)	23:38:11
2008	Sandra Brown (100M track)	19:59:29
2009	Sandra Brown (100M road)	19:57:24
2010	Sandra Brown (100M road)	20:23:30
2011	Sandra Brown (100M road)	20:18:23

CROSS COUNTRY

(Event instituted in 1927)
(Distance varied; Individual and team winners)

1927	Anne Williams	15:25	Middlesex Ladies
1928	Lillian Styles	20:50	Middlesex Ladies & London Olympiades
1929	Lillian Styles	17:16	Middlesex Ladies
1930	Lillian Styles	21:00	Westbury
1931	Gladys Lunn	21:05	London Olympiades
1932	Gladys Lunn	19:15	Birchfield
1933	Lillian Styles	21:23	Airedale
1934	Lillian Styles	21:26	London Olympiades
1935	Nellie Halstead	15:40	London Olympiades
1936	Nellie Halstead	22:12	Small Heath
1937	Lillian Styles	28:40	Birchfield
1938	Evelyne Forster	21:58	Birchfield
1939	Evelyne Forster	20:33	Birchfield
1946	Pat Sandall	17:01	Birchfield
1947	Ruby Wright	21:13	Birchfield
1948	Ivy Kibbler	20:53	Birchfield
1949	Enid Johnson	19:25	Birchfield
1950	Avery Gibson	16:46	Birchfield
1951	Phyllis Green	19:54	Ilford
1952	Phyllis Green	15:16	Ilford
1953	Diane Leather	15:17	Birchfield
1954	Diane Leather	19:16	Birchfield
1955	Diane Leather	15:47	Ilford
1956	Diane Leather	15:53	Ilford
1957	June Bridgland	16:55	Ilford
1958	Roma Ashby	19:10	Highgate
1959	Joyce Byatt	19:30	London Olympiades
1960	Joyce Byatt	15:22	Ilford
1961	Roma Ashby	22:51	London Olympiades
1962	Roma Ashby	20:07	London Olympiades
1963	Madeline Ibbotson	19:20	Mitcham
1964	Madeline Ibbotson	19:43	Bury & Radcliffe
1965	Pam Davies	23:51	Maryhill Ladies
1966	Pam Davies	19:38	Maryhill Ladies
1967	Pam Davies	21:34	Barnet & District
1968	Pam Davies	21:26	Cambridge Harriers
1969	Rita Lincoln	22:05	Barnet & District
1970	Rita Ridley (Lincoln)	21:01	Cambridge Harriers
1971	Rita Ridley	18:43	Coventry Godiva
1972	Rita Ridley	19:15	Cambridge Harriers
1973	Joyce Smith (Byatt)	22:10	Cambridge Harriers
1974	Rita Ridley	20:03	Barnet & District
1975	Deirdre Nagel IRL (2, Chris Tranter 18:35)	18:25	Cambridge Harriers

1976	Ann Ford	17:23	London Olympiades
1977	Glynis Penny	20:16	Sale
1978	Mary Stewart	18:32	Sale
1979	Kath Binns	18:00	Aldershot Farnham & D
1980	Ruth Smeeth	21:50	Birchfield
1981	Wendy Smith (later Sly)	22:09	Sale
1982	Paula Fudge	20:20	Sale
1983	Chris Benning (Tranter)	21:35	Sale
1984	Jane Furniss	16:35	Aldershot Farnham & D
1985	Angela Tooby	18:25	Crawley
1986	Carole Bradford	15:06	Sale
1987	Jane Shields (Furniss)	21:03	Sale
1988	Helen Titterington	20:57	Birchfield
1989	Angie Pain	23:58	Parkside
1990	Andrea Whitcombe	19:03	Parkside
1991	Andrea Whitcombe	19:55	Parkside (Harrow)
1992	Lisa York	19:49	Parkside (Harrow)
1993	Gillian Stacey	19:53	Parkside (Harrow)
1994	Paula Radcliffe	20:51	Parkside (Harrow)
1995	Katy McCandless USA	19:55	
	(2, Alison Wyeth 20:13)		Parkside (Harrow)
1996	Alison Wyeth	21:59	Parkside (Harrow)
1997	Andrea Whitcombe	21:07	Leeds City
1998	Mara Myers (later Yamauchi)	28:59	Shaftesbury Barnet
1999	Angela Newport	29:33	Shaftesbury Barnet
2000	Tara Krzywicki	27:21	Shaftesbury Barnet
2001	Liz Yelling	28:08	Sale Manchester
2002	Liz Yelling	27:36	Shaftesbury Barnet
2003	Hayley Yelling	32:18	Chester-le-Street & D
2004	Birhan Dagne	32:28	Bristol
2005	Hayley Yelling	28:21	Bristol & West
2006	Lizzie Hall	32:12	Charnwood
2007	Liz Yelling	28:56	Winchester & District
2008	Liz Yelling	23:44	Winchester & District
2009	Hatti Dean	29:34	Charnwood
2010	Steph Twell	27:52	Charnwood
2011	Louise Damen	23:49	Charnwood
2012	Gemma Steel	27:06	Hallamshire

Most titles won: 6 Lillian Styles 1928–1930, 1933, 1934, 1937

ROAD RUNNING

5 KILOMETRES

(Event instituted in 2005)

2005	Vicky Gill	16:05
2006	Kate Reed	15:45

10 KILOMETRES

(Event instituted in 1992)

1992	Nicky Morris	33:39
1993	Jo Thompson	33:10
1994	Angie Hulley (Pain)	34:16
1995	Cath Mijovic	34:18
1996	Caroline Herbert	34:57
1997	Heather Heasman	34:23
1998	Heather Heasman	33:23
1999	Birhan Dagne	33:19
2000	Liz Yelling	33:10
2001	Amanda Allen	33:13
2002	Miriam Wangari KEN	33:48
	(2, Sharon Morris 33:50)	
2003	Caroline Hoyte	33:39
2004	Natalie Harvey	33:02
2005	Natalie Harvey	33:15
2006	Hayley Yelling	32:31
2007	Kate Reed	32:07
2008	Caroline Hoyte	33:27
2009	Freya Murray	32:28
2010	Faye Fullerton	33:03
2011	Claire Hallissey	32:36
2012	Getenesh Tamirat	33:26

10 MILES

(Event instituted in 1981; discontinued after 1999)

1981	Julie Barleycorn	56:32
1982	Paula Fudge	54:06
1983	Angela Tooby	55:31
1984	Véronique Marot	54:20
1985	Véronique Marot	54:21
1986	Paula Fudge	54:56
1987	Paula Fudge	55:08
1988	Sandra Branney	55:32
1989	Angie Pain	54:32
1990	Andrea Wallace	55:12
1991	Sheila Catford	55:41
1992	Julia Sakara ZIM	56:28
	(2, Karen Macleod 56:55)	
1993	Danielle Sanderson	56:53
1994	Angie Hulley (Pain)	54:41

1995	Carol Holmes	58:53
1996	Heather Heasman	59:09
1997	Marian Sutton	54:42
1998	Maria Bradley	55:59
1999	Lynn Williams	58:28

HALF MARATHON

(Event instituted in 1993)

1993	Sue Dilnot	1:13:57
1994	Linda Rushmere	1:14:31
1995	Carol Holmes	1:16:58
1996	Suzanne Rigg	1:13:04
1997	Danielle Sanderson	1:16:07
1998	Heather Heasman	1:15:59
1999	Beth Allott	1:14:38
2000	Sue Reinsford	1:14:21
2002	Jo Lodge	1:14:01
2003	Bev Jenkins	1:13:08
2004	Penny Thackray	1:19:28
2005	Jo Kelsey	1:18:19
2006	Birhan Dagne	1:15:01
2007	Liz Yelling	1:10:46
2008	Hayley Haining	1:11:28
2009	Michelle Ross-Cope	1:12:35
2010	Michelle Ross-Cope	1:12:02
2011	Julie Briscoe	1:13:29

MARATHON

(Event instituted in 1978; where different, first Briton to finish London Marathon is also listed)

1978	Margaret Lockley	2:55:08
1979	Joyce Smith	2:41:37
1980	Joyce Smith	2:41:22
1981	Leslie Watson	2:49:08
	(London: Joyce Smith 2:29:57)	
1982	Kath Binns	2:36:12
	(London: Joyce Smith 2:29:43)	
1983	Glynis Penny	2:36:21
1984	Priscilla Welch	2:30:06
1985	Sarah Rowell	2:28:06
1986	Ann Ford	2:31:40
1987	Priscilla Welch	2:26:51
1988	Ann Ford	2:30:38
1989	Véronique Marot	2:25:56
1990	Nicky McCracken	2:33:07
1991	Sally Ellis	2:34:42
1992	Andrea Wallace	2:31:33
1993	Gillian Horovitz	2:42:14
	(London: Liz McColgan 2:29:37)	

1994	Sally Ellis	2:37:06
1995	Liz McColgan	2:31:14
1996	Liz McColgan	2:27:54
1997	Marian Sutton	2:35:45
	(London: Liz McColgan 2:26:52)	
1998	Nicola Brown	2:43:18
	(London: Liz McColgan 2:26:54)	
1999	Jo Lodge	2:45:46
	(London: Nicola Scales 2:44:28)	
2000	Jo Lodge	2:40:51
	(London: Lynne MacDougall 2:38:32)	
2001	Bev Hartigan	2:37:45
	(London: Lynne MacDougall 2:37:20)	
2002	Paula Radcliffe	2:18:56
2003	Paula Radcliffe	2:15:25
2004	Birhan Dagne	2:34:45
	(London: Tracey Morris 2:33:52)	
2005	Paula Radcliffe	2:17:42
2006	Mara Yamauchi	2:25:13
2007	Mara Yamauchi	2:25:41
2008	Liz Yelling	2:28:33
2009	Mara Yamauchi	2:23:12
2010	Mara Yamauchi	2:26:16
2011	Jo Pavey	2:28:24
2012	Claire Hallissey	2:27:44

4-STAGE ROAD RELAY

(Event instituted in 1963; stage standardised at 4.314km since 2001; * 3-stage relay)

1963	Mitcham	
1965	Ilford	49:36
1966	Ilford	42:56
1967	Essex Ladies	46:38
	Barnet & District	33:04*
1968	Feltham	40:20*
1969	Barnet & District	33:50*
1970	Barnet & District	34:39*
1971	Barnet & District	32:52*
1972	Aldershot Farnham & D	31:30*
1973	Aldershot Farnham & D	35:11*
1974	Barnet & District	30:17*
1975	Barnet & District	31:04*
1976	Feltham	33:22*
1977	Feltham	32:49*
1978	Feltham	27:50*
1979	Stretford	31:11*
1980	Sale	30:48*
1981	Aldershot Farnham & D	27:56*
1982	Borough of Hounslow	29:42*

1983	Cardiff	39:01*
1984	Bracknell	39:38*
1985	Sale	42:36*
1986	Aldershot Farnham & Dt	39:57*
1987	Borough of Hounslow	42:35*
1988	Essex Ladies	41:39*
1989	Sale	39:39*
1990	Westbury	43:27*
1991	Leicester Coritanian	43:18*
1992	Parkside (Harrow)	42:56*
1993	Tipton	43:18*
1994	Parkside (Harrow)	58:37
1995	Shaftesbury Barnet	58:47
1996	Birchfield	59:31
1997	Bedford & County	58:22
1998	Sale Manchester	59:19
1999	Shaftesbury Barnet	59:07
2000	Sale Manchester	58:34
2001	Charnwood	58:44
2002	Windsor Slough Eton & Hounslow	59:40
2003	Chester-le-Street & District	59:09
2004	Bristol & West	57:46
2005	Bristol & West	59:16
2006	Birchfield	59:33
2007	Aldershot Farnham & D	57:15
2008	Aldershot Farnham & D	57:24
2009	Aldershot Farnham & D	57:09
2010	Aldershot Farnham & D	58:14
2011	Aldershot Farnham & D	57:17

6-STAGE ROAD RELAY

(Event instituted in 2000; 6 stages of 3 miles)

2000	Shaftesbury Barnet	1:40:33
2001	Charnwood	1:42:47
2002	Bristol	1:39:22
2003	Sale Manchester	1:41:00
2004	Coventry Godiva	1:42:46
2005	Bristol & West	1:43:32
2006	Chester-le-Street & District	1:44:12
2007	Charnwood	1:41:14
2008	Aldershot Farnham & D	1:41:48
2009	Charnwood	1:38:14
2010	Aldershot Farnham & D	1:40:30
2011	Aldershot Farnham & D	1:41:21
2012	Aldershot Farnham & D	1:36:30

WAAA INDOOR CHAMPIONS

WAAA/AAA title winners from 1935 to 2006 inclusive; UK champions from 2007 to 2012

(Where the title was won by an overseas athlete, the highest placed UK athlete is shown in brackets)

Venues: 1935–1939 & 1962–1964 London (Wembley); 1965–1991 Cosford; 1992–2001 & 2003 Birmingham; 2002 Cardiff; 2004–2012 Sheffield. No Championships were held in 1968

60 METRES

(Event instituted in 1935; held at 60 yards from 1962 to 1966 = y)

1935	Kathleen Stokes	8.2
1936	Eileen Hiscock	8.1
1937	Barbara Burke SAF	8.1
	(2, Doris Watson)	
1938	Betty Lock	8.0
1939	Betty Lock	7.9
1962	Daphne Arden	7.1y
1963	Daphne Arden	7.1y
1964	Daphne Arden	7.1y
1965	Liz Gill	6.9y
1966	Daphne Slater (Arden)	7.1y
1967	Della James (later Pascoe)	7.5
1969	Madeleine Cobb	7.5
1970	Janet Stroud	7.4
1971	Sonia Lannaman	7.5
1972	Madeleine Cobb	7.4
1973	Andrea Lynch	7.4
1974	Sonia Lannaman	7.5
1975	Andrea Lynch	7.30
1976	Andrea Lynch	7.3
1977	Wendy Clarke	7.4
1978	Heather Hunte	7.39
1979	Eleanor Thomas	7.34
1980	Wendy Clarke	7.34
1981	Wendy Hoyte (Clarke)	7.30
1982	Wendy Hoyte	7.30
1983	Bev Kinch	7.29
1984	Bev Kinch	7.26
1985	Heather Oakes (Hunte)	7.24
1986	Bev Kinch	7.20
1987	Bev Kinch	7.27
1988	Paula Dunn	7.29
1989	Paula Dunn	7.28
1990	Bev Kinch	7.26
1991	Stephanie Douglas	7.25
1992	Stephanie Douglas	7.31
1993	Sanna Hernesniemi FIN	7.33

	(2, Marcia Richardson 7.36)	
1994	Bev Kinch	7.35
1995	Stephanie Douglas	7.28
1996	Marcia Richardson	7.34
1997	Endurance Ojokolo NGR	7.27
	(2, Sophia Smith 7.44)	
1998	Joice Maduaka	7.34
1999	Christine Bloomfield	7.40
2000	Marcia Richardson	7.25
2001	Marcia Richardson	7.28
2002	Joice Maduaka	7.33
2003	Joice Maduaka	7.32
2004	Joice Maduaka	7.33
2005	Jeanette Kwakye	7.27
2006	Emily Maher IRL	7.40
	(2, Christine Ohuruogu 7.43)	
2007	Laura Turner	7.25
2008	Laura Turner	7.32
2009	Joice Maduaka	7.36
2010	Joice Maduaka	7.29
2011	Jodie Williams	7.24
2012	Jeanette Kwakye	7.20

Most titles won: 6 Bev Kinch 1983, 1984, 1986, 1987, 1990, 1994 & Joice Maduaka 1998, 2002–2004, 2009, 2010

200 METRES

(Event instituted in 1966 at 220 yards = y; held over 200m from 1969 but not contested between 1970 and 1978)

1966	Maureen Tranter	24.8y
1967	Jenny Pawsey	25.2y
1969	Della James	25.5
1979	Christine Warden	25.0
1980	Linsey Macdonald	24.3
1981	Carmen Smart	24.5
1982	Ruth Patten	24.07
1983	Joan Baptiste	24.24
1984	Simmone Jacobs	23.87
1985	Carmen Smart	24.44
1986	Jenny Stoute	24.67
1987	Sally Gunnell	24.37
1988	Rachel Kirby	24.89
1989	Grace Jackson JAM	23.37
	(2, Jenny Stoute 24.21)	
1990	Merlene Ottey JAM	23.07
	(2, Clova Court 24.46)	
1991	Angela Williams TRI	24.08
	(2, Simmone Jacobs 24.29)	
1992	Rochelle Stevens USA	23.59
	(2, Geraldine McLeod 24.34)	

1993	Sanna Hernesniemi FIN	23.54
	(2, Marcia Richardson 24.16)	
1994	Maria Staafgard SWE	23.78
	(2, Marcia Richardson 23.94)	
1995	Jacqui Agyepong	24.22
1996	Catherine Murphy	23.69
1997	Katharine Merry	23.50
1998	Donna Fraser	23.15
1999	Shani Anderson	23.90
2000	Christine Bloomfield	23.31
2001	Catherine Murphy	23.35
2002	Amy Spencer	23.74
2003	Ciara Sheehy IRL	23.17
	(2, Amy Spencer 23.20)	
2004	Ciara Sheehy IRL	23.41
	(2, Joice Maduaka 23.72)	
2005	Susan Deacon	23.67
2006	Ciara Sheehy IRL	23.20
	(2, Christine Ohuruogu 23.56)	
2007	Kadi-Ann Thomas	23.68
2008	Joice Maduaka	23.43
2009	Donna Fraser	23.48
2010	Joice Maduaka	23.48
2011	Joice Maduaka	23.63
2012	Margaret Adeoye	23.36

Most titles won: 3 Ciara Sheehy IRL 2003, 2004, 2006 & Joice Maduaka 2008, 2010, 2011

400 METRES

(Event instituted in 1966 at 440 yards = y; held over 400m from 1969)

1966	Gloria Dourass	58.0y
1967	Rosemary Stirling	56.3y
1969	Rosemary Stirling	56.0
1970	Marilyn Neufville	54.9
1971	Jannette Roscoe	56.1
1972	Verona Bernard	55.9
1973	Verona Bernard	54.6
1974	Sharon Colyear	57.2
1975	Verona Elder (Bernard)	53.5
1976	Verona Elder	54.1
1977	Verona Elder	54.3
1978	Liz Eddy	54.8
1979	Verona Elder	54.3
1980	Liz Barnes	55.3
1981	Verona Elder	53.2
1982	Verona Elder	52.77
1983	Janine MacGregor	54.83
1984	Ruth Patten	53.47
1985	Linsey Macdonald	54.74

1986	Angela Piggford	54.50
1987	Dawn Gandy	55.67
1988	Sally Gunnell	53.28
1989	Merlene Ottey JAM	52.21
	(2, Sally Gunnell 52.58)	
1990	Suzanne Guise	55.24
1991	Sandra Douglas	55.20
1992	Jillian Richardson CAN	52.72
	(3, Jenny Stoute 54.12)	
1993	Louise Fraser	54.14
1994	Tracy Goddard	54.05
1995	Melanie Neef	52.82
1996	Melanie Neef	52.50
1997	Phylis Smith	52.85
1998	Vicki Jamison	53.04
1999	Sinead Dudgeon	53.51
2000	Michelle Thomas	55.26
2001	Catherine Murphy	52.31
2002	Catherine Murphy	52.54
2003	Jenny Meadows	53.31
2004	Catherine Murphy	52.54
2005	Kim Wall	53.45
2006	Nicola Sanders	50.72
2007	Nicola Sanders	50.60
2008	Meghan Beesley	54.88
2009	Donna Fraser	52.83
2010	Kim Wall	53.07
2011	Kelly Sotherton	53.46
2012	Shana Cox	52.38

Most titles won: 8 Verona Elder (Bernard) 1972, 1973, 1975–1977, 1979, 1981, 1982

800 METRES

(Race held over 712.5 yards, 5 laps of Wembley track, in 1938 & 1939; 600 yards from 1962 to 1964; 880 yards = y from 1965 to 1967; 800m from 1969)

1938	Evelyne Forster	1:56.4
1939	Evelyne Forster	1:55.0
1962	Phyllis Perkins	1:28.6
1963	Brenda Cook	1:28.4
1964	Pam Piercy	1:27.3
1965	Mary Campbell	2:22.1y
1966	Mary Campbell	2:16.6y
1967	Sheila Taylor	2:14.8y
1969	Sheila Carey (Taylor)	2:10.8
1970	Rosemary Stirling	2:06.5
1971	Rosemary Stirling	2:08.0
1972	Margaret Beacham	2:09.4
1973	Norine Braithwaite	2:10.4
1974	Rosemary Wright (Stirling)	2:07.2

1975	Marion Barrett	2:11.5
1976	Mary Stewart	2:08.2
1977	Sue Smith	2:08.4
1978	Verona Elder	2:08.4
1979	Gillian Dainty	2:08.9
1980	Cherry Hanson	2:05.8
1981	Kirsty McDermott	2:07.1
1982	Julie Asgill	2:09.8
1983	Teena Colebrook	2:08.40
1984	Karin Steer	2:11.06
1985	Kirsty McDermott	2:02.70
1986	Kirsty McDermott	2:03.09
1987	Janet Prictoe	2:04.18
1988	Dawn Gandy	2:05.62
1989	Mary Kitson	2:05.45
1990	Dawn Gandy	2:07.65
1991	Paula Fryer	2:08.96
1992	Dawn Gandy	2:07.80
1993	Linda Keough	2:05.22
1994	Kirsty Wade (McDermott)	2:05.60
1995	Abigail Hunte	2:08.06
1996	Vicky Sterne	2:06.41
1997	Hayley Parry (later Tullett)	2:04.14
1998	Hayley Parry	2:02.91
1999	Paula Fryer	2:08.99
2000	Emma Davies	2:07.34
2001	Kelly Holmes	2:05.26
2002	Jenny Meadows	2:05.07
2003	Jo Fenn	1:59.74
2004	Kelly Holmes	2:01.40
2005	Jenny Meadows	2:04.43
2006	Jenny Meadows	2:02.41
2007	Marilyn Okoro	2:04.39
2008	Jenny Meadows	2:01.97
2009	Jenny Meadows	2:01.67
2010	Jenny Meadows	2:00.91
2011	Marilyn Okoro	2:04.36
2012	Marilyn Okoro	2:04.01

Most titles won: 6 Jenny Meadows 2002, 2005, 2006, 2008–2010

1500 METRES

(Insituted at mile in 1966 = y; changed to 1500m in 1969)

1966	Joyce Smith	5:03.6y
1967	Dian Elliott	5:02.1y
1969	Carol Gould	4:42.4
1970	Gillian Tivey	4:32.8
1971	Margaret Beacham	4:20.5
1972	Jean Lochhead	4:26.9
1973	Jean Lochhead	4:30.6

1974	Norine Braithwaite	4:37.4
1975	Mary Stewart	4:21.0
1976	Lynne Harvey	4:29.8
1977	Mary Stewart	4:15.9
1978	Jo White	4:16.2
1979	Mary Stewart	4:18.7
1980	Sandra Arthurton	4:21.2
1981	Alison Wright	4:16.7
1982	Janet Marlow	4:20.8
1983	Jane Finch (Colebrook)	4:15.73
1984	Lynne MacDougall	4:16.89
1985	Zola Budd	4:11.20
1986	Zola Budd	4:06.87
1987	Kirsty Wade	4:09.26
1988	Bev Nicholson	4:25.74
1989	Karen Hutcheson	4:14.98
1990	Debbie Gunning	4:27.55
1991	Jo Dering	4:13.31
1992	Chris Cahill (Boxer)	4:12.34
1993	Carol-Ann Gray	4:30.09
1994	Lynn Gibson	4:17.01
1995	Lynn Gibson	4:18.41
1996	Angela Davies	4:16.24
1997	Ann Griffiths	4:18.86
1998	Shirley Griffiths	4:23.56
1999	Rachel Jordan	4:25.88
2000	Shirley Griffiths	4:25.69
2001	Freda Davoren IRL	4:19.85
	(2, Zoe Jelbert 4:23.16)	
2002	Natalie Lewis	4:25.49
2003	Hayley Ovens	4:16.53
2004	Jo Fenn	4:12.67
2005	Hayley Ovens	4:19.11
2006	Hayley Ovens	4:15.50
2007	Katrina Wootton	4:17.90
2008	Jemma Simpson	4:13.99
2009	Susan Scott	4:12.85
2010	Helen Clitheroe	4:13.90
2011	Stacey Smith	4:22.96
2012	Claire Gibson	4:17.38

Most titles won: 3 Mary Stewart 1975, 1977, 1979 & Hayley Ovens 2003, 2005, 2006,

3000 METRES

(Event instituted in 1973)

1973	Liz Connors	9:36.0
1975	Christine Haskett	9:40.2
1976	Mary Stewart	9:07.6
1977	Mary Stewart	9:09.4

1978	Helen Fielon	9:47.0
1979	Sara Harris	9:57.6
1980	Thelwyn Bateman	9:37.4
1981	Thelwyn Bateman	9:44.7
1982	Julie Rose	9:34.6
1983	Sharon Harvey	9:27.8
1984	Yvonne Murray	9:22.0
	(Carol Haigh 9:12.1 ineligible for title)	
1985	Sue Crehan	9:27.63
1986	Roisin Smyth IRL	9:22.05
	(2, Jill Clarke 9:22.70)	
1987	Karen Macleod	9:30.98
1988	Wendy Sly	8:55.49
1989	Nicky Morris	9:05.73
1990	Debbie Peel	9:45.00
1991	Sonia McGeorge	9:05.99
1992	Karen Hutcheson	9:11.99
1993	Una English	9:15.68
1994	Erika König AUT	9:25.58
	(2, Julie Briggs 9:30.15)	
1995	Angela Davies	9:25.65
1996	Sonia McGeorge	9:04.69
1997	Angela Davies	9:26.04
1998	Sarah Singleton	9:35.04
1999	Zara Hyde Peters	9:30.76
2000	Zara Hyde Peters	9:16.89
2001	Maria Lynch IRL	9:35.92
	(2, Emma Ford 9:42.42)	
2003	Kerry Gillibrand	9:39.56
2004	Jo Pavey	8:43.23
2005	Jo Pavey	8:50.28
2006	Lisa Dobriskey	9:10.44
2007	Lisa Dobriskey	8:55.22
2008	Helen Clitheroe	8:56.13
2009	Deidre Byrne IRL	9:04.78
	(2, Katrina Wootton 9:05.27)	
2010	Hazel Murphy IRL	9:02.06
	(2, Gemma Turtle 9:02.81)	
2011	Helen Clitheroe	8:55.26
2012	Hannah England	9:06.04

Most titles won: 2 Mary Stewart 1976, 1977, Thelwyn Bateman 1980, 1981, Sonia McGeorge 1991, 1996, Angela Davies 1995, 1997, Zara Hyde Peters 1999, 2000, Jo Pavey 2004, 2005, Lisa Dobriskey 2006, 2007 & Helen Clitheroe 2008, 2011

60 METRES HURDLES

(Event instituted in 1935 at 60 yards = y with 2'6" hurdles; changed to 60m with 2'6" hurdles in 1967 and with 2'9" hurdles from 1969)

1935	Violet Webb	9.5y
1936	Eveline Ball	8.9y

WAAA Champions

1937	Barbara Burke SAF	8.6y
	(2, Kate Robertson)	
1962	Dorothy Window	8.2y
1963	Pat Nutting	8.1y
1964	Maxine Botley	7.9y
1965	Maxine Botley	7.9y
1966	Mary Rand	7.8y
1967	Pat Whitehead	8.9
1969	Chris Perera	8.8
1970	Mary Peters	8.5
1971	Ann Wilson	8.9
1972	Ann Wilson	8.6
1973	Judy Vernon	8.6
1974	Judy Vernon	8.3
1975	Lorna Boothe	8.54
1976	Liz Sutherland	8.3
1977	Lorna Boothe	8.5
1978	Lorna Boothe	8.36
1979	Lorna Boothe	8.46
1980	Yvette Wray	8.33
1981	Yvette Wray	8.33
1982	Yvette Wray	8.33
1983	Lorna Boothe	8.30
1984	Kerry Robin-Millerchip	8.38
1985	Judy Simpson	8.25
1986	Lesley-Ann Skeete	8.22
1987	Lesley-Ann Skeete	8.21
1988	Kerry Robin-Millerchip	8.29
1989	Lesley-Ann Skeete	8.15
1990	Jacqui Agyepong	8.16
1991	Lesley-Ann Skeete	8.19
1992	Jackie Humphrey USA	8.23
	(2, Kay Morley-Brown 8.25)	
1993	Clova Court	8.20
1994	Sam Farquharson	8.19
1995	Clova Court	8.22
1996	Jacqui Agyepong	8.17
1997	Denise Lewis	8.41
1998	Diane Allahgreen	8.21
1999	Keri Maddox	8.36
2000	Diane Allahgreen	8.24
2001	Melani Wilkins	8.20
2002	Diane Allahgreen	8.01
2003	Sarah Claxton	8.12
2004	Sarah Claxton	8.11
2005	Sarah Claxton	7.96
2006	Derval O'Rourke IRL	7.98
	(2, Sarah Claxton 8.01)	
2007	Sara McGreavy	8.03

2008	Sarah Claxton	8.09
2009	Gemma Bennett	8.06
2010	Derval O'Rourke IRL	8.11
	(2, Gemma Bennett 8.20)	
2011	Gemma Bennett	8.22
2012	Jessica Ennis	7.95

Most titles won: 5 Lorna Boothe 1975, 1977–1979, 1983

HIGH JUMP

(Event instituted in 1935)

1935	Mary Milne	1.50
1936	Mary Dumbrill (Milne) & Dorothy Odam	1.57
1937	Dorothy Odam	1.59
1938	Dorothy Odam	1.55
1939	Dorothy Odam	1.55
1962	Frances Slaap	1.70
1963	Linda Knowles	1.62
1964	Frances Slaap	1.67
1965	Dorothy Shirley	1.62
1966	Mary Rand	1.65
1967	Linda Knowles	1.69
1969	Barbara Inkpen	1.73
1970	Barbara Inkpen	1.69
1971	Ann Wilson	1.70
1972	Ros Few	1.71
1973	Barbara Inkpen	1.86
1974	Ann Wilson	1.75
1975	Ros Few	1.80
1976	Denise Cooper	1.74
1977	Ros Few	1.78
1978	Gillian Hitchen	1.80
1979	Louise Miller	1.75
1980	Louise Miller	1.82
1981	Louise Miller	1.80
1982	Ann-Marie Cording	1.91
1983	Barbara Simmonds	1.83
1984	Diana Elliott	1.84
1985	Olga Turchak URS	1.88
	(2, Diana Davies (Elliott) 1.85)	
1986	Diana Davies	1.85
1987	Janet Boyle	1.90
1988	Debbie McDowell	1.88
1989	Sharon Hutchings (McPeake)	1.82
1990	Julia Bennett	1.92
1991	Debbie Marti	1.94
1992	Debbie Marti	1.91
1993	Jo Jennings	1.89
1994	Hanne Haugland NOR	1.94
	(2, Julia Bennett 1.85)	

1995	Lea Haggett	1.86
1996	Michelle Dunkley	1.85
1997	Debbie Marti	1.91
1998	Susan Jones	1.89
1999	Michelle Dunkley	1.86
2000	Wanita May CAN	1.84

(2=, Jo Jennings, Susan Jones & Aileen Wilson 1.79)

2001	Susan Jones	1.85
2002	Susan Jones	1.90
2003	Susan Jones	1.93
2004	Susan Jones	1.87
2005	Susan Jones	1.90
2006	Susan Moncrieff (Jones)	1.84
2007	Jessica Ennis	1.87
2008	Jessica Ennis	1.92
2009	Stephanie Pywell	1.82
2010	Vikki Hubbard	1.87
2011	Jessica Ennis	1.88
2012	Jessica Ennis	1.91

Most titles won: 7 Susan Moncrieff (Jones) 1998, 2001–2006

POLE VAULT

(Event instituted in 1994)

1994	Kate Staples	3.46
1995	Kate Staples	3.80
1996	Kate Staples	3.70
1997	Janine Whitlock	3.70
1998	Janine Whitlock	4.11
1999	Janine Whitlock	4.13
2000	Janine Whitlock	4.20
2001	Janine Whitlock	4.05
2002	Janine Whitlock	4.20
2003	Tracey Bloomfield	4.00
2004	Tracey Grant (Bloomfield)	4.15
2005	Janine Whitlock	4.25
2006	Kate Dennison	4.10
2007	Kate Dennison	4.35
2008	Kate Dennison	4.25
2009	Kate Dennison	4.45
2010	Kate Dennison	4.40
2011	Holly Bleasdale	4.36
2012	Holly Bleasdale	4.70

Most titles won: 7 Janine Whitlock 1997–2002, 2005

LONG JUMP

(Event instituted in 1935)

| 1935 | Ethel Raby | 5.03 |
| 1936 | Ethel Raby | 5.15 |

1937	Ethel Raby	5.14
1938	Ethel Raby	5.35
1939	Ethel Raby	5.48
1962	Sheila Parkin (later Sherwood)	5.81
1963	Sheila Parkin	5.78
1964	Alix Jamieson	6.07
1965	Sheila Parkin	5.86
1966	Mary Rand	6.14
1967	Barbara Inkpen	5.74
1969	Sue Scott	5.87
1970	Ann Wilson	5.99
1971	Ruth Martin-Jones	6.02
1972	Maureen Chitty	6.36
1973	Barbara-Anne Barrett	6.02
1974	Maureen Chitty	5.79
1975	Julie Jay	5.78
1976	Sue Reeve (Scott)	6.28
1977	Sue Reeve	6.09
1978	Sue Reeve	6.20
1979	Sharon Colyear	6.05
1980	Allison Manley	6.13
1981	Sue Longden	5.85
1982	Bev Kinch	6.11
1983	Carol Earlington	6.38
1984	Sue Hearnshaw	6.50
1985	Liao Wenfen CHN	6.26
	(2, Kim Hagger 6.13)	
1986	Mary Berkeley	6.21
1987	Mary Berkeley	6.38
1988	Kim Hagger	6.17
1989	Nicole Boegman AUS	6.51
	(2, Mary Berkeley 6.32)	
1990	Kim Hagger	6.28
1991	Kim Hagger	6.39
1992	Jo Wise	6.27
1993	Renata Nielsen DEN	6.28
	(3, Jacqui White 5.86)	
1994	Denise Lewis	6.07
1995	Denise Lewis	6.28
1996	Ann Brooks	6.01
1997	Jo Wise	6.41
1998	Denise Lewis	6.29
1999	Jo Wise	6.32
2000	Jade Johnson	6.46
2001	Ann Danson	5.97
2002	Kelly Sotherton	6.22
2003	Ruth Irving	6.24
2004	Fiona May ITA	6.68
	(2, Sarah Claxton 6.31)	

2005	Jade Johnson	6.50
2006	Kelly Sotherton	6.53
2007	Amy Harris	6.47
2008	Kelly Sotherton	6.41
2009	Kelly Proper IRL	6.44
	(2, Amy Woodman 6.40)	
2010	Kelly Proper IRL	6.48
	(2, Amy Woodman 6.20)	
2011	Kelly Proper IRL	6.35
	(2, Dominique Blaize 6.25)	
2012	Shara Proctor	6.68

Most titles won: 5 Ethel Raby 1935–1939

TRIPLE JUMP

(Event instituted in 1991)

1991	Michelle Griffith	13.07
1992	Michelle Griffith	13.16
1993	Rachel Kirby	13.52
1994	Rachel Kirby	13.21
1995	Ashia Hansen	13.61
1996	Michelle Griffith	13.18
1997	Michelle Griffith	13.20
1998	Ashia Hansen	14.19
1999	Ashia Hansen	14.23
2000	Debbie Rowe	12.47
2001	Michelle Griffith	13.25
2002	Ashia Hansen	13.53
2003	Sandra Swennen BEL	13.51
	(2, Rebecca White 12.94)	
2004	Trecia Smith JAM	14.13
	(5, Stephanie Aneto 12.17)	
2005	Taneisha Scanlon IRL	13.28
	(2, Emily Parker 13.02)	
2006	Tiombé Hurd USA	13.67
	(2, Rebecca White 13.18)	
2007	Ashia Hansen	13.68
2008	Nadia Williams	13.39
2009	Nony Mordi	13.23
2010	Trecia Smith JAM	13.69
	(2, Nadia Williams 13.41)	
2011	Laura Samuel	13.24
2012	Yamilé Aldama	14.09

Most titles won: 5 Michelle Griffith 1991, 1992, 1996, 1997, 2001 & Ashia Hansen 1995, 1998, 1999, 2002, 2007

SHOT

(Event instituted in 1935)

| 1935 | Kitty Tilley | 9.35 |
| 1936 | Kitty Tilley | 9.40 |

1937	Kitty Tilley	10.48
1938	Bevis Reid	11.09
1939	Bevis Reid	11.24
1962	Suzanne Allday	13.76
1963	Suzanne Allday	14.13
1964	Mary Peters	14.97
1965	Mary Peters	14.10
1966	Mary Peters	15.30
1967	Brenda Bedford	13.90
1969	Brenda Bedford	14.49
1970	Mary Peters	15.86
1971	Brenda Bedford	14.14
1972	Mary Peters	16.26
1973	Brenda Bedford	14.59
1974	Janis Kerr	15.80
1975	Brenda Bedford	15.08
1976	Janis Kerr	15.80
1977	Judy Oakes	15.87
1978	Judy Oakes	16.41
1979	Judy Oakes	16.44
1980	Judy Oakes	16.45
1981	Angela Littlewood	16.90
1982	Judy Oakes	16.50
1983	Venissa Head	17.67
1984	Judy Oakes	17.67
1985	Jusy Oakes	17.85
1986	Judy Oakes	18.11
1987	Judy Oakes	18.05
1988	Judy Oakes	18.19
1989	Myrtle Augee	17.40
1990	Judy Oakes	18.55
1991	Judy Oakes	17.83
1992	Yvonne Hanson-Nortey	16.33
1993	Maggie Lynes	15.65
1994	Maggie Lynes	15.82
1995	Judy Oakes	17.81
1996	Judy Oakes	18.57
1997	Judy Oakes	17.71
1998	Judy Oakes	18.23
1999	Judy Oakes	17.36
2000	Judy Oakes	18.30
2001	Lieja Koeman NED (2, Julie Dunkley 15.47)	17.26
2002	Helena Engman SWE (2, Jo Duncan 16.01)	16.27
2003	Eva Massey	16.29
2004	Helena Engman SWE (2, Denise Lewis 14.59)	15.42
2005	Jo Duncan	15.27

2006	Julie Dunkley	15.89
2007	Jo Duncan	16.45
2008	Eden Francis	16.11
2009	Alison Rodger	15.79
2010	Alison Rodger	16.02
2011	Eden Francis	15.85
2012	Eden Francis	16.72

Most titles won: 18 Judy Oakes 1977–1980, 1982, 1984–1988, 1990, 1991, 1995–2000

PENTATHLON

(Event instituted in 1987)

1987	Jackie Kinsella	3909
1988	Kim Price	3634
1989	Wendy Laing	3787
1990	Kim Price	3673
1991	Brid Hallissey IRL	3869
	(2, Emma Beales 3778)	
1992	Brid Hallissey IRL	3847
	(2, Emma Beales 3800)	
1993	Emma Beales	4012
1994	Emma Beales	3808
1995	Vikki Schofield	4238
1996	Sarah Damm	4058
1997	Pauline Richards	3988
1998	Julia Bennett	4297
1999	Diana Bennett	4110
2000	Julia Bennett	4216
2001	Kelly Sotherton	4116
2002	Kelly Sotherton	4166
2003	Kelly Sotherton	4226
2004	Kate Brewington	4070
2005	Jessica Ennis	4089
2006	Katia Lannon	3868
2007	Katia Lannon	3944
2008	Kate Cowley	3974
2009	Catherine Holdworth	3838
2010	Grace Clements	3915
2011	Lydia Chamberlin	3694
2012	Gemma Weetman	3997

Most titles won: 3 Kelly Sotherton 2001–2003

570 YARDS RELAY

(Event contested only between 1937 & 1939)

1937	Atalanta	1:13.2
1938	Atalanta	1:14.5
1939	Mitcham	1:12.3

WALK

(1.5 miles 1966 & 1967; 3000m 1997–2002; discontinued after 2002)

1966	Judy Farr	12:29.2
1967	Diane Cotterill	12:33.8
1997	Sylvia Black	14:09.58
1999	Sharon Tonks	14:29.44
2000	Gillian O'Sullivan IRL	12:33.11
	(2, Sharon Tonks 14:17.50)	
2001	Gillian O'Sullivan IRL	12:23.45
	(2, Sharon Tonks 14:02.55)	
2002	Gillian O'Sullivan IRL	12:17.56
	(2, Niobe Menéndez 13:08.64)	

UNDER-23

(Instituted in 1999)

100 METRES

1999	Susie Williams	11.61w
2000	Amanda Forrester	11.71
2001	Abi Oyepitan	11.17w
2002	Susan Burnside	11.61w
2003	Jeanette Kwakye	11.69
2004	Jeanette Kwakye	11.7
2005	Jeanette Kwakye	11.58
2006	Montell Douglas	11.57
2007	Kadi-Ann Thomas	11.52w
2008	Louise Dickson	12.12
2009	Elaine O'Neill	11.59
2010	Torema Thompson	11.86
2011	Ashleigh Nelson	11.45w
2012	Ashleigh Nelson	11.46

200 METRES

1999	Susie Williams	23.95
2000	Melanie Purkiss	24.00
2001	Helen Roscoe	23.4w
2002	Emily Freeman	23.51w
2003	Danielle Norville	24.52
2004	Laura Turner	24.59
2005	Jeanette Kwakye	24.07
2006	Kadi-Ann Thomas	23.80
2007	Katherine Jones	24.44
2008	Stacey Downie	24.90w
2009	Joey Duck	23.65
2010	Annabelle Lewis	24.44
2011	Niamh Whelan IRL	24.47
	(2, Joey Duck 24.82)	
2012	Emily Diamond	23.60

400 METRES

1999	Louretta Thorne	54.37
2000	Karen Gear	54.03
2001	Helen Thieme	53.27
2002	Jenny Meadows	54.13
2003	Helen Karagounis (Thieme)	52.47
2004	Marilyn Okoro	54.67
2005	Christine Ohuruogu	52.43
2006	Marilyn Okoro	52.57
2007	Kelly Massey	53.82
2008	Henrietta Kodilinye-Sims	54.41
2009	Henrietta Kodilinye-Sims	53.88
2010	Laura Maddox	53.89
2011	Emma Pullen	53.69
2012	Laura Wake	55.15

800 METRES

1999	Emma Davies	2:09.65
2000	Emma Davies	2:07.38
2001	Alex Carter	2:07.10
2002	Joanna Ross	2:10.88
2003	Catherine Riley	2:06.09
2004	Hannah Whitmore	2:08.42
2005	Marilyn Okoro	2:03.65
2006	Victoria Griffiths	2:04.19
2007	Charlotte Best	2:05.02
2008	Emma Jackson	2:04.64
2009	Tara Bird	2:03.00
2010	Lucy Yates	2:07.82
2011	Lynsey Sharp	2:06.06
2012	Rebecca Linney	2:11.52

1500 METRES

1999	Susan Scott	4:25.87
2000	Ellen O'Hare	4:24.40
2001	Alex Carter	4:23.0
2002	Natalie Lewis	4:25.82
2003	Lisa Dobriskey	4:16.96
2004	Natalie Lewis	4:24.23
2005	Katrina Wootton	4:21.66
2006	Faye Fullerton	4:21.30
2007	Hannah England	4:19.28
2008	Stacey Johnson	4:31.30
2009	Emma Pallant	4:27.13
2010	Stacey Smith	4:29.26
2011	Stacey Smith	4:24.22
2012	Gemma Kersey	4:35.56

3000/5000 METRES

1999	Emma Ford (3000)	9:33.06
2000	Gillian Palmer (3000)	9:35.03
2001	Gillian Palmer (3000)	9:39.4
2002	Gillian Palmer	16:13.87
2003	Susannah Evans (3000)	9:53.07
2004	Jade Wright	16:33.82
2005	Alexa Joel	16:31.94
2006	Victoria Webster	17:10.38
2007	Susie Hignett	16:26.43
2008	Lucy O'Gorman	17:04.21
2009	Emily Pidgeon	16:31.80
2010	Naomi Taschimowitz	16:41.28
2011	Stevie Stockton	16:10.63
2012	Katie Good	17:03.62

3000 METRES STEEPLECHASE

2003	Barbara Parker (2000)	6:50.33
2004	Barbara Parker	10:48.79
2005	Lizzie Hall	10:35.18
2006	Carolyn Boosey	10:48.41
2007	Jessica Sparke	10:29.17
2008	Lucy Mayho	11:05.02
2009	Alice Mason NZL	10:13.10
	(2, Caryl Jones 10:33.74)	
2010	Laura Parker	10:21.33
2011	not held	
2012	Emily Stewart	10:02.63

100 METRES HURDLES

1999	Julie Pratt	13.62
2000	Julie Pratt	13.50
2001	Julie Pratt	13.5w
2002	Tamsin Stephens	13.67
2003	Kate Brewington	14.02
2004	Sara McGreavy	13.51w
2005	Gemma Bennett	13.62
2006	Katey Read	14.53w
2007	Jessica Ennis	13.04
2008	Gemma Werrett	13.32w
2009	Zara Hohn	13.37
2010	Ashley Helsby	13.39w
2011	Serita Solomon	13.53
2012	Serita Solomon	13.28

400 METRES HURDLES

1999	Tracey Duncan	60.48
2000	Tracey Duncan	58.84
2001	Hannah Wood	60.5

2002	Michelle Carey IRL	58.7
	(2, Hannah Wood 58.8)	
2003	Michelle Carey IRL	58.76
	(2, Hannah Wood 59.73)	
2004	Nicola Sanders	59.08
2005	Sian Scott	57.45
2006	Sian Scott	58.79
2007	Eilidh Child	57.81
2008	Eilidh Child	59.18
2009	Perri Shakes-Drayton	55.34
2010	Ese Okoro	59.41
2011	Caryl Granville	58.43
2012	Megan Southwart	59.06

HIGH JUMP

1999	Susan Jones	1.82
2000	Michelle Dunkley	1.89
2001	Gayle O'Connor	1.75
2002	Natalie Clark	1.69
2003	Natalie Clark	1.83
2004	Aileen Wilson	1.76
2005	Aileen Wilson	1.76
2006	Emma Morris	1.74
2007	Sharon Heveran IRL	1.78
	(2, Rachael MacKenzie 1.70)	
2008	Jayne Nisbet	1.82
2009	Adele Lassu	1.82
2010	Adele Lassu	1.78
2011	Liz Lamb NZL	1.82
	(2, Bethan Partridge 1.78)	
2012	Emma Nuttall	1.86

POLE VAULT

1999	Jenni Dryburgh NZL	4.00
	(2,Rhian Clarke 3.70)	
2000	Tracey Bloomfield	3.80
2001	Gael Davies	3.70
2002	Ellie Spain	3.85
2003	Zoe Brown	3.90
2004	Kate Dennison	3.80
2005	Zoe Brown	4.05
2006	Jennifer Graham	3.75
2007	Louise Butterworth	4.10
2008	Emma Lyons	3.90
2009	Emma Lyons	4.11
2010	Sophie Upton	3.95
2011	Holly Bleasdale	4.53
2012	Abigail Haywood	3.75

LONG JUMP

1999	Sarah Claxton	5.99
2000	Jade Johnson	6.48
2001	Sarah Wellstead	6.02w
2002	Natasha May	6.17w
2003	Kate Brewington	6.10w
2004	Henrietta Paxton	6.37w
2005	Henrietta Paxton	6.02
2006	Louise Bloor	6.25
2007	Amy Harris	6.32
2008	Amy Harris	6.16w
2009	Amy Harris	5.93
2010	Abigail Irozuru	6.01
2011	Lorraine Ugen	6.39
2012	Lorraine Ugen	6.15

TRIPLE JUMP

1999	Jodie Hurst	12.59
2000	Leandra Polius	12.52
2001	Rebecca White	13.09w
2002	Rebecca White	12.90
2003	Zainab Ceesay	12.38
2004	Zainab Ceesay	12.28
2005	Karlene Turner	12.98
2006	Denae Matthew	12.82
2007	Nony Mordi	13.01
2008	Sineade Gutzmore	13.02w
2009	Claire Linskill	12.78
2010	Claire Linskill	12.63
2011	Hannah Frankson	13.44
2012	Laura Samuel	13.75

SHOT

1999	Julie Dunkley	16.11
2000	Julie Dunkley	15.96
2001	Julie Dunkley	16.31
2002	Eva Massey	15.49
2003	Rebecca Peake	14.59
2004	Rebecca Peake	14.53
2005	Rebecca Peake	15.21
2006	Alison Rodger	15.03
2007	Sally Hinds	14.48
2008	Eden Francis	15.51
2009	Eden Francis	15.74
2010	Eden Francis	15.83
2011	Rachel Wallader	16.08
2012	Shaunagh Brown	16.31

DISCUS

1999	Philippa Roles	55.08
2000	Philippa Roles	51.79
2001	Rebecca Roles	49.06
2002	Emma Carpenter	53.56
2003	Claire Smithson	50.76
2004	Claire Griss	50.80
2005	Claire Smithson	55.58
2006	Kirsty Law	46.03
2007	Kirsty Law	50.37
2008	Dani Samuels AUS	58.26
	(2, Eden Francis 52.74)	
2009	Eden Francis	54.90
2010	Eden Francis	58.99
2011	Shaunagh Brown	49.11
2012	Shadine Duquemin	50.63

HAMMER

1999	Rachael Beverley	60.27
2000	Suzanne Roberts	54.03
2001	Zoe Derham	57.05
2002	Zoe Derham	60.57
2003	Carys Parry	58.03
2004	Laura Douglas	60.13
2005	Laura Douglas	61.39
2006	Susan McKelvie	58.62
2007	Susan McKelvie	59.94
2008	Rachel Gair	55.20
2009	Sara Holt	63.60
2010	Hayley Murray	50.53
2011	Sophie Hitchon	67.07
2012	Myra Perkins	56.06

JAVELIN

1999	Joanna Bruce	45.58
2000	Chloe Cozens	49.24
2001	Jenny Kemp	48.97
2002	Goldie Sayers	58.20
2003	Goldie Sayers	55.09
2004	Goldie Sayers	57.09
2005	Jo Chapman	47.73
2006	Lauren Therin	50.97
2007	Lianne Clarke	50.96
2008	Louise Watton	48.14
2009	Rosie Semenytsh	46.90
2010	Sam Cullinane	45.55
2011	Tesni Ward	47.40
2012	Izzy Jeffs	53.58

TRACK WALK

(5000m 1999–2009; 10,000m from 2010)

1999	Nikki Huckerby	25:30.07
2000	Sally Warren	25:22.68
2005	Jo Jackson	22:55.89
2006	Jo Jackson	23:22.42
2007	Jo Jackson	22:38.19
2008	Fiona McGorum	29:46.81
2009	Rebecca Mersh	27:05.17
2010	Fiona McGorum	54:37.61
2012	Bethan Davies	52:32.33

JUNIORS

(Under-19 Instituted in 1984; under-20 in 1988)

100 METRES

1984	Louise Stuart	12.1
1985	Lynne Draper	11.9
1986	Sharon Dolby	11.83w
1987	Kim Goodwin	12.14
1988	Stephanie Douglas	11.45w
1989	Louise Fraser	11.88
1990	Diane Smith	11.79
1991	Marcia Richardson	11.62w
1992	Donna Hoggarth	11.66
1993	Katharine Merry	11.40w
1994	Diane Allahgreen	11.89
1995	Rebecca Drummond	11.88
1996	Rebecca Drummond	11.69w
1997	Rebecca Drummond	11.93
1998	Rebecca White	11.45w
1999	Emily Freeman	11.69w
2000	Kelly Thomas	12.06
2001	Vernicha James	11.44w
2002	Vernicha James	11.45w
2003	Jade Lucas-Read	11.59
2004	Joey Duck	12.06
2005	Kadi-Ann Thomas	11.72
2006	Asha Phillip	11.79
2007	Asha Philip	11.37
2008	Ashlee Nelson	11.58
2009	Jodie Williams	11.48
2010	Jodie Williams	11.28
2011	Jodie Williams	11.33w
2012	Sophie Papps	11.47

200 METRES

1985	Lynne Draper	24.0w
1986	Sally-Ann Frisby	24.49w
1987	Kim Goodwin	25.18
1988	Stephanie Douglas	23.97
1989	Donna Fraser	24.14w
1990	Diane Smith	23.94w
1991	Katharine Merry	23.74w
1992	Katharine Merry	23.90
1993	Katharine Merry	23.43w
1994	Susie Williams	24.27
1995	Victoria Shipman	24.08
1996	Victoria Shipman	24.20
1997	Sarah Wilhelmy	23.44
1998	Sarah Wilhelmy	23.31w
1999	Emma Whitter	24.10
2000	Vernicha James	23.81w
2001	Amy Spencer	23.3w
2002	Amy Spencer	23.58w
2003	Anyika Onuora	24.36
2004	Mandy Crowe IRL	24.51w
	(2, Sabina Astarita 24.57w)	
2005	Lucy Sargent	23.93
2006	Hayley Jones	24.00
2007	Hayley Jones	23.61
2008	Ashlee Nelson	23.83
2009	Shaunna Thompson	23.87
2010	Jodie Williams	23.15
2011	Jodie Williams	24.13
2012	Sophie Papps	23.48

400 METRES

1984	Diane Edwards (later Modahl)	55.9
1985	Ann Evison	57.8
1986	Caroline Kidd	57.38
1987	Alanna Cooke	56.34
1988	Tracy Goddard	54.81
1989	Paulette McLean	54.52
1990	Claire Raven	56.33
1991	Katharine Reeves	55.85
1992	Helen Frost	54.77
1993	Donna Adamson AUS	56.00
	(2, Katharine Eustace 56.14)	
1994	Tamsyn Lewis AUS	54.52
	(2, Jo Sloane 55.12)	
1995	Jo Sloane	55.17
1996	Emma Symonds	54.86
1997	Lesley Owusu	55.23

1998	Carey Easton	55.90
1999	Helen Thieme	54.23
2000	Jenny Meadows	54.53
2001	Lisa Miller	54.02
2002	Kim Wall	54.63
2003	Marilyn Okoro	53.97
2004	Gemma Nicol	55.20
2005	Gemma Nicol	53.79
2006	Katie Flower	54.28
2007	Carmen Gedling	55.83
2008	Shelayna Oskan	57.07
2009	Laura Wake	54.07
2010	Katie Snowden	54.59
2011	Katie Kirk	53.69
2012	Kirsten McAslan	54.11

800 METRES

1985	Michelle Faherty	2:12.5
1986	Paula Fryer	2:09.94
1987	Paula Fryer	2:10.23
1988	Paula Fryer	2:08.5
1989	Natalie Tait	2:08.27
1990	Natalie Tait	2:11.11
1991	Michelle Harries	2:08.98
1992	Charlotte Mayock	2:09.86
1993	Vicky Kirk	2:13.57
1994	Jeina Mitchell	2:05.85
1995	Alison Chiu AUS	2:10.35
	(2, Jane Groves 2:11.37)	
1996	Amanda Pritchard	2:07.59
1997	Emma Davies	2:07.11
1998	Emma Ward	2:12.08
1999	Becky Lyne	2:07.29
2000	Jemma Simpson	2:08.37
2001	Becky Lyne	2:09.64
2002	Jemma Simpson	2:09.65
2003	Jemma Simpson	2:04.59
2004	Laura Finucane	2:03.73
2005	Laura Finucane	2:05.0
2006	Emma Jackson	2:06.54
2007	Emma Jackson	2:05.81
2008	Alison Leonard	2:06.85
2009	Alison Leonard	2:04.50
2010	Leigh Lennon	2:10.10
2011	Rowena Cole	2:07.93
2012	Emily Dudgeon	2:04.95

1500 METRES

1984	Elise Lyon	4:26.6

1985	Anne Reason	4:30.3
1986	Debbie Farren	4:35.93
1987	Sue Parker	4:29.13
1988	Lisa York	4:23.93
1989	Lisa York	4:25.90
1990	Gillian Stacey	4:23.4
1991	Natalie Tait	4:25.97
1992	Jeina Mitchell	4:25.43
1993	Jeina Mitchell	4:25.47
1994	Susie Power AUS	4:19.54
	(2, Catherine Berry 4:25.58)	
1995	Juliette Oldfield	4:27.16
1996	Juliette Oldfield	4:30.1
1997	Ellen O'Hare	4:20.17
1998	Caroline Walsh	4:30.37
1999	Alex Carter	4:26.94
2000	Emma Ward	4:21.58
2001	Emma Ward	4:26.1
2002	Lisa Dobriskey	4:23.22
2003	Dani Barnes	4:23.17
2004	Dani Barnes	4:23.50
2005	Morag MacLarty	4:23.37
2006	Hannah England	4:17.31
2007	Emma Pallant	4:25.28
2008	Steph Twell	4:24.91
2009	Stacey Smith	4:18.54
2010	Laura Weightman	4:32.55
2011	Georgia Peel	4:19.82
2012	Jessica Judd	4:29.14

3000 METRES

1988	Andrea Whitcombe	9:40.74
1989	Sue Parker	9:31.05
1990	Kerry Mackay	9:34.81
1991	Hayley Haining	9:31.52
1992	Kerry Mackay	9:38.55
1993	Heidi Moulder	9:27.07
1994	Nikki Slater	9:21.20
1995	Alice Braham	9:35.77
1996	Michelle Mann	9:43.23
1997	Katie Skorupska	9:36.91
1998	Amber Gascoigne	9:46.06
1999	Collette Fagan	9:53.78
2000	Jane Potter	9:30.13
2001	Collette Fagan	9:36.1
2003	Katrina Wootton	9:35.27
2004	Victoria Webster	9:37.06
2005	Steph Twell	9:47.11
2006	Sian Edwards	9:16.38

2007	Jessica Coulson	9:24.30
2008	Emily Pidgeon	9:45.0
2009	Beth Potter	9:17.59
2010	Emelia Gorecka	9:25.65
2011	Emelia Gorecka	9:25.35
2012	Emelia Gorecka	9:22.11

5000 METRES

1996	Birhan Dagne ETH	16:40.00
	(3, Tanya Povey 17:43.9)	
2002	Kathryn Frost	17:17.92
2004	Laura Kenney	16:45.15
2005	Danielle Sale	17:09.11
2006	Sian Edwards	15:42.48
(discontinued after 2006)		

3000 METRES STEEPLECHASE

2003	Kathryn Frost (2000m)	6:55.52
2004	Becky Ellis	11:04.04
2005	Emily Pidgeon	10:06.12
2006	Ruth Senior	10:32.96
2007	Louise Webb	10:40.51
2008	Lucy Mayho	11:05.02
2009	Nicola Hood	10:31.90
2010	Mel Newbery	10:46.25
2011	Nicole Roberts	11:17.43
2012	Katie Ingle	10:25.48

100 METRES HURDLES

1984	Gillian Rhind	14.8
1985	Michelle Stone	13.9w
1986	Stephanie Douglas	14.49w
1987	Lisa Griffiths	14.66
1988	Jacqui Agyepong	13.89
1989	Louise Fraser	13.45w
1990	Keri Maddox	13.32w
1991	Keri Maddox	13.34
1992	Bethan Edwards	14.05
1993	Diane Allahgreen	13.58
1994	Diane Allahgreen	13.64
1995	Tasha Danvers	13.51w
1996	Tasha Danvers	13.78
1997	Julie Pratt	13.61w
1998	Sarah Claxton	13.28w
1999	Tamsin Stephens	14.29
2000	Helen Worsey	13.76w
2001	Helen Worsey	13.8w
2002	Gemma Fergusson	13.76
2003	Jessica Ennis	14.03

2004	Nicola Robinson	13.81
2005	Heather Jones	13.70
2006	Zara Hohn	13.75
2007	Jade Surman	13.77
2008	Meghan Beesley	13.83w
2009	Lauren Dewdney	13.90
2010	Rebecca Liddell	13.79w
2011	Katarina Johnson-Thompson	13.90
2012	Yasmin Miller	13.74w

400 METRES HURDLES

1985	Debra Cook	63.4
1986	Sarah Pennington	63.43
1987	Hayley Patterson	61.26
1988	Sara Elson	60.25
1989	Tracy Allen	59.12
1990	Clare Bleasdale	61.5
1991	Vyv Rhodes	60.26
1992	Vyv Rhodes	59.93
1993	Allison Curbishley	59.16
1994	Rebecca Campbell AUS	59.09
	(2, Allison Curbishley 59.16)	
1995	Josephine Fowley AUS	59.00
	(2, Vicki Jamison 59.81)	
1996	Vicki Jamison	57.27
1997	Cicely Hall	62.01
1998	Rachael Kay	60.83
1999	Nicola Sanders	60.94
2000	Nicola Sanders	59.68
2001	Gemma Dooney	60.6
2002	Sian Scott	61.06
2003	Sian Scott	58.36
2004	Faye Harding	60.42
2005	Eilidh Child	59.78
2006	Perri Shakes-Drayton	59.29
2007	Meghan Beesley	57.33
2008	Meghan Beesley	60.92
2009	Lauren Bouchard	59.76
2010	Christine McMahon IRL	59.66
	(2, Katrina Cosby 59.97)	
2011	Megan Southwart	59.49
2012	Aisha Naibe-Wey	61.00

HIGH JUMP

1985	Debbie Marti	1.80
1986	Michele Wheeler	1.76
1987	Jo Jennings	1.76
1988	Jo Jennings	1.75
1989	Julia Bennett	1.83

1990	Lea Haggett	1.84
1991	Lea Haggett	1.84
1992	Hazel Melvin	1.76
1993	Carolyn May	1.76
1994	Julie Crane	1.78
1995	Rachael Forrest	1.85
1996	Rachael Forrest	1.85
1997	Michelle Dunkley	1.87
1998	Aileen Wilson	1.79
1999	Emily Jackson	1.76
2000	Aileen Wilson	1.79
2001	Aileen Wilson	1.82
2002	Rebecca Jones	1.83
2003	Elizabeth Sweeney	1.73
2004	Emma Morris	1.74
2005	Charis O'Connor	1.80
2006	Jessica Leach	1.82
2007	Adele Lassu	1.78
2008	Adele Lassu	1.74
2009	Katarina Johnson-Thompson	1.74
2010	Isobel Pooley	1.82
2011	Emma Nuttall	1.82
2012	Evie Grogan	1.72

POLE VAULT

1993	Dawn-Alice Wright	2.80
1994	Clare Ridgley	3.40
1995	Rhian Clarke	3.40
1996	Rhian Clarke	3.50
1997	Becky Ridgley	3.35
1998	Emma Draisey NZL	3.70
	(4, Tracey Bloomfield 3.50)	
1999	Laura Patterson	3.30
2000	Ellie Spain	3.55
2001	Kate Dennison	3.65
2002	Kate Dennison	3.95
2003	Kate Dennison	3.75
2004	Natalie Olson	3.70
2005	Rachel Gibbens	3.80
2006	Emma Lyons	3.70
2007	Sally Scott	3.80
2008	Jade Ive	3.80
2009	Sally Scott	4.05
2010	Sally Scott	4.20
2011	Katie Byres	4.00
2012	Katie Byres	4.36

LONG JUMP

| 1984 | Leeanne Crutchley | 5.55 |

1985	Debbie Marti	6.14
1986	Lorraine Lynch	5.75w
1987	Julia Robertson	5.55
1988	Jo Wise	6.32w
1989	Denise Lewis	5.91
1990	Yinka Idowu	6.32w
1991	Jayne McCoy	6.12
1992	Lisa Armstrong	6.15
1993	Jo Dear	6.31w
1994	Adele Forester	6.03
1995	Adele Forester	5.87
1996	Sarah Claxton	6.23
1997	Sarah Claxton	6.09
1998	Sarah Claxton	6.34w
1999	Emma Hughes	6.07w
2000	Fiona Westwood	5.77
2001	Elaine Smith	5.92w
2002	Elaine Smith	5.97w
2003	Emily Parker	5.97w
2004	Louise Bloor	6.06w
2005	Amy Harris	6.30w
2006	Amy Harris	6.40w
2007	Jade Surman	6.27
2008	Abigail Irozuru	6.29w
2009	Lorraine Ugen	6.29
2010	Lorraine Ugen	6.42w
2011	Katarina Johnson-Thompson	6.44
2012	Jazmin Sawyers	6.42

TRIPLE JUMP

1991	Lorna Turner	12.48w
1992	Shani Anderson	11.95
1993	Shani Anderson	12.35
1994	Nicole Mladenis AUS	12.46
	(2, Shani Anderson 12.16)	
1995	Gillian Ting AUS	12.62
	(Liz Gibbens 12.42)	
1996	Liz Gibbens	12.17
1997	Julia Johnson	12.05
1998	Judy Kotey	12.61w
1999	Leandra Polius	11.85
2000	Rachel Peacock	11.98w
2001	Rachel Peacock	12.10w
2002	Emily Parker	12.19w
2003	Emily Parker	12.63w
2004	Yasmine Regis	12.64w
2005	Yasmine Regis	13.13
2006	Claire Linskill	12.62w
2007	Melissa Carr	12.45w

2008	Melissa Carr	12.67
2009	Laura Samuel	12.64
2010	Laura Samuel	12.71w
2011	Naomi Reid	12.76
2012	Ahtolla Rose	12.88

SHOT

1984	Kathryn Farr	13.14
1985	Sharon Andrews	13.50
1986	Ann Gardner	12.48
1987	Carol Cooksley	14.11
1988	Carol Cooksley	14.45
1989	Jayne Berry	13.66
1990	Alison Grey	13.55
1991	Alison Grey	14.28
1992	Alison Grey	15.08
1993	Denise Passmore AUS	13.88
	(2, Uju Efobi 13.72)	
1994	Kylie Standing AUS	13.76
	(3, Helen Wilding 12.66)	
1995	Philippa Roles	14.11
1996	Philippa Roles	13.76
1997	Julie Dunkley	14.36
1998	Julie Dunkley	14.81
1999	Valerie Adams NZL	14.15
	(2, Eva Massey 13.90)	
2000	Claire Smithson	13.72
2001	Rebecca Peake	14.13
2002	Charlotte Spelzini	13.72
2003	Alana Smith	12.63
2004	Chloe Edwards	13.61
2005	Sally Hinds	14.72
2006	Eden Francis	14.94
2007	Eden Francis	15.48
2008	Rachel Wallader	14.23
2009	Shaunagh Brown	13.74
2010	Sophie McKinna	14.37
2011	Sophie McKinna	14.51
2012	Sophie McKinna	16.16

DISCUS

1985	Belinda Hockley	44.60
1986	Belinda Hockley	45.90
1987	Rosanne Lister	46.04
1988	Rosanne Lister	46.42
1989	Natalie Hart	45.70
1990	Emma Merry	48.90
1991	Emma Merry	48.66
1992	Emma Merry	49.22

1993	Emma Merry	50.84
1994	Monique Nacsa AUS	49.38
	(2, Philippa Roles 44.90)	
1995	Monique Nacsa AUS	48.28
	(2, Philippa Roles 48.16)	
1996	Lauren Keightley	48.24
1997	Philippa Roles	50.94
1998	Lauren Keightley	49.58
1999	Joanne Street	45.93
2000	Claire Smithson	48.65
2001	Claire Smithson	54.81
2002	Claire Smithson	53.91
2003	Ellisha Dee	40.82
2004	Kirsty Law	40.78
2005	Lauren Therin	46.57
2006	Jade Lally	46.60
2007	Eden Francis	49.01
2008	Shaunagh Brown	48.00
2009	Shaunagh Brown	47.79
2010	Tesni Ward	47.17
2011	Tina Hakeai NZL	47.97
	(3, Charlotte Gair 42.59)	
2012	Shadine Duquemin	51.31

HAMMER

1993	Diana Holden	49.44
1994	Lyn Sprules	54.48
1995	Brenda MacNaughton AUS	53.36
	(3, Samantha Burns-Salmond 47.56)	
1996	Helen Arnold	50.62
1997	Rachael Beverley	53.88
1998	Rachael Beverley	56.35
1999	Zoe Derham	51.10
2000	Mhairi Walters	52.88
2001	Katy Lamb	52.17
2002	Nicola Dudman	54.22
2003	Susan McKelvie	50.58
2004	Susan McKelvie	55.28
2005	Samantha Hynes	51.05
2006	Victoria Thomas	56.78
2007	Hayley Murray	52.39
2008	Sophie Hitchon	60.49
2009	Sophie Hitchon	61.36
2010	Sophie Hitchon	63.74
2011	Abbi Carter	55.87
2012	Abbi Carter	59.21

JAVELIN

1984	Catherine Garside	46.84

1985	Michelle Poole	42.96
1986	Angelique Pullen	47.08
1987	Sally Painter	39.84
1988	Mandy Liverton	52.24
1989	Mandy Liverton	53.70
1990	Mandy Liverton	55.94
1991	Shelley Holroyd	51.16
1992	Karen Martin	55.72
1993	Kirsty Morrison	54.74
1994	Kirsty Morrison	53.88
1995	Kelly Morgan	46.94
1996	Tammie Francis	45.74
1997	Tammie Francis	46.24
1998	Kelly Morgan	50.32

JAVELIN
current model

1999	Jenny Kemp	52.54
2000	Goldie Sayers	51.37
2001	Goldie Sayers	53.74
2002	Samantha Redd	47.66
2003	Jo Chapman	47.12
2004	Becky Bartlett	49.72
2005	Lianne Clarke	47.10
2006	Lianne Clarke	45.77
2007	Jade Dodd	47.48
2008	Kelly Pagdin	44.98
2009	Tesni Ward	45.41
2010	Sanni Utriainen FIN	49.99
	(2, Tesni Ward 48.87)	
2011	Izzy Jeffs	49.61
2012	Freya Jones	52.73

HEPTATHLON

1988	Jenny Kelly	5364
1989	Yinka Idowu	5313
1990	Emma Beales	4916
1991	Yinka Idowu	5384
1992	Anne Hollman	4914
1993	Anne Hollman	5187w
1994	Julie Hollman	4851
1995	Kelly Sotherton	4940
1996	Nicola Gautier	5080
1997	Katherine Livesey	5215
1998	Danielle Freeman	4915
1999	Laura Redmond	4781
2000	Lara Carty	4401
2001	Roz Gonse	4875
2002	Phyllis Agbo	4868

2003	Louise Hazel	4698
2004	Catherine Holdsworth	5100w
2005	Catherine Holdsworth	5005
2006	Dominique Blaize	5164
2007	Jenny Lumley	5105
2008	Katarina Johnson-Thompson	5192
2009	Katarina Johnson-Thompson	5481
2010	Rebecca Curtis-Harris	4910
2011	Katarina Johnson-Thompson	5577
2012	Emma Buckett	5199

TRACK WALK

(5000m 1986–2009; 10,000m from 2010)

1986	Karen Dunster	27:43.33
1987	Louise Carr	26:26.22
1988	Julie Drake	24:07.22
1989	Vicky Lupton	25:06.27
1990	Vicky Lupton	23:41.5
1991	Carla Jarvis	25:13.8
1992	Theresa Ashman	25:32.95
1993	Kate Horwill	26:49.41
1994	Natalie Saville AUS	23:12.03
	(3, Kate Horwill 25:31.47)	
1995	Nikki Huckerby	26:03.46
1996	Rosaleigh Comerford IRL	24:40.2
	(2, Nina Howley 24:48.1)	
1997	Nikki Huckerby	25:01.55
1998	Katie Ford	25:30.29
1999	Amy Hales	24:35.55
2000	Serena O'Keeffe IRL	25:07.32
	(2, Sophie Hales 26:54.67)	
2001	Sophie Hales	26:29.35
2002	Sophie Hales	25:18.56
2003	Sophie Hales	25:16.90
2004	Sophie Hales	24:54.62
2005	Rebecca Mersh	25:32.85
2006	Chelsea O'Rawe-Hobbs	26:22.51
2007	Rebecca Mersh	27:26.11
2008	Rebecca Mersh	27:33.43
2009	Rebecca Mersh	27:05.17
2010	Emma Doherty IRL	52:15.26
	(4, Lauren Whelan 52:54.26)	
2011	Heather Lewis	54:27.48
2012	Heather Lewis	51:57.20

INTERMEDIATES (Under 17)
(later married name in brackets for selected athletes)

100 METRES
(Event instituted in 1949; y = 100 yards)

Year	Athlete	Time
1949	Barbara Schofield	12.8
1950	June Foulds (Paul)	12.6
1951	Shirley Hampton (Pirie)	13.1
1952	Jean Scrivens	11.1wy
1953	P Head	11.8y
1954	Christine Simpson	12.3y
1955	S Burroughs	11.9y
1956	Madeleine Weston (Cobb)	11.5y
1957	Dorothy Hyman	10.9y
1958	Debra Turner	11.1y
1959	Jenny Smart	11.2y
1960	Jenny Taylor	11.0y
1961	Sheila Cooper	11.4y
1962	Sheila Cooper	11.4y
1963	Christine Moore	11.6y
1964	Barbara Jones	11.3y
1965	Della James (Pascoe)	11.3y
1966	Kathryn Nelson	11.0y
1967	Denise Ramsden	11.2y
1968	Janet Stroud	11.1y
1969	Helen Golden	12.2
1970	Ruth Morris	12.4
1971	Linda Nash	12.3
1972	Linda Nash	11.8
1973	Wendy Clarke (Hoyte)	12.1
1974	Averil McClelland	12.4
1975	Heather Hunte (Oakes)	12.1
1976	Carmen Smart	12.04
1977	Michelle Walsh IRL	11.89
	(2, Philippa Baker 12.08)	
1978	Patricia Amond IRL	12.09
	(2, Philippa Baker 12.09)	
1979	Linsey Macdonald	11.94
1980	Linsey Macdonald	11.75
1981	Jane Parry	11.89
1982	Lisa Goreeph	11.98
1983	Simmone Jacobs	11.8
1984	Sallyanne Short	11.88
1985	Hayley Clements	11.77
1986	Danaa Myhill	11.99w
1987	Annabel Soper	12.06
1988	Fiona Page	12.02
1989	Renate Chinyou	11.87w

1990	Katharine Merry	11.64w
1991	Sophia Smith	11.99
1992	Debbie Mant	12.41
1993	Leanne Eastwood	12.00
1994	Rebecca Drummond	11.9
1995	Tatum Nelson	11.92
1996	Abi Oyepitan	12.06
1997	Donna Maylor	12.17
1998	Donna Maylor	11.76w
1999	Cherie Pierre	12.08
2000	Danielle Selley	12.00
2001	Amala Onuora	12.02
2002	Montell Douglas	11.77
2003	Natalie Jowett	11.94
2004	Joscelynn Hopeson	11.70
2005	Chinedu Monye	11.93
2006	Ashlee Nelson	11.96
2007	Rebekah Wilson	11.94
2008	Jodie Williams	11.56
2009	Angie Tagoe	11.61
2010	Bianca Williams	11.87w
2011	Sophie Papps	11.95

200 METRES

(Event instituted in 1956; y = 220 yards)

1956	Valerie Cutting (Surety)	26.2y
1959	Mary Hall	24.9y
1960	Jenny Taylor	25.3y
1961	Janet Simpson	25.5y
1962	Beryl Wear	25.4y
1963	Maureen Tranter	24.9y
1964	Barbara Jones	25.2y
1965	Della James (Pascoe)	25.8y
1966	Kathryn Nelson	25.2y
1967	Denise Ramsden	25.5y
1968	Marilyn Neufville	23.9y
1969	Helen Golden	24.7
1970	Sharon Colyear	25.0
1971	Barbara Martin	25.0
1972	Linda Nash	24.5w
1973	Hazel Oakes	24.9
1974	Elaine Douglas	24.6
1975	Susan Howells	25.0
1976	Michelle Probert (Scutt)	23.6
1977	Michelle Walsh IRL	24.12
	(2, Fay Nixon 24.23)	
1978	Debbie Bunn	24.12
1979	Debbie Warner	24.83
1980	Linsey Macdonald	23.89

1981	Jane Parry	24.24
1982	Lisa Goreeph	23.97
1983	Simmone Jacobs	23.58
1984	Sallyanne Short	24.21w
1985	Hayley Clements	24.12
1986	Tracy Goddard	24.81
1987	Annabel Soper	24.28w
1988	Donna Fraser	24.14
1989	Donna Fraser	24.76
1990	Katharine Merry	24.10
1991	Sophia Smith	24.47
1992	Debbie Mant	24.57
1993	Jo Sloane	24.66
1994	Lesley Owusu	24.99
1995	Lesley Owusu	24.43
1996	Helen Roscoe	25.2
1997	Karlene Palmer	24.47
1998	Kim Wall	24.52w
1999	Kim Wall	24.13w
2000	Eleanor Caney	24.29
2001	Jemma Sims	24.86
2002	Montell Douglas	24.33
2003	Sabina Astarita	24.58
2004	Joscelynn Hopeson	24.24
2005	Lucy Sargent	23.61w
2006	Jazmine Rowe	24.12
2007	Jo White	24.21w
2008	Shaunna Thompson	23.69w
2009	Angie Tagoe	24.25
2010	Desiree Henry	24.23
2011	Sophie Papps	23.93

400 METRES

(Event instituted in 1969; event switched to 300m from 1990)

1969	Dawn Webster	57.0
1970	Dawn Webster	56.1
1971	Paula Lloyd	56.2
1972	Julie Spiers	56.8
1973	Janet Ravenscroft	55.8
1974	Jane Colebrook (Finch)	55.5
1975	Karen Williams	55.17
1976	Liz Beton	55.46
1977	Sian Waters	55.53
1978	Carol Pendleton	55.3
1979	Linsey Macdonald	54.99
1980	Angela Bridgeman	54.01
1981	Carol Candlish	54.84
1982	Carol Candlish	54.85
1983	Ruth Elder	55.36

1984	Michelle Cooney	56.21
1985	Caroline Kidd	56.98
1986	Sharron Davenport	56.63
1987	Jillian Reynolds	58.00
1988	Donna Fraser	55.03
1989	Charlotte Knowles	57.68
1990	Katharine Eustace	41.89
1991	Alison Shingler	40.03
1992	Sophie Cocker	39.40
1993	Ruth Nicholson	40.8
1994	Lesley Owusu	38.71
1995	Lesley Owusu	38.54
1996	Rebecca White	39.25
1997	Gabi Howell	39.29
1998	Kim Wall	38.55
1999	Kim Wall	38.68
2000	Eleanor Caney	38.41
2001	Faye Harding	40.01
2002	Gemma Nicol	38.49
2003	Ni-Kysha Ferguson	39.21
2004	Laura Scougall	39.65
2005	Hayley Jones	39.33
2006	Holly Croxford	39.07
2007	Savannah Echel-Thomson	39.07
2008	Victoria Ohuruogu	39.77
2009	Joanna Mills IRL	39.77
2010	Katie Kirk	38.97
2011	Sabrina Bakare	39.28

800 METRES

(Event instituted in 1949; y = 880 yards)

1949	Iris Williams	2:23.9
1950	Hazel Needham (Rider)	2:32.0
1951	M Garver	2:34.3
1952	Mary Nusser	2:34.5y
1953	Mary Flin	2:31.0y
1954	Olwyn Foster	2:27.9y
1955	Violet Murphy	2:27.2y
1956	Susan Etherton	2:30.8y
1957	Marlene Swailes	2:33.1y
1958	Marlene Swailes	2:30.1y
1959	Margaret Easson	2:20.4y
1960	Valerie Tomlinson	2:18.2y
1961	Isobel Inwood	2:20.6y
1962	Marilyn Chaney	2:22.7y
1963	Jane Perry	2:19.0y
1964	Elizabeth McGarry	2:27.6y
1965	Jane Caffall	2:23.8y
1966	Margaret MacSherry	

	Coomber)	2:18.2y
1967	Norine Braithwaite	2:15.8y
1968	Christine Ansell	2:18.4y
1969	Mary Sonner	2:13.2
1970	Mary Sonner	2:10.9
1971	Chris Tranter (Benning)	2:13.3
1972	Chris Boxer (Cahill)	2:11.3
1973	Jane Colebrook (Finch)	2:12.8
1974	Janet Lawrence	2:11.0
1975	Angela Mason	2:11.3
1976	Sue Parker	2:11.4
1977	Sally Ludlam	2:08.31
1978	Kirsty McDermott (Wade)	2:07.74
1979	Lorraine Baker	2:09.69
1980	Lorraine Baker	2:05.38
1981	Tonia McCullough	2:09.86
1982	Phillipa Weaver-Smith	2:10.36
1983	Sally Wheeler	2:10.39
1984	Lynne Robinson	2:09.54
1985	Lynne Robinson	2:08.69
1986	Jayne Heathcote	2:08.77
1987	Jayne Heathcote	2:09.20
1988	Emma Langston	2:09.04
1989	Arlene Smith IRL	2:09.21
	(2, Michelle Wilkinson 2:09.69)	
1990	Joanne Davis (Pavey)	2:10.60
1991	Jeina Mitchell	2:11.33
1992	Isabel Linaker	2:12.75
1993	Dorothea Lee	2:10.87
1994	Maria Lynch IRL	2:13.95
	(2, Lucy Pringle 2:14.23)	
1995	Rachael Ogden	2:12.70
1996	Simone Hardy	2:15.19
1997	Suzanne Hasler	2:14.96
1998	Claire Taylor	2:12.52
1999	Lisa Dobriskey	2:10.46
2000	Charlotte Best	2:11.52
2001	Morag MacLarty	2:08.42
2002	Rachael Thompson	2:11.32
2003	Laura Kirk	2:08.90
2004	Danielle Christmas	2:08.02
2005	Emily Goodall	2:09.14
2006	Alison Leonard	2:07.52
2007	Kerrie Harris	2:07.52
2008	Rowena Cole	2:07.23
2009	Georgia Peel	2:07.35
2010	Grace Rodgers	2:13.38
2011	Loren Bleaken	2:07.88

1500 METRES

(Event instituted in 1971)

1971	Betty Price	4:35.70
1972	Teena Colebrook	4:39.9
1973	Monica Joyce	4:44.10
1974	Anne Tunnicliffe	4:33.58
1975	Gillian Dainty (Green)	4:31.76
1976	Christine Brace	4:28.7
1977	Denise Kiernan	4:23.25
1978	Carole Meagan IRL	4:21.02
	(2, Sandra Arthurton 4:21.8)	
1979	Carole Meagan IRL	4:19.94
	(2, Wendy Lodge 4:28.62)	
1980	Lynne MacDougall	4:25.76
1981	Lynne MacDougall	4:27.10
1982	Elise Lyon	4:22.51
1983	Diane Critchlow	4:30.93
1984	Bridget Smyth	4:24.20
1985	Clare Keller	4:31.67
1986	Lisa York	4:35.77
1987	Dawn Hargan	4:33.23
1988	Louise Watson	4:27.93
1989	Gillian Stacey	4:30.16
1990	Joanne Davis (Pavey)	4:37.16
1991	Jeina Mitchell	4:28.20
1992	Isabel Linaker	4:30.85
1993	Nikki Slater	4:30.10
1994	Maria Lynch IRL	4:37.4
	(2, Dawn Adams 4:38.7)	
1995	Maria Lynch IRL	4:36.51
	(2, Karen Montador 4:38.54)	
1996	Camilla Waite	4:36.61
1997	Aoife Byrne IRL	4:32.87
	(2, Emma Ward 4:33.62)	
1998	Emma Ward	4:38.32
1999	Kate Reed	4:32.29
2000	Charlotte Dale	4:30.87
2001	Rosie Smith	4:40.10
2002	Rachel Jones	4:33.74
2003	Charlotte Browning	4:25.61
2004	Nikki Hamblin	4:22.41
2005	Sarah Hopkinson	4:32.82
2006	Jessica Coulson	4:28.12
2007	Charlotte Purdue	4:28.40
2008	Sarah Kelly	4:31.35
2009	Melissa Courtney	4:32.90
2010	Jessica Judd	4:33.54
2011	Jessica Judd	4:20.34

3000 METRES
(Event instituted in 1985)

1985	Sue Jordan	10:06.54
1986	Helen Titterington	9:40.96
1987	Julie Adkin	9:50.07
1988	Julie Adkin	9:46.80
1989	Kerry Mackay	9:50.13
1990	Jessica Mills	10:15.25
1991	Catherine Berry	10:10.35
1993	Jennifer Heath	10:20.88
1994	Caroline McNulty	10:08.96
1995	Nicola Lilley	10:16.38
1996	Kate Grimshaw	10:04.48
1997	Jodie Swallow	9:59.67
1998	Collette Fagan	10:33.75
1999	Gemma Taylor	10:22.10
2001	Emma Hunt	10:00.65
2002	Rachael Nathan	9:55.38
2003	Leonie Smith	9:50.72
2004	Jessica Sparke	9:52.65
2005	Emily Pidgeon	9:38.81
2006	Charlotte Purdue	9:45.70
2007	Ciara Mageean	9:39.48
2008	Laura Park	9:45.47
2009	Lauren Proctor	9:34.89
2010	Charlotte Taylor	10:02.83
2011	Natalia Hackett	9:59.21

80 METRES HURDLES
(Event instituted in 1948; 2' 6" hurdles; y = 80 yards)

1948	Jean Oldfield	11.9y
1949	Jean Oldfield	12.0y
1950	Jean Edgerley	11.6y
1951	Pam Seaborne (Elliott)	11.9y
1952	Pamela Fry	11.7y
1953	Sylvia Dawes	12.0y
1954	Sylvia Mackay	11.3y
1955	Christine Simpson	11.7y
1956	Alma Osborne	11.7y
1957	Maxine Botley	11.4y
1958	Brenda Hamilton	11.4y
1959	Barbara Moser	11.3y
1960	Angela Charman	11.0y
1961	Rosemary Kimberley	11.2y
1962	Beryl Jenkins	11.2y
1963	Pauline Williams	11.3y
1964	Sheila Garnett	11.5
1965	Ann Wilson	11.7

1966	Christine Perera (Bell)	11.7
1967	Jackie Philp	12.1
1968	Susan Turpin	11.4
1969	Julie Rainford	11.7
1970	Myra Nimmo	11.7
1971	Lorna Drysdale	12.1
1972	Sue Mapstone	11.4
1973	Liz Eddy	11.4
1974	Shirley Strong	12.1
1975	Maureen Prendergast	11.7
1976	Maureen Prendergast	11.54
1977	Wendy McDonnell	11.03w
1978	Sarah Brennan	11.48
1979	Claire St John	11.39
1980	Sarah Dean	11.46
1984	Alison Glasgow	11.72
1985	Stephanie Douglas & Sam Farquharson	11.16
1986	Amanda Parker	11.07
1987	Louise Brunning	11.20
1988	Nina Thompson	11.29
1989	Bethan Edwards	11.46
1990	Catherine Murphy	11.36
1991	Diane Allahgreen	11.57
1992	Orla Bermingham	11.64
1993	Liz Fairs	11.40
1994	Liz Fairs	11.48
1995	Claire Pearson	11.44
1996	Sarina Mantle	11.62
1997	Helen Worsey	11.41
1998	Helen Worsey	11.02
1999	Sara McGreavy	11.17
2000	Symone Belle	11.20
2001	Channelle Garnett	11.31
2002	Heather Jones	11.56
2003	Heather Jones	11.30
2004	Zara Hohn	11.31
2005	Serita Solomon	11.04w
2006	Ashley Helsby	11.20w
2007	Helen Van Kempen	11.38
2008	Kirsty Warland	11.32
2009	Georgia Atkins	11.28
2010	Yasmin Miller	11.02
2011	Shirin Irving	11.29

100 METRES HURDLES

(Event instituted in 1978; 2' 6" hurdles; discontinued after 1989)

1978	Claire St John	14.43
1979	Claire St John	13.82

1980	Lynne Roper	14.24
1981	Ann Girvan	13.66
1982	Pam St Ange	13.91
1983	Pam St Ange	13.87
1984	Michelle Stone	14.51
1985	Stephanie Douglas	14.05
1987	Lauraine Cameron	14.14
1988	Lauraine Cameron	13.97w
1989	Angie Thorp	13.84

200 METRES HURDLES

(Event instituted in 1973; discontinued after 1987)

1973	Liz Eddy	30.5
1974	Fiona Macaulay	28.5
1975	Yvette Wray	28.6
1976	Maureen Prendergast	28.0w
1977	Diane Wade	28.90
1978	Aileen Mills	28.51
1979	Susan Trickett	28.5
1980	Mandy Lewis	28.35
1981	Noelle Morrissey IRL	27.80
	(2, Ann Girvan 28.06)	
1982	Noelle Morrissey IRL	28.27
	(2, Michelle Grant 28.73)	
1983	Michelle Stone	28.19
1984	Michelle Stone	28.68
1985	Sam Farquharson	27.83
1986	Sam Farquharson	28.14
1987	Louise Fraser	27.31

400/300 METRES HURDLES

(Event instituted in 1981; 300m from 1988)

1981	Kay Simpson	61.27
1982	Karin Hendrickse	60.87
1983	Jacqui Parker	62.37
1984	Susan Fowlie	63.25
1985	Debra Duncan	61.32
1986	Sara Elson	63.09
1987	Clare Bleasdale	64.02
1988	Keri Maddox	43.12
1989	Val Theobalds	43.03
1990	Helen Frost	45.83
1991	Allison Curbishley	42.91
1992	Allison Curbishley	43.68
1993	Natasha Danvers	42.61
1994	Natasha Danvers	42.60
1995	Tracey Duncan	44.44
1996	Yewande Ige	43.79
1997	Rachael Kay	41.8

1998	Wendy Davidson	44.27
1999	Wendy Davidson	43.03
2000	Gemma Dooney	42.96
2001	Joanne Erskine	43.71
2002	Eilidh Child	42.49
2003	Eilidh Child	41.97
2004	Claire Triggs	42.64
2005	Perri Shakes-Drayton	42.44
2006	Meghan Beesley	41.41
2007	Nicola Hill	44.50
2008	Megan Rogers	43.16
2009	Megan Rogers	43.19
2010	Hayley McLean	43.38
2011	Claire Murphy IRL	42.25
	(2, Hayley McLean 42.63)	

HIGH JUMP

(Event instituted in 1948)

1948	Christine Wheeler	1.52
1949	Jean Cowan	1.55
1950	M Quaife	1.45
1951	Ursula Hynes	1.47
1952	J.D.Turner	1.47
1953	Maureen Hudson	1.50
1954	Jennifer Fraser	1.47
1955	Dorothy Shirley	1.55
1956	Mary Bignal (Rand)	1.55
1957	Janet Gaunt	1.55
1958	Frances Slaap	1.57
1959	Pauline Sibley	1.52
1960	Gwenda Matthews (Hurst/Ward)	1.66
1961	Diane Warnock	1.55
1962	Margaret Symonds	1.50
1963	June Ratcliffe	1.60
1964	Kathleen Killian	1.50
1965	Ann Wilson	1.62
1966	Janet Oldall (Honour) ?	1.62
1967	Yvonne Saunders	1.60
1968	Yvonne Saunders	1.65
1969	Rachel Edwards	1.55
1970	Gillian Lansdowne	1.57
1971	Penny Dimmock	1.62
1972	Carol Mathers	1.72
1973	Carol Mathers	1.67
1974	Val Mullin	1.75
1975	Ann-Marie Devally (Cording)	1.72
1976	Janet Sykes	1.74
1977	Heather Spencer	1.71
1978	Heather Spencer	1.78

1979	Bridget Corrigan IRL	1.80
	(2, Susan Brown 1.80)	
1980	Denise Wilkinson	1.76
1981	Claire Summerfield	1.75
1982	Louise Manning	1.76
1983	Debbie Marti	1.83
1984	Claire Bessant	1.72
1985	Jo Jennings	1.83
1986	Jo Jennings	1.73
1987	Lea Haggett	1.75
1988	Lea Haggett	1.77
1989	Wendy MacDonald	1.73
1990	Tracy Flin	1.71
1991	Olivia Scully IRL	1.71
	(2, Emma Whitworth 1.68)	
1992	Lindsay Evans	1.73
1993	Julie Crane	1.70
1994	Susan Jones (Moncrieff)	1.70
1995	Rachel Martin	1.74
1996	Antonia Bemrose	1.73
1997	Samantha Adamson	1.65
1998	Deirdre Ryan IRL	1.73
	(2, Rebecca Jones 1.70)	
1999	Rebecca Jones	1.79
2000	Stephanie Higham	1.78
2001	Emma Perkins	1.74
2002	Shani Rainford	1.71
2003	Stephanie Pywell	1.71
2004	Charis O'Connor	1.74
2005	Adele Lassu	1.77
2006	Grainne Moggan IRL	1.69
	(2, Rebecca Pottinger 1.69)	
2007	Cathriona Farrell IRL	1.69
	(2, Jill Brooks 1.69)	
2008	Katarina Johnson-Thompson	1.76
2009	Katarina Johnson-Thompson	1.79
2010	Ffion Bodilly	1.73
2011	Camellia Hayes	1.77

POLE VAULT

(Event instituted in 1993)

1993	Clare Ridgley	3.30
1994	Clare Ridgley	3.20
1995	Becky Ridgley	2.90
1996	Fiona Harrison	3.45
1997	Sarah Hartley	3.00
1998	Lindsay Hodges	3.20
1999	Lindsay Hodges	3.55
2000	Kate Dennison	3.20

2001	Erin Kinnear IRL	3.50
	(2, Natalie Olson 3.50)	
2002	Hannah Olson	3.80
2003	Hannah Olson	3.70
2004	Kim Skinner	3.65
2005	Jasmin Hicks	3.30
2006	Abigail Haywood	3.50
2007	Jade Ive	3.80
2008	Jade Ive	3.80
2009	Ellie Besford	3.70
2010	Lucy Bryan	3.81
2011	Lucy Bryan	3.80

LONG JUMP

(Event instituted in 1948)

1948	Juance Perry	4.92
1949	Valerie Webster	5.18
1950	Audrey Cashmore	5.07
1952	Sheila Hoskin	4.85
1953	Sheila Hoskin	5.40
1954	Jean Whitehead	5.62
1955	C Roe	5.17
1956	Mary Bignal (Rand)	5.43
1957	Rosemary Jordan	5.21
1958	Marian Needham	5.89
1959	Janice Catt	5.32
1960	Anne Wilson	5.28
1961	Anne Wilson	5.49
1962	Sandra Anderson	5.19
1963	Patricia Wilson	5.41
1964	Maureen Barton	5.55
1965	Anita Neil	5.74
1966	Anita Neil	5.88
1967	Sue Scott (Reeve)	5.71
1968	Barbara-Anne Barrett	5.55
1969	Janis Murray	5.81
1970	Myra Nimmo	5.60w
1971	Julie Roberts	5.46
1972	Sue Mapstone	5.85
1973	Gill Regan	5.56
1974	Joy Bowerman	5.83w
1975	Karen Murray	5.73
1976	Sue Hearnshaw	5.95
1977	Kim Hagger	5.58
1978	Kim Hagger	5.73
1979	Sandy French	5.77
1980	Karen Glen	6.09
1981	Sally Gunnell	5.72
1982	Georgina Oladapo	5.84w

1983	Georgina Oladapo	6.29
1984	Margaret Cheetham	6.42
1985	Margaret Cheetham	5.84
1986	Fiona May	6.21w
1987	Jo Wise	5.98
1988	Jackie Harris	6.00
1989	Jackie Harris	5.56
1990	Jo Dear	5.66
1991	Claire Ingerton IRL	5.86
	(2, Stephanie Dobson 5.70)	
1992	Adele Forester	5.70
1993	Julie Hollman	5.82
1994	Rebecca Lewis	5.69
1995	Jade Johnson	5.69
1996	Emma Hughes	5.67
1997	Rachel Peacock	5.57
1998	Aimee Cutler	5.84w
1999	Lara Richards	5.82w
2000	Symone Belle	5.74
2001	Phyllis Agbo	5.77w
2002	Catherine Holdsworth	5.83w
2003	Amy Harris	5.69
2004	Jade Surman	5.99
2005	Jade Surman	5.85w
2006	Jade Nimmo	5.68
2007	Hannah Lewis	5.68
2008	Katarina Johnson-Thompson	6.07w
2009	Katarina Johnson-Thompson	6.19
2010	Micaela Brindle	5.79
2011	Jahisha Thomas	5.85

TRIPLE JUMP

(Event instituted in 1993)

1993	Pamela Anderson	11.50w
1994	Jayne Ludlow	11.14
1995	Jayne Ludlow	11.76w
1996	Julia Johnson	11.65
1997	Rachel Peacock	11.38
1998	Rachel Peacock	11.47
1999	Lara Richards	11.60w
2000	Emily Parker	11.70
2001	Rachel Brenton	11.86w ?
2002	Sally Peake	11.89w
2003	Rebekah Passley	12.19
2004	Tanine Nicholas	11.69
2005	Hannah Frankson	12.19w
2006	Kayley Alcorn	11.78
2007	Desola Bakre	11.79
2008	Emma Pringle	12.08

2009	Sophie Brown	11.93w
2010	Naomi Reid	12.23
2011	Mary Fasipe	12.18

SHOT

(Event instituted in 1948)

1948	Rita Hurley	9.34
1949	Gwen Buddle	9.55
1950	Diane Coates	9.31
1951	Suzanne Farmer (Allday)	10.59
1952	Josephine Brocklehurst	10.02
1953	Patricia Legg	8.56
1954	Judy Pridie	9.60
1955	Maureen Costard	10.29
1956	Alma Osborne	10.88
1957	Carole Saunders	10.82
1958	Rosemary Morgan	10.96
1959	Sandra Fraser	10.13
1960	Valerie Woods	10.97
1961	Moira Kerr	10.82
1962	Kathy Duckett	11.16
1963	Janis Quick (Kerr)	11.14
1964	Helen Walker	10.82
1965	Christine Fisher	11.59
1966	Mary Scott	11.05
1967	Jill Lucas	12.55
1968	Debbie Kerr	11.49
1969	Wendy Blackwood	11.71
1970	Chris Chalk	11.82
1971	Judith Potts	11.34
1972	Judith Potts	12.25
1973	Ereka Service	11.40
1974	Judy Oakes	11.95
1975	Lana Newton	13.17
1976	Marita Walton IRL	13.25
	(3, Fiona Condon 11.20)	
1977	Maureen Tree	11.92
1978	Susan Bracey	11.85
1979	Susan Bracey	12.26
1980	Cynthia Gregory	13.39
1981	Susan King	13.27
1982	Terri Salt	13.00
1983	Terri Salt	13.57
1984	Mary Anderson	13.70
1985	Carol Cooksley	12.64
1986	Justine Buttle	13.83
1987	Natalie Hart	12.84
1988	Natalie Hart	12.63
1989	Alison Grey	12.53

1990	Emma Capes	12.61
1991	Kelly Kane	12.15
1992	Julie Robin	12.61
1993	Natasha Smith	11.98
1994	Philippa Roles	12.82
1995	Catherine Garden	11.94
1996	Julie Dunkley	12.59
1997	Amy Wilson	11.92
1998	Claire Smithson	12.73
1999	Shaunette Richards	12.24
2000	Frances Miller	11.37
2001	Frances Miller	12.31
2002	Sally Hinds	12.10
2003	Chloe Edwards	12.28
2004	Eden Francis	12.90
2005	Eden Francis	13.95
2006	Rachel Wallader	12.44
2007	Jade Weston	11.85
2008	Yasmin Spencer	12.26
2009	Yasmin Spencer	12.62
2010	Simi Pam	12.54
2011	Annabel Sherry	13.49

DISCUS

(Event instituted in 1949)

1949	Gwen Buddle	30.15
1950	Sylvia Needham	31.08
1951	Suzanne Farmer (Allday)	37.77
1952	Josephine Brocklehurst	31.72
1953	Dorothy Smyth	30.81
1954	Dorothy Smyth	32.82
1955	Maureen Brazier	32.11
1956	Alma Osborne	29.02
1957	Brenda Hampton	37.90
1958	Antoinette Coombes	37.71
1959	Ann Waters	33.48
1960	Wendy Thomas	40.81
1961	Margaret Walsh	34.48
1962	Kathy Duckett	37.08
1963	Carol Mitchell	35.53
1964	Angela Hooks	34.96
1965	Angela Hooks	33.79
1966	Jill Lucas	36.86
1967	Jill Lucas	37.31
1968	Susan Carter	38.56
1969	Wendy Blackwood	36.82
1970	Jackie Elsmore	40.00
1971	Linda King	35.58
1972	Erica Ball	37.90

1973	Karen Mallard	35.16
1974	Karen Mallard	39.38
1975	Val Watson	41.74
1976	Marita Walton IRL	44.50
	(2, Fiona Condon 40.86)	
1977	Fiona Condon	46.64
1978	Janette Picton	42.40
1979	Janette Picton	43.74
1980	Debbie Bushnell	40.92
1981	Karen Pugh	43.66
1982	Karen Pugh	45.32
1983	Catherine Bradley	43.66
1984	Catherine Bradley	43.98
1985	Jane Aucott	46.56
1986	Charladee Clarke	38.94
1987	Charladee Clarke	41.46
1988	Emma Beales	43.22
1989	Emma Merry	43.56
1990	Sarah Winckless	43.38
1991	Charlotte Davies	38.96
1992	Julie Robin	41.96
1993	Helen Wilding	40.06
1994	Philippa Roles	44.40
1995	Lauren Keightley	44.10
1996	Natalie Kerr	44.44
1997	Carly Burton	39.14
1998	Emma Carpenter	41.30
1999	Claire Smithson	45.91
2000	Angela Lockley	36.44
2001	Danielle Hall	41.28
2002	Lucy Sutton	37.00
2003	Kirsty Law	39.80
2004	Eden Francis	41.27
2005	Eden Francis	43.80
2006	Shaunagh Brown	44.95
2007	Hannah Evenden	40.52
2008	Claire Fitzgerald IRL	39.07
	(2, Tyne Breen 36.23)	
2009	Samantha Milner	43.19
2010	Pheobe Dowson	40.24
2011	Shadine Duquemin	46.02

HAMMER

(Event instituted in 1993)

1993	Cheryl Cunnane	33.32
1994	Rachael Beverley	41.26
1995	Helen Arnold	46.98
1996	Clara Thompson IRL	42.52
	(2, Zoe Derham 42.10)	

1997	Zoe Derham	48.66
1998	Lucy Marshall	43.10
1999	Laura Douglas	42.78
2000	Nicola Dudman	44.40
2001	Frances Miller	48.18
2002	Laura Chalmers	45.23
2003	Catherine Marvin	44.44
2004	Anna Johnson	47.22
2005	Katie O'Shea IRL	43.23
	(3, Nicola Stevenson 42.45)	
2006	Hayley Murray	48.79
2007	Sophie Hitchon	53.18
2008	Myra Perkins	50.69
2009	Abbi Carter	52.00
2010	Abbi Carter	55.03
2011	Kimberley Reed	52.76

JAVELIN

(Event instituted in 1948; current specification javelin used from 1999)

1948	Una Kirk	25.75
1949	Diane Coates	30.49
1950	Diane Coates	38.19
1951	Suzanne Farmer (Allday)	27.81
1952	Patricia Legg	30.09
1953	Yvonne Kaye	36.73
1954	E Pitfield	34.95
1955	M Cattle	39.88
1956	Margaret Callender	
	(Whitbread)	38.16
1957	Sue Platt	39.36
1958	Rosemary Morgan	38.83
1959	Barbara Nicholls	37.93
1960	Mary Adams	35.93
1961	Carol Wilkie	34.38
1962	Cynthia Patrick	38.51
1963	Cynthia Patrick	35.78
1964	Susan Paul	35.99
1965	Christine Slater	36.78
1966	Marion Pearson	37.13
1967	Marlene Garner	36.40
1968	Jean Schofield	39.04
1969	Dorothy Pendlebury	38.76
1970	Anne Goodlad	37.98
1971	Tessa Sanderson	42.02
1972	Tessa Sanderson	42.04
1973	Laurie Kern CAN	46.88
	(2, Christine Green 41.92)	
1974	Julie King	44.80
1975	Julie Walker	40.90

1976	Yvonne Gregory	42.76
1977	Fatima Whitbread	48.28
1978	Sara Fry	45.18
1979	Joanne Harding	40.22
1980	Joanne Harding	42.42
1981	Maxine Worsfold	43.44
1982	Jacqui Barclay	46.22
1983	Karen Hough	45.92
1984	Karen Hough	46.30
1985	Angelique Pullen	43.40
1986	Janette McClean	43.64
1987	Nicky Emblem	48.70
1988	Mandy Liverton	51.22
1989	Shelley Holroyd	48.70
1990	Debbie Boomer	42.96
1991	Kirsty Morrison	46.24
1992	Kirsty Morrison	53.22
1993	Angharad Richards	46.20
1994	Nicola Mackay	42.60
1995	Sian Lax	44.78
1996	Lucy Rann	40.86
1997	Goldie Sayers	45.10
1998	Michelle Lonsdale	41.93
1999	Samantha Redd	40.58
2000	Samantha Redd	42.23
2001	Jo Chapman	41.78
2002	Louise Watton	43.39
2003	Hayley Thomas	42.93
2004	Laura Scott	38.48
2005	Jade Dodd	37.75
2006	Sarah-Anne de Kremer	42.22
2007	Sadie Watts	39.87
2008	Izzy Jeffs	42.69
2009	Freya Jones	49.66
2010	Laura McDonald	45.52
2011	Kerry Murch	42.64

HEPTATHLON

(Event instituted as Pentathlon in 1966; Heptathlon from 1981)

1966	Vivien Knowles	4056
1967	Sue Scott (Reeve)	4118
1968	Yvonne Saunders	4079
1969	Janis Murray	3952
1970	Shirley Biggs	4167
1971	Stephanie Dyer	3746
1972	Sue Mapstone	3709
1973	Joy Bowerman	3848
1974	Joy Bowerman	3772
1975	Kathy Warren	3790

1976	Manndy Laing	3780
1977	Kim Hagger	3781w
1978	Kim Hagger	3770
1979	Sarah Rowe	3786
1980	Joanne Taylor	3673
1981	Suzanne Sherratt	4661
1982	Sarah Booth	4597
1983	Claire Smith	4609
1984	Michelle Stone	5147
1985	Jackie Kinsella	4839
1986	Jenny Kelly	4521w
1987	Louise Schramm	4111
1988	Denise Lewis	4915
1989	Ade Rawcliffe	4270
1990	Carolyn May	4578
1991	Natasha Turner	4523
1992	Krissy Owen	4440
1993	Clover Wynter-Pink	4620
1994	Claire Everett	4435
1995	Jackie Tindal	4409
1996	Chloe Cozens	4668
1997	Vickie Williams	4466
1998	Nicola Sanders	4298
1999	Jemma Scott	4558
2000	Hannah Barnes	4338
2001	Emily Parker	4436
2002	Naida Bromley	4574
2003	Naida Bromley	4749
2004	Jade Surman	4918w
2005	Mairead Murphy IRL	4832
	(2, Sophie Skinner 4306)	
2006	Chelsea Cooper	4752
2007	Alice Lennox	4601
2008	Katy Marchant	4384
2009	Becky Curtis-Harris	4600
2010	Tanisha Clayton	4720
2011	Georgina Westwood	4604

TRACK WALK

(Event instituted at mile in 1949; discontinued after 1955; revived in 1961; 2000m 1969–1972, 2500m 1973–1974, 3000m 1975–1989, 5000m since 1990; mixed races since 1998)

1949	Zoe White	?
1950	Zoe White	8:49.4
1951	Irene McCormack	9:22.0
1952	Pauline Williams	9:39.0
1955	Pat Myatt	8:53.0
1961	Jennifer Keen	9:11.4
1962	Jennifer Keen	8:45.6

1963	Sheila Higgleton	10:14.5
1964	Susan Dyer	8:36.0
1965	Jennifer Peck	9:01.8
1966	Jane Matthews	8:58.4
1967	Doris Froome	8:23.4
1968	Catherine Russell	8:45.2
1969	Barbara Brown	10:58.4
1970	Catherine Daniels	11:11.0
1971	Kim Braznell	10:31.6
1972	Marion Davis	12:20.0
1973	Pamela Branson	12:42.8
1974	Sylvia Saunders	12:47.8
1975	Bev Francis	16:27.0
1976	Elaine Cox	15:29.46
1977	Joanna Wickham	15:30.0
1978	Carol Brooke	16:43.8
1979	Jillian Mullins	15:47.5
1980	Jill Barrett	15:34.8
1981	Karen Nipper	14:59.32
1982	Helen Ringshaw	15:05.82
1983	Elizabeth Ryan	15:41.66
1984	Kim Macadam	15:24.3
1985	Susan Ashforth	14:35.5
1986	Nicola Massey	15:38.79
1987	Andrea Crofts	15:01.22
1988	Tracy Devlin	15:06.71
1989	Tracy Devlin	14:33.76
1990	Carla Jarvis	27:08.29
1991	Kate Horwill	26:48.37
1992	Lisa Crump	28:42.12
1993	Nina Howley	26:54.99
1994	Nina Howley	25:25.07
1995	Sarah Bennett	27:01.1
1996	Sarah Bennett	27:53.40
1997	Serena O'Keeffe IRL	25:00.6
	(2, Rebecca Tisshaw 25:52.8)	
1998	Serena O'Keeffe IRL	24:35.02
	(2, Katie Ford 26:13.07)	
1999	Nicola Phillips	26:32.96
2000	Natalie Evans	27:24.88
2001	Bryna Chrismas	27:42.35
2002	Katie Stones	25:57.11
2003	Jenny Gagg	25:03.91
2004	Rebecca Mersh	24:47.75
2005	Laura Reynolds IRL	25:19.67
	(2, Rebecca Mersh 25:57.64)	
2006	Chelsea O'Rawe-Hobbs	26:44.55
2007	Fiona Dennehy IRL	26:52.49
	(2, Chelsea O'Rawe-Hobbs 27:20.96)	

2008	Emma Doherty	26:23.72
2009	Katie Veale IRL	23:27.58
	(3, Kelsey Howard 28:11.41)	
2010	Heather Lewis	26:24.26
2011	Tasha Webster	26:10.69

4 x100 METRES RELAY

(Event instituted in 1949; y = 4 x 110 yards)

1949	Birchfield	?
1950	Spartan Ladies	51.9y
1952	Spartan Ladies	50.8y
1953	Spartan Ladies	50.8y
1954	Darlington	50.8y
1955	Spartan Ladies	50.4y
1956	Selsonia Ladies	51.1y
1957	Selsonia Ladies	49.0y
1958	Mitcham	50.5y
1959	London Olympiades	50.6y

JUNIOR GIRLS (Under 15)

(later married name in brackets for selected athletes)

60 YARDS

(Event instituted in 1949; discontinued after 1955)

1949	Mavis Elcock	7.4
1950	W. Richings	7.6
1951	Carole Quinton	8.0
1952	M. Astell	7.4
1953	June Pearson	7.5
1954	Dorothy Wood	7.6
1955	Madeleine Weston (Cobb)	7.7 ?

100 METRES

(Event instituted in 1949; y = 100 yards)

1949	Mavis Elcock	11.8y
1950	M. Hunt	12.3y
1951	Carole Quinton	12.5y
1952	M. Astell	12.2y
1953	June Pearson	11.9y
1954	Dorothy Wood	12.9y
1955	Madeleine Weston (Cobb)	12.0y
1956	Dorothy Hyman	12.0y
1957	Christine Theaker	11.8y
1958	Beryl Wear	11.4y
1959	Helen Harris	11.4y
1960	Jill Hall	11.3y
1961	Beryl Wear	11.4y
1962	Christine Moore	11.1y

WAAA Champions

1963	Christina Amos	11.4y
1964	Marilyn North	11.5y
1965	Wendy Kavanagh	11.2y
1966	Linda Barratt	11.4y
1967	Marilyn Neufville	11.5y
1968	Christine Smith	11.4y
1969	Sonia Lannaman	12.5
1970	Sonia Lannaman	12.2
1971	Gillian Spurgin	12.8
1972	Averil McClelland	12.2w
1973	Valerie Smith	12.5
1974	Janis Walsh	12.1
1975	Debbie Bunn	12.5
1976	Joanne Gardner	12.03
1977	Joanne Gardner	11.89
1978	Jane Parry	12.10
1979	Delmena Doyley	12.24
1980	Etta Kessebeh	12.33
1981	Dawn Flockhart	12.30
1982	Bernadette Ross	12.31
1983	Margaret Cheetham	12.10
1984	Kerrie Hughes	12.62
1985	Annabel Soper	12.28w
1986	Annabel Soper	12.14w
1987	Jane Riley	12.20
1988	Katharine Merry	12.04
1989	Katharine Merry	11.97
1990	Myra McShannon	12.2w
1991	Helen Seery	12.42
1992	Rebecca Drummond	12.42
1993	Tatum Nelson	12.00
1994	Sarah Wilhelmy	12.0
1995	Chantell Manning	12.4
1996	Fiona Harrison	12.25
1997	Kim Wall	12.62
1998	Danielle Selley	12.15
1999	Kara Dunn	12.10w
2000	Amy Spencer	12.02
2001	Sinead Johnson	11.92w
2002	Carley Wenham	12.08
2003	Joey Duck	12.07
2004	Chinedu Monye	12.09
2005	Ashlee Nelson	11.82
2006	Shaunna Thompson	11.89
2007	Jodie Williams	12.03
2008	Makeda Lewis	12.38
2009	Dina Asher-Smith	12.10
2010	Dina Asher-Smith	12.00
2011	Maya Bruney	12.29

150 YARDS

(Event instituted in 1959; discontinued after 1968)

1959	Beryl Wear	17.0
1960	Beryl Wear	16.9
1961	Beryl Wear	17.0
1962	Maureen Tranter	16.8
1963	Shena Willshire	17.1
1964	Marilyn North	17.0
1965	Wendy Kavanagh	16.6
1966	Linda Barratt	17.1
1967	Marilyn Neufville	17.3
1968	Sheila Richardson	17.0

200 METRES

(Event instituted in 1969)

1969	Sharon Colyear	25.5
1970	Sonia Lannaman	25.0
1971	Gillian Spurgin	26.1
1972	Jane Colebrook (Finch)	25.0
1973	Anne Baldock	25.5
1974	Susan Howells	24.9
1975	Fay Nixon	25.5
1976	Debbie Bunn	24.4w
1977	Jane Parry	24.49
1978	Jane Parry	24.57
1979	Elaine Mitchell	25.47
1980	Simmone Jacobs	25.03
1981	Simmone Jacobs	24.58
1982	Bernadette Ross	24.68
1983	Hayley Clements	24.40
1984	Tracy Goddard	25.15
1985	Annabel Soper	25.28
1986	Annabel Soper	24.84w
1987	Donna Fraser	24.59w
1988	Lisa Armstrong	25.53
1989	Katharine Merry	23.74w
1990	Catherine Murphy	25.53w
1991	Jo Sloane	25.42
1992	Emma Ania	25.63
1993	Tatum Nelson	24.51
1994	Sarah Wilhelmy	24.54
1995	Karlene Palmer	25.03
1996	Kimberley Canning	25.07
1997	Vernicha James	25.28
1998	Cherie Pierre	25.03w
1999	Amy Spencer	24.71
2000	Amy Spencer	24.50
2001	Nicola Gossman	24.85

2002	Joey Duck	25.49
2003	Joey Duck	24.74
2004	Chinedu Monye	24.50
2005	Shaunna Thompson	24.81
2006	Shaunna Thompson	24.40
2007	Jodie Williams	24.57w
2008	Jodie Williams	24.45
2009	Desiree Henry	24.22
2010	Dina Asher-Smith	24.77w
2011	Maya Bruney	25.24

800 METRES

(Event instituted at 880 yards in 1967; y = 880 yards)

1967	Doris Dixon	2:21.1y
1968	Mary Sonner	2:22.6y
1969	Chris Tranter (Benning)	2:17.8
1970	Lesley Cobden	2:19.0
1971	Chris Boxer (Cahill)	2:14.8
1972	Pat Byrne	2:15.7
1973	Elisabeth Spurgin	2:12.0
1974	Fay Nixon	2:15.2
1975	Sally Ludlam	2:11.9
1976	Kirsty McDermott (Wade)	2:11.1
1977	Maria Hennessy IRL	2:11.56
	(2, Judith Croasdale 2:11.97)	
1978	Lorraine Baker	2:09.77
1979	Karen Hughes	2:12.93
1980	Tonia McCullough	2:11.30
1981	Stacey Zartler USA	2:08.91
	(2, Hope Wallace 2:13.60)	
1982	Bernadette Hayes	2:15.52
1983	Karen Hill	2:13.55
1984	Sharron Davenport	2:12.17
1985	Emma Langston	2:10.91
1986	Emma Langston	2:09.90
1987	Michelle Wilkinson	2:13.42
1988	Joanne Davis (Pavey)	2:12.94
1989	Tiffany Davey	2:14.17
1990	Esther Merchant	2:17.7
1991	Hannah Curnock	2:12.62
1992	Hannah Curnock	2:09.80
1993	Jennifer Ward	2:16.61
1994	Amanda Pritchard	2:12.2
1995	Jenny Meadows	2:15.13
1996	Nikki Daniels	2:15.59
1997	Iona McIntyre	2:13.98
1998	Lisa Dobriskey	2:12.79
1999	Charlotte Moore	2:13.64
2000	Hayley Beard	2:10.89

2001	Elizabeth McWilliams	2:16.26
2002	Laura Crowe IRL	2:10.37
	(2, Nikki Hamblin 2:11.29)	
2003	Gillian Moss	2:13.63
2004	Lynsey Sharp	2:09.98
2005	Ciara Cronin IRL	2:11.97
	(2, Lucy McLoughlin 2:14.78)	
2006	Alexandra Turner	2:10.65
2007	Adelle Tracey	2:12.90
2008	Mel Wood	2:11.45
2009	Lauren Bell	2:14.57
2010	Sophie Riches	2:12.62
2011	Bobby Clay	2:08.75

1500 METRES

(Event instituted in 1972)

1972	Helen Hill	4:41.7
1973	Anne Tunnicliffe	4:36.0
1974	Sally Ludlam	4:39.7
1975	Janice Moody	4:43.9
1976	Sara Harris	4:36.5
1977	Carole Meagan IRL	4:32.54
	(Julie Clarke 4:37.7)	
1978	Amanda Alford	4:39.07
1979	Lynne MacDougall	4:34.34
1980	Elise Lyon	4:35.45
1981	Helen Appleby	4:38.18
1982	Rachel Hughes	4:32.12
1983	Claire Pattison	4:37.46
1984	Suzanne Healey	4:37.23
1985	Julie Adkin	4:38.98
1986	Julie Adkin	4:34.90
1987	Claire Nicholson	4:32.82
1988	Joanne Davis (Pavey)	4:30.23
1989	Claire Allen	4:37.79
1990	Isabel Linaker	4:32.3
1991	Sarah Willicombe	4:40.94
1992	Hannah Curnock	4:36.92
1993	Dawn Adams	4:40.89
1994	Emma Alberts	4:38.60
1995	Emma Ward	4:41.58
1996	Jenny Mockler	4:39.47
1997	Louise Damen	4:39.6
1998	Charlotte Moore	4:44.12
1999	Courtney Birch	4:35.98
2000	Melissa Wall	4:39.80
2001	Charlotte Browning	4:35.85
2002	Charlotte Browning	4:35.83
2003	Emily Pidgeon	4:29.28

2004	Joanne Harvey	4:34.82
2005	Louise Webb	4:40.21
2006	Katie Holt	4:34.20
2007	Melissa Courtney	4:33.01
2008	Emelia Gorecka	4:27.90
2009	Jessica Judd	4:29.48
2010	Abbie Hetherington	4:39.03
2011	Sian Rainsley	4:43.81

75 METRES HURDLES

(Event instituted at 75 yards in 1947; 70 yards from 1952; 80 yards from 1964; 75m from 1970; 2' 6" hurdles)

1947	Beryl Stoner	12.0
1948	M. Law	11.8
1949	Mavis Stafford	11.5
1950	H. Mitchell	11.4
1951	Sylvia Dawes	12.1
1952	S. Sibbett	10.8
1953	Alma Osborne	10.6
1954	Sheila Gould	11.3
1955	Cherie Rowlands	10.6
1956	Ann Charlesworth	10.6
1957	Cynthia Kempson	10.3
1958	Cynthia Kempson	10.2
1959	Angela Charman	10.2
1960	Susan Beldham	10.2
1961	Sandra Anderson	10.3
1962	Josephine Kendle	10.2
1963	Ann Wilson	10.2
1964	Ann Wilson	11.5
1965	Jane Matthews	11.4
1966	Susan Turpin	11.4
1967	Denise Etheridge	11.3
1968	Blondelle Thompson (Caines)	11.2
1969	Nnenna Njoku	11.3
1970	Ann Firman	11.6
1971	Sue Mapstone	11.6
1972	Helen Murray	11.5
1973	Susan Nomo	11.4
1974	Jill Duffield	11.5
1975	Wendy McDonnell	11.4
1976	Pat Campbell	11.35
1977	Caroline Porter	11.51
1978	Lynda Playel	11.22
1979	Noelle Morrissey IRL (2, Lynn Parry 11.44)	11.24
1980	Noelle Morrissey IRL (2, Natalie Byer 11.01)	10.92
	Noelle Morrissey IRL (80m)	11.48

	(2, Juliet Kay 12.26)	
1981	Olive Burke IRL (80m)	11.75
	(2, Sonia Maynard 11.84)	
1982	Michelle Stone (80m)	11.9
1983	Paula Khouri (80m)	11.7w
1984	Julie Mulcock	11.28w
1985	Rachel Halstead-Peel	10.98
1986	Lydia Chadwick	11.13
1987	Angie Thorp	11.17w
1988	Catherine Murphy	11.09
1989	Diane Allahgreen	11.16
1990	Orla Bermingham	11.2
1991	Julie McAughtrie	11.40
1992	Liz Fairs	11.43
1993	Julie Pratt	11.51
1994	Leanda Adams	11.30
1995	Naomi Hodge-Dalloway	11.13
1996	Helen Worsey	11.48
1997	Lauren McLoughlin	11.42
1998	Danielle Selley	11.08
1999	Symone Belle	11.20
2000	Heather Jones	11.1
2001	Heather Jones	10.95
2002	Clare Cooper	11.17
2003	Natalie Doyle	11.20
2004	Senta Solomon	11.24
2005	Helen van Kempen	10.91
2006	Jenny White	11.40
2007	Grace Christopher	11.16
2008	Jasmin Miller	11.45
2009	Hayley McLean	11.13
2010	Alicia Tymon-McEwan	11.07
2011	Moesha Howard	11.00

HIGH JUMP

(Event instituted in 1945)

1945	M. Brewer	1.45
1946	Christine Wheeler	1.42
1947	M. Trendall	1.40
1948	M. Ingram	1.40
1949	S. Lapidge	1.42
1950	Ursula Hynes	1.50
1951	Brenda Cox	1.47
1952	S. Moore	1.47
1953	S. Moore	1.40
1954	S. Rundley	1.47
1955	Nina Bliss	1.50
1956	Irish Welsh	1.52
1957	Patricia Ford	1.55

1958	Gwenda Matthews	
	(Hurst/Ward)	1.60
1959	Gwenda Matthews	1.57
1960	Christine Osbourne	1.52
1961	Janet Brown	1.50
1962	Janet Hopkins	1.47
1963	Ann Wilson	1.57
1964	Ann Wilson	1.57
1965	Leonie Esdaile	1.47
1966	Barbara-Anne Barrett	1.55
1967	Sylvia Rampton	1.50
1968	Christine Bird	1.50
1969	Ann Wetherall	1.48
1970	Gillian Howell	1.45
1971	Gillian Howell	1.53
1972	Jackie Matthews	1.62
1973	Jacqueline Buss	1.58
1974	Val Kelly	1.71
1975	Gail Sumner	1.67
1976	Barbara Simmonds	1.73
1977	Lorinda Matthews	1.74
1978	Claire Summerfield	1.73
1979	Claire Summerfield	1.78
1980	Julia Charlton	1.70
1981	Louise Manning	1.69
1982	Ursula Fay	1.80
1983	Sarah Bailiff	1.66
1984	Jo Jennings	1.78
1985	Tracey Clarke	1.70
1986	Lea Haggett	1.81
1987	Janice Anderson	1.65
1988	Jane Falconer	1.68
1989	Jane Falconer	1.73
1990	Alison May	1.60
1991	Lindsay Evans	1.70
1992	Kellie Durham	1.68
1993	Lee McConnell	1.70
1994	Antonia Bemrose	1.70
1995	Alison Kerboas	1.65
1996	Deirdre Ryan IRL	1.70
	(2, Sophie McQueen 1.69)	
1997	Sonia Crawley	1.63
1998	Aileen Wilson	1.75
1999	Michelle Doherty IRL	1.61
	(2, Jessica Ennis 1.61)	
2000	Jessica Ennis	1.60
2001	Shani Rainford	1.64
2002	Dominique Blaize	1.65
2003	Vikki Hubbard	1.72

2004	Maureen Farrell IRL	1.63
2005	Hannah Dickson	1.63
2006	Katarina Johnson-Thompson	1.64
2007	Katarina Johnson-Thompson	1.72
2008	Jazmin Sawyers	1.61
2009	Jordanna Morrish	1.65
2010	Morgan Lake	1.65
2011	Morgan Lake	1.75

POLE VAULT

(Event instituted in 2007)

2007	Ellie Besford	3.30
2008	Katie Byres	3.35
2009	Lucy Bryan	3.48
2010	Naomi Lee	3.11
2011	Clare Dyer	3.30

LONG JUMP

(Event instituted in 1945)

1945	P. Giles	4.46
1946	Jennifer Monday	4.90
1947	Lorna Cornell	4.84
1948	B. I. Marles	4.68
1949	Audrey Cashmore	5.03
1950	Shirley Hampton (Pirie)	4.61
1951	M. Parker	4.52
1952	Pamela Drew	4.70
1953	A. Brett	4.91
1954	A. Smith	5.33
1955	C. Fox	4.68
1956	Patricia Martin	5.34
1957	S. Cave	5.01
1958	Margaret Blatcher	5.07
1959	L Harrington	5.14
1960	Helen Harris	5.24
1961	Maureen Barton	5.41
1962	Patricia Wilson	5.03
1963	Ann Vincent	5.38
1964	Ann Wilson	5.45
1965	Valerie Fox	5.50
1966	Sue Scott (Reeve)	5.42
1967	Frances Young	5.69w
1968	Shirley Biggs	5.28
1969	Susan King	5.60
1970	Teresa Goodson	5.32w
1971	Sue Mapstone	5.35
1972	Patricia Northall	5.15
1973	Mandy Killoran	5.27
1974	Mandy Killoran	5.29

1975	Kim Hagger	5.42
1976	Kim Hagger	5.85
1977	Sandy French	5.72
1978	Sandy French	5.81
1979	Yvonne Anderson	5.48
1980	Sally Gunnell	5.56
1981	Georgina Oladapo	5.45
1982	Debbie Marti	5.76
1983	Margaret Cheetham	6.20
1984	Fiona May	6.07
1985	Jo Wise	5.41
1986	Samantha Bird	5.31
1987	Jackie Harris	5.83
1988	Lisa Armstrong	5.30
1989	Claire Ingerton IRL	5.49w
	(3, Nicola Walton 5.17)	
1990	Linzie Kerr	5.56
1991	Tammy McCammon	5.86
1992	Rebecca Lewis	5.49
1993	Sarah Wilhelmy	5.72w
1994	Jade Johnson	5.68
1995	Caroline Pearce	5.47
1996	Fiona Harrison	5.78w
1997	Elaine Smith	5.17
1998	Zainab Ceesay	5.55w
1999	Symone Belle	5.82w ?
2000	Aimee Palmer	5.23
2001	Rebekah Passley	5.86
2002	Amy Harris	5.59w
2003	Kim Murray	5.54
2004	Alexandra Russell	5.71
2005	Jade Nimmo	5.63w
2006	Jill Brooks	5.44
2007	Katarina Johnson-Thompson	5.57
2008	Gabby Rowsell	5.49w
2009	Jahisha Thomas	5.43
2010	Morgan Lake	5.60
2011	Morgan Lake	5.93

SHOT

(Event instituted in 1958; 6lb/2.72kg until 1963; 7lb/3.175kg 1964-1970; 3.25kg since 1971)

1958	Rona Fuller	9.88
1959	Valerie Woods	10.92
1960	Moira Kerr	11.39
1961	Kathy Duckett	11.79
1962	Jean Davies	11.49
1963	Hilary Fairclough	12.91
1964	Elaine Bridges	10.40

1965	Jenny Bloss	12.18
1966	Margaret Smith	10.97
1967	Debbie Kerr	12.08
1968	Sheila Kaye	10.67
1969	Betsy Lyons	12.43
1970	Judith Potts	11.61
1971	Ann Kidger	11.27
1972	Ereka Service	10.41
1973	Yvonne Stewart	11.37
1974	Marita Walton IRL	11.26
	(2, Ionie Samuels 10.85)	
1975	Maureen Tree	12.43
1976	Amanda Franks	11.80
1977	Susan Bracey	11.53
1978	Cynthia Gregory	12.69
1979	Susan King	13.12
1980	Iona Doyley	12.75
1981	Terri Salt	12.91
1982	Sarah Eldridge	12.24
1983	Jane Shepherd	11.37
1984	Justine Buttle	12.38
1985	Sara Allen	11.79
1986	Natalie Hart	11.89
1987	Claire Burnett	11.84
1988	Sira Robinson	11.71
1989	Rebecca Shreeve	11.78
1990	Donna King	10.64
1991	Julie Robin	12.04
1992	Philippa Roles	12.85
1993	Catherine Garden	12.28
1994	Frances Reid-Hughes	11.16
1995	Amy Wilson	11.93
1996	Rachel Harley	11.37
1997	Claire Smithson	12.41
1998	Gillian Austin IRL	11.58
1999	Frances Miller	11.68
2000	Lucy Sutton	11.57
2001	Chloe Edwards	11.70
2002	Tolani Agoro	11.83
2003	Eden Francis	13.76
2004	Rachel Wallader	12.07
2005	Jenny Brown	12.29
2006	Claire Fitzgerald IRL	12.61
	(2, Amber-Louise O'Brien 11.37)	
2007	Lauren Sammout	11.29
2008	Abbi Carter	11.96
2009	Shadine Duquemin	12.62
2010	Annabel Sherry	12.88
2011	Adele Nicoll	14.12

DISCUS

(Event instituted in 1956)

Year	Name	Mark
1956	Carole Saunders	29.72
1957	S. Harvey	27.22
1958	Wendy Thomas	34.09
1959	Elizabeth-Mary Robertson	30.44
1960	Pamela Quelch	32.99
1961	Kathy Duckett	32.72
1962	Heather Horsburgh	34.02
1963	Heather Horsburgh	33.53
1964	Patricia Denton	31.93
1965	Linda Enever	30.75
1966	Linda Pears	30.71
1967	Carol Richardson	31.47
1968	Jackie Elsmore	33.35
1969	Ann Wetherall	30.80
1970	Lesley Mallin	32.40
1971	Yvonne Page	33.48
1972	Lynn Robertson	34.36
1973	Val Watson	32.50
1974	Fiona Condon	33.60
1975	Fiona Condon	34.48
1976	Amanda Franks	38.12
1977	Sandra McDonald	36.80
1978	Sandra McDonald	38.46
1979	Linda Higman	36.98
1980	Karen Pugh	38.72
1981	Mandy Hampton	36.10
1982	Belinda Hockley	34.66
1983	Rosanne Lister	32.22
1984	Jayne Thornton	31.52
1985	Charladee Clarke	38.46
1986	Natalie Hart	35.34
1987	Ann-Marie Flannery IRL (2, Alix Gallagher 35.94)	36.26
1988	Emma Merry	37.98
1989	Leanne Hughes	31.06
1990	Charlotte Davies	31.20
1991	Julie Robin	38.86
1992	Philippa Roles	42.06
1993	Lauren Keightley	37.04
1994	Natalie Kerr	37.12
1995	Joan McPherson	35.90
1996	Emma Carpenter	35.96
1997	Claire Smithson	37.62
1998	Angela Lockley	33.66
1999	Donna Swatheridge	34.53
2000	Christina Carding	33.33

2001	Christina Carding	36.70
2002	Ruth Hay	34.40
2003	Eden Francis	38.49
2004	Lucy Underdown	33.42
2005	Katie Wickman	37.45
2006	Tyne Breen	32.84
2007	Charlotte Gair	32.23
2008	Abbi Carter	35.48
2009	Shadine Duquemin	37.72
2010	Emily Lupton	36.81
2011	Adele Nicoll	39.97

HAMMER

(Event instituted in 2006)

2006	Helen Broadbridge	43.22
2007	Gaby McNally	49.17
2008	Louisa James	49.81
2009	Kimberley Reed	45.73
2010	Alice Akers IRL	47.68
	(2, Zoe Dakin 42.39)	
2011	Alice Akers IRL	56.20
	(2, Rebecca Keating 48.87)	

JAVELIN

(Event instituted in 1956; current specification javelin used from 1999)

1956	Rosemary Morgan	32.57
1957	A. Turner	30.52
1958	A. James	33.14
1959	Margaret White	35.40
1960	Susan Tadd	32.85
1961	Cynthia Patrick	38.71
1962	Jackie Wainwright	35.38
1963	Veronica Powell	34.65
1964	Fiona Smith	29.40
1965	Shara Spragg	31.56
1966	Marlene Garner	35.36
1967	Rosemary Cole	29.36
1968	Lynda Bennett	31.85
1969	Anne Goodlad	35.40
1970	Susan James	39.14
1971	Christine Green	34.16
1972	Marian Mendham	34.32
1973	Gillian Grey	33.88
1974	Christine Whitmore	34.70
1975	Jackie Brown	39.42
1976	Joan Kenyon	38.34
1977	Julie Hawkins	37.18
1978	Karen Miller	35.92
1979	Julie Tayler	33.48

1980	Maxine Worsfold	38.30
1981	Catherine Garside	33.92
1982	Karen Hough	38.70
1983	Alison Moffitt	36.90
1984	Alison Moffitt	36.04
1985	Rebecca Foster	35.46
1986	Kerry Tudor	38.00
1987	Mandy Liverton	40.02
1988	Debbie Boomer	34.52
1989	Kirsty Morrison	39.04
1990	Kirsty Morrison	46.98
1991	Angharad Richards	38.78
1992	Jenny Foster	40.80
1993	Kelly Morgan	36.66
1994	Kelly Morgan	36.08
1995	Lucy Rann	37.36
1996	Melanie Vaggers	35.72
1997	Carol Wallbanks	35.76
1998	Samantha Redd	39.81
1999	Lauren Therin	38.01
2000	Christine Lawrence	34.84
2001	Louise Watton	38.29
2002	Lucy Boggis	32.09
2003	Lucy Boggis	35.99
2004	Peta Lundgren	35.61
2005	Robyn Purchase	36.11
2006	Claire Fitzgerald IRL	36.39
	(2, Izzy Jeffs 35.45)	
2007	Kike Oniwinde	37.74
2008	Freya Jones	43.42
2009	Laura McDonald	41.89
2010	Natasha Wilson	39.20
2011	Isobel McHattie	38.21

PENTATHLON

(Event instituted in 1967)

1967	Debbie Kerr	3684
1968	Shirley Biggs	3840
1969	Nnenna Njoku	4000
1970	Ann Hull	3680
1971	Sue Mapstone	3718
1972	Joy Bowerman	3315
1973	Geraldine Gray	3154
1974	Brenda Gauntlett	3453
1975	Angela Rothwell	3694
1976	Kim Hagger	3917
1977	Wendy Laing	3399w
1978	Sandy French	3389
1979	Julie Frampton	3281

1980	Linda Wong	3309
1981	Catherine Brown	3388
1982	Claire Smith	3586
1983	Jane Shepherd	3671
1984	Jacqueline Cotton	3174
1985	Kate Barlow	2848
1986	Kate Barlow	2942w
1987	Jackie Harris	3311
1988	Tanya Lazar	2929
1989	Jane Falconer	2874
1990	Leone Dickinson	2850
1991	Teresa Andrews	2888
1992	Louise Dixon	3023
1993	Claire Everett	3196
1994	Katherine Livesey	3142
1995	Tina Thirwell	2613
1996	Tina Thirwell	2867w
1997	Rebecca Jones	2811
1998	Aileen Wilson	3027
1999	Symone Belle	3158
2000	Jessica Ennis	3109
2001	Cherri Morrison	2861
2002	Jade Surman	3126
2003	Kalyn Sheehan IRL	3054w
	(3, Kathryn Davies 2925)	
2004	Kalyn Sheehan IRL	3309
	(2, Meghan Beesley 3069)	
2005	Alice Lennox	3056
2006	Jill Brooks	3087
2007	Katarina Johnson-Thompson	3418
2008	Katie Gardner	3064
2009	Hayley McLean	3143
2010	Morgan Lake	3676

TRACK WALK

(Event instituted at 2500m in 1973; 3000m from 1990; mixed races since 1998)

1973	Dorothy Ilderton	13:26.2
1974	Elaine Cox	12:53.2
1975	Elaine Cox	13:09.4
1976	Karen Eden	13:34.27
1977	Karen Eden	13:17.0
1978	Jillian Mullins	13:07.6
1979	Angela Copeland	13:26.0
1980	Karen Bowers	12:43.0
1981	Lisa Langford	13:04.52
1982	Sally Clark	12:53.83
1983	Susan Ashforth	12:55.77
1984	Susan Ashforth	11:59.8

1985	Julie Snead	12:40.5
1986	Tracy Devlin	12:49.49
1987	Tracy Devlin	12:21.94
1988	Nicola Greenfield	13:01.12
1989	Carla Jarvis	12:56.32
1990	Nikki Parsons	16:28.92
1991	Lucy Butterley	16:27.48
1992	Nina Howley	16:16.52
1993	Sarah Bennett	15:47.0
1994	Sarah Bennett	15:28.31
1995	Kelly Mann	15:41.0
1996	Katie Ford	16:07.95
1997	Nicola Phillips	15:40.37
1998	Natalie Evans	15:41.71
1999	Natalie Geens	16:03.49
2000	Carol Burtonshaw IRL (2, Natasha Fox 17:03.12)	16:43.43
2001	Rebecca Mersh	16:03.25
2002	Rebecca Mersh	15:26.01
2003	Rebecca Mersh	15:09.10
2004	Kathryn Granger	16:04.35
2005	Kathryn Granger	15:43.76
2006	Natalie Myers	16:08.65
2007	Lauren Whelan	16:07.97
2008	Katie Veale IRL (2, Kelsey Howard 16:46.58)	14:16.63
2009	Katie Funnell	16:03.07
2010	Emma Achurch	16:40.68

4x110 YARDS RELAY

(Event instituted in 1949)

1949	Chesterfield	52.5
1950	Spartan Ladies	53.2
1951	Spartan Ladies	51.5
1952	Spartan Ladies	53.4
1953	Spartan Ladies	52.0
1954	Spartan Ladies	52.8
1955	Selsonia Ladies	51.0
1956	London Olympiades	52.2
1957	London Olympiades	50.8
1958	Middlesex Ladies	51.1
1959	Southend	50.5

INDOORS

WAAA/AAA title winners from 1966 to 2006 inclusive; England champions from 2007 to 2012
(Where the title was won by an overseas athlete, the highest placed UK athlete is shown in brackets)
Main Venues: 1966–1991 Cosford; 1992–2012 Birmingham

JUNIORS (UNDER 20)

60 METRES

(Event instituted in 1985)

Year	Athlete	Time
1985	Helen Miles	7.55
1986	Sue Briggs	7.5
1987	Christine Chambers	7.5
1988	Christine Chambers	7.58
1989	Aileen McGillivary	7.58
1990	Vivienne Francis	7.52
1991	Lisa Armstrong	7.48
1992	Joice Maduaka	7.59
1993	Diane Allahgreen	7.55
1994	Diane Allahgreen	7.53
1995	Ellena Ruddock	7.75
1996	Malgorzata Rostek	7.55
1997	Rebecca Drummond	7.50
1998	Rebecca White	7.55
1999	Ciara Sheehy IRL	7.54
	(2, Susan Burnside 7.66)	
2000	Donna Maylor	7.65
2001	Danielle Norville	7.54
2002	Jeanette Kwakye	7.52
2003	Montell Douglas	7.62
2004	Sinead Johnson	7.57
2005	Montell Douglas	7.50
2006	Claire Brady IRL	7.70
	(2, Amy Godsell 7.73)	
2007	Jennifer Taker	7.52
2008	Anike Shand-Whittingham	7.47
2009	Folaki Akinyemi NGR	7.45
	(3, Corinne Humphreys 7.61)	
2010	Marilyn Nwawulor	7.47
2011	Annie Tagoe	7.41
2012	Jodie Williams	7.47

200 METRES

(Event instituted in 1985)

Year	Athlete	Time
1985	Lesley-Ann Skeete	25.05
1986	Sue Briggs	24.9
1987	Michelle Hammond	25.3

1988	not held	
1989	Ruth Williams	24.94
1990	Lisa Armstrong	25.11
1991	Val Theobalds	24.65
1992	Sophia Smith	25.03
1993	Sophia Smith	24.40
1994	Debbie Mant	24.78
1995	Victoria Shipman	25.16
1996	Victoria Shipman	24.39
1997	Dion Graham JAM	24.63
	(3, Eleanor Mardle 25.02)	
1998	Rebecca White	24.17
1999	Ciara Sheehy IRL	23.96
	(2, Emma Whitter 24.27)	
2000	Lowri Jones	24.60
2001	Vernicha James	23.80
2002	Claire Bergin IRL	24.38
	(2, Jemma Sims 24.81)	
2003	Anyika Onuora	24.30
2004	Montell Douglas	24.00
2005	Lucy Sargent	23.78
2006	Joey Duck	24.24
2007	Joey Duck	24.05
2008	Niamh Whelan IRL	23.92
	(2, Meghan Beesley 23.97)	
2009	Niamh Whelan IRL	23.98
	(2, Emily Diamond 24.00)	
2010	Jennie Batten	23.82
2011	Desiree Henry	23.92
2012	Hannah Thomas	24.51

400 METRES

(Event instituted in 1988)

1988	Sally-Ann Frisby	57.76
1989	Tanya Blake	57.01
1990	Claire Raven	56.71
1991	Claire Raven	55.30
1992	Vyv Rhodes	57.10
1993	Sarah Smith	58.29
1994	Allison Curbishley	54.78
1995	Allison Curbishley	54.43
1996	Vicki Jamison	56.13
1997	Lesley Owusu	55.66
1998	Carey Easton	55.29
1999	Helen Thieme	56.31
2000	Jenny Meadows	55.34
2001	Lesley Clarkson	56.39
2002	Lindsey Singer	55.81
2003	Victoria Griffiths	54.28

2004	Faye Harding	55.75
2005	Laura Gillhespy	55.75
2006	Emma Cloggie	55.27
2007	Erica Smith	56.93
2008	Meghan Beesley	53.84
2009	Shelayna Oskan	55.79
2010	Victoria Ohuruogu	55.36
2011	Kirsten McAslan	54.66
2012	Megan Rogers	56.13

800 METRES

(Event instituted in 1985)

1985	Sonia Cundy	2:16.01
1986	Bev Nicholson	2:10.8
1987	Michelle Faherty	2:11.7
1988	Lynn Gibson	2:12.64
1989	Jody Allen	2:09.86
1990	Helen Whitley	2:15.93
1991	Arlene Smith IRL	2:08.74
	(2, Natalie Tait 2:09.48)	
1992	Arlene Smith IRL	2:09.07
	(2, Lesley Mallows 2:10.39)	
1993	Hannah Curnock	2:12.66
1994	Dorothea Lee	2:10.67
1995	Rhonda MacPhee	2:11.96
1996	Emma Davies	2:13.08
1997	Emma Davies	2:08.55
1998	Joanna Ross	2:11.20
1999	Catherine Riley	2:10.18
2000	Iona McIntyre	2:13.88
2001	Becky Lyne	2:10.67
2002	Nisha Desai	2:16.33
2003	Rachael Thompson	2:09.19
2004	Rachael Thompson	2:06.96
2005	Carolyn Plateau	2:07.27
2006	Carolyn Plateau	2:14.73
2007	Rachel Stringer	2:12.92
2008	Rachel Stringer	2:06.91
2009	Leigh Lennon	2:11.36
2010	Ciara Mageean IRL	2:07.79
	(2, Leigh Lennon 2:09.85)	
2011	Jenny Beckingham	2:11.79
2012	Madeleine Austin	2:12.39

1500 METRES

(Event instituted in 1989)

1989	Adele Rankin	4:38.67
1991	Natalie Tait	4:34.52
1992	Amanda Crowe	4:30.46

1993	Sarah Bouchard	4:44.43
1994	Jeina Mitchell	4:32.11
1995	Anne Connolly	4:40.98
1996	Juliette Oldfield	4:27.71
1997	Anne Connolly	4:36.21
1998	Camilla Waite	4:53.57
1999	Leanne Appleton	4:36.39
2000	Lisa Dobriskey	4:33.95
2001	Jo Ankier	4:31.79
2002	Zoe Jelbert	4:34.40
2004	Isabel Stoate	4:44.42
2005	Hannah England	4:35.59
2006	Emily Pidgeon	4:30.87
2007	Sarah Hopkinson	4:43.43
2008	Katie Clark	4:33.94
2009	Vicky Fouhy	4:28.93
2010	Gemma Kersey	4:37.54
2011	Gemma Kersey	4:36.90
2012	Laura Farrar	4:55.09

3000 METRES

(Event instituted in 1989; discontinued after 2001)

1989	Jenny Hawthorne	10:07.39
1993	Isabel Linaker	9:57.42
1994	Charlotte Goff	10:24.70
1995	Anne Welsh	10:24.47
1996	Paula Gowing	10:23.71
1997	Christina Radon	9:47.60
2000	Zoe Jelbert	9:37.54
2001	Zoe Jelbert	9:48.55

60 METRES HURDLES

(Event instituted in 1987; 2ft 9in hurdles)

1987	Karen Gibbs	9.0
1988	Carol Whiteway	9.08
1989	Susan Smith IRL	8.63
	(2, Angie Thorp 8.67)	
1990	Angie Thorp	8.44
1991	Sam Baker & Angie Thorp	8.42
1992	Bethan Edwards	8.47
1993	Jane Hale	8.57
1994	Diane Allahgreen	8.47
1995	Natasha Danvers	8.60
1996	Natasha Danvers	8.39
1997	Julie Pratt	8.59
1998	Sarah Claxton	8.53
1999	Derval O'Rourke IRL	8.46
	(2, Tamsin Stephens 8.74)	
2000	Helen Worsey	8.69

2001	Lauren McLoughlin	8.61
2002	Symone Belle	8.58
2003	Symone Bell	8.47
2004	Channelle Garnett	8.68
2005	Nicola Robinson	8.49
2006	Zara Hohn	8.42
2007	Serita Solomon	8.38
2008	Tale Orving NOR	8.66
	(2, Meghan Beesley 8.60)	
2009	Stephanie Gaynor	8.52
2010	Sandra Seaton	8.62
2011	Marilyn Nwawulor	8.47
2012	Yasmin Miller	8.45

HIGH JUMP

(Event instituted in 1989)

1989	Julia Bennett	1.81
1990	Kelly Mason	1.80
1991	Claire Phythian	1.75
1992	Alison Evans	1.74
1993	Diana Bennett	1.72
1994	Lindsay Evans	1.73
1995	Michelle Dunkley	1.79
1996	Rachael Forrest	1.80
1997	Michelle Dunkley	1.89
1998	Chloe Cozens	1.75
1999	Chloe Cozens	1.78
2000	Aileen Wilson	1.79
2001	Deirdre Ryan IRL	1.81
	(2, Stephanie Higham 1.70)	
2002	Stephanie Higham	1.75
2003	Aileen Wilson	1.78
2004	Sarah Fielding-Smith	1.76
2005	Vikki Hubbard	1.78
2006	Stephanie Pywell	1.77
2007	Vikki Hubbard	1.85
2008	Pamela Hughes IRL	1.75
	(3, Bethan Partridge 1.65)	
2009	Amy Marchant	1.72
2010	Katarina Johnson-Thompson	1.81
2011	Isobel Pooley	1.86
2012	Katarina Johnson-Thompson	1.85

POLE VAULT

(Event instituted in 1994)

1994	Dawn-Alice Wright	2.85
1995	Clare Ridgley	3.00
1996	Clare Ridgley	3.51
1997	Rebecca Roles	3.10

1998	Laura Patterson	3.25
1999	Becky Ridgley	3.40
2000	Ellie Spain	3.65
2001	Lindsay Hodges	3.66
2002	Kate Dennison	3.91
2003	Kate Dennison	3.70
2004	Natalie Olson	3.60
2005	Kim Skinner	3.80
2006	Kim Skinner	3.80
2007	Jessica Abraham	3.50
2008	Maria Seager	3.70
2009	Sophie Upton	3.80
2010	Katie Byres	4.01
2011	Ellie Besford	3.50
2012	Lucy Bryan	3.80

LONG JUMP

(Event instituted in 1985)

1985	Jacqui Stokes IRL	5.41
1987	Lorraine Lynch	5.50
1988	Karen Hambrook	5.94
1989	Julia Bennett	5.75
1990	Michelle Griffith	6.02
1991	Ruth Irving	5.80
1992	Ruth Irving	5.94
1993	Jo Dear	5.93
1994	Jo Dear	5.94
1995	Tammy McCammon	5.76
1996	Grainne O'Malley IRL	5.66
	(2, Claire Everett 5.40)	
1997	Sarah Claxton	5.94
1998	Danielle Freeman	5.96
1999	Denise Andrews	5.66
2000	Rachel Hogg	5.64
2001	Danielle Humphreys	5.78
2002	Symone Belle	5.94
2003	Karlene Turner	5.69
2004	Louise Bloor	5.97
2005	Jade Surman	5.76
2006	Amy Harris	6.15
2007	Kelly Proper IRL	6.17
	(2, Emily Martin 5.62)	
2008	Abigail Irozuru	5.97
2009	Lorraine Ugen	5.80
2010	Katarina Johnson-Thompson	6.25
2011	Katarina Johnson-Thompson	6.28
2012	Katarina Johnson-Thompson	6.30

TRIPLE JUMP
(Event instituted in 1991)

1991	Kate Evans	11.31
1992	Kate Evans	11.54
1993	Shani Anderson	12.14
1994	Kathryn Blackwood	11.28
1995	Catherine Burrows	11.72
1996	Liz Gibbens	12.20
1997	Julia Johnson	11.64
1998	Judy Kotey	12.07
1999	Leandra Pollus	11.74
2000	Angela Williams	12.00
2001	Rachel Peacock	12.01
2002	Linsi Robinson	11.84
2003	Karlene Turner	12.41
2004	Anna Kelly	12.00
2005	Yasmine Regis	12.65
2006	Denae Matthew	12.56
2007	Jayne Nisbet	12.37
2008	Mia Nielsen Haave NOR	12.89
	(2, Melissa Carr 12.10)	
2009	Laura Samuel	12.40
2010	Laura Samuel	12.74
2011	Naomi Reid	12.16
2012	Ahtollah Rose	12.28

SHOT
(Event instituted in 1985; 4kg)

1985	Kathryn Farr	13.91
1986	Mary Anderson	14.88
1988	Jayne Thornton	14.01
1989	Jayne Berry	14.54
1990	Dawn Grazette	13.01
1991	Dawn Grazette	14.42
1992	Emma Merry	13.06
1993	Ujo Efobi	14.13
1994	Eleanor Gatrell	11.18
1995	Philippa Roles	13.72
1996	Natasha Smith	14.09
1997	Christina Bennett	14.27
1998	Julie Dunkley	14.30
1999	Eva Massey	12.71
2000	Claire Smithson	13.09
2001	Charlotte Spelzini	13.10
2002	Charlotte Spelzini	13.59
2003	Alison Rodger	12.73
2004	Chloe Edwards	13.76
2005	Chloe Edwards	14.04

2006	Eden Francis	13.98
2007	Eden Francis	14.85
2008	Rachel Wallder	14.43
2009	Shaunagh Brown	14.51
2010	Hannah Evenden	13.35
2011	Sophie McKinna	15.70
2012	Sophie McKinna	14.82

PENTATHLON

(Event instituted in 1995)

1995	Teresa Andrews	3564
1996	Nicola Gautier	3624
1997	Nicola Gautier	3702
1998	Danielle Freeman	3430
1999	Chloe Cozens	3707
2000	Rebecca Jones	3236
2001	Rebecca Jones	3592
2002	Jenny Pacey	3195
2003	Jessica Ennis	3719
2004	Samantha Backwell	3581
2005	Elizabeth Sweeney	3665
2006	Kelly Proper IRL	3666
	(2, Gemma Weetman 3643)	
2007	Jenny Lumley	3767
2008	Meghan Beesley	3908
2009	Sophie Wilkins	3543
2010	Alice Lennox	3633
2011	Marilyn Nwawulor	3606
2012	Katy Marchant	3935

3000 METRES WALK

(Event instituted in 1995; discontinued after 2006)

1995	Sarah Bennett	15:22.58
1996	Sarah Bennett	15:22.20
1997	Sarah Bennett	15:07.08
1998	Katie Ford	15:01.32
1999	Serena O'Keeffe IRL	15:06.55
	(2, Katie Ford 15:22.73)	
2000	Nicola Phillips	14:38.22
2001	Nicola Phillips	14:49.40
2002	Sophie Hales	14:34.11
2003	Sophie Hales	14:20.83
2004	Sophie Hales	13:36.43
2005	Rebecca Mersh	14:28.70
2006	Rebecca Mersh	14:40.94

INTERMEDIATES (UNDER 17)

60 METRES

(Event instituted in 1966; y = 60 yards)

1966	Anita Neil	7.2y
1967	Jacqueline Chidlow	7.7
1970	Christine Sprigg	7.7
1971	Rosemary Leech	7.6
1972	Gillian Spurgin	7.6
1973	Diane Heath	7.8
1974	Averil McClelland	7.6
1975	Janine MacGregor	7.7
1976	Fay Nixon	7.6
1977	Fay Nixon	7.6
1978	Pippa Baker	7.57
1979	Linsey Macdonald	7.5
1980	Jane Parry	7.56
1981	Nathalie Byer	7.5
1982	Nathalie Byer	7.63
1983	Georgina Oladapo	7.55
1984	Georgina Oladapo	7.50
1985	Stephanie Douglas	7.73
1986	Stephanie Douglas	7.64
1987	Lesley Lewis	7.72
1988	Kathleen Lithgow	7.69
1989	Renate Chinyou	7.59
1990	Lisa Armstrong	7.64
1991	Sophia Smith	7.64
1992	Jo Sloane	7.68
1993	Rebecca Drummond	7.78
1994	Tatum Nelson	7.61
1995	Sarah Wilhelmy	7.54
1996	Sarah Wilhelmy	7.59
1997	Donna Maylor	7.63
1998	Natalie Smellie	7.66
1999	Danielle Selley	7.70
2000	Vernicha James	7.58
2001	Amy Spencer	7.54
2002	Montell Douglas	7.59
2003	Sinead Johnson	7.56
2004	Joey Duck	7.62
2005	Chinedu Monye	7.73
2006	Asha Phillip	7.59
2007	Shaunna Thompson	7.55
2008	Shaunna Thompson	7.51
2009	Jodie Williams	7.53
2010	Olivia Callaghan	7.67
2011	Dina Asher-Smith	7.61
2012	Dina Asher-Smith	7.56

200 METRES

(Event instituted in 1983)

1983	Dawn Flockhart	24.81
1984	Jakki Harman	24.9
1985	Fiona Boswell	25.19
1986	Michelle Hammond	25.26
1987	Kim Goodwin	25.33
1988	Emma Langston	25.71
1989	Claire Phythian	25.70
1990	Lisa Armstrong	25.32
1991	Sophia Smith	25.03
1992	Jo Sloane	24.86
1993	Jo Sloane	24.98
1994	Laura Seston	25.04
1995	Sarah Wilhelmy	24.52
1996	Sarah Wilhelmy	24.69
1997	Emily Freeman	24.19
1998	Sarah Zawada	24.30
1999	Kim Wall	24.79
2000	Samantha Gamble	24.93
2001	Amy Spencer	24.14
2002	Phyllis Agbo	25.06
2003	Nicola Gossman	24.86
2004	Joey Duck	24.38
2005	Hayley Jones	24.44
2006	Chelsea Cooper	24.28
2007	Shaunna Thompson	24.59
2008	Shaunna Thompson	24.02
2009	Jennie Batten	24.32
2010	Desiree Henry	23.93
2011	Dina Asher-Smith	24.67
2012	Dina Asher-Smith	24.61

400/300 METRES

(Event instituted in 1971; 300m from 1990)

1971	Tina Greisen	61.4
1972	Christine McMeekin	58.9
1973	Jane Colebrook (Finch)	58.1
1974	Ann Robertson	56.7
1975	Deborah Bain	57.0
1976	Susan Howells	55.4
1977	Kim Bissell	57.1
1978	Linda Callow	58.9
1979	Linsey Macdonald	55.9
1980	Lorraine Baker	55.4
1981	Kay Simpson	57.0
1982	Carol Candlish	56.5
1983	Carol Candlish	55.62

1984	Georgina Honley	58.72
1985	Loreen Hall	55.89
1986	Lisa Hankin	57.48
1987	Amanda Salter	57.78
1988	Emma Langston	56.78
1989	Sonya Bowyer	59.07
1990	Samantha Taylor	42.59
1994	Ruth Nicholson	41.20
1995	Gael Davies	40.58
1996	Lindsay Impett	40.77
1997	Karlene Palmer	40.22
1998	Nicola Sanders	39.95
1999	Kim Wall	39.84
2000	Samantha Gamble	40.22
2001	Gemma Nicol	39.97
2002	Amy Spencer	37.72
2003	Holly Barlow	40.29
2004	Laura Gillhespy	40.26
2005	Lucy Sargent	39.37
2006	Alexandra Stuková SVK	39.93
	(Carmen Gedling 40.53)	
2007	Lucy James	39.97
2008	Katrina Thompson	38.56
2009	Victoria Ohuruogu	39.82
2010	Katie Kirk	39.2
2011	Sabrina Bakare	38.99
2012	Sabrina Bakare	39.16

800 METRES

(Event instituted in 1972)

1972	Evelyn McMeekin	2:18.4
1973	Evelyn McMeekin	2:11.9
1974	Jane Colebrook (Finch)	2:14.6
1975	Lesley Pamment	2:13.6
1976	Vivienne Weston	2:15.7
1977	Jo White	2:13.0
1978	Alison Clifford	2:12.6
1979	Jane Walker	2:11.1
1980	Lorraine Baker	2:10.3
1981	Lynne MacDougall	2:13.7
1982	Tonia McCullough	2:14.5
1983	Phillipa Weaver-Smith	2:13.20
1984	Anne Winter	2:12.90
1985	Michelle Faherty	2:11.90
1986	Lynne Robinson	2:11.62
1987	Jayne Heathcote	2:11.33
1988	Helen Whitley	2:14.82
1989	Della Butcher	2:15.86
1990	Arlene Smith IRL	2:16.67

	(2, Clare McBride 2:20.87)	
1991	Carolyn May	2:13.92
1992	Lucy Edge	2:19.30
1993	Helen Todd	2:15.30
1994	Helen Parsons	2:16.12
1995	Emma Davies	2:16.36
1996	Simone Hardy	2:15.58
1997	Karlene Tromans	2:18.90
1998	Catherine Riley	2:15.11
1999	Roisin Quinn IRL	2:19.35
2000	Jemma Simpson	2:12.92
2001	Rachael Thompson	2:12.53
2002	Hayley Beard	2:07.98
2003	Linzi Snow	2:14.10
2004	Charlotte Browning	2:09.31
2005	Emily Goodall	2:10.48
2006	Sarah Hopkinson	2:10.25
2007	Beth Duff	2:13.71
2008	Calli Thackery	2:13.07
2009	Katie Kirk	2:14.38
2010	Katie Snowden	2:15.49
2011	Emily Jenkinson	2:13.84
2012	Loren Bleaken	2:06.75

1500 METRES

(Event instituted in 1972)

1972	Pam Davis	4:39.7
1973	Teena Colebrook	4:46.2
1974	Marion Barrett	4:44.2
1975	Janet Lawrence	4:39.6
1976	Jane Donovan	4:45.8
1977	Denise Kiernan	4:37.8
1978	Sandra Arthurton	4:27.1
1979	Amanda Alford	4:35.4
1980	Amanda Alford	4:32.8
1981	Karen Hughes	4:26.8
1982	Karen Hutcheson	4:36.3
1983	Carol Haigh	4:32.13
1984	Michelle Faherty	4:41.09
1985	Wendy Wright	4:29.77
1986	Anita Philpott IRL	4:36.63
	(2, Susan Parker 4:40.03)	
1987	Julie Morris	4:29.74
1988	Wendy Farrow	4:47.33
1991	Nicola Jones	4:54.55
1992	Helen Todd	4:38.51
1993	Juliette Oldfield	4:42.43
1994	Caroline McNulty	4:48.37
1995	Maria Lynch IRL	4:46.79

	(2, Georgina Salmon 4:52.63)	
1996	Emma Alberts	4:40.74
1997	Jenny Mockler	4:38.53
1998	Jenny Mockler	4:35.33
1999	Leanne Appleton	4:36.39
2000	Emma King	4:52.70
2001	Dani Barnes	4:33.73
2002	Emily Pidgeon	4:49.06
2003	Nikki Hamblin	4:47.83
2004	Charlotte Browning	4:29.90
2005	Sarah Hopkinson	4:35.80
2006	Sarah Hopkinson	4:33.28
2007	April Stevenson	4:55.88
2008	Hannah Alderson	4:40.33
2009	Natasha Cockram	4:40.03
2010	Melanie Wood	4:48.92
2011	Chelsea Jarvis	4:46.83
2012	Chelsea Jarvis	4:36.91

60 METRES HURDLES

(Event instituted in 1966; y = 60 yards; (1) 80m spacings; (2) 100m spacings; 2ft 6in hurdles)

1966	Irene Powder	8.6y
1967	Vivien Knowles	9.5
1970	Gaynor Blackwell	9.3
1971	Jennifer Richardson	8.9
1972	Bridget Ruttledge	9.2
1973	Sue Mapstone	8.9
1974	Jane Long	8.8
1975	Jill Duffield	9.0
1976	Jill Duffield	8.6
1977	Wendy McDonnell	8.6
1978	Debbie Baker	8.80
1979	Claire St John	8.6
1980	Sarah Dean	8.71
1981	Ann Girvan	8.6
1982	Ann Girvan	8.7
1983	Pam St Ange	8.66
1984	Lesley-Ann Skeete	8.45
1985	Brid Hallissey IRL	8.88(1)
	(2, Andrea May 8.95)	
	Stephanie Douglas	8.68(2)
1986	Amanda Parker	8.65(1)
	Stephanie Douglas	8.56(2)
1987	Catherine Rotheram	8.75(1)
	Amanda Parker	8.56(2)
1988	Louise Brunning	8.62
1989	Angie Thorp	8.58
1990	Catherine Murphy	8.61

1991	Patricia Naughton IRL	8.89
	(2, Tracy Fradley 8.99)	
1992	Orla Bermingham	8.75
1993	Vicki Jamison	8.90
1994	Louise Colledge	8.89
1995	Julie Pratt	8.82
1996	Rachael Kay	8.71
1997	Rachael Kay	8.65
1998	Helen Worsey	8.53
1999	Sara McGreavy	8.65
2000	Symone Belle	8.61
2001	Symone Belle	8.52
2002	Phyllis Agbo	8.74
2003	Heather Jones	8.74
2004	Kylie Robilliard	8.67
2005	Serita Solomon	8.62
2006	Chelsea Cooper	8.56
2007	Danielle Rooney	8.66
2008	Grace Christopher	8.73
2009	Grace Christopher	8.55
2010	Yasmin Miller	8.61
2011	Hayley McLean	8.64
2012	Alicia Tymon-McEwan	8.60

HIGH JUMP

(Event instituted in 1972)

1972	Teresa Dainton	1.63
1973	Teresa Dainton	1.65
1974	Fiona Stacey	1.71
1975	Gillian Hitchen	1.72
1976	Ann-Marie Devally (Cording)	1.66
1977	Deborah Friar	1.70
1978	Kim Hagger	1.68
1979	Susan Brown	1.70
1980	Bridget Corrigan IRL	1.78
	(2, Gillian Blount 1.73)	
1981	Claire Summerfield	1.70
1982	Jackie Robinson	1.72
1983	Louise Manning	1.81
1984	Debbie Marti	1.83
1985	Jo Jennings	1.81
1986	Fiona Ross	1.72
1987	Tracey Clarke	1.76
1988	Alison Purton	1.70
1989	Alison Purton	1.70
1990	Jane Falconer	1.76
1991	Carolyn May	1.70
1992	Nicola Jupp	1.73
1993	Susan Jones (Moncrieff)	1.73

1994	Cathy Boulton	1.76
1995	Lee McConnell	1.74
1996	Hayley Young	1.75
1997	Beth Orford	1.72
1998	Lisa Marsh IRL	1.66
	(2, Natalia Norford 1.65)	
1999	Aileen Wilson	1.78
2000	Claire Wright	1.73
2001	Rebecka Bell	1.70
2002	Shani Rainford	1.66
2003	Sarah Fielding-Smith	1.69
2004	Dominique Blaize	1.74
2005	Vikki Hubbard	1.78
2006	Kayley Alcorn	1.66
2007	Hannah Dickson	1.70
2008	Katarina Johnson-Thompson	1.73
2009	Katarina Johnson-Thompson	1.79
2010	Cosmina Berry	1.70
2011	Isobel Brown	1.71
2012	Poppy Lake/Georgina Westwood	1.70

POLE VAULT

(Event instituted in 1994)

1994	Katharine Horner	2.40
1995	Becky Ridgley	2.60
1996	Becky Ridgley	2.90
1997	Sarah Hartley	3.10
1998	Kia Wnuk	2.90
1999	Lindsay Hodges	3.30
2000	Natalie Olson	2.90
2001	Natalie Olson	3.25
2002	Kim Skinner	3.50
2003	Hannah Olson	3.81
2004	Hannah Olson	3.70
2005	Hannah Abraham	3.20
2006	Abigail Haywood	3.60
2007	Sally Scott	3.70
2008	Jade Ive	4.00
2009	Katie Byres	3.60
2010	Lucy Bryan	3.80
2011	Lucy Bryan	3.90
2012	Ailis McGovern	3.50

LONG JUMP

(Event instituted in 1966)

1966	Anita Neil	5.54
1967	Sue Scott (Reeve)	5.87
1970	Shirley Biggs	5.39
1971	Julie Roberts	5.62

1972	Jill Ferneyhough	5.59
1973	Gill Regan	5.71
1974	Joy Bowerman	5.80
1975	Karen Murray	5.77
1976	Janet Frank-Lynch	5.65
1977	Kim Hagger	5.61
1978	Alison Licorish	5.69
1979	Trudie Donaldson	5.61
1980	Karen Glen	5.63
1981	Joanne Mulliner	5.49
1982	Joanne Mulliner	5.73
1983	Georgina Oladapo	6.03
1984	Michelle Stone	5.90
1985	Margaret Cheetham	6.25
1986	Fiona May	5.96
1987	Fiona May	5.89
1988	Jackie Harris	5.72
1989	Jackie Harris	5.69
1990	Ruth Irving	5.58
1991	Jo Dear	5.76
1992	Tammy McCammon	5.65
1993	Tammy McCammon	5.36
1994	Helen Pryer	5.50
1995	Jade Johnson	5.61
1996	Sarah Claxton	5.75
1997	Emma Hughes	5.54
1998	Aimee Cutler	5.70
1999	Anne-Marie Lynch IRL	5.58
	(2, Siobhan McVie 5.55)	
2000	Zainab Ceesay	5.63
2001	Symone Belle	5.71
2002	Rebekah Passley	5.86
2003	Amy Harris	5.39
2004	Amy Harris	5.87
2005	Jade Surman	5.90
2006	Alice Lennox	5.61
2007	Jade Nimmo	5.82
2008	Katarina Johnson-Thompson	6.02
2009	Katarina Johnson-Thompson	5.92
2010	Andrea Gaffmey	5.70
2011	Lisa James	5.50
2012	Morgan Lake	5.72

TRIPLE JUMP

(Event instituted in 1994)

1994	Jayne Ludlow	11.74
1995	Rebecca White	11.34
1996	Julia Johnson	11.40
1997	Syreeta Williams	11.68

1998	Mary McLoone IRL	11.67
	(2, Rachel Peacock 11.41)	
1999	Carol Loscher IRL	11.49
	(2, Natalie Brant 11.30)	
2000	Linsi Robinson	11.58
2001	Emily Parker	12.01
2002	Angela Barrett	11.85
2003	Anna Kelly	11.48
2004	Tanine Nicholas	11.55
2005	Hannah Frankson	11.76
2006	Kayley Alcorn	11.48
2007	Jade Ellams	11.41
2008	Shazana Mariam SIN	11.75
	(2, Gemma Smith 11.42)	
2009	Ahtolla Rose	11.48
2010	Naomi Reid	11.46
2011	Kate Anson	11.13
2012	Nikita Campbell-Smith	11.66

SHOT

(Event instituted in 1970; 4kg)

1970	Margaret Cook	10.66
1971	Judith Donkin	8.86
1972	Judith Potts	11.13
1973	Beverley Wadeson	10.38
1974	Judy Oakes	12.18
1975	Lana Newton	12.53
1976	Maureen Tree	10.65
1977	Maureen Tree	11.02
1978	Elaine Tinkler	11.36
1979	Susan Bracey	11.97
1980	Cynthia Gregory	12.84
1981	Susan King	13.25
1982	Iona Doyley	12.20
1983	Terri Salt	14.03
1984	Terri Salt	14.48
1985	Susan Coyne	13.25
1986	Justine Buttle	14.07
1987	Justine Buttle	14.97
1988	Natalie Hart	13.58
1989	Alison Grey	13.06
1990	Emma Capes	12.99
1991	Kelly Kane	12.09
1992	Helen Wilding	11.52
1993	Helen Wilding	12.74
1994	Philippa Roles	13.26
1995	Helen Arnold	11.72
1996	Julie Dunkley	12.02
1997	Amy Wilson	11.59

1998	Claire Smithson	12.72
1999	Claire Smithson	12.48
2000	Shelley Moles	11.01
2001	Frances Miller	12.80
2002	Sally Hinds	11.57
2003	Chloe Edwards	12.27
2004	Eden Francis	13.51
2005	Liz Millward	12.50
2006	Jenny Brown	12.09
2007	Clare Fitzgerald IRL	12.09
	(3, Hannah Evenden 10.87)	
2008	Tesni Ward	12.66
2009	Anesa Wanogho	11.65
2010	Sophie McKinna	13.24
2011	Annabel Sherry	12.43
2012	Adele Nicoll	13.14

PENTATHLON

(Event instituted in 1992)

1992	Michala Gee	3342
1993	Denise Bolton	3238
1994	Angie Nyhan	3039
1996	Katherine Livesey	3350
1997	Laura Curtis	3136
1998	Samantha Adamson	3331
1999	Aileen Wilson	3517
2000	Aileen Wilson	3527
2001	Hollie Lundgren	3101
2002	Faye Harding	3386
2003	Stephanie Owen	3262
2004	Lucy Boggis	3590
2005	Amy Hill	3372
2006	Kalyn Sheehan IRL	3429
	(2, Meghan Beesley 3291)	
2007	Kaneesha Johnson	3377
2008	Kaneesha Johnson	3478
2009	Katy Marchant	3440
2010	Hayley McLean	3291
2011	Hayley McLean	3346
2012	Shirin Irving	3570

JUNIORS (UNDER 15)

60 METRES

(Event instituted in 1975)

1975	Debbie Bunn	7.8
1976	Joanne Gardner	7.6
1977	Joanne Gardner	7.5
1978	Linsey Macdonald	7.82
1979	Elaine Mitchell	7.8
1980	Noelle Morrissey IRL	7.79
	(2, Angela Turner 7.80)	
1981	Simmone Jacobs	7.6
1982	Georgina Oladapo	7.55
1983	Mandy Haslam	7.84
1984	Janet Levermore	7.87
1985	Aileen McGillivary	7.85
1986	Danaa Myhill	7.72
1987	Vivienne Francis	7.88
1988	Katharine Merry	7.70
1989	Katharine Merry	7.35
1990	Catherine Murphy	7.85
1991	Jo Sloane	7.80
1992	Joanne Bevan	7.94
1993	Tatum Nelson	7.68
1994	Sarah Wilhelmy	7.64
1995	Dione Howell	7.81
1996	Fiona Harrison	7.82
1997	Chevette Mais	8.01
1998	Danielle Selley	7.77
1999	Claire Bergin IRL	7.85
	(2, Amy Spencer 7.92)	
2000	Amy Spencer	7.75
2001	Sinead Johnson	7.74
2002	Nimneh Hyde	7.94
2003	Joey Duck	7.78
2004	Rebekah Wilson	7.79
2005	Asha Phillip	7.72
2006	Shaunna Thompson	7.69
2007	Jodie Williams	7.75
2008	Jodie Williams	7.57
2009	Yasmin Miller	7.71
2010	Kate Wasykiw	7.80
2011	Hannah Brier	7.75
2012	Hannah Brier	7.74

200 METRES

(Event instituted in 1990)

1990	Catherine Murphy	26.27
1991	Jo Sloane	25.75

1992	Melanie Clarke	25.93
1993	Sarah Wilhelmy	25.42
1994	Sarah Wilhelmy	25.01
1995	Karlene Palmer	25.38
1996	Sarah Zawada	25.4
1997	Danielle Norville	26.03
1998	Sarah Bell	25.59
1999	Amy Spencer	25.58
2000	Amy Spencer	25.03
2001	Nicola Gossman	24.81
2002	Nimneh Hyde	25.53
2003	Joey Duck	25.08
2004	Morgan Brown	25.57
2005	Chelsea Cooper	25.30
2006	Twinelle Hopeson	24.88
2007	Jennie Batten	25.26
2008	Sarah Lavin IRL	25.19
	(2, Makeda Lewis 25.80)	
2009	Yasmin Miller	24.85
2010	Sabrina Bakare	25.18
2011	Hannah Brier	25.14
2012	Hannah Brier	24.85

800 METRES

(Event instituted in 1989)

1989	Colette Whitley	2:20.64
1990	Lucy Edge	2:20.3
1991	Helen Todd	2:24.19
1992	Hannah Curnock	2:14.91
1993	Charlotte Reeks	2:21.22
1994	Sarah Mead	2:18.19
1995	Aoife Byrne IRL	2:16.30
	(2, Jenny Meadows 2:16.30)	
1996	Jenny Mockler	2:20.49
1997	Iona McIntyre	2:13.57
1998	Jennifer Tunstill	2:26.41
1999	Lucy Thomas	2:19.31
2000	Rachael Thompson	2:19.78
2001	Ciara Durkan IRL	2:17.66
	(2, Claire Macauley 2:22.87)	
2002	Laura Crowe IRL	2:16.43
	(2, Emma Cloggie 2:17.60)	
2003	Gillian Moss	2:16.03
2004	Lynsey Sharp	2:12.79
2005	Jessica Hicks	2:17.24
2006	Alexandra Turner	2:16.93
2007	Frederica Foster	2:13.18
2008	Emily FitzHugh	2:19.73
2009	Lauren Bell	2:15.32

2010	Emily Jenkinson	2:15.25
2011	Amy Cooper	2:19.81
2012	Chelsea Nugent	2:12.71

1500 METRES

(Event instituted in 1975; discontinued after 1988)

1975	Deborah Watson	4:51.4
1976	Sandra Arthurton	4:50.8
1977	Louise Parker	4:43.2
1978	Amanda Alford	4:47.3
1979	Lynda O'Connor	4:46.9
1980	Phillipa Weaver-Smith	4:48.4
1981	Helen Appleby	4:47.5
1982	Rachel Hughes	4:36.0
1983	Wendy Wright	4:35.21
1984	Sue Burtonwood	4:42.80
1985	Alanna Cooke	4:44.92
1986	Katherine Tulloh	4:33.96
1987	Hayley Haining	4:40.89
1988	Colette Whitley	4:45.14

60 METRES HURDLES

(Event instituted in 1979; 2ft 6in hurdles)

1979	Diana Warnett	9.2
1980	Noelle Morrissey IRL	8.8
	(2, Natalie Byer 8.9)	
1981	Sharon Robinson	9.5
1982	Louise Manning	8.99
1983	Maria Jordan	9.06
1984	Janet Levermore	9.00
1985	Sam Farquharson	8.77
1986	Claire Mackintosh	9.19
1987	Lydia Chadwick	8.83
1988	Elaine Murphy IRL	9.22
	(2, Paula Wilkin 9.47)	
1989	Katharine Merry	8.84
1990	Catriona Burr	9.25
1991	Jodi Lester	9.28
1992	Liz Fairs	9.33
1993	Maria Bolsover	9.28
1994	Nicola Hall	9.20
1995	Rachael Kay	8.99
1996	Helen Worsey	9.26
1997	Lauren McLoughlin	9.16
1998	Danielle Selley	8.94
1999	Symone Belle	8.87
2000	Amy Beighton	9.07
2001	Heather Jones	8.85
2002	Joanna Kirby	9.27
2003	Helen Asher	9.07

2004	Ashley Helsby	9.06
2005	Stephanie Gaynor	9.11
2006	Chanel Taite	9.20
2007	Grace Christopher	9.34
2008	Sara Otung	9.01
2009	Lilyann O'Hara IRL	9.14
	(2, Hayley McLean 9.17)	
2010	Steph Clitheroe	9.06
2011	Morgan Lake	9.10
2012	Alicia Barrett	8.92

HIGH JUMP
(Event instituted in 1989)

1989	Suzie Filce	1.68
1990	Kerry McCabe	1.62
1991	Anna Morby	1.61
1992	Susan Jones (Moncrieff)	1.60
1993	Louise Gentle	1.63
1994	Antonia Bemrose	1.63
1995	Lynsey Rankine	1.60
1996	Rachel Harris	1.70
1997	Carol Loscher IRL	1.66
	(2=, Odelle DeJonghe & Stephanie Higham 1.60)	
1998	Aileen Wilson	1.75
1999	India Hadland	1.58
2000	Jessica Ennis	1.60
2001	Stephanie Pywell	1.67
2002	Dominique Blaize	1.68
2003	Juliet Fielden	1.58
2004	Hatty Scaramanga	1.58
2005	Paula Dalgleish	1.58
2006	Klára Abelová SVK	1.67
	(2, Hannah Dickson 1.61)	
2007	Katarina Johnson-Thompson	1.68
2008	Jazmin Sawyers	1.65
2009	Alice Jennings	1.62
2010	Jordanna Morrish	1.69
2011	Morgan Lake	1.71
2012	Kierra Barker	1.67

POLE VAULT
(Event instituted in 2007)

2007	Ellie Besford	3.10
2008	Katie Byres	3.41
2009	Lucy Bryan	3.42
2010	Abigail Roberts	2.90
2011	Jade Brewster & Abigail Roberts	2.90
2012	Natalie Hooper	3.30

LONG JUMP

(Event instituted in 1989)

1989	Leigh Blaney	5.16
1990	Fiona Allan	5.20
1991	Michelle Margison	5.22
1992	Kathryn Dowsett	5.19
1993	Sarah Wilhelmy	5.15
1994	Kelly Williamson	5.35
1995	Emma Hughes	5.26
1996	Fiona Harrison	5.52
1997	Katie Richardson	5.01
1998	Monique Parris	5.76
1999	Channelle Garnett	5.08
2000	Leah McGuire	5.14
2001	Stephanie Madgett	5.17
2002	Dominique Blaize	5.49
2003	Jade Surman	5.37
2004	Alexandra Russell	5.35
2005	Jade Nimmo	5.23
2006	Lisa Sabel	5.38
2007	Katarina Johnson-Thompson	5.30
2008	Jazmin Sawyers	5.48
2009	Morgan Lake	5.04
2010	Morgan Lake	5.61
2011	Morgan Lake	5.48
2012	Amy Williams	5.54

SHOT

(Event instituted in 1982; 3.25kg)

1982	Terri Salt	14.16
1984	Amanda Barnes	11.49
1985	Carol Cooksley	12.61
1986	Sara Allen	12.00
1987	Yvonne Anekwe NGR	13.99
	(2, Natalie Hart 13.41)	
1988	Tracey Walters	10.64
1989	Elisabeth Weldon	11.15
1991	Nicola Warriner	11.74
1992	Navdeep Dhaliwal	12.50
1993	Helen Arnold	11.06
1994	Frances Reid-Hughes	11.06
1995	Amy Wilson	11.32
1996	Elizabeth Bowyer	10.90
1997	Joanne Street	11.24
1998	Gillian Austin IRL	10.76
	(2, Cherie Pierre 10.52)	
1999	Kylie West	10.89
2000	Debbie Collinson	10.63
2001	Chloe Edwards	12.45

2002	Kayleigh Southgate	11.26
2003	Liz Millward	12.74
2004	Susie Scott	11.56
2005	Aoife Hickey IRL	11.38
	(3, Hannah Evenden 10.81)	
2006	Clare Fitzgerald IRL	12.31
	(2, Laura Baker 10.25)	
2007	Yasmin Spencer	11.66
2008	Abbi Carter	12.48
2009	Shadine Duquemin	11.85
2010	Adele Nicoll	12.32
2011	Adele Nicoll	13.36
2012	Sophie Merritt	12.46

PENTATHLON

(Event instituted in 1989)

1989	Suzie Filce	3064
1990	Jessie Aru	2969
1991	Nicola Alcock	2961
1992	Karen Lawful	2677
1993	Natalie Butler	2652
1994	Sarah Wilhelmy	2985
1995	Katie Lawful	2677
1996	Helen Thieme	2770
1997	Sara McGreavy	2986
1998	Danielle Selley	3229
1999	Ruth Laybourne	2873
2000	Louise Hazel	3194
2001	Caroline Smith	2556
2002	Dominique Blaize	3208
2003	Alice Simpson	3291
2004	Sophie Skinner	3055
2005	Alice Lennox	3011
2006	Jess Devaney	2854
2007	Katarina Johnson-Thompson	3351
2008	Jazmin Sawyers	3383
2009	Hayley McLean	3135
2010	Morgan Lake	3379
2011	Ellie Rayer	3183
2012	Emily Borthwick	3327